Airs & Places

people and music in Berkshire

For a Dancer
Charlotte Ruth Curtis (1981-1994)

Published by Corridor Press
The Arts Centre
21 South Street
Reading
Berkshire RG1 4QU
England

Tel: (0118) 901 5177
Fax: (0118) 901 5175
E-mail: corridor@dircon.co.uk

November 1999

Printed and bound in Great Britain by
Antony Rowe Ltd,
Bumper's Farm,
Chippenham,
Wiltshire, England

ISBN 1 897715 55 2

Airs & Places

people and music in Berkshire

CORRIDOR PRESS

Foreword

The subject of this latest book project by Corridor Press, chosen as always by the volunteers themselves, seemed a good idea at the time.... Writing about music in all its many forms across Berkshire was a daunting prospect but what we hope to have achieved is a taste of the tremendous variety of music-making that is going on all around us.

Apart from the many fine choirs and orchestras in the county, there is an abundance of music from many cultures, contemporary pop, historical brass bands and all those unusual and individual stories Corridor Press delights in – the Friends of Mendelssohn, the hurdy-gurdy maker, the street musicians, the bellringers, the German POW carol singers, and the people who simply love music. They all tell their own stories, either writing or taping their information, anecdotes and memories. Our aim was, as ever, to capture the diversity of the voices as well as the music.

We hope you will find something within the book to enjoy, to inform and to surprise you.

■ Corridor Press is a non-profit-making community publisher funded by Southern Arts and Reading Borough Council and run by volunteers. We always welcome more people to join our book projects and take part in our training courses and workshops.

You can contact Corridor Press at The Arts Centre, 21 South Street, Reading RG1 4QU, Berkshire, or telephone (0118) 901 5177.

Corridor Press Publications:

See It! Want It! Have It! (1992)

Bricks & Mortals (1994, reprinted 1994, 1996)

Moments of Glory (1996)

A Book of Cuttings (1997)

A Haystack of Young Poets (1998)

Potions & Notions (1998)

Real Estate (1998)

Islands of Order (1999)

Under the imprint Corridor Poets (1997)

The Dark Larder Lesley Saunders

Einstein's Eyes Tim Masters

Scratched Initials Susan Utting

Small Infidelities Kristina Close

Introduction
by Shirley, Lady Beecham

This is a fascinating book which deals with music-making and entertainment in the county. The articles span so many fields, with each one painting a picture of its own.

In some one can trace the origins of the contributors and their progress in the world of entertainment and the people they have met and worked with.

In others you are treated to an interesting narrative of a truly Berkshire enterprise. Institutions like Reading School give a wonderful insight into the changing world of education and the part that music has played over the centuries. The pop and light entertainment scene is not overlooked, with an inside view of how one group got started.

We learn that the concerts sponsored by the John Lewis Partnership were started by a chance meeting between John Spedan Lewis and the conductor Boyd Neel. Choirs abound, each with an interesting tale to tell.

The bagpipes are not forgotten and there is a good account of the local Salvation Army Band. Some of the many enterprising ventures now, sadly, belong to the past but it is good that they are recorded here for it is only with publications like this one that future generations will have the opportunity to learn of the diversity of music-making, in all its forms, which has always flourished in Berkshire.

The story of Reading Town Hall brings back a happy and amusing memory for me. In the 1960s I brought the Royal Philharmonic Orchestra to the town. The conductor was Herman Lindars, whose association with Reading is recalled in the article by Graham Ireland. The soloist was Joan Hammond and the hall was sold out. One of the ladies in the audience became so excited by Joan Hammond's rendering of *Oh Silver Moon* that she rushed to the front of the hall and removed one of the potted plant decorations provided by the council which she then handed to Joan. Naturally it was replaced to its rightful position after the concert!

I would like to offer my congratulations to everyone who has contributed to this book and to the production team.

Shirley Beecham

Contributors

Carol Whelan

Peter White

Graham Whyte

Ken Wickens

David Wilson

Design and layout:

Imogen and Damian Clarke

Typography and transcription:

Anne-Marie Dodson

Alison Haymonds

Ron Pearce

Beryl Pearson

Jackie Tate

Christine Taylor

Photography:

Ron Pearce

Illustrations:

Marianne Ziffo

Proofreading:

William Campbell

Dermot O'Rourke

Ron Pearce

Jackie Tate

Picture editor

Linda Maestranzi

Editor:

Alison Haymonds

Acknowledgements

Our grateful thanks go as always to our loyal funders , Southern Arts and Reading Borough Council; to The Paul Hamlyn Foundation which gives invaluable support for training; Reading Evening Post which sponsors our projects, gives us wide publicity and allows us access to their photo library; and Slough Borough Council for giving us financial support. We thank all our loyal volunteers for their continuing help and encouragement.

We particularly thank Marianne Ziffo for her original illustrations for the book, especially in tackling some obscure instruments; Anne-Marie Dodson for her unflustered administrative help; Ron Pearce for 34 hours of proofreading (he counted them) and for all his help in tracking down and chasing musicians and carrying out hours of research; Marigold Pearce for putting up with the phone calls; William Campbell who became an invaluable 'Slough connection' spending hours contacting and interviewing musicians in the area; Jackie Tate for appearing in our office and offering help just exactly when we needed it most; and Ken Wickens for his enthusiastic support for the project despite adversity.

Once again we are indebted to Imogen and Damian Clarke, of Imaging Design – you can run but you can't hide! Even though they have moved on they continue to support the work of Corridor Press and their design and layout skills have been invaluable.

We thank Graham Ireland of Reading School for his cheerful help and for introducing us to Shirley, Lady Beecham; and to Lady Beecham for so willingly writing our introduction, for her kindness and immense professionalism.

We would like to give special thanks to Reading Over 55's Writers Group, now sadly defunct, which donated funds towards the publishing costs of the book.

As usual Margaret Smith of Local Studies, Reading Central Library, was a tremendous help and we shall miss her now she has retired. The Music and Drama section of Reading Central Library was also very helpful.

We thank Tim Bennett-Goodman, Amrit Maghera-Johal, Mike Thompson and Bob Edwards, the 21 South Street team for their unfailing good humour and helpfulness, and send good wishes to Tim and Bob.

Grateful thanks go to the following people who contributed towards the book: Russell Alsop, Lennie Attrill, Margaret Carruthers, Librarian of Newbury Weekly News, Malcolm Clarke, Mandy Craine, Les Daniels , Judy Faraday, John Lewis Partnership Archivist, Friends of Reading Youth Orchestra, Ian Graham, Paul Hancock, Arthur Hands, John Hann, Rachel Hicks, Ian McGirr, Dr Margaret Laurie, Music Library, The University of Reading University, Antony and Olwen Mundye, Maurice Powell, John Ryall, Ken Turton.

Contents

'No different to being Michael Jackson' The Avengers

DERICK ANDREWS came to England in 1964 and by 1974, aged 17, he had started his first soul/pop group in Reading called The Avengers (later ESP). Although Derick's main instrument is the guitar, he is also a drummer, bass player and steel pan player and is a self-taught keyboard/synthesiser player, which helped him with his music computer programming skills. He is now programming and producing new material for an international artiste as well as his own projects

The Avengers was a very young group and the first black youth band to play in adult circles. All the other bands were fully-grown members of the community who had been playing since they left the Caribbean – Hurricane Force, The Flamingos; it was groups like that we were up against. But the difference was that we played quite a variety of music; we had a style. We were the first group in the black community, probably even to this day, who actually had the name of the band in lights and flashing. Dad made that! I remember him cutting out the box, doing the letters, putting the lights on and trying out a little gadget to make that timer flash so it would spell the name in coloured light bulbs, A-V-E-N-G-E-R-S, and then flash 'AVENGERS!' and stay on. Bam! The joke was that the box was so big, it took up half the stage and we had to try to find somewhere unobtrusive to put it! But it used to fascinate people.

I had started playing guitar when I was 14, and at 16 I teamed up with Eric Walker. He wanted to play lead guitar but I said to him, "Why don't you play bass because I already play guitar. You should end up being good because if you try to play the lead on the bass it will improve your speed." After a year, we decided to make a band with my sister Flavia as lead singer, Erling Duncan (who lived in my road) as rhythm guitarist, and Carl Leacock, who already played drums. I have no idea why we called ourselves The Avengers – it could have been the influence of the TV show which I was hooked on at the time.

My Dad decided he would manage us. He said: "If you are going to be a group, this is the way to do it and you need to practise." So he found us a place to practise in St Bartholomew's Church hall, in London Road, and we would to load up all the gear in Dad's car.

I bought my first electric guitar from Norman Hackett's in town, an Avon copy of a Gibson Les Paul, which I covered in monster stickers. It was black and looked like a flower

power guitar. Eric had this big old Columbus bass. Mr Francis (Dad's friend) sold his bass cabinet amp and a microphone to the group. Duncan, who had joined us, played an acoustic guitar. He had a manual pick-up underneath the strings before he got an electric guitar. My first amplifier was a 'Slider' which I bought at Rumbelows. It was a poxy little upright thing, probably just as powerful as a headphone, but we used that to start off with. You could plug a microphone in it, which was quite good at that time. It had three inputs; you could get three guitars and a microphone and it would strain the poor thing to bits. We used to practise with it in my room in between the times when we weren't at the hall.

> I remember going to see the Motown singer Mary Wells at Top Rank in Station Road when I was young before I ever had an electric guitar. I was sitting upstairs, looking over at the guitarist who was playing this semi-acoustic electric guitar. I didn't know anything about guitars except they had strings. He glanced up and saw me admiring him. The next week in town I passed Woolworth's and they had a guitar just like that man was playing. Probably some cheap old plywood rubbish with the strings about half a mile from the fretboard and impossible to press but I wanted to go and buy it just because his had sounded good. That just shows I didn't know the difference between that and a real guitar.

We played various types of music. Duncan loved reggae, I loved soul music, and anything else really as long as it had a lot of chords in it to play. I was into that. I just loved melody and chords. Flavia liked a lot of Gladys Knight and all the classic singers. Carl liked Kool & the Gang songs. It was a fairly good mixture. There were so many songs we used to play – *Can't Get Enough* (of that funky stuff), *Boogie Nights*, *The Way We Were*, calypso songs by Sparrow – *Good Morning, Mrs Walker*, etc, and various lovers' reggae like *Country Living* and *Oh Margaret*. I can't believe the different songs we used to play – even Max Bygraves!

The nice thing was that Dad helped us

Derick Andrews

buy new equipment. I don't know where he got the money or whether he re-mortgaged his house; we never thought about it. We bought these H&H amps, which were a new brand. They were pretty because when we switched them on, all the controls had green lights on the front.

We were riding high. The first gig was in a pub somewhere, just to try it out. Our first real gig for a dance was for Mrs Walker, who gave us a spot at Watford Hall, in Carey Street. Headlining was the Hurricane Force, a popular local steel band, and they were already playing when we arrived and wouldn't get off the stage. So Mrs Walker asked them to let us play. Emmerson (Emmy) Ashby was their drummer at that time – I knew him from the growing-up scene – and he put his foot down and said to give us a chance. So we played. I believe Carl even played Emmy's drums. We started with *The Sound of Philadelphia*, an instrumental, which was our theme tune – we always started with that. But they didn't dance; everybody just watched. Dad even made my two younger sisters dance to encourage the crowd, but that didn't work either!

We played lots of different things including Country and Western – Dad always told us we should play music for all types of people. We had two guitars, a bass and a drum; no keyboards but we did a good imitation. We got quite a full sound; Duncan used to mimic the organ on the reggae tracks with his guitar.

It was good when we got the H&H equipment because it

Derick Andrews and The Avengers complete with flares

was almost like a uniform. We were all wearing giant flares and Afros, light grey flared trousers with the flowered shirt, which blended nicely with my guitar. I was like a lollipop stick I was so skinny, the flares were bigger than my waist. Although platform shoes were in we did not wear them on stage. Flavia would change clothes between sets, so she would go off to the dressing room to change and come back like Shirley Bassey with her second dress and we were still sweaty in our old stuff. But we looked the part.

Everything we did with that band was well ahead of its time. We were the first ones to use synthesisers and I used a flanger pedal to make the guitar sound like one of those fairground organs; little things that I'd never seen anyone else do. We used to play with reverb on the amps to lighten up the sound and make it travel. We were the first ones to start doing it. There were no other bands like us.

We had a regular spot at the dances held at the AUEW Hall, Oxford Road, and also played many times at the Caribbean Club in London Street (now the After Dark club). The first time we played AUEW we opened with, *Good Morning, Mrs Walker*, and I was playing the intro for about half an hour because nobody could sing a note because of our nerves. In the end Dad came on stage, picked up the microphone and started singing the song. It was so embarrassing that he had to start it for us.

We also played in High Wycombe Community Centre, at Slough, and Acklam Hall in West London; we used to hire a van from Clifton in George Street to travel out of Reading. Carl played the bongos sometimes so I would swap and play drums. You felt really good. To me, it was no different to being Michael Jackson on stage with his audience of billions. You would look and see people of the same age who had actually paid to come in and see you play and entertain and they were loving it and you felt: "Wow, this is the life."

Because Dad used to manage us, we had someone to look after us. That's why we got the respect from organisers and other bands. Even when reggae sound systems started, they never disrespected the band, which was amazing. Maybe it was because we played a bit of everything for people (including a lot of reggae) or maybe because Dad was our manager. He would deal with them, and say "Excuse me, it's the group's time to play." We played a lot of reggae music, particularly Burning Spear's *No One Remembers Old Marcus Garvey*. We had a kind of a following, especially with young people, but at the time we didn't even realise the influence we had. I remember when Colin Watson (aka local reggae artist Aqua Livi) said to me: "I used to come to watch you guys. You were the pioneers for youth music in Reading; nobody was doing that stuff in those days. We all wished we could play like that."

Dad never controlled how we rehearsed, that was down to me, but we began having problems. We had a timing problem on the drums and we often found it difficult to end songs as Carl was like a runaway train. In the end, Carl left because he felt he was keeping the band back. Then Duncan decided he wouldn't play any more. Tony Hinds came into the picture, and said: "I can play man; I played drums in Barbados." Years later he told me that was the first time he saw a drum kit! And he had the same timing problem. We then got Dave King, a male nurse from Broadmoor. He was a keen guitarist, played well, was a nice person and very patient, considering I was a real hothead as a leader.

That's when we bought the uniform guitars and when The Avengers changed to ESP. There was Eric, Tony, Dave, Flavia and me. We wore these turquoise T-shirts stamped with a heart with wings on either side and ESP with the 'S' in the middle like superman though, of course, the guitar used to cover it. We also had red short-sleeved shirts as a change of clothes and Tony had his red drums (which he still has after all these years).

A major gig for us was when ESP played in the new Hexagon for the Carnival Queen dance in 1977. I've never seen other bands with the equipment we had. We had the H&H amps that glowed green when they were switched on, the PA system and the speakers on poles for the vocals. We had a metal rack, which used to hold the amplifier for the mikes with about 10 inputs. We had mikes and mike stands and boom stands. It was just looking hard!

The group went on for a while but I got fed up. Everyone was headstrong. Dad didn't know but we just stopped going to rehearsals because nothing was progressing. None of us knew what to do to make it work. Every week I'd tell the drummer "play it like this" and ended up having to learn to play drums because the drummer couldn't play. Something was wrong. So I simply decided the band was over. Looking back at it, it wasn't done very nicely. I suppose it was impetuous youth.

Round that time I was getting into more soul and funk. I was thinking about my playing more seriously. Flavia was still into more classic soul songs. Dave and Tony weren't anywhere. Only Eric and I were doing anything similar. If I think about it, I was goaded by him into ending it.

There was a time in the early days with Duncan when I was playing my guitar but I wasn't really playing it as an art form. I was just playing the music because I heard it. I wasn't studying my sound – "does my guitar sound all right?" I didn't think about it. I'd just play the tune. When I think about the way I play now, I try to move on

ESP supporting Gonzales at the Henwick Club, Thatcham

from that. When I started playing solos, particularly funk, I started listening properly. There wasn't anyone teaching me - it was always 'me' teaching me. Sitting down with somebody and learning would have been nicer.

Musically, I listened to a lot of George Benson and Stevie Wonder who has been my main inspiration. However, my musical influences were developed as I went through my Earth Wind & Fire phase. They brought out the single Saturday Night and when I heard the song I had to find out who it was. I loved their harmony structure and how they arranged things, the conversation between the music and the big horn section in the background. I spent months practising their musical style.

Then Eric and I got into a funk band – I think the band was Emmy's idea. He asked me what I was doing: "Why don't we start a band?" This became the funk band ESP which started in 1978 and finished around 1981. We still practised at St Bartholomew's in London Road. Eric and I were on bass and guitar and Emmy on drums. He knew Jeff Hawkins and Dean as saxophone players and also introduced Ricky Greaves as rhythm guitarist. We never had any keyboards. I remember ESP playing outside at The University of Reading, the sun beaming down and the PA sounding crisp. It was the first time we had played with a PA and it sounded great. Everyone was enjoying the music and we were playing things like Love You All Over. We had lots of gigs like that.

The next main ESP gig was at the Henwick Club in Thatcham in October 1979 as support act to Gonzales, a session band who were in the pop charts at the time (their bass player, Hughie, was from Reading). Already by then we had a small following and our Reading fans came to Thatcham to see us perform. We used a PA and as we play quite loud it started squeaking and we screamed to the engineer: "It's too loud on stage!" He shouted back: "Well it would help if you turned it down!". Eventually you learn things like that. It was a hard gig but we all felt really good. It was probably the most exciting thing that ever happened in Thatcham because there's nothing out there! I remember that gig especially since the club burned down soon after the show.

Then ESP played as support act for the US band Odyssey, first in Wales and then at Reading Top Rank Nightclub in 1981. Top Rank, in Station Road, was the best venue in Reading – why did they turn it into a bingo hall? The place was buzzing with liveliness . All major touring pop groups came there.

When we played with Odyssey we had a revolving stage and there was a 'superstar quality' feeling. My grandmother, my mother, my sisters and all my friends were in the audience. Joyce (now my wife) was also there; I had just started seeing her. You felt that all those girls you fancied were going to see you playing and they would like you. 'Course, that never worked, but it felt like that.

We'd never played to a crowd like that before – 2,000 people participating in what you did. For the first time we were playing music that we wanted to play. Some of it was covers. For me it was brilliant because it was as good as what I heard in my head. It was really enjoyable, as if you were floating. That Reading show with Odyssey was brilliant.

When ESP, the funk band, broke up, it broke me in half. I couldn't see a reason why Eric and Ricky simply left to join an African band, Kabala. It made me numb – particularly the split with Eric as we had played together for so long. Later the name ESP was revived for a while when I teamed up again with Ricky after he left Kabala, to work on our own material.

In the meantime I had played with Hurricane Force, and during my time with them Emmy had suggested we start our own calypso band to tour the summer season.

Hot Steel was unique. It combined steel, pop and jazz set, and toured the UK. Emmy was on drums, Jeff Hawkins back playing sax, and Miles Hawkins (his son) on bass. Jimmy Harry (former lead player for Hurricane Force) was on 'tenor 'pan, my sister Claudette played the rhythm on two 'guitar' pans and Ainsley 'Young' Lampkin (who we called 'Lammy') on the 'cello' pans. We had a lead singer called Neil who was particularly good at calypso.

We had a winning formula. Here were people who really could play their instruments and we worked hard practising twice a week at the Caribbean Club (now After Dark). Hot Steel played its first gig there and afterwards had a regular spot. We were really good and, though we played mainly for fun, by the time the group ended in 1985 it had built up quite a serious following.

The Reading Rota

Abbey music

Many people have walked though the Abbey ruins in Reading at one time or another, perhaps noticing the plaques and memorials to kings and archbishops of many years ago. In addition to the memorials to the great, the good, and the not-so-good, is a stone containing a piece of music, Sumer is icumen in, which is celebrated as the oldest known piece of secular (non-religious) music in English.

In musical circles, this piece of music is known as the Reading Rota, and is certainly the earliest known composition written in six parts. The top melody is sung as a four-part round (hence, rota) by four voices. It works in a similar way to the round London's Burning, which many of us will have sung at school. The music is recorded with a Latin and an English text, to the same notation, but totally unrelated in subject matter. Perhaps the English text was sneaked in?

The song itself celebrates the coming of summer:

Sumer is icumen in, lhude sing, cucu;
Growe sed and blowe med and sprin e wude nu;
Sing, cucu.
Awe blete after lomb, lbou after calue cu;
Bulluc sterte bucke uerte, murie sing cucu.
Cucu, cucu.
Well singes u cucu; ne swik u nauer nu.

Summer is a-coming in, loudly sing, cuckoo;
Groweth seed and bloweth mead and springeth the woodland now;
Sing cuckoo.
Ewe bleateth after lamb, lows after calf the cow;
Bullock starteth, buck darteth, merry sing, cuckoo.
Cuckoo, cuckoo,
Well singest thou, cuckoo; cease you never now.

Sumer is icumen in is believed to have been the work of a 13th-century monk at Reading Abbey. It may seem odd to us that it is not particularly religious or spiritual but it was not uncommon for monks to record secular works, sometimes of a rude or bawdy nature, alongside sacred hymns and psalms. Often this was the only way that traditions would be recorded for future generations. The manuscript is now in the British Library.

The secular lives of 13th-century monks has been made most famous by the monks of Beuron in Bavaria, whose songs, discovered in 1847, celebrated far from what we would consider to be an ideal monastic existence, and which inspired the composer Carl Orff to write Carmina Burana. Perhaps the monks at Reading were more spiritual in nature than those in Bavaria – or maybe the bawdy drinking songs written by the Reading monks have never been found?

John Davey

A Medley of Memories Bulmershe Girls' Choir 1965-85

GWYN ARCH started Bulmershe Girls' Choir in 1965 soon after he arrived at the college of Higher Education as Director of music. He recalls a score of musical years

They were all young ladies, aged between 18 and 21. I wonder how they would wish to be described were the choir to be formed today, but in 1965 they were very clear that they wanted to be called girls for a little longer, and over 20 years no one complained, or anyway, not to me.

Bulmershe was set up in September 1964 as a teacher-training college with a particular brief to prepare students for the primary school. The initial intake was 225 first year students, of whom 157 were female. This proportion mirrored the national picture at the time, and although the college resolved to move towards a ratio of two men to three women by 1970, it was pretty well pie in the sky. One to three or thereabouts it firmly remained for most of those 20 years. The 'main' college choir was invariably disadvantaged. In the early days we made records of some of the more significant musical events, the record being a quaintly-large disc of vinyl with plenty of room for information on the sleeve. I see that I conducted Bernstein's *Chichester Psalms*, Constant Lambert's *The Rio Grande* and other bits and pieces in the college hall in February 1969. There were 53 sopranos, 50 altos, 17 tenors and 22 basses – 103 women to 39 men. I will always be grateful to the male members of staff who submitted to being cajoled into making these performances viable. In this case, without them the ratio would have been slightly worse than five to one and I dread to think…

In these circumstances, the rationale for forming a separate girls' choir was compelling. It would meet the demand for more singing opportunities which invariably came from the distaff side. It would create a viable artistic unit and enable the students (especially those taking music as their main subject) to explore the choral repertoire for upper voices. It didn't quite work out like that, though. Invariably there was a high proportion of students studying History, or Science, or Physical Education, etc, in the choir, and as for the female choir repertoire, there wasn't very much of it, so I landed myself with having to write endless arrangements for sopranos and altos in order to produce enough material to fill a concert.

From the start I recognised that one of the functions of the Music Department was to advertise the existence of the brand-new college to the outside world in order to

achieve more applicants to its courses. This intention was shared with the Drama and Sports departments, and we all hoped that our concerted effort would help to put the strange name of Bulmershe on the academic map. As far as music activities were concerned, Bulmershe Girls' Choir was the front runner, and from the very early days concerts were given far and wide.

It was a very early decision to restrict the size of the choir to 50, because if you add the conductor and the accompanist, 52 was the most seats you could get on a bus in those days, and it was most unlikely that concert organisers would be willing to pay for two of them! As the choir became more popular (aided, no doubt by the glamour of yearly foreign tours and regular broadcasts), the demand for places in the choir grew rapidly, and I had to introduce auditions for potential members, difficult to justify on educational grounds, but easy on economic ones. I always felt extremely unhappy in having to exclude many perfectly adequate voices pretty well arbitrarily, but the really keen ones sang in other groups for a year or so and re-applied, and re-applied, and eventually they got in, albeit for a shorter time.

The choir's first big challenge, to compete in the biggest choral festival in the country, the Llangollen International Eisteddfod of 1966, is seared in my memory. BGC (work it out) had been formed for a year. It had given several concerts in the locality and had rehearsed twice a week. I was a young man of extremely limited experience but one who knew it all. I wasn't quite sure that we would win, but imagined a second or third place well within grasp. After all, the girls had prepared the music exactly according to my instructions. The occasion was the choir's first really long bus ride, the first of what turned out to be hundreds and hundreds of ever longer bus rides.

The girls sang to a huge audience in a huge tent pitched on the only flat field on the edge of a small and pretty Welsh town. We had entered the International Female Choir competition, and there were groups from all over Europe, mostly bedecked in their national costumes, and mostly looking terrific. BGC's approach to dress was a touch more informal. "Anything you like as long as it's some shade of blue". It looked, shall we say, terrible, but never mind, the judges were only interested in what they heard, the sound of the choir, and after all, the girls had prepared the music exactly according to my instructions. Now for the seared-in bit. There were 18 choirs in that particular contest. BGC came 17th and they had exactly the same number of (distressingly few) marks as one other (local, school) choir. In other words, equal bottom of the list.

I now think that was the best thing that has ever happened to me musically, and probably personally as well. On the one hand my insufferable ego had been deflated; on the other, I had experienced the privilege of hearing at close quarters some of the finest female choirs in the world. The goalposts had been moved, further away than I had ever imagined, but I now knew where they were. Chastened, we returned to Reading, but determined to bounce back.

The choir entered the International Female competition for ten years running after that. BGC never won, but gained one second and one third prize. Going to Llangollen became a routine. Conveniently, the festival coincided with the last week of the summer term, when all the exams were out of the way, and students needed distractions while awaiting their results. The choir stayed for three days in a Youth Hostel owned by the Liverpool Education Authority, and the college kitchens provided enough food and equipment for the students to do their own catering. It became a tradition on the final night to climb the mountain overlooking Llangollen, sit in the ruins of Dinas Brân and sing madrigals. I seem to remember that hillside getting steeper over the years, but the students never seemed to notice this curious phenomenon.

I must confess that I have never enjoyed competitions. I do not believe that the purpose of music-making is to win things. Music is a social activity. The choir learns a song, gets to know its every detail, every nuance, every delicious moment, and thus comes to love it. The concert is an opportunity to demonstrate that love, to share it, to communicate it to others, to hope that they will love it, too. The competition exists in order to hope to demonstrate superiority, surely a less worthy objective. However, we live in a competitive world, and in the case of Llangollen, it was also a learning experience. The girls learned as much from it as I did, and their pursuit of excellence became more focused and informed.

There was another form of competition which I found much more palatable than the usual format. Indeed I never felt I was actually in a contest. It was a competition run every year by the BBC on Radio 3, and it was called *Let the Peoples Sing*. What happened was that following a preliminary audition certain choirs were invited to London to record four or five items. The recording was usually in the main concert hall of Broadcasting House or in the number one studio at Maida Vale, at that time the home of the BBC Symphony Orchestra. Once the recording was in the can, that was that. Parts of the same recording were used in every single round of the competition. BGC usually found itself competing in the 'equal voice' sector (female and male voice choirs) and started off representing the south-east of England in knock-out heats against other regions of the country. Eventually one choir emerged to represent the UK in the international rounds against the 35 other competing nations.

In one way it was extremely frustrating. There was the choir making the same mistakes in exactly the same places every time that particular song was being used, and there was absolutely nothing I could do about it except wince on cue. But it was wonderful free publicity for the college and many generations of students got very used to singing to microphones as well as to people. For the record, the choir managed to represent the UK seven times in the 12 years when they participated, and once (1978) they were judged to be the outstanding British choir, chosen from all the different categories of the competition.

The girls got used to singing for television cameras, too, especially during the 70s. They made eight or nine programmes for what was irreligiously called 'The God Slot', and were normally transmitted on Sunday mornings. The shows were structured around a central theme like 'Winter' or 'Numbers', or were mini-musicals based on biblical stories and legends. Of course, anything broadcast on a Sunday morning was watched by nobody except maybe the parents of the girls, but there was one peak viewing engagement that blazoned the name of the college to unsuspecting millions when BGC sang two numbers on the Val Doonican show, and just by chance they were all wearing informative T-shirts!

Every teacher will tell you that the best part of the academic year is its end, and the end of most years at Bulmershe was celebrated with a choir tour. I can't begin to calculate how many miles I travelled in a bus filled to capacity with successive generations of BGC members. During the year they gave 15 concerts in the UK, appearing in Wolverhampton, Wokingham or wherever . Requests for their services greatly exceeded the time available to give them, so 15 became the official limit. Something I have been able to calculate is the extent to which the choir covered the repertoire while criss-crossing the country. In the 20 years of its existence, BGC sang from memory well over 300 items. What it is to be young! Incidentally, they also learned the soprano and alto parts of works such as the *Bach B minor Mass* and *Mahler's Eighth Symphony* and sang them in the Royal Festival Hall and the Albert Hall along with other choirs. For these events they were *not* expected to learn the music by heart.

What the students loved most were the foreign tours. They all lasted two or three weeks, were absolutely exhausting but invariably exhilarating. It astonishes me just thinking about the countries BGC visited. They sang in Denmark, Sweden, Finland, Lapland, Austria, Holland, Germany, Bavaria, Hungary, Ireland, Poland, the USA and Canada. I expect I have forgotten one or two others. For all the European tours we had the same bus driver (Dave Lee) and he adapted his vehicle to the circumstances by rigging up a pole across the rear seats so that the choir dresses could be hung up (and sometimes grabbed in a hurry when we were late arriving for a concert in an unfamiliar location). Dresses were the bane of my life. Every year the girls wanted a new uniform. Given a free hand, they would have cheerfully spent all the rehearsal time of the whole of the autumn term discussing what it was to be, time that was truly precious. How the issue was resolved was difficult – and contentious.

There must be a host of memories of specific events that the girls treasure to this day. I say 'girls' when a moment's reflection reminds me that some of them are now old enough to have daughters who themselves have been through college – and married – and had children. I'll start again. There must be a few grannies who have memories of BGC that they treasure to this day. Taking photos of each other at 1am by the light of the midnight sun in Lapland; singing in the Wieliczka Salt Mine outside Krakow in southern Poland to an audience of 200 asthma patients from a hospital within the mine; giving a concert in mad King Ludwig's opera salon within the fairy-tale castle of Neuschwanstein in Bavaria – more exciting than Disneyland.

The American tours (all four of them) were perhaps the most memorable of all. Why? They were the longest and most arduous. For example, in July 1973 BGC gave a concert every night for three weeks, travelled over 5000 miles by Greyhound bus and were heard by over 5000 people. They sang in Ontario, New York, New Jersey, Pennsylvania, Michigan, Indiana, Illinois, Iowa, South Dakota, Nebraska, Colorado, Kansas, Missouri and Ohio. They performed in universities, theatres, churches and concert halls and they gave presents of packets of biscuits to all their hosts, kindly donated by Huntley and Palmer, and bearing the name of Reading on the labels.

It was the hosting that made the tour possible. The girls had only the cost of the flight and the chartered bus to persuade their parents to cover. BGC never stayed a single night in a hotel in the USA. They were always billeted in pairs or threes in the houses of people associated with the concert in some way – church members, Rotary Club associates, university staff, charity committee people, etc. The hospitality was overwhelming. The girls usually carried a food-filled bag on to the bus in the morning – no need to spend any of the diminishing supply of pocket money at the lunchtime stop en route to the next stopover. Of course, the insatiable curiosity of many of the hosts about all things English ("We gotta friend livin' in London. Name o' Smith. Do ya know him?") meant that many of the girls didn't get to bed until way after midnight, but you could always sleep on the bus, couldn't you, and anyway, Kansas consisted of 700 miles of what appeared to be one continuous wheat field.

I expect that in the 20 years BGC gave at least 500 concerts. Nearly all of them involved a bus trip, so it is the memory of the bus that endures. I never needed to ask the girls how they thought the concert had gone. If it had been a good one they would begin an informal singsong within two minutes of the bus starting on its return journey, and they would continue to sing as they walked across the Bulmershe campus to the college hostels. I can hear them now, and count myself singularly fortunate to have been part of it.

The official photograph of Bulmershe Girls' choir at the Llangollen International Eisteddfod in July 1979

All Things Bright and Beautiful   Musical memories

NORA COATES is now in her 80s and registered blind but still enjoys life and music. She lives in Caversham where she was born and brought up, and finds music can prompt many memories of her early life

Every time I sing *All Things Bright and Beautiful* I'm a child again, five years old sitting in a little armchair in the Sunday school, with bare boards and a big roaring fire with a fireguard around it. I've always loved singing – I never had a good voice but it was a strong one. I suppose you always remember the first time you sing a song. We lived in Southview Avenue, Caversham, and I walked to Sunday school at St Peter's through South Street. Caversham was a nice little village in those days.

I began learning piano at about eight so I could read music right from the start. I always wanted to be an Yvonne Arnaud, but I never was. I used to practise and kid myself but I wasn't a good pianist. We had a piano in the front room, no electric lights so we had a lamp standing on the table behind us when the teacher came in the winter months. My eldest brother and I learned the piano with Mr Thomas Waite, who had a music shop in King's Road, Reading, years ago. He was a lovely old man with a beard. He always called me Sissy because that's what the family called me. My brother couldn't say Nora so my mother would say, "Go and see what your little sissy is doing," and it stuck.

Mr Waite rode over to our house on a tricycle and when I was having my lesson, my brother used to pop out and have a ride on it. Once he didn't get back in time for the lesson and eventually appeared on the tricycle carrying a sack of potatoes which he had collected from Elliot's where my dad worked.

He was naughty my brother. I always remember him singing *The First Noel* in church: "No ale, no beer, no stout, sold out, born is the King of Brussels sprouts!"

I joined Reading Children's Choir when I was 12 and had started going to Wilson Central School, in Reading. You had to audition for the choir, which was run by the council and took children from all the Reading schools. Mr Marsh was the conductor and Miss Dunn was the pianist. We practised twice a week on Tuesdays and Thursdays. I went to both and never missed. I remember one pouring wet night my mother said, "You're not going to practise unless you can get your Russian boots on." My mother had bought me these Russian boots but I could never get the blessed things on. So I struggled and got them on and she had to let me go.

We practised from September to March when there were three children's concerts held each year in Reading Town Hall. I can remember going in at the Valpy Street end underneath the town hall, walking along the passages and coming up some funny little steps right behind the organ. We all sat on either side of the stage, wearing our best Sunday dresses, no uniforms. Every school in Reading was there. We sang all sorts, excerpts from *The Gondoliers* and *The Mikado, English Country Garden*, spirituals. We learned them all off by heart because we didn't have books on the stage. The ones that knew their words were in the front row and so my friend Beryl and I were in the front row all the time.

I gave up when I was 15 and didn't have time for choir but they held the concerts for years. Later on they used to hold schools' music festivals when my son was in the choir and we were up in the balcony. We joined in the final hymn, *Praise My Soul the King of Heaven*.

My whole family was musical. My dad was a wonderful whistler. We had a big orchard and when my dad pruned the apple trees he'd climb up to the top of the tree and whistle like a bird – Handel's *Largo, Tales of Hoffman*. My cousin was the violinist Marcel Gardner (his name was really Herbie). He played in the cinemas in the silent days, and in the Dorchester, and was on the radio in *Music for Bedtime* and *Music While You Work*.

My late brother Gerald Gardner was also a musician. He played the saxophone and ran a dance orchestra, Geraldo's Revels, in Reading in the 1930s with a good pianist Doug Illsley, a clarinettist and a drummer. I had to make his music stand for him. My mother gave me her wedding photo for the backing and I put a velvet fringe round it. He played in all the little halls and his signature tune was *Whispering*. It was the wrong era for him really; he would have been a good jazz player.

Music always reminds me of people and places. *Red Sails in the Sunset* makes me think of the time I went for an interview at Blakey Morris's, the wallpaper shop in the Market Place, in 1936. All the time I was being interviewed a barrel organ was playing *Red Sails*. I got the job, at 25 shillings a week, and after that every Wednesday morning it was there playing that tune.

The song *All The Things You Are* reminds me of my three evacuees who lived with me in Mayfield Drive during the war. Marie used to sing that.

I was never a musician but I love music and it brings back so many memories. Music and art bring you back together, back to earth, and back to people.

Millennium Choice Nora Coates

My favourite is Handel's Messiah. I used to sing it in choirs

A Most Unusual Instrument   Reading Accordion Group

You either like the accordion or loathe it. One of its great fans is BOB BROWN, who has been secretary of Reading Accordion Group (RAG) for many years, and he explains its attraction

The problem with the accordion is that it's an unusual instrument. A lot of people are a bit toffee-nosed and say: "Accordion? You don't expect me to listen to that." My son's one of them. One year an accordionist reached the final of the Young Musician of the Year competition and people said: "What a waste of space having an accordion in the final six." This was a top-flight accordionist playing a difficult piece of Russian modern music. This attitude is disappointing but reflects the lack of knowledge about a very versatile instrument.

The age range for folk who really like the intrument is 50-plus, like me, because they remember the period during and just after the war when they heard the accordion on radio programmes like Workers' Playtime. Then there was a period when accordion playing was almost forgotten until about 15 years ago when there was a resurgence. Now you can find accordion clubs and ensembles all over the country.

Basically, I am a classical music enthusiast but I love the accordion. It all started for me in January 1987 at Mike Rackley's Studio Accordé School of Accordions in Tilehurst. I was getting towards early retirement and my mother died and left me some money. I'd always wanted to play the accordion but they're very expensive things to buy if you don't know whether you can actually play them or not .

I bought a cheap 'Parrott' accordion but I still needed someone to teach me to play it. I picked up the Chronicle and there was an advert from Mike Rackley saying he was starting group tuition. It was just meant to be. I joined up with him, six or eight of us paying for group tuition every Monday night in Tilehurst. It isn't as difficult as it looks. The keyboard is the same as a piano keyboard so once you have got the hang of the bellows, the right hand is easy enough.

After six or nine months, I said to Mike: "It'd be nice to form a little group now we've learnt a bit, just to play among ourselves." He said: "I'm no good at organising." I said: "My music is not so good but I'm good at organising." So that's how it started. We called a general meeting in Tilehurst in January 1987, and about 14 people came along. At first there was a problem

between those who didn't want to take it too seriously and the rest of us who never even thought about entertaining people but just wanted to master the art of playing orchestrated music. After a while, the problem resolved itself. Mike, who's a brilliant accordionist and a real character, became our musical director and I became secretary and have been ever since.

After a few months we were invited to play at an old people's club in Oxford Road. We said we'd give it a go but you've never seen such a terrified group of people in all your life. There were 90 people expecting us to entertain them. It was just frightening. We didn't have much in the way of music, a few sing-alongs, but we managed to get through it sufficiently well for them to ask us to come back again.

We did eight or nine performances the first year and after that it was 50 a year at least. In 1990 we took the plunge and decided to go for a public charity concert. We went to the Victoria Town Hall and held our first concert with Mike as our conductor.

When Mike left, we invited Tony Banks to become our musical director. He had been a Licentiate of the British College of Accordionists since he was 16 and when he joined us, he was appointed leader on the spot. When we asked him to take over, he said: "I've only done a little bit of conducting. I'll give it a fortnight and see how we get on." He was about 28 years old and some of us were in our 50s, 60s and 70s, so you can imagine it was

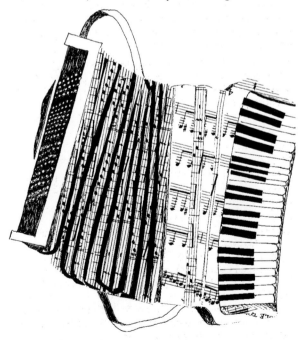

difficult for him. He's a very charming chap, not one to rant and rave, and we had to plead with him: "For Heaven's sake, tell us off if we're doing it wrong." He won't do it; he's got his own way of bringing us on. He became our musical director in 1991, just before our first concert at the Coronation Hall in Woodley, and he's still our musical director today.

That's how it all started to evolve. My forte is organising. I was an administrator all my life so it comes easy to me. The others don't want to get too involved but are very co-operative. A constitution was agreed which laid out the ground rules and the group commenced on a proper footing.

We did get a community grant from Reading Borough Council for £500 to buy some loudspeaker equipment to emphasise the bass part and to facilitate announcements. That helped us a lot. Not knowing what we were doing we bought one speaker incorporating the amplifier which you need a crane to lift. As we were getting older it was getting heavier and heavier so eventually we sold

it and bought two speakers and a separate amplifier. We're currently building up the money to buy a bass accordion. It has the most wonderful sound. We're not rushing because we don't have anybody to play it at the moment. If we find someone who is happy to do oompah-oompah, we'll buy one.

We ask for a donation wherever we play. Our policy is that if a charitable organisation wants to raise money at a concert, we'll play for nothing. If it wants to entertain its members, we ask for a donation. For instance we've got a regular booking at Mortimer Day Centre every month except July and August and they'd have us every week if we could. The money buys us all the equipment and music we need. Every time a new piece of music is introduced, it costs £30 or £40 for each set. We've bought some good equipment over the years. Otherwise, the charity concerts and any other money is given to charity. In rough terms over the 12 years we've raised £10,000. We're principally there to enjoy ourselves and I reckon we entertain 1,500 to 2,000 people every year.

Back row, left to right: Adrian Forrester, Cyril Leeke (Chair), Tony Banks (Musical Director), Walter Morris, Bob Brown (Secretary), Ray Hutchins. Front row, left to right: Joan Owen, Pearl Morris, Sue Titorenko

Seven years ago we started touring, the first time to Jersey. Some didn't want to go by ship and some didn't want to fly so I said: "I don't think the little aeroplane will be very happy if it had ten accordions in it. Why don't some of us go by sea, take all the gear and the rest can fly."

We had a hotel in St Helier and that's where we made our first mistake. I'd written to the Health Authority and said we're available for old folk's homes and so on, and they were very good and gave us contacts. We played at three different hospitals, geriatric departments, a residential home, a day centre, and at the Jersey Accordion Club's club night. The only problem was the evening meal at the hotel. The meal was half-past six, not a minute before. They wouldn't budge, not even a bit of salad. so we did a bit of running round and gobbling down food.

On the way back home, we decided not to use an hotel again. If we could rent a large enough house, we could have our meals to suit our commitments. Having been a Scout leader, it seemed obvious to organise a kind of a patrol system where duties such as preparing vegetables, waiting at table, washing up, etc, were allocated. This meant being on duty only twice during the week. My wife had experience in catering for numbers in the Guide Movement and became our cook.

We've been to places like North Devon, South Derbyshire, Norfolk, Weston-super-Mare and Cornwall. It's been the making of the group. When you're away for a week together, either you fall out with each other or you gel. Although we have our differences of opinion now and again, basically we're a friendly lot who do well.

We're going for a Millennium Grant. What we want is six accordions to lend out to people for six months or so to find out if they really want to play it. The problem really is that an accordion looks very difficult to play and people need to have one to find out if they like playing it.

The size is identified by the number of bass buttons. My accordion has 120. Some have 96 bass. The one that is ideal for a six-year-old plus, according to my supplier, is 48 bass. That's plenty to learn up to maybe Grade Three. After that, you will know for yourself if you want to continue. You've got to be sure that you want to play the accordion before committing yourself to spending anything up to £5,000 plus. After a year, I was able to purchase a new 'Sonola' which is currently valued at£2,000. A 48-bass is about £600 so we're asking for a £3,500 grant.

Recently we produced our second tape cassette recording which is selling well and helps to swell our funds.

We have entered one or two competitions but we're not over keen on them. It means you've got to practise one or two pieces over a long period just for ten minutes. We won a cup at Maidenhead Festival and were placed in the National Accordion Organisation's Area Festivals in the Thames Valley, but we decided that's not what we joined for. There's a lot of argument, about whether competitions are a good thing. Well, they do apply your mind and make you play things properly.

We're very aware of the growing age of our existing membership. the majority of members are in the 60 to 80 age range so we need to attract new younger members. What we're proposing to do as a Millennium project is to start a school of accordions within our group, and target the young people particularly.

We realise that it is necessary to convince young people that it is a good instrument to play but over the country you'd be surprised at the number and quality of the young players around. We hope to target children from about six years upwards as well as adults.

We propose to do group training with the emphasis on ensemble playing. Where necessary, the theory of music will be taught in addition to mastering the accordion as far as we can. Anyone who wishes to progress further will be passed on to suitable advanced accordion teachers such as Mike Rackley,who is still teaching and knows his stuff.

Years ago, OAPs stayed at home – "that's me had it". But now, they're not. They're the new 'young set' with money, but they need something to occupy their minds. In our group for instance, Joan, who plays accompanying rhythm at the back, played with the Marie Hyde Band during the war in Reading but she more or less gave up playing after the war. After she lost her husband, she was persuaded to join RAG and she loves every minute. She'd play every day if you wanted her to.

Cyril Leeke, our chairman, recently found out that Ray Hutchins, who plays in the 'seconds', actually played in the Barnes and Avis Accordion Orchestra with him all those years ago – it's a small world!

The group's members are all enthusiastic and, when you think, there's seven of us in retirement playing in the group who would otherwise not be doing very much. On top of that we have the bonus of making a lot of other people very happy.

Millennium Choice

Reading Accordion Group

**The Dambusters March by Eric Coates (1942) is always
very popular with audiences**

A Steadying Effect Army Cadet Force Band

PETER 'CHALKY' WHITE remembers his happy times as drum major with the Army Cadet Force band in the 1940s

I had no musical experience but I was brought up with music – my uncle, Ashley Church, used to play in the Royal Berks Band and the Reading Temperance Band. When I was a boy I used to stay with them for a month in the summer in Tilehurst and when my uncle was practising on the bassoon there had to be dead silence, no talking, no doing anything: "Just sit still, while I'm practising."

We used to go to the Forbury Gardens in Reading every Sunday afternoon to listen to the band. I was only a little boy, and I remember I was playing up a bit and my aunt told me to sit down. Then they played *The Battle of Waterloo* which starts up with a terrific beat on the drum. There was this terrific 'boom' as I was walking past and I jumped, then I sat down and never moved again.

I remember Mr Needham conducting the Royal Berks Regimental Band. He used to spring three foot in the air he got so carried away when he was conducting. It used to be packed on a Sunday afternoon and evening in the Forbury with everybody sitting down and behaving, apart from one or two silly little boys like me. That's what gave me the real interest in music.

I joined the Army Cadet Force band in 1944 when I was about 14 and stayed there until 1947 when I went into the Army. They took us cadets in without musical experience; that was the only way. When I joined the band, they taught me the trumpet first, then the drums and then, I suppose because I was pretty tall, they took me on as drum major. We went to band practice every Wednesday night in the army drill hall in St Mary's Butts behind what was the fire station.

The first time I went to band practice I was introduced to Jack, an ex-bandsman from the Royal Berks, who was the bandmaster. He said to me: "Can you blow a trumpet?" and I said: "No, I can't." He said: "Well, you do it like this." He showed me and from then on you just had to pick it up as you went along. I didn't find it difficult; it's fairly easy when you get going especially when there's a lot playing and you can sort of mingle in with them and get lost in the crowd.

I couldn't read music; you don't have to with a trumpet. I suppose you would if you played a trumpet with valves but you didn't with a cavalry trumpet . It worked all right, and we had a good band. My favourite pieces were *All for a Shilling A Day* and *Ganges*; I liked those tunes.

November 1946. Church parade for the British Legion,

I was moved on to the drums – I didn't mind as long as it was in the band – and then the drum major dropped out and Jack said: "White, do you want to swing the mace?" and I said: "Well, I might as well." I used to wear a white belt, white gaiters and white gloves and we would march on Remembrance Day parades for the British Legion, as it was then, in Spencers Wood and in Newtown.

I joined the cadets because the Army was always me, right from when I was a boy, but I only served six years at the end of it all. I joined up in 1947 at Brock Barracks. I was with the Royal Armoured Corps, first with the 5th Dragoon Guards and then the 8th Hussars and I went with them to to Korea. I was in Korea for 13 months – two winters because they said that was all we could stand. They said really only one but we had two.

The Army Cadet band was the first and last band I played in but they were great days. My uncle stopped playing in 1946 and the Reading Temperance Band went downhill after that – lack of interest, I suppose, or lack of temperance! My uncle wouldn't drink but I encouraged him into the pub one day and he had a half pint of ale and said: "Whatever you do don't tell your aunt." I still listen to music, classical music, I don't like this pop stuff.

When my boy Alan went to Ashmead School I insisted he went into the band. George Watkins taught him and he played French horn, trumpet and the euphonium. He stayed with that band till he left school at 18 and he also played in the Spring Gardens band.

I insisted he joined the band because I believe music's got a steadying effect on people – and I think it worked.

Millennium Choice Peter White

St Patrick's Day by Bidgood

Let the people ring Bellringing

Bellringer BOBBIE MAY, writing about 100 years of bellringing in Berkshire, explains that for three-quarters of that time Berkshire contained large areas of what is now Oxfordshire and was without Slough. Bellringers in the area owe their allegiance to the Oxford Diocesan Guild of Church Bell Ringers – there is no Berkshire association – but more importantly they are part of an international freemasonry promoting what is good for The Exercise at large

The story of 'modern' church bellringing begins shortly before the last 100 years. Most of the ringing associations have their inception in the last quarter of the 19th century as a direct result of the Oxford Movement. In practical terms, the Oxford Movement did much to tidy up irregularities which were creeping into church services. Church musicians had long been holding the church to ransom and demanding a greater emphasis on the musical aspects of the service than was warranted. These characters, very much on the lines of Thomas Hardy's Mellstock church band, were rapidly replaced by an organ and robed choir.

However, the ringers posed a greater problem and weren't so easily ousted. For a start, ringing had become detached from its original purpose and the bells were far more often rung for secular or civic celebrations and the ringers paid accordingly. They often had competitions with neighbouring villages and the prize was serious money for men who were, in the main, labourers. Ringing lacked finesse and was the preserve of the hoi-polloi, who rang when it suited them, often into the small hours and refused to stop, often the worse for drink, because many of them 'brewed up' in the belfry and, on at least one occasion, locked the vicar out of his own tower.

There are many tales of the exclusive societies, who owned their bells, but not the tower, of course. When not using the tower themselves, they would chain up the bells so that other ringers could not use them. It took a determined group of clergymen, who learned to ring and were prepared to stand cheek by jowl with the local rough-necks, to absorb them gradually into the church community.

Thus the diocesan associations were formed, bringing the ringers into communion with the rest of the church. The standard of bellringing also improved as the Guild produced paid trainers who were to introduce the very English art of change ringing, which had previously been the preserve of only the 'gentlemen' ringers, men of substance and leisure, who did it for the exercise. To this day, the ringing fraternity is referred to as The Exercise by its members.

The Oxford Diocesan Guild of Church Bell Ringers was founded in Reading on January 17, 1881. Reading had for some time been an important centre for ringing among the gentlemen ringers. St Laurence's Church, Reading, contains some historic peal boards, the oldest dating back to 1734, which commemorated the first peal rung in Berkshire. The artwork of these peal boards is, in many ways, as noteworthy as the contents, often containing paintings and beautifully intricate decorations in gold leaf. Some of the artwork was done by Charles Hounslow, himself a ringer of note, who conducted the first peal for the newly-formed Guild.

In general bells tended, in the past, to be added piece-meal. The first mention of any bells at St Laurence is in 1433. By 1499 it had become a ring of five. Change ringing as such had not been invented and the number of bells in a church tower was more closely related to the importance of the town and church than to the music which could be rung on them. Bells were added to St Laurence through the ages and in 1929 it became a ring of 12, the only one in Berkshire.

Even among good ringers it requires a very high degree of proficiency to ring 12 bells well. There are only four rings of 12 bells in the whole of the diocese of Oxford –

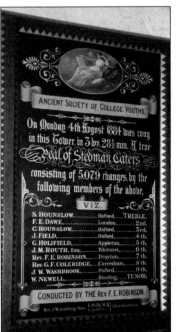

Peal board. Photo by William Butler

Christchurch Cathedral, Amersham and High Wycombe in addition to St. Laurence, Reading – and there are only about 100 rings of 12 bells in the entire world where change ringing is practised in the English style.

If we were to return to the year 1899 we would discover that bands in the population centres, such as Reading and Oxford, would have had ringers of greater expertise than those in the rural areas. In some ways this is still true today. Good ringers will always be attracted to good ringing where the bells are better or the tradition on higher numbers is good. Often the talent of one or two exceptional ringers helps to perpetuate the standard of ringing in one area. However, at the turn of the century, the attitude of the elite bands was somewhat supercilious and the country bands were definitely struggling and inferior. The newly-formed Guild produced its own teachers and went forth to evangelise.

When the Reading Branch of the ODG was formed shortly after the Guild itself was established, the ' branch' consisted of four towers;: Reading St Laurence, Reading St Mary in the Butts, Reading St Giles in Southampton Street, and Caversham St Peter. Shortly after this Tilehurst St Michael, which had a flourishing ringing tradition and a good leader, was added. Today there are 26 towers in the Reading Branch, most of which are affiliated to the Oxford Diocesan Guild of Church Bell Ringers.

Before the Guild was established there were territorial associations already in existence. Sonning Deanery was established in 1880 and East Berkshire with South Buckinghamshire in 1879. They amalgamated with the newly-formed diocesan association, bringing its membership up to 314 in 1881. Newbury Branch was created in 1882 and North Berkshire in 1904. When the county boundaries changed in 1974 and they suddenly found themselves in Oxfordshire, they voted to retain their heritage and rename themselves Old North Berks.

By 1962 the Guild had 15 branches, its present number, those not mentioned being in Oxfordshire and Buckinghamshire. The Guild territory covers some 2,323 square miles and includes over 370 churches with bells hung for change ringing. The membership now stands at about 2,400.

From time to time bells fall into disrepair and lie silent, often for years before anything is done about them. Many new rings of bells were created with the beginning of the Guild, including the two towers at Stratfield Mortimer, where the ringers celebrated the hundredth anniversary of the first peals in their towers during the last few years. Bells were often provided by wealthy men, including the first Master of ODG, the Rev F E Robinson, a gentleman clergyman of some substance, one time vicar of Drayton near Abingdon and buried in All Saints' Churchyard, Wokingham.

Robinson could be legitimately granted a chapter all to himself. Not only was he the Oxford Guild's first Master, but he was made of stern stuff, sufficient, like many of the ringing clergymen of the time, to stand beside the local toughs and ring their 'stony' or 'churchyard bob' (both euphemisms for the most basic and unimaginative ringing) and lead them on to better things, or at least see that their wicked ways remained outside the realms of

the church! He was one of the early instructors of the Guild, who was prepared, at a price, to initiate the local ringers into the art of change ringing, though he was happier to help existing ringers onto the path of even more complicated methods.

In this capacity he was a notable 'conductor', the ringer in charge of the ringing who can help to keep the other ringers right. He was a prolific peal ringer in his day and was the first man ever to have achieved the total of 1000 peals, performances which, on average, each take about three hours to achieve and he conducted many of them, including several 'long lengths' of more than the standard 5000 or so changes.

Peal board. Photo by William Butler

The peal boards at Appleton give testimony to their great and glorious achievements in the ringing of long lengths and include peals of 15,041 changes (nine hours and 16 minutes) three times the normal peal length. Speaking as someone who finds the normal three-hour peal a sore-hands job, my mind boggles at the thought of more than nine hours of continuous ringing. To satisfy the rules of peal ringing, the ringing has to be continuous with the same band of people and no substitutes and in those days the bells would have been hung on plain bearings and would have been much harder work than the average ring today.

Appleton is home to the Guild's own resident family firm of bell hangers, White's, who have served ringing for 175 years. Peal boards contain names of generations of Whites, who were not only craftsmen, but talented ringers in their own right.

Robinson's favourite method was Stedman, a principle notoriously difficult to keep free from error. Whenever the peal was successful, his band would be fêted and taken triumphantly back to the vicarage and feasted. If the peal was lost, then the ringers got nothing; callous ruling for a band, many of them ordinary working men who had, in all likelihood, walked anything up to ten miles before ringing the peal and who would then have to walk home again with empty bellies. Robinson's dictum was a harsh one; no peal, no meal.

So how have things changed in the last 100 years? The working parts of a bell tend to last about a century and we have recently come to the uncomfortable position of having to renew quite a lot of the original fittings and fixtures and often the bells themselves. Benefactors of Robinson's ilk do not exist in the same way that they did 100 years ago. However, the new Millennium and all the excitement that this has engendered, together with a renewed interest in church bells, has made restoring and replacing possible once more. Many churches throughout the land have benefited from millennium funding, and old installations refurbished, silent bells restored and new rings are all on the agenda for the year 2000.

Three years ago a ladies' band of ringers in Reading rang a centenary peal in honour of Alice White of Basingstoke, first lady to ring a peal in a church tower and who did so in the Reading branch. The centenary peal was achieved at Goring-on-Thames. A band of ladies from the East Berkshire and South Buckinghamshire branch also rang a peal for this at Burnham. Ladies' peals are something of a rarity and The Ringing World, newspaper to the ringing exercise, contained an unprecedented full page of peals rung by ladies in honour of Alice White.

Women have for some time rung peals, but more often than not they are at the lighter or front end of the ring. To prove that technique and not brawn are what really counts, some of the best female heavy bell ringers in the country (among them our own Claire Edwards of Twyford) got together to ring a peal of *Cambridge Surprise Minor* at St Buryan in Cornwall, at 37 cwt, the heaviest six bell tower in the world and brought the ringing round in three hours and 48 minutes.

There has recently been a trend to produce much smaller, lighter rings of bells which exist as an entity in themselves, known as mini-rings. Enthusiasts have had these bells installed in their garages, bedrooms and sheds. One such exists in Crowthorne and is the property of the deputy editor of The Ringing World. It has been named the Coleridge Campanile as a tribute to Canon Coleridge, deputy master to the Guild in Robinson's time, peal-ringer, teacher, clergyman and rector at Crowthorne for 40 years.

Bibliography:

100 Years of the Oxford Diocesan Guild by William Butler
The Church Bells of Berkshire by Frederick Sharpe
The Ringing World 1996

Millennium Choice Bobbie May

Monteverdi's Beatus Vir, because I love early church music

A Bundle of Contradictions
Baron Berners

One of the great eccentrics of the 20th century, Gerald, ninth Baron Berners was a composer of some originality. His music has been described as "light music of a very superior type" and some resemblance can be traced to the early styles of Igor Stravinsky and William Walton, both of whom Berners knew. The music he wrote to a ballet, The Triumph of Neptune, once enjoyed considerable popularity and is still occasionally played.

As a person, Gerald Berners was a bundle of contradictions. He was capable of great charm and, in general, seems to have been loyal to his friends, but his eccentricities were not always entirely amiable and some of his behaviour ill became his rank. He took little interest in politics but allowed himself to be talked into composing some kind of anthem or marching-song for the Fascists. It is possible that his aim was partly ironic. Many years before, Percy Grainger had written a Marching Song of Democracy and Dame Ethel Smythe (who came from Frimley, just over the Surrey border) had-written a March of the Women for the Suffragette movement. Berners viewed such music as cheap and vulgar and it could be that his own composition was not completely serious. None the less it did his reputation great damage.

At about the same period it was widely believed (Berners himself may have encouraged the rumour) that Gerald Berners had lunched with Adolf Hitler in the course of which they had a row about the composer Hindemith. Sir John Betjeman stated that the story was a fabrication, and he was in a better position than most to give an opinion, for he had been one of the Berners' circle of friends for many years.

Many other stories are told about Gerald Berners. For example, the success of Radclyffe Hall's lesbian novel, The Well of Loneliness, aroused some public excitement at the end of the 1920s. A year or two later Berners wrote and published (using the name Adela Quebec) The Girls of Radcliff Hall, a school story in questionable taste written in a style resembling that of Angela Brazil, whose schoolgirl tales were very popular. Copies of this work are now, I believe, quite valuable collectors' items.

Constant Lambert said of Gerald Berners that he had an ingenious plan for getting a compartment to himself on the pre-war GWR from Paddington to Oxford. He would put on dark glasses and stand beckoning people in. Anyone who dared to enter would find him reading The Times upside-down and taking his own temperature with a thermometer every few minutes. This usually caused the intruder to retreat and the ninth Baron then had the compartment to himself all the way to Oxford.

Gerald Berners died at his home in Faringdon in 1950.

Tony Barham

Playing for the People   Bandsman Stanley Harding

STANLEY HARDING, who lives in Southcote, is now registered blind, but he still gets pleasure from music. Born in 1920, he played with brass bands for more than 60 years, starting with the Boys' Brigade and finishing with the popular and long-established East Woodhay Silver Band

Music has been my life. When I was playing with the Salvation Army, they would try to get me to join the Army, and I always said; "You can't talk me into the Kingdom but you can sing me or play me into it." I can listen to all sorts of music – I hate people who only go for one thing. To be musically minded you need to encompass the lot. I haven't got my eyesight any more but my ears are okay and I can still listen to an orchestra and itemise all the instruments. I get a lot of pleasure out of it.

My introduction to music was in the Boys' Brigade drum and bugle band at Norcot Mission Hall, in Reading. I played them both. You had someone to show you the rudiments but you picked up the rest yourself. You shut yourself in the bedroom and annoyed everybody. No one else in the family played but I was a natural. I was about nine and went to the Mission Hall until I was about 13.

I was taught to play an instrument properly when I joined Reading West Salvation Army band and Mr Allen, the bandmaster, took me under his wing. I played the cornet at first, pure and simple and then one by one the horn, the tenor horn, the baritone, the trombone, the trumpet, the euphonium, the bass. If we were short of any instrument on a Sunday I'd fill in. I enjoyed the challenge.

When I was playing in the Sandhurst Silver Band, the musical director, Jim Brewer, used to come the old soldier to me and say, "We're going to be short on so and so this afternoon, can you bring your trumpet? Can you bring your trombone?" My instrument really is the trombone. That's the one I would choose but I ended up playing the big double-bass tuba; it's a lovely instrument. All the time I was with East Woodhay Silver Band I played the bass. I used to love playing the old bass but it got a bit heavy towards the end. I've got a French horn and a trumpet and though I can't read music now I can play by ear.

We were taught to read music properly in the Reading West Salvation Army band before they would give us an instrument. There was no question you got an instrument unless you satisfied them that you knew what you were doing. You learned the C scale and the F scale ,

one or two flats and naturals thrown in with it, then you were allowed to pick up your instrument, learn how to articulate and play it, and put the two together. After that they gave you a music book and you played a tune in a short space of time. You could do that with proper tuition. I have taught youngsters and you only get out of them what you put in. You have got to work with them.

During the war years, I was a signalman so I was on reserved occupation. Reading West band went down to about four and I took over teaching about seven youngsters and they could all play hymn tunes in a short space of time, then marches and selections. I enjoyed those war years. I moved to Maidenhead Citadel and was a cornet player in the band. The bandmaster, Walter Steventon, was a special constable and a marvellous cornet player. His son Trevor who was 13, and I, were the cornet section. Before the war they had a band of about 18-20 and during the war the most we had was 11 or 12. But if you've got 10 good players you have got the balance and you can make a nice sound. The Reading West band had only 13 members at that time but those 13 were real players and the band could play practically everything. There is an affinity within the band and to get good results you listen to the player next to you. You've got to balance each other. That's the secret of good playing, balance.

I used to love going to the old citadel in the Butts. I don't like the new citadel; it's a concrete jungle. The old Victorian hall was marvellous but it was pulled down to build the Butts shopping centre. We had some lovely times there. I saw the composer Eric Ball in person at the old citadel. He was a lovely pianist . He said, "Give me three tunes" and he'd put them all together and play them. He was bandmaster of the International Staff band at one time, a marvellous musician. He got interested in spiritualism and the Salvation Army didn't like that so he was more or less forced to resign. But his interest was there. He was one of my favourite composers. I particularly liked the Old Wells. I used to play that on the bass and there's a lovely bass part in it. It's an old tune with the words,"Come back to the Old Wells, to the Old Wells."

Working for the railway mucked up my banding for a while because I was always on call and we moved around a bit. I played in the Llanelli Citadel Young People's band in South Wales for about two years but we came back to Reading and settled here. It was when I joined Sandhurst Silver Band as bandmaster under Jim Brewer that I started to conduct. Old Jim used to say: "I'll play and you conduct. You get more out of them than I do." Conducting needs flair. Some people can and some people can't. The best bet is not to keep looking at the score. Look at it beforehand so you know what you're doing and then you can bring the bandsmen in. I studied the scores first and then had the music up in my head.

When I first went to Sandhurst we took part in a competition in Portsmouth and did a fine job. Old Jim said, "I reckon you're wasting your time here. You could get a place in Black Dyke or Grimethorpe." I said, "You get lost, mate. I've got a nice job on the railway and a nice family. I've moved five times now and I'm not moving again." I liked being amateur status and I liked what I did with the music. All sort of things have cropped up musically.

My longest stint was with East Woodhay Silver Band and I was there for many years. I had the farthest to go of all the members and I used to travel from Reading, backwards and forwards, all those years. Eventually I had to pack it up when I lost my car because of my eyesight. They were a nice crowd at East Woodhay. It was like going to a social club when you walked into the bandroom. I was happy to stay with them for a long time. They were a well-known band, and still are, and were always in the prizes. If we weren't first or second in a competition, it was hard luck.

The funny thing is while town bands are struggling, East Woodhay, which is right out in the country, is still going strong. When I was there it had 90 playing members. There was the senior band, the youth band, and the training band. You never went on the bandstand at East Woodhay without about 30 members. If you were short in the senior band, you took some out of the junior band.

The long-established East Woodhay Silver Band started life as a village band known as East Woodhay Mechanics Band in 1884. In 1904 it was renamed St Martin's Band after the local church and did not take on its present name until after the First World War. The band has been long associated with the Webb family and three generations have played with the band since 1908. The late Desmond Webb was bandmaster from 1947, following his father, and his two sons still play. It has always been a thriving band and in the '80s built its own bandroom on a site donated to it. Its music has been enjoyed by thousands of people over the years at carnivals, fêtes and shows and it plays regularly in the Forbury Gardens in Reading.

We had some lovely times at East Woodhay. We played the music that the public liked. It didn't necessarily mean the band as a whole enjoyed that sort of music but if the people wanted it, that's what we gave them. To tell you the truth I wasn't interested in contests. I'd sooner go to the bandstand at Newbury Park and if the band was playing on a nice day and there were lots of people crowding round, I was happy. I enjoyed those concerts most of all. We were giving pleasure and we were getting pleasure.

Des Webb was a good bandmaster and lovely man. He was a milkman by trade and musically he was marvellous. He really was something on the bandstand. You had to

Stanley Harding playing in the East Woodhay Band in 1984
Photo by Reading Evening Post

sort out all your music before you started, no messing about. In some bands there is about ten minutes between each piece. With Des, you played one bit and you only had the chance to blow the water out of your instrument and he was on again. If Des was ready, he started.

Just before I retired from the band, I said to him: "When are you going to get me off this bass? I'm getting an old man now, 70 odd." And his wife Shirley said: "The time you come off that bass, Stan, you'll break Des's heart. He depends on you." I'll always remember whenever we were on the bandstand, Old Des had his beady eyes on me. The bass is the rhythm of the band; if you are playing a tango for instance, the bass sets the rhythm. If that's not right, look out.

I have been out playing when they have had a full band and just one bass – me. I just had to put more puff through it. Afterwards old Des said: "We could hear you." Playing the bass is like singing. You can get away playing a cornet with your mouth and throat but you can't with a bass. Singers train their breathing and take deep breaths and it's the same with the bass. Old Des would say: "Play a note" and I took a deep breath and that went on for six bars. Des said: "Are you still playing?" and I said: "Only just !" He said: "I didn't think you'd last that long." Mind you, I didn't put double 'ff' on it, a medium 'pp' perhaps.

It broke my heart when Des died. I missed him. I couldn't carry on. It wasn't the same without him.

East Woodhay still competes but they're in the top section now. I went to hear them two years ago at the Christmas concert in St Martin's Church and I was thrilled at their playing. Their bandmaster plays in the Grenadier Guards and he's marvellous. They played *Jupiter* from the *Planet Suite*, and I thought, Crikey, they're asking for trouble. Do you know, they played it perfectly and when they got to that magnificent ending, they lifted the roof. I went round to see them afterwards and they were pleased to see me. They hadn't forgotten me.

I've always had a reasonable baritone voice. When I was with Reading West I sang with the Songsters and I was roped into a little choir run by Mrs Richards from Tilehurst, who had been a concert pianist. I still do a bit of entertaining though my wife has to help me because I can't read the small print. The only thing I haven't got is eyesight.

Happy Band of Orphans

Bearwood College band

The band of the Royal Merchant Navy School first made its mark in the 1890s when, from its former home at Snaresbrook, it won acclaim after being adjudged the best boys' band in the United Kingdom. At that time the school was known as the Merchant Seamen's Orphan Asylum and the band, then trained by the headmaster, helped to bring in much-needed donations by playing at fundraising events including garden parties, steamer excursions on the Thames and dinners at West End hotels.

When the school moved to Bearwood, near Wokingham, in 1921, the band continued to flourish, heading the weekly church parade to St Catherine's and leading the march through London to the annual Service for Seafarers at St. Paul's Cathedral. It was also a frequent 'turn' at variety concerts at the Palace Theatre, Reading, as well as providing music for events at the Royal Albert Hall.

During the Second World War the musicians were in constant demand for special War Week parades throughout the county, (like the War Weapons Parade in 1942 pictured below). Sadly, when in the '60s, the school began to admit students unconnected with the Merchant Navy, some traditions were inevitably lost and one of the things to go was the band.

However, music continues to play an important role at Bearwood College, as it is now called. It is taught as a general subject and provides a choir which, among other events, sings each year at St. Paul's.

The splendid Music and Drama Centre, opened by the Queen in 1991, is also a much sought after venue and is used for concerts and rehearsals by bands and orchestras throughout Berkshire and the surrounding area.

The band from the Royal Merchant Navy School at Bearwood leads a War Weapons parade through Wokingham town centre in 1942

'It's not all George Formby'   Banjo Festival

JULIAN VINCENT ran the first Reading Banjo Festival as a fringe event of the Reading Festival of Arts in 1983. It has moved from venue to venue over the years and although it has now become the Reading International Banjo and Fiddle Festival, it is still the most informal of festivals open to anyone banjoist or not

I remember the first Reading Banjo Festival very clearly. It was 12th June 1983 and was the first event ever held at the Radstock Lane Community Centre (local residents were in panic at the prospect of a loud all-night party until told that the average age of banjo players was about 50) and my wife was heavily pregnant with our daughter. It was a fringe event of the Reading Festival of the Arts (RFA) and I had been persuaded to organise it by the readership of a magazine I edit and publish.

Based on that first Festival, the main function is to bring together all sorts of banjo players in a family atmosphere where they can sit around and play to and alongside each other, be warm, dry and well fed. As a biologist I see no difference between our wants and those of the locusts I used to breed. The locusts even make music! Then in the evening there's a concert which displays the various styles of playing by some of the best players in the world. At various times we have had some of the definitive musicians of the banjo world, many like Buddy Wachter and Cynthia Sayers visiting from the USA in order to play for us. They may play solo or in bands, and most of the soloists are accompanied at the piano by Keith Nichols, a well-known and highly experienced professional musician who specialises in stride and ragtime piano, and has broadcast, arranged and taught widely.

Now accepted as a permanent feature of the RFA, we went from Radstock Lane to the Great Hall of The University of Reading. Although the acoustics were pretty awful, there were many other facilities such as the space and peaceful lawns which made this a popular venue. But when the university sold the site it became necessary to move, so we had two superb years at the old Town Hall. Unfortunately the finances proved impossible, so we went to the social club of Royal Berkshire Hospital. This was demolished, so on we went to the Ramada hotel. For three years they were welcoming, but then became more difficult and put the price up (we had been getting a *very* good deal) and we moved back to the university, this time to the Buttery, a large room on the Whiteknights site, where we became the Reading International Banjo and Fiddle Festival. This worked quite well, but was not

ideal, so we decided to go to 21 South Street, Reading's own arts centre. Perhaps we'll stay there.

Most years the festival starts on Friday evening with a welcome session, and continues on the Sunday. Then the serious business of playing starts on the Saturday. In the course of organising these Banjo Festivals I have built up an archive of photos (donated by the various people who attended) and recordings.

The festival is, of course, open to all who wish to attend, banjoist or not. Some of the best times have been with players of other instruments who blend in with the hardened banjo players and broaden greatly the range of music played. It's not all George Formby!

The banjo is a strange instrument, at once the pariah and the clown of instruments, reviled and laughed at. Yet I have played it with classical musicians who have been charmed and excited by its virtuosity, and an American friend of mine has played Brahms *Hungarian Dances* with a symphony orchestra in Carnegie Hall in New York – and at the end of the concert the whole orchestra stood up spontaneously and applauded him.

Just remember – the banjo is a musical instrument, no more, no less. So you play music on it. Classical, ragtime, jazz, avant-garde, folk. It's just this instrument, y'know. Mozart, Bach, Joplin, Formby, Brahms, Gershwin, Lerner and Lowe, Morton, Ellington. It's all music. And there are the specialist composers such as Reser, Mandell, Thomas and Grimshaw, who wrote and adapted some highly technical pieces, derived from the dance bands and piano novelty music of the '20s.

Even today there are professional musicians composing for the banjo. Geoff Freed, who gives recitals in Boston and New York, is a classically trained pianist who traded the 88 keys for the five banjo strings. He plays pieces which were written by Alfred Cammeyer for the rich and regal in Edwardian England, and modern works by Timothy Mainland, the Professor of Music at Concord College, West Virginia.

A Crusade for British Music   The Broadheath Singers

Not only are The Broadheath Singers unique in Berkshire but they are unique in the country. People come from great distances to their annual concert at Eton College to hear rarely performed and neglected works, mainly by British composers born between 1848 and 1900. This is the remit for an unusual choral group which was founded in 1971 by ROBERT TUCKER who explains how the Singers came about and why he enjoys, above all, searching through attics for obscure musical works

It all started because of my enthusiasm for the music of Elgar, a new friendship with another music lover and a tinge of envy over a 14-year-old impresario. I had recently moved to take up a job in Uxbridge as Music Librarian for the London Borough of Hillingdon and was living in digs in Iver.

At the time I was particularly keen on the music of Elgar. Although Elgar is extremely popular today, in those days hardly anything beyond a certain core number of works such as *Dream of Gerontius*, *Enigma Variations* and the *Cello Concerto* were performed. I was particularly interested in hearing three works I'd read about: *The Light of Life*, an oratorio written in 1896; *Romance for Bassoon and Orchestra*; and a work called *Polonia*, which was written during the First World War to raise money for the Polish people. There were no recordings of these pieces.

I had talked about this music with Mary Pearce who had a house a couple of doors up from where I was staying. She was a research assistant at the British Library and sang in the Windsor and Eton Choral Society.

I saw a headline in the local paper, which said something like: *David (14) takes on Messiah*. There was a picture of this golden-haired lad, David Lacey, who I later got to know, who had got together a group of friends and conducted Handel's Messiah in St Mary's, Slough, where he was the organist. I must have been about 25 years old and thought: if a boy of fourteen can do something like this ... After all I had been involved in music since the age of seven. I played the piano, the organ, and I'd been involved in choirs over the years in various churches.

So Mary Pearce said: "The only way you're going to hear The Light of Life is if you actually do it yourself." I'd never conducted an orchestra before but I thought that perhaps this *was* the only way I would hear it.

The long and the short of it was we got hold of the scores, gathered a group of singers together and an orchestra, and put on a performance in Windsor Parish Church in September 1971. We had a choir of just under 70. The orchestra was mainly made up of local amateur players.

We named the choir after Elgar's birthplace, Broadheath in Worcestershire. The orchestra was called the Windsor Sinfonia. From about 1979 the orchestra has become professional and the amateur element was gradually reduced. Although it costs us much more to get professional players you get a much better sound. We have one rehearsal with the orchestra, in the concert hall on the Saturday afternoon and they play all this unfamiliar music they have never seen before.

That first concert was meant to be a one-off. I'd heard The Light of Life at last and that was it. But at the end of the concert, people asked: "What are you going to do next year? You've got all these people together, you must do something."

I said: "I'm only prepared to do it if we concentrate on doing things that other people don't do. I see no point becoming yet another choral society doing the same standard repertory. If you're prepared for me to come along and suggest rarely performed and neglected works, mainly by British composers born between 1848 and 1900, then I will."

So they said: "Yes, we're willing to go along with this." And I said: "I won't put anything in your way that will be unpleasant. You may never have heard of the composer, or you may never have heard of the piece but it will be tuneful, singable music."

The rest, as they say is history. We have specialised in that area and held a concert every year since then.

After the first year, I decided it was not a good idea to put things on in Windsor Parish Church, mainly because it had fixed pews which were difficult and expensive to move. Also, I realised why they didn't have concerts there on a regular basis. It was because it was on a direct flight path to Heathrow and there were aircraft coming over every few minutes.

We moved to St Mary's in Slough and all the concerts after the first one were put on there until 1980, when we moved to our current venue, which is the School Hall at Eton College.

Broadheath Singers meet from May to September. We have to have a longer rehearsal season than most other choirs, eighteen to nineteen weeks rehearsal, whereas most choirs have about twelve to thirteen, because we are doing it during the time when choir members invariably take weeks out to go on holiday.

We also stick to one concert a year because I spend the rest of the year doing research, tracking down various pieces of music. Although you may find the vocal score of a piece, when you start making enquiries with the publishers about orchestral material, in a lot of cases they don't have it any more, or they've thrown it away, or it's gone back to the composer who's subsequently died and their relatives have said: "Oh, nobody's interested in this", and put it on the bonfire at the end of the garden.

I spend lots of time going through attics and discover lots of treasures that way. In certain cases we've had to have pieces re-orchestrated in order to perform them which is rather expensive.

For example if you take this year's (1999) concert, it has a Pre-Raphaelite theme. One of the pieces, *The Lady of Shalott* by Cyril Rootham, has never been performed, although it was written in 1909. The manuscript full score was at St John's College, Cambridge, and the manuscript vocal score was at Cambridge University. We subsequently managed to get a photo-copy of both of these and they've been put on to Sibelius 7, a computerised music setting system, which has produced a completely new full score and set of parts and vocal score, and we'll be giving the first performance of it.

With another piece we're doing this year, Armstrong Gibbs's *La Belle Dame sans Merci*, the publisher no longer exists. Although you could still trace copies of the vocal score, the orchestral score had disappeared. I know the composer's daughter and she hadn't got it.

However, we discovered that the British Library have got a set of string parts and we have gained permission from the people who now own the copyright, to get copies. We commissioned somebody to re-orchestrate the piece based on those string parts because we know what instrumentation it was to have. Obviously it may not come out exactly as it was, but it will be as near as we can get.

The other piece that we are doing is a setting of *The Blessed Damozel* by Edgar Bainton, who spent the last years of his life in Australia. The full score and parts were in Sydney and they wouldn't risk photo-copying the parts because they were in manuscript so they had to be microfilmed, then photo-copied, and they've been sent over from Australia for us.

Alexander Brent Smith (1889-1950) is a composer in whom I'm particularly interested. I come from Lancing in West Sussex and he was for a time Director of music at Lancing College, and he'd written a piece called *Elegy* (in Memory of Edward Elgar). The combination of Elgar and Lancing intrigued me. I couldn't find very much information about him but I eventually tracked down his niece, who lives just outside Gloucester, where he was born and subsequently died. She'd got all his music, in the same house where he lived.

I visited the house and discovered many works of his that I had never heard of. Much of it had never been

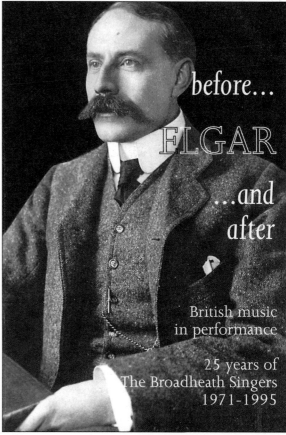

before...
ELGAR
...and after

British music in performance

25 years of The Broadheath Singers 1971-1995

The Broadheath Singers produced a booklet to celebrate their 25th anniversary in 1995

published and most of it was stored in an amazing attic where it had lain since his death.

We've performed two pieces by him and in his centenary year I managed to persuade a number of organisations in the Gloucester area to do some of his music.

There's such a lot of music out there from this period which for some reason never caught on. This may be because the composers weren't particularly good self publicists, or they didn't have publishers who promoted their music as much as they should have. Some things just take off and others don't. For example, there's a work I want to do next year, by the composer Eric Fogg called *The Seasons*, which he wrote in 1931 for the Leeds Festival. It sank without trace because that was the year that Walton's *Belshazzar's Feast* was performed at the Leeds Festival and everything was overshadowed by this.

He died in 1939 at the age of 36 falling under a tube train at Waterloo station. He was on his way to get married for the second time the next day in

Bournemouth, which made it even more tragic. We don't know whether he committed suicide or became ill and just fell. It was an open verdict. I tried to track down his fiancée, but have never been able to trace her.

Music is subject to fashion. What may be of no interest today may become popular in ten years time. We are probably ahead of fashion. In the past some publishers may have disposed of music that had lain on their hire library shelves for fifty years or more in the belief that nobody had any further interest in it. However, nowadays it is possible to store music on computers to save storage space so that it can be retrieved in the future when there is a revived interest in it. Music need never go 'out of print' any longer.

We always record our concerts just for our own archive. A couple of years ago the National Sound Archive approached me about whether they could have a list of the music we'd done. They discovered that there were 30 pieces we had done of which they had no other recordings, including commercial recordings, off-air broadcasts or private recordings. They took our original tapes and transferred them to compact disc.

They are now available for anyone to hear in the new British Library at St Pancras. We are very proud of this achievement which shows that the importance of our crusade for British music has at last been recognised nationally.

We've had reviews in the *Musical Times* and last year for the first time we got a review in a national daily newspaper, which I think is pretty rare for an amateur group.

We have a core audience who come to the concerts year after year from as far afield as Worcestershire, Leicestershire, Gloucestershire, Sussex and Essex. They realise that it will probably be their only opportunity to hear many of the pieces in the foreseeable future.

For some years now we have been part of the Windsor Festival Fringe.

My ultimate challenge is to get into a situation, which I found myself in some years ago going to a concert in the Sheldonian Theatre in Oxford. The concert was so popular they turned people away at the door. That's always been my challenge for the concerts to be so well supported that it would be difficult to get in. It will never happen but it gives us something to aim for.

We would like to see more local people attending and more support from the local press and other media.

There are still many unexplored attics out there waiting to yield up their treasures. We have only uncovered the tip of the iceberg so far. However, it has been a very enjoyable experience and I can thoroughly recommend it to other musical explorers.

Singing down the river
Boulter's Lock

Early in the 20th century, Ascot Sunday became a splendid occasion, a riverside gathering of the fashionable and the notorious and an opportunity for everyone to see the "swells" they could read about in the gossip-columns of the newspapers. The gathering centred upon Maidenhead Bridge, Skindles and Boulter's Lock.

During the afternoon of Ascot Sunday, in 1932, the fine old Edwardian steamer Empress of India was filmed, for a newsreel, passing through Boulter's Lock. The people on the steamer were apparently singing The Battle Hymn of the Republic. Some may think that this hardly suited the lavish, imperial celebration which Ascot Sunday used to be.

Were the passengers on the steamboat a party of touring Americans? Was it a non-conformist church outing using the hymn to remind others to observe the Sabbath? There is another possible explanation.

In the late '20s there was a craze for "community singing". It was vaguely associated with left-wing politics, co-operation, open-air activities and there was even a slogan for it , Let the People Sing, attributed to J B Priestley.

One of the songs which proved popular in the community singing era was John Brown's Body, the song which had preceded the Battle Hymn and which has a similar tune and chorus.

It may be that this was what the people on the steamer were singing that Sunday afternoon.

The community singing movement did not last but one legacy of that time remains – the tradition of singing Abide With Me at important football matches.

Tony Barham

Remembering Boozy's Boozy Blues Bar

Musician PETER LINCOLN, who has been backing vocalist for Cliff Richard and other stars, recalls six unforgettable years at The late lamented Boozy Blues Bar in London Road, Reading, during the early 1990s

"…So they want me to continue running the downstairs part," said Paul, "but I'm going to have to change the name."

"Oh yeah, got anything in mind?" I inquired innocently.

"I'm going to call it The Boozy Blues Bar," he said.

My first reaction was "You can't be serious!" I'd been doing the odd gig both as a solo performer and as a duo with my old mate Hugh at what was then dubiously called 'The Studio Bistro'. All wooden floors and French-stick-in-a-basket. It was about to undergo a transformation both dramatic and bizarre.

Upstairs was to become a haven for the local curry connoisseurs – The Raj – and downstairs The Boozy Blues Bar. Surely the strangest marriage.

I resigned myself to the fact that what had been a reasonable local gig was about to bite the dust and I would have to look elsewhere to replace it.

How wrong can a man be?

Paul called. "I've had a word with the new proprietor and convinced him to let you do the opening night," he said.

The opening night was a somewhat surreal occasion. The wooden floor had been replaced by fitted carpet, the French stick by Naan bread. Exotic Tikka smells wafted down the staircase and the walls of the back room were adorned with framed black and white prints of the great Blues legends.

I shared the bill that evening with Steve George and we still talk about it to this day. Our audience, there by invitation, were treated to a scintillating combination of *Hotel California* and onion bahjees, and the evening was a huge success.

Now, this happened to take place on a Thursday. As I was leaving, Mr Raja, the aforementioned new proprietor, asked me if I would like to come back and play the following Thursday – and the following Thursday – and…

"How long do you think we should do this for?" I inquired innocently.

"Well, I'm sure we'll soon realise if it's not working any more," said Raja.

The Thursday gig at Boozy's became part of my weekly routine. It was my equivalent of 'a night out with the lads'; it was where I could let off steam, have a few beers – and get paid for it. The back room was small enough to create an instant atmosphere, and it was always full, some people coming straight from work to unwind and sing their hearts out.

Downstairs I beat hell out of my guitar and you all stamped and clapped, bellowing out the choruses to *Pinball Wizard* and *Hey Jude*. Upstairs the plates of Chicken Madras bounced across the tables to the vibrations from below.

It became commonplace for certain hoodlums to have regular guest spots. Remember Pete singing *The Killing of Georgie*, and Tony's rendition of *Easy (Like a Sunday Morning)*, and of course Stevie's inimitable *Summer of '69*?

Suddenly I'd been doing the damned gig for a year! Then another! And another! Faces came and went, sometimes to return a year later and find that I was still there, singing the same old bollocks!

To say I got a buzz out of all this would be a massive understatement. It was a sufficient ego booster to last the whole week …and then I got to do it all over again.

On and on it went, for more than six years. It became too hard to leave it, even though I sometimes felt like throwing in the towel. So it didn't end on a high as we would all have wished, and towards the end of its era, things did go a bit stale. However, I have no regrets. I made a great many friends there and have some cherished memories of those Thursday nights.

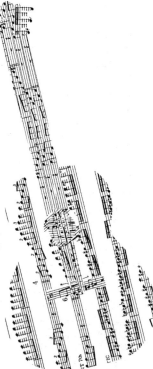

My thanks and best wishes go to Raja and Paul who kicked it all off, to Derek and Juliet who kept the beer flowing in the heyday, to Stevie for being a complete nutter, and of course to my dear friend Sid who kept the rest of the nutters away, and a bemused smile on his face.

If you were there singing along, I thank you. Keep on supporting live music, there's nothing like it.

On Parade Regimental Bands

It was a sad day when regimental bands were abolished in 1994 to be replaced by new divisional bands. In The Royal Berkshire Regiment, bands are recorded as far back as the mid-18th century

An inspection report dating from 1769 records that the 49th Foot had a band, and it is believed that some eight or ten musicians accompanied the Regiment on its posting early the next decade to Mhow in India. Thereafter the bandsmen could have had little opportunity for music, for the 49th fought against the French in the 1790s, in the American War of 1812-1814 and then in the Chinese Opium War. There were occasional breaks in the military activity, however, and it is reported that in August 1824 the bands of the 6th and 49th Foot played at a ball given by the wife of the Governor of the Cape Province.

The first known Bandmaster of the 49th was James Gibbon, who had enlisted into the Regiment in the mid-1850s and attended a Kneller Hall course before returning in 1867. He remained for eight years and seems to have been successful in his work, with a final annual report saying that he 'gives satisfaction in every way'.

The reports of the first recorded Bandmaster of the 66th Foot, Frederick Hynes, were less impressive. Under the headings of Musical Ability and General Usefulness he was adjudged adequate, but there was a repeated complaint under Conduct that he was 'unsteady'; quite what this meant is unclear but it was a problem not resolved until 1870 when, after just five years in the job, he was reduced in rank, continuing to serve with the Regiment in a lesser role. His replacement was Michael Kleinstuber, who was to serve through the Second Afghan War.

At the time of the 1881 amalgamation Mr Gibbon was still Bandmaster of the 1st Battalion, then serving in Gibraltar. Following some time in Malta and the Egyptian campaign of 1882, Mr Gibbon retired the following year, to be replaced by Richard Francis. During his ten years at the post he, too, was denied a stable posting to build up the band: he accompanied the Battalion to Gibraltar, Egypt, Malta, Cyprus and Bermuda, and it was not until a return to England in 1903 that there was a chance to settle down.

The 2nd Battalion also ended the century overseas - it was in South Africa when fighting broke out in 1899 and the bandsmen were switched to stretcher-bearer duties. From there it was sent on to Egypt and then India, where

The Royal Berkshire Regiment

1742 49th or Cotterell's Marines

1743 disbanded

1744 63rd, or Trelawney's Foot

1748 49th Foot

1782 49th (Hertfordshire) Foot

1816 49th (Princess of Wales's) Hertfordshire Foot

1755 2nd Bn, 19th Foot

1758 66th Foot

1782 66th (Berkshire) Foot

1881 (May) The Berkshire Regiment (Princess Charlotte of Wales's)

1881 (July) Princess Charlotte of Wales's (Berkshire Regiment)

1885 Princess Charlotte of Wales's (Royal Berkshire Regiment)

1921 The Royal Berkshire Regiment (Princess Charlotte of Wales's)

1959 amalgamated to form The Duke of Edinburgh's Royal Regiment (Berkshire and Wiltshire)

The Royal Berkshire Regimental
Regimental music
The quick march was the popular song The Dashing White Sergeant, with words by General Burgoyne and music by Henry Bishop (composer of Home, Sweet Home). Probably written in the early years of the 19th century, it is believed that it was adopted by the 49th Foot during the Peninsular War. The 2nd Battalion used The Young May Moon (also used by The Sherwood Foresters)

The regimental slow march was the troop, 'Les Hugenots. Arranged by Dan Godfrey (snr), it is based on themes from Meyerbeer's opera Les Huguenots and has been used as the slow troop on almost every Trooping the Colour ceremony by the Guards this century.

The Duke of Edinburgh's Royal Regiment
Regimental music
The quick march is The Farmer's Boy, played in an arrangement by Bandmaster George Haile. This tune had previously been used by The Royal Berkshire Regiment to march troops off parade. The slow march is Auld Robin Gray, inherited from The Wiltshire Regiment.

Bandmaster Sidney Dore — who had been in his post for 17 years – was succeeded by Ernest Barrett, formerly Bandmaster of the 3rd Battalion, The Manchester Regiment. That Mr Barrett made a good showing in his new job is apparent from a letter written by his commanding officer to Sir Alfred Balfour, Commandant of Kneller Hall, on 1st August 1907:

> I want to write and tell you what a great success our new bandmaster, Mr Barrett, has proved. You were so kind as to say you would ensure our getting a good man, when Mr Dore, our former bandmaster, retired last December and we are all most grateful for the man you sent us. He has done wonders for our band aready and is also most popular and tactful.

The 2nd Battalion returned to Europe in 1914 to fight in the war, a difficult period for Ernest Weaver who had taken over from Mr Barrett earlier in the year. He was, however, to prove one of the successes of the Regiment, remaining for 20 years. A photograph taken in 1923 shows his band standing at a strength of 29, and during the inter-war years he built it into a popular attraction all over the country, playing seasons in towns from Edinburgh to Torquay to Brighton. The following programme was put on at Prince's Street Gardens, Edinburgh in 1929, and illustrates Mr Weaver's careful mix of popular and classical works:

March Triumphant *The Spirit of Pageantry* Fletcher
Excerpts from *The Pathetic Symphony* Tschaikovsky
    Andante from the 1st movement
    March from the 3rd movement
Selection *Hit the Deck* Youmans
Two Hindoo Pictures Hansen & Lotter
    The Shepherdess of the Himalayas
    Approaching and passing a Hindoo Temple
Selection *Cavaleria Rusticana* Mascagni
Japanese Romance *Poppies* Moret
Polonaise in A Chopin
Selection *Chu Chin Chow* Norton
Rule Britannia
God Save The King

The band and drums of the Royal Berkshire Regiment

Equally typical of the period was a march around the recruiting area in 1928, on which the band was expected not only to play on the march but also at concerts in the evenings. The 1st Battalion shared the same kind of experience, though with the added difficulty of the Indian climate to contend with: 'We marched both ways (76 miles),' recorded the regimental journal in 1930 of an exercise. 'We played to the troops every evening and (judging by the applause that we received) it was very much appreciated.'

The 1st Battalion returned home in time to take part in the 50th anniversary of the granting of the Royal title in 1935. It then found regular work on the South Coast where Bandmaster Joseph Needham acquired a reputation of playing to the gallery. One of the last peace-time engagements of the Band in 1914 had been a Massed Bands Review in Aldershot; in 1939 history repeated itself with an appearance at the Aldershot Tattoo, shortly followed by a departure for war in Europe.

Both battalions saw most of their fighting in the Far East, but it was the 1st that ended the war in the weaker condition: when the cut-backs came in the first years of peace, it was therefore the 1st that was put in suspended animation. On 5th March 1949 an Amalgamation Parade took place at Asmara Airport, Eritrea, with the 2nd Band under William Freeth becoming the Regimental Band.

Uniquely, it is believed, the band at this time contained four brothers; the Sprys were the sons of a former bandsman, and one of them - William - was later to become Bandmaster of The Buffs.

On 21st July 1956 the Queen presented new colours to the Regiment at Windsor Castle; three years later the Royal Berkshires amalgamated to become The Duke of Edinburgh's Royal Regiment.

For the Amalgamation Parade at Albany Barracks on the Isle of Wight in June 1959 the band was conducted by George Haile of the Wiltshires, but shortly afterwards he retired and Roy Hibbs of the Berkshires took up the baton.

During the '60s the band travelled extensively, visiting Canada, Malta, Libya, Cyprus, Holland and Germany, building a reputation as one of the best line infantry bands. When Mr Hibbs finally retired in 1971, Nigel Borlase took over and led the band through most of the major tattoos and massed bands events in Britain and Germany.

Time was also spent in the '70s and '80s in Northern Ireland, but the major posting of the period was to Hong Kong in February 1988. During the next 30 months the Band played more than 350 engagements, including a trip to South Korea and a three-week tour of Japan. It also raised £1500 for the Royal Marines' School of Music.

Under Options for Change the Regiment was amalgamated in April 1994 with The Gloucestershire Regiment to form The Royal Gloucestershire, Berkshire and Wiltshire Regiment, and for a while Mr Clegg of the Glosters was the Bandmaster. Later that year, however, regimental bands were abolished and most of the musicians were absorbed into the new divisional bands.

Gordon Turner and Alwyn W Turner
© Spellmount Publishing

Bandmasters

The 1st Battalion The Royal Berkshire Regiment

1868-1883 James Gibbon, d 1904

1883-1893 Richard Francis, 1850-1934

1893-1912 Arthur Vincent Barwood, 1867-1938

1912-1922 Charles White, 1879-19??

1922-1945 Joseph Ernest Needham LRAM ARCM, 1893-9??.

1947-1949 1st Battalion in suspended animation

1949-1958 William Herman Freeth, 1912-1982

1958-1959 Roy Hibbs, b 1927

The 2nd Battalion TheRoyal Berkshire Regiment

1865-1870 Frederick Hynes

1870-1880 M Kleinstuber

1880-1889 Matthew Larter, 1847-1910

1889-1907 Sidney Dore, 1861-1943

1907-1914 Ernest Arthur Barrett, 1870-1936

1914-1934 Ernest Augustus Weaver LRAM ARCM, 1883-19??

1934-1945 Joseph Bertram George O'Keefe FTCL, 1904-19??

1945-1949 William Herman Freeth, 1912-1982

The Duke of Edinburhg's Royal Regiment

1959-1971 Roy Hibbs, b 1929

1971-1980 Nigel Anthony Borlase ARCM, b 1940

1980-1987 Robert Charles Nother, b 1947

1987-1994 Keith Hatton, FTCL ARCM BBCM psm, b 1957

Putting Bach in Berkshire Reading Bach Choir

The Reading Bach Choir has been singing for 33 years, and has just appointed Mark Shepherd as its fourth Musical Director. Each of his predecessors brought particular characteristics to the 50-strong choir's direction, but all have subscribed to the objectives of its founder: to perform choral music to the highest standards (members are auditioned every year) and to promote the enjoyment of music in the Reading area.

It was the founder of Reading Bach Choir, Simon Johnson, who taught music at The University of Reading's School of Education, who instituted the ambitious programming policy which has remained a hallmark of the choir. His first concert, in 1966, set the standard for the years to come: Bach's *B minor Mass*, with soloists including John Carol Case and Wilfred Brown.

Bach figured prominently in the early years, an original intention being to perform one of the three major choral works every two years; but despite its name the choir has always sung a wide repertoire, and Simon's programmes featured challenging works by Malcolm Williamson, Palestrina, Stravinsky and Britten. A notable achievement was the first performance in Reading of Tippett's *A Child of Our Time* in 1972: a difficult work which the choir found extremely challenging, but enormously rewarding.

In 1973 Simon moved on to further his career and was replaced by Julian Williamson, a freelance conductor from London, who remained with the choir for 19 years. Adventurous programming continued to be the norm: as well as a wide range of early music there were many 20th century pieces, including works by Phyllis Tate, Ligeti, Geoffrey Burgon and Peter Maxwell Davies, and the first British performance of Iain Hamilton's *Requiem*. The choir began its now regular practice of presenting a Christmas concert of carols and readings, and there were a number of other interesting and original themed programmes with well-known readers such as Gabriel Woolf, Marius Goring, Robert Hardy and David Kossoff.

During Julian's regime the choir ventured further afield, giving several concerts in London, at the Royal Festival and Queen Elizabeth Halls and the Barbican. They enjoyed weekends working with the Rehearsal Orchestra to give concert performances of operas, including *Carmen*, the *Force of Destiny* and *La Bohème*. The longest journey they undertook in the cause of music-making was a week-long trip to Philadelphia in 1982, to sing Bach's *St Matthew Passion* with the Philadelphia Festival Chorus. Some members took the opportunity to

Julian Williamson

visit the town of Reading in Pennsylvania, bringing greetings from the old country.

Julian resigned in 1992 and was replaced by Sarah Tenant-Flowers, a talented and ambitious young conductor with a background in arts administration. Her experience and professionalism in this field were of great value in concert promotion and planning; the choir was soon back to full strength, and audience numbers became healthier. Along with her administrative skills Sarah brought a lively and intelligent interest in singing technique, and as well as coaching in rehearsals, she arranged vocal workshops for choir members. Her interest in choral conducting led to the choir's winning a BT award, which was used to appoint a trainee conductor, Paul Stephenson, for six months; he benefited from Sarah's tuition and gained valuable experience conducting the choir at several concerts.

Repertoire continued to be varied and exciting, with a leaning towards the contemporary (Gorecki, Jonathan Harvey) and new departures into the Russian church repertoire, including a memorable Rachmaninov Vespers in the wonderful setting of Douai Abbey. But Bach has never been neglected, and the two *Passions* and the *B minor Mass* all received performances under Sarah.

The choir has often joined forces with others to present larger-scale works. In Reading, it has sung with the Festival Chorus and the Haydn Choir, and a number of concerts were performed in Winchester Cathedral with the Waynflete Singers under Martin Neary, including Elgar's *Dream of Gerontius*. Under Julian Williamson, concerts were given with his other choirs from Camden and Ware.

In 1979 the choir first made contact, via the Reading-Düsseldorf Association, with the Kantorei der Friedenskirche, and since then visits and joint concerts have been exchanged with our German friends roughly every two years. The highlight of this association was Britten's *War Requiem*, put on in the Hexagon in May 1995 and repeated later in Düsseldorf's Tonhalle, to mark the 50th anniversary of VE day. These performances brought together two Düsseldorf and two Reading choirs under the baton of Jonathan Grieves-Smith, at that time conductor of the Reading Festival Chorus. It was a tremendous and moving occasion, and many choir members felt privileged to take part.

In the early years the choir sang in the old Reading Town Hall, which for all its faults (especially backstage and front-of-house) had a very sympathetic acoustic for choral singing. The Hexagon seemed a good and comfortable replacement when it opened, but it has never been an ideal space in which to sing, and has become uneconomic for smallish groups to hire. The choir is now looking forward to the reopening of the Town Hall; in the meantime it has relied heavily on local churches, though in recent years two new venues, Dorchester and Douai Abbeys, have proved very successful in terms of both ambience and audience.

It has been a policy from the start to employ professional orchestras. Simon used the Bristol Sinfonia; Julian preferred a London band, and many concerts were given with the London Bach and English Symphony Orchestras. Sarah has brought in I Fiori, a period instrument ensemble, to provide brilliant and authentic accompaniments to the earlier end of the choir's repertoire. Soloists have included Emma Kirkby, Lesley Garrett, Martyn Hill, Ian Partridge, Philip Langridge, Alfreda Hodgson, Neil Jenkins and many others.

Putting on concerts with professional musicians is expensive, and the choir has constantly had to raise funds and seek sponsorship in order to perform the works it has wanted to sing. Support from local and national arts associations has dwindled over the years, and sponsorship is hard-won though gratefully received. The choir's own fund-raising is made as pleasurable as possible through singing at weddings and doing performances from

scratch. Social events such as barn dances help to keep up morale as well as raise money, and there was even a time when the choir parties were considered more successful than the concerts.

The membership has naturally changed a great deal over the years, as people move into and away from Reading, but three founder members are still singing with the choir. Many old friends, including former accompanists, chairmen and the previous conductor, came back for its 30th birthday party in 1997. As the Millennium approaches the choir is saying a sad farewell to Sarah and at the same time looking forward with excitement to a new beginning with a new conductor.

Members of the choir remember –

'...the time all the lights fused in the middle of a concert in Christchurch, in the presence of the composer of one of the works we were singing. We had to decamp, performers and audience together, to Leighton Park School (our rehearsal venue) and sing the second half of the concert there.'

'Sarah producing a potato gun to chivvy up choir members who failed to watch her beat.'

'The excitement of singing David Fanshawe's African Sanctus.'

'The magic of Rachmaninov's Vespers in the candlelit space of Douai Abbey.'

'The look on the faces of our two young German friends when they heard the full magnitude of the Britten War Requiem for the first time.'

'Present and former choir members singing together and sharing memories at the choir's 30th birthday party in the Old Town Hall.'

'Celebrating VE day through an act of reconciliation – Germans and English singing together.'

Steps in Time Cadence Drum and Bugle Corps

It is all too easy to make puns about champions when writing on the subject of Cadence Drum and Bugle Corps, for the Champion family are the inspiration behind Reading's top marching band, and have been the driving force which has made the corps a champion in its own right.

This autumn (1999) the band became British champions, winning the premier event in Europe for marching music, the Drum Corps United Kingdom championship, in Northampton. Only four years before, the band was near the bottom of the second division of marching bands in the country but with hard work, dedication and talent, the young members of Cadence have managed to produce the perfect story-book ending after years of struggle.

The band, under corps director David Champion, has made enormous strides since the early days. It was at the end of the '60s, when David's father Tony Champion first mooted the idea of introducing the Caversham Boys' Brigade to music and the late Tony Nicks began teaching the lads at Gosbrook Road Methodist Church. He instructed them how to play simple bugle tunes, accompanied by marching rhythms from the two drums that they then possessed.

The first major step in the band's short but dramatic history came in 1980, when it joined the British Youth Band Association and changed its name to Caversham Ambassadors, whilst retaining a connection with its church base.

By this time girls were also admitted to membership, and here the band faced its first minor conflict. Boys had to be members of the brigade, but without a similar organisation at the church for the opposite sex, girls joined without the need for association ties.

As a result of regularising this anomaly, recruitment of boys became easier, and in 1986 the band became members of Drum Corps United Kingdom, joining as an independent youth band.

The next big step was in 1991, when the Caversham Ambassadors joined forces with the Starisers Drum and Bugle Corps to form Cadence for, until that date, the two Reading-based bands had both struggled to recruit individually within the same catchment area.

Cadence was further strengthened in 1996, when it was supplemented by former members of the Raiders Drum and Bugle Corps from the Woking and Guildford area. As well as the main corps, two vibrant cadet units now operate, one in Caversham and the other in Guildford.

By now, the instrumentation had progressed from the five-note bugles and sidedrums of the sixties to larger-bore brass instruments in a range from soprano to contrabass, plus a percussion section of snare, tenor and bass drums, a static tuned percussion ensemble and a colour guard.

The band's appearance had also undergone a transformation with smart scarlet and gold tunics and black trousers adorned with scarlet and gold stripes and topped off with plumed hats which were based on the old uniforms of the Emerald Knights American Drum Corps.

The quality and availability of tuition has also come a long way since the days when Tony Nicks taught two-note bugle tunes, for the band is now tutored by 16 instructors, each with his own particular responsibilities but none, perhaps, more important than John Barclay, who joined Cadence from a Boys' Brigade Corps in Glasgow.

John was conductor of Cadence for four years and is now responsible for the band's annual ten-minute

Cadence in competition at Leicester cycledrome in 1997

competition showpiece, which must combine the highest qualities of music and choreography.

It is in this area that technology has come to the band's aid, for all the intricate marching manoeuvres are originated on computers before being rehearsed by the musicians. Cadence is fortunate to have Alan Layng, a brilliant computer programmer, among its many supporters, who has also helped very considerably with the enormous cost of equipping and running the band. To give an idea of expenditure involved, the price of just one of the American-manufactured brass contrabasses is currently £5,000.

DrillPro, a computer software teaching aid, marketed by Cadence and written by Alan is now sold to marching bands worldwide and the package is continually being updated to complement technological advances. It is fortunate Cadence has this unexpected source of income because their application for lottery aid was rejected, even though a prospectus carefully planned to meet every demand and requirement was enthusiastically received by the reviewing panel.

However, the biggest headache faced by Cadence has been the difficulty of finding practice space, for as Tony Champion said: "We soon outgrew the church premises and the sound of the band had become so loud that it was unfair on the neighbours."

After Reading Borough Council had banned the youngsters from using any of its parkland, the search was on for a suitable venue and at one period the difficulty was overcome by the kindness of the Americans at Greenham Common who loaned Cadence an aircraft hangar for rehearsals. This fortuitous generosity was perhaps understandable for the tradition of drum corps marching bands originated from American High Schools. Now, however, permission has been obtained to use military land at Pirbright, Surrey, and the teething problems that have beset Cadence since its formation seem well behind them.

Practice has, as they say, almost made perfect, and the young people – there are about 45 members aged between 13 and 25 – don't stint on practice, going through their routines for six hours a week with a full weekend camp each month throughout the winter. It is during these dark and cold months that the musicians and dancers put in most of their hard work, preparing and perfecting their 12-minute competition display of classical music and choreographed dance for the coming summer season. It is then that Cadence begins its travels throughout Britain to compete against other bands in the long – and ultimately successful – march towards a place in the National Finals.

Ron Pearce

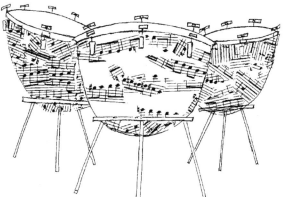

Millennium Choice

Tony Champion

My choice is Tchaikovsky's 1812 Overture because it is so very dramatic

Colour and Harmony

"One of the most popular orchestras in Reading in the '20s was at The Vaudeville Electric Theatre in Broad Street, Reading's oldest cinema which was opened in 1908."

"The Vaudeville was undergoing a major transformation. Over a period of two years, a larger and more elaborate cinema was constructed round and over the old one, and when, in September 1921, the new Vaudeville was at last revealed, it was greeted with rapturous applause...."

"The Vaudeville was given the splendid title of Reading's Temple of Colour and Harmony, and was one of the town's principal attractions in the 1920s. Its orchestra, which was quite as famous as its decor, was led by Lionel Falkman, an accomplished violinist from the Royal Opera, Covent Garden, and all the members were experienced professional musicians. Their work was not easy; they were billed to 'play continuously from 2 to 10.15 daily'.

"A particular favourite with the public was the pianist, Eduard Parlovitz, 'little Parlo', who eventually succeeded Falkman as musical director. Long after sound films had made them redundant, the members of this orchestra were remembered with affection and admiration, and, not surprisingly, the Vaudeville was one of the last cinemas to go over to sound films."

[The Vaudeville was eventually closed in 1957 and converted into a hardware and chemist's store.]

**Reading Theatres, Cinemas and other Entertainments
Daphne Phillips
© Reading Libraries**

Singing for the King Peter Davies

PETER DAVIES left his home in Newbury to become a chorister at St George's School, Windsor, in 1927 at the age of nine. Now president of Newbury Symphony Orchestra Peter looks back on his five happy years as a chorister, his memories of King George V and Queen Mary and the many famous musical figures he met

I can remember singing Sunday matins for King George V and Queen Mary in their private chapel when they were in residence in Windsor Castle and the King wasn't well enough to attend the service at St George's Chapel. He needed a lot of warmth, although it must have been quite an expense to heat those staterooms, and it was very stuffy in there. This was the private chapel where the fire broke out in 1993 and I thought it wasn't particularly interesting. It was quite small so when six choristers and six lay clerks were gathered there to sing, we were at very close quarters with the King. To reach it we had to go in the tradesmen's entrance near the quadrangle and find our way through a labyrinth of staterooms and St George's Hall. One of the rooms we passed through had a magnificent display of gold plate and I can remember once when I was going through there by myself, I ran into Queen Mary round the corner and had to disappear pretty quickly.

I became a chorister at St George's School, Windsor, in 1927 at the age of nine and stayed for five years. I went up for my voice trial earlier in that year but I remember little, except for singing *The Blacksmith* by Brahms, even though it was taken by Sir Henry Walford Davies, who was to become Master of the Choristers and organist at St George's Chapel soon after I started in September. The takeover period must have been a little uncertain. For my first few weeks the choirmaster was Dr EH (Edmund) Fellowes, a minor canon and a very good musician who almost single-handedly revised and republished all the Tudor church music and madrigals we now have in print. It was a marvellous beginning. Then Sir Walford Davies came along and he was very different from Dr Fellowes. I remember at one concert Dr Fellowes was accompanying us on the lute as we were singing *Never Weather-beaten Sail* by Thomas Campion. Sir Walford Davies introduced it to the audience and said: "We are accompanied by Dr Fellowes." And he put his hand on Dr Fellowes' head and said: "He's an old master himself, isn't he?" I know what I feel like when people put their hands on my head. It annoys me very much and it annoyed Fellowes too, you could see.

I can remember the first thing I ever sang at Windsor in 1927 was *Oh Clap Your Hands Together* by Orlando Gibbons and that really started me on my interest in Early Music. When Early Music was revived in the 1950s by people like David Munrow, it was put across as something quite new but we were singing church music all the time at St George's that had a continuous history right back to the Tudors. I've got an 18th century edition of William Boyce's *Cathedral Music* (1788) of music recovered from old manuscripts which had been in cathedrals right back to the 16th century and we sang many of those pieces.

St George's was a boarding school and although I was very homesick to begin with, I grew to love it almost fervently. What I didn't love were the games; I was always trying to get out of those. I'm not at all sure I had a strong religious faith then but I enjoyed going to chapel every day and the religion came with everything else. You couldn't avoid it. There is a set order of services at the chapel laid down by the clerics under the Tudors and it has followed that form ever since. I got to know a lot of the Bible lessons and psalms by heart, and of course we sang many anthems but hardly ever a hymn; it took me until fairly recently to know anything about hymns.

King George V

We had all sorts of ceremonial occasions in the chapel when I was there. The first one of all was the funeral of the Governor and Constable of Windsor Castle, the Marquess of Cambridge, brother of Queen Mary, who died in 1927. The chapel was so full of the Knights of the Garter and members of the Royal Household that there was no room for the choir. We had to stand up in the organ loft, which was a benefit because the smallest boys were in the front and we could look over the side and see all this panorama of colour and costume. Although it was a funeral and the Knights wore dark cloaks in Garter blue there were still splashes of scarlet and brightness.

Another splendid occasion was in 1930 when St George's Chapel was reopened ceremonially by George V and Queen Mary after a long period of restoration work which had started in 1921. The celebrations started on November 3, 1930, with Sunday matins, and concerts, and evensongs were held throughout the week. At one service all the choirs associated with St George's were there: King's College, Cambridge, Eton College choir, St Paul's, Westminster Abbey, and, I think, Winchester and New College, Oxford, because King's, Eton and New College have an 'amicable concord'. The choirmasters all took it in turns to conduct. I remember Boris Ord, who was my choirmaster later when I went to King's on a choral scholarship, sitting there looking rather like a Staffordshire pottery cat – he had an awful singing voice. Sir Ernest Bullock, who was organist of Westminster Abbey, showed us how he wanted us to sing but he sang through his nose! Sir Sidney Nicholson, who was the founding principal of the Royal College of English Church Music, was also there. It was a wonderful gathering but funnily enough I have taken those people for granted ever since.

We had even more distinguished conductors visiting us for the concerts which were held each year for the benefit of the lay clerks. I think these concerts were left over from Victorian times when the lay clerks, who are the men in the choir, were badly paid, although I don't suppose they were very well paid in my time. These concerts were held in the Albert Institute, Sheet Street, a miserable Gothic revival of a place in those days, with dark brown and dirty-white paint, really depressing.

The first year that I remember, in about 1929, Elgar came to conduct us. We were a choir of 36 altogether and he conducted us mainly in a programme of his own works – *As Torrents in Summer* was one of them. Elgar looked just like his photographs, taciturn with his nose jutting out over that big white moustache. I can't remember that he did anything much except sit in the back room when he wasn't conducting. I got his autograph and that of Ralph Vaughan Williams who came the next year. Vaughan Williams was portly and benevolent looking and we probably sang some of the music from Windsor Forest. The following year Sir Edward German was our guest conductor. He wore his bowler hat slightly to the side, jaunty looking in keeping with his music. His hair was silvery grey and very crinkled. I don't know whether it was permed. I very much doubt it.

Apart from the music we had a normal prep school education at St George's School; in fact we didn't have as much music then as there is now. It was a lot of work, only one never realised it, and sometimes we must have been exhausted. We used to get up early each morning to sing matins, with a practice before it, and then back to school to do our lessons, followed by games every afternoon. Then we went up to the chapel again for a practice, followed by evensong, and back to school for a rather nauseating tea. All the food was terrible. The cook, Miss Bush, had a kitchen which had to be seen to be believed with a stuffed owl in a glass case. That was

Young Peter Davies (centre) in a play at St George's School in 1929

typical of the whole ambience. On Sundays, we had a practice on Sunday morning, matins and choral communion, from 9.30 to midday, which was fairly exhausting – matins was the one service I didn't like very much anyway – and then went down to school to have cold beef for lunch. We called it Pink Horse and it looked slightly iridescent. On Thursdays at lunchtime we had alternating round and rectangular meat pies, plenty of pastry, not all that much meat, and they were called Long Pig and Short Pig – Long Pig is the South Sea islanders' name for human flesh.

There were 36 boys in the school altogether and four classes, so we had plenty of attention. We had a marvellous grounding in music from Sir Walford Davies, who in 1934 became Master of the King's Musick. We virtually had the run of his house with a room of our own downstairs with encyclopaedias, books and a gramophone. It was marvellous. In addition I learned piano from Alwyn Surplice, whose family had a garage in Sheet Street, Windsor, and who later became assistant organist at Windsor and then organist at Winchester. I also learned the cello – I've still got the one my mother bought me from a market gardener in Newbury – and I had lessons regularly from Miss Hetherington, whose family ran an estate agency in High Street, Eton. It was a rather stiff era for teaching strings but at least it started me off and I have loved it ever since.

We heard less serious music as well. There was a funny old master, Mr Bridge, who had a banjo and he occasionally used to play it to us and sing some very old-fashioned, pre-First World War songs, about the man who sent his teeth to the wash and all that kind of thing. He used to read to us too, all sorts of books, including one I've never been able to trace about a detective named Holmlock Sheres.

Another master, James Webb-Jones, who later became headmaster, also read to us in the dormitory including Winnie the Pooh , which had just been published, and a superb book, The Midnight Folk by John Masefield.

We had to be quite hardy. Our dormitories were very cold and in the winter the matron used to come round to wake us in the morning with a large enamel jug which she poured into our wash basins to melt the ice on the water. We had one bath a week and when we came in from playing games with muddy knees, we had to wash in a washroom with a row of cold water washbasins in a great big slate top. There were press-down taps which sprang up immediately you let go. If you took a hand off to wash properly there was no water so you just did your knees in a casual way and put on your trousers. They didn't see the dirt under trousers and cassocks in chapel.

We saw the King and Queen quite often in the chapel and, in 1931, when we went to Boscombe to sing at the wedding of Lady May Cambridge, Queen Victoria's granddaughter, and Captain Henry Abel in the village church, King George and Queen Mary were sitting there in the front pew. They looked exactly as you'd expect from their pictures. Queen Mary always wore a toque on her head, in varying colours. A lot of the women who came to matins on Sundays in Windsor wore toques like Queen Mary. The same congregation used to come from the castle community and from the town every Sunday wearing the same clothes, month after month, year in year out and if they didn't, you noticed it. Practically nobody attended weekday evensong, but there was a little old lady who always used to sit in the same pew who was known to us as Mrs Tummy Pain because she was rather bent and slightly convulsive.

On Sunday mornings, we enjoyed seeing the Military Knights of Windsor march into matins. They were retired officers who in summer wore uniforms with a lot of scarlet in them and in the winter changed to uniforms of of bluey-grey with a cloak. They would march stiffly down the north aisle and up into their pews next to ours under the command of Major-General Carteret Carey, Governor of the Military Knights. The song school where we practised was on the Lower Ward opposite the Military Knights' quarters. Major-General Carey as Governor had the best one and we overlooked his bedroom which had a rather large bay window. It used to delight us as boys to see Lady Carey putting her wig on at her dressing table mirror.

At that time, the Dean of Windsor was The Very Rev Albert Victor Baillie and he had been dean for a long

Michael Redgrave, Peter Davies's languages master at Cranleigh in the school production of HMS Pinafore in 1932

time and was chaplain to the king. He was a large imposing man who used to gad about a bit, visiting Hollywood and entertaining interesting people, like the writer Hector Bolitho. At Christmas he always held the Dean's party for the Choristers – we had to stay on at school until Christmas Eve night. The catering for the boys was slightly different at that time and I remember one of the canons, Dr Alexander Nairne, a very old, ascetic man, who was also professor of divinity at Cambridge, ordered our meals from Fortnum and Mason. But we didn't like them because they were too good. That shows you how bad the food was.

After St George's I went to Cranleigh because Mr Webb-Jones had been at Cranleigh and recruited boys to go there. I won a music scholarship and my music master, who later became my housemaster, Maurice Allen, did a lot for me. My modern languages master was Michael Redgrave who directed us in a performance of Pinafore and took the lead in several Shakespeare plays before resigning in 1934 to start his distinguished career as an actor. The thing I liked about Cranleigh was the opportunity to do music out of hours. There is a great deal said against public schools now but it did give you the opportunity to practise your music, to sing and to play in the orchestra. I did all the big standard choral

Peter Davies (left) in HMS PInafore (1932) at Cranleigh

works when I was there. We had sung Bach's *St Matthew Passion* and Handel's *Messiah* at Windsor and then at Cranleigh we went on to sing Brahms *Requiem*, *Rio Grande* by Constant Lambert, *St John Passion*, and many other works. It gave you the chance to do the things properly and, like St George's, it provided a marvellous grounding in music that lasted for life.

Millennium Choice

Peter Davies

I would pick Brahms' Requiem – it was a favourite of my father, Arthur Davies, who played the timpani part when he was with Newbury Symphony Orchestra. My father was a very musical player of the timps; he could cajole them, draw the music out of them. I have done four things in the Requiem, I sang in it as a treble, as a bass and as an alto (a marvellous alto part) and played cello and timpani in it and conducted bits of it.

There are certain works which are absolutely marvellous. One is Tallis's Forty Part Motet Spem in Alium, and another is the St Matthew Passion of Bach, particularly the first and last movements. The Forty Part Motet I first sang at King's in 1938 and it was quite an experience with 40 singers and a choir all round the west end of the chapel and your having responsibility for your own voice out of the 40. It was thrilling and it is a marvellous work but it has to be done just right.

The Matthew Passion, the first movement particularly. I've paid the cello and sung in that. It is such an inspiring movement. It's the feeling of the cello being the foundation of everything there with pedal points and scales, and to sing it's good. There is a lovely sustained chorale for the trebles only on top. I get the same feeling in the Brahms's Haydn Variations and Dvorak's Symphonic Variations. It is such a marvellous feeling.

Songs Sacred and Profane

Bob Russell

Music, although totally restricted to singing, formed a significant part of my primary school education at Christ Church School, Reading, during the early 1940s.

We always sang a hymn at daily assembly, which on Fridays was usually conducted by the Vicar, the Reverend Jocelyn Woods. He was a tall, benevolent-looking man who had a deep bass voice which resonated against the background of treble and soprano voices. He was assisted by a member of my class who sang in the church choir, Tom Foley. Tom appeared to have been born with a bass voice and he and the Vicar gave full volume to the morning's music.

One of the favourite hymns was Holy, Holy, Holy, Lord God Almighty which lent itself to the bass contribution. The headmistress, Miss Lamport-Gilbert always thanked Tom for "helping us with the singing". In fact most of the 'us' listened to the thunderous bass duet, which became known as Holy, Holy, Holy, Jocelyn Woods and Foley.

Not so praiseworthy was the musical contribution, in a fourth year singing lesson, of one of the well-known class saboteurs. Miss Eason taught the top class for almost everything including singing. She was a very tall thin lady with a very long neck. Like all her colleagues she attempted to instill total 'correctness' and nothing less than attainment of the 'high moral ground' in all that she did.

During one of her singing lessons she attempted to teach Ariel's song from The Tempest, Where The Bee Sucks, There Suck I. Miss Eason played the piano while we struggled with the words, apart from our class comedian, who had invented his own version. Suddenly Miss Eason slammed down the lid of the piano, stood up, and shaking with rage demanded to know "who is singing the wrong word?". No one was. Some, out of ignorance or innocence hardly knew what the 'wrong' word was.

Further enraged inquiries elicited no further response. The veins on Miss Eason's neck stood out like pieces of black string, her face fluctuated from bright puce to deep beetroot. We were marched back to the classroom and made to sit in silence with 'hands on heads', a punishment more associated with 'Stalag luft' than enlightened education, so enraged was the good Miss Eason. We never attempted to sing Ariel's song again.

When we were let out at the end of the afternoon the culprit loudly regaled the residents of Spring Gardens with his fully unexpurgated version. I can only imagine that his original song sheet was printed in olde English script!

The Disappearing Conductor   Reading Concert Orchestra

The early sixties saw a change to the traditional concerts performed In Reading with the formation of Reading Concert Orchestra (started in 1959). The founder of this orchestra was Les Lawrence who had been involved with music in Reading for many years. A percussionist and timpanist, he began with Reading Youth Orchestra and played with most of the local music societies. He produced a series of concerts known as Moods in Music to introduce people to music who had never been to a live concert. KEN WICKENS remembers playing in these concerts as a young musician

Having found my collection of concert programmes it was with great surprise that I discovered it was over 30 years ago that I played in my first orchestral concert. Les Lawrence was responsible for producing a series of concerts in Reading called *Moods in Music*. These concerts, performed by Reading Concert Orchestra, were designed to introduce music to a wider audience and included both serious and light music. They also provided the opportunity for other musical groups in the area to perform in a concert setting.

The mainstay of each concert was the 100-piece Reading Concert Orchestra but often included local choirs and other music groups and soloists which helped to develop the interest of the young performers and listeners. Between eight and ten concerts a year were presented and, with the exception of two concerts, were played to a full house. They ranged from serious to popular classics through to show and film music with one lecture-concert on the percussion department of the orchestra.

My first concert as a new young player was in a Tchaikovsky *Moods in Music* in Reading Town Hall on Sunday, 5th March, 1967. I played the bass drum in the *1812 Overture* along with 150 other musicians made up of the Reading Concert Orchestra and other local players.

The *1812* was the last piece to be played and my apprehension grew throughout the concert. The overture started quietly like a church hymn and the tension built up as the music grew to represent the Battle of Borodino. The sound of the first cannon fire over the noise of the battle was enough to lift most of the audience off their very uncomfortable seats. The cannon effects were produced by maroons electrically fired in dustbins to the side of the stage. With the full augmented orchestra, many bass drums, sets of tubular bells, hand bells and a recording of Sonning church bells played over the public address system, the firing of the

maroons added to the sound which was incredible in the final stages of the music.

As the maroons were fired, large amounts of smoke issued into the hall. With the final few bars being played, the conductor began to disappear into the smoke. As the conductor brought down the baton to finish the piece both he and the audience disappeared, leaving the string players in a fog of white smoke and the sound of applause from an audience that could not be seen.

I was to play the *1812 Overture* on a number of occasions. Other memories of this great piece of music include the time when the maroons set off the fire system, which resulted in the fire service entering the concert hall in full breathing apparatus, to the great amusement of the audience. On another occasion large amounts of dust from the roof were deposited upon the orchestra as a result of the maroons exploding.

The largest concert I performed in with the Reading Concert Orchestra, which included the *1812,* was an outdoor concert held in Hills Meadows in 1971. This was part of the Festival of Reading and the celebrations for the opening of the Butts Centre (now Broad Street Mall) and was the largest performance ever seen in Reading with 400 musicians and an audience of 5,000. The Royal Artillery 25-pounder guns were used for the cannon effects with over 250 musicians playing.

The Reading Concert Orchestra also travelled to places such as Portsmouth and Hemel Hempstead to give concerts, and the woodwind, brass and percussions section formed the Reading Concert Band which also gave concerts in and around Reading.

Reading Town Hall was the main venue for the *Moods in Music* concerts. It had a capacity of just over 1,000 uncomfortable seats of which only a small number provided good vision because the stage was not tiered. There were also inadequate toilet, restaurant and bar facilities. However, the popularity of the concerts grew to such an extent that people were turned away,

Throughout the sixties and seventies a great debate was held as to whether Reading needed a new hall. Reading Town Council of the day had strong reservations and spent a very small amount on the arts in the town. Les Lawerence, through the *Moods in Music* concerts, regularly raised this debate and eventually the argument was won and the Hexagon was built.

Sadly Reading Concert Orchestra and *Moods in Music* concerts are no more. Reading is much the poorer place without concerts like these. They provided a platform for young musicians, like myself, to experience playing in public and gave the people of Reading the opportunity to enjoy a variety of music. Let us hope that when the Town Hall is refurbished, the sound of concerts like these may be heard once again.

Nut Rocker Clayson and the Argonauts

Chanteur, auteur and raconteur ALAN CLAYSON tells the strange story of his artistic odyssey

My walk with destiny began in 1965 with the formation of Ace and the Crescents with other pupils at Farnborough Grammar School. Yet I wasn't to make a public appearance with a group until 1969, two years before I became lead vocalist with Turnpike, a folk-rock quintet gettIng-it-together-in-the-country in Upper Basildon.

As an escape valve from earnest Turnpike, I had created Billy and the Conquerors to perform items from a record collection that had grown during my scouring of the area for any emporium bearing the sign 'junk', 'second-hand' or 'bric-à-brac' in an obsessive search for artefacts from musical eras as far back as the 1920s – anything to keep the ghastly Woodstock Generation present at arm's length.

"I can honestly say that I've never seen anything like it in my life." gasped a *Wokingham News* newshound after an 18-piece Billy and the Conquerors hit the town's Rock Club. Of every ensemble in which I have played a part, the Conquerors, titans of trash though we were, remain my favourite – and as long as I survive as an entertainer, so will mythical Billy.

The next venture, Average Joe and the Men in the Street, also absorbed the Conquerors' ramshackle grandeur – as did Clayson and the Argonauts, the more enduring entity that followed. During a fleeting sojourn in its string section, I noticed that the Portsmouth Sinfonia were victims of much the same passion.

Another vital element in my cultural meltIng pot was Gallic chanson after I stumbled upon Jacques Brel via Scott Walker, and Charles Aznavour through his spot on a ITV variety show in 1972. Six years on, Clayson and the Argonauts' go at 'The Ham' was to be dismissed by a *New Musical Express* critic, damn his impudence, as 'a slice of Aznavourian breast-beating that was all too appropriate under the circumstances.' By then, the group was mutating into a kind of travelling asylum. Ironically, we had been championed by *Melody Maker*'s Allan Jones for occupying 'a premier position on rock's Lunatic Fringe', not quite a year after an incident that had concluded with us being hustled out of one Reading venue at gunpoint.

Regardless, we muddled on, and, after making a London debut (with the then-unsigned Jam) on 9th January, 1977, I held Eldorado in the hollow of my hand fleetingly with a Radio One In Concert spot, and a long run of

Alan Clayson

headlining treks round Britain and Europe.

En route, we found time to record our only (and very disinclined) single, an arrangement of Wild Man Fischer's *The Taster* (coupled with a track from a hitherto unissued in-concert LP at the Roundhouse). This rose to number three in *Time Out*'s chart, but fast comes the hour when fades the fairest flower. A lengthy lay-off prefaced the first of many attempted Clayson and the Argonauts comebacks and the protraction of the group's intermittent recording schedule that climaxed with 1985's valedictory *What a Difference a Decade Made* album.

While this door was closing, another creaked open when a *Record Collector* feature about the Dave Clark Five came about after I'd run into their former bass guitarist in a Camberwell music shop in 1981. More articles followed, and a parallel second career as an author left the runway with my first book, *Call Up The Groups!*

From 1979, I was also producing the records of others. More far-reaching, however, was a tenure on keyboards in Dave Berry and the Cruisers after its leader 'covered' a Clayson opus, *On the Waterfront* from *What a Difference a Decade Made*. Later, I climbed up the ranks to write and produce the lion's share of Dave's *Hostage To The*

Beat album and his 1988 revival of *Out of Time*.

Because of Dave and *Call Up The Groups*!, I became something of a 'face' on the Sounds of the Sixties circuit, and after distance forced my exit from the Yorkshire-based Cruisers, such networking paid off in sporadic engagements hammering piano as one of Screaming Lord Sutch's Savages; a string of one-nighters in the north-east as Denny Laine's support act in 1996, and, before that, rehearsing a group – the Wild Ones – to back Twinkle, now a grande dame of the 1960s nostalgia scene. I chose to pluck bass mainly because I could conduct by eye-contact with greater ease than from behind a bank of keyboards. These were played by the gifted Chris Gore from Newbury – who was to have a bearing on my output, both in the studio and on the boards, after grave internal problems scattered the Wild Ones like rats disturbed in a granary.

This was regrettable but not disastrous as I was now scratching a living from my pen at an alarming pace. Books alone ranged from supermarket potboilers to *Aspects of Elvis* (with its excerpt from a projected novel, *The Thistledown Flash*) and the only English language life of Jacques Brel. The biggest commercial success has been the film tie-in, *Backbeat*, but a spin-off from 1995's *Beat Merchants* was a CD compilation that kicked off with *The Man of the Moment* (which rhymes 'Nashville Teens' with 'Swinging Blue Jeans') by Clayson and an ad-hoc resurrected Argonauts. *Beat Merchants* also contained an Alan Clayson-Jim McCarty songwriting credit for Dave Berry's *The Moonlight Skater*; a nascent version of which was to turn up on *Raindreaming* by Stairway (with vocals by Jane Relf, ex-Renaissance). McCarty and fellow Stairway-farers, Clifford White (a New Age colossus) and Louis Cennamo (ex-Renaissance), were roped in for the Berry session.

I attended too as a general nuisance, and, shortly afterwards, 'sat in' on keyboards with Jim's R&B group – a sort of ersatz Yardbirds – during its residency in a West London niterie. This was one of many artistic diversions around the turn of the decade. I functioned too as guitarist and vocalist with two local groups, Poacher's Packet and then Parisian Fishnets, whose stock-in-trade was French café music. In my own right, I was attempting to reach and widen my work spectrum as a 'performance artist', peddling an act that defied succinct explanation.

During four visits to the United States – ostensibly to plug my books – those at this convention hall or that exposition centre could hardly believe I was real as I plunged into onstage excesses that occurred in the knowledge that I was unlikely to see any of these folk again — or was I? Within days of shaking off jet-lag back in England the first time in 1992, I received a package from two ladies from Minnesota who'd been among the

Clayson and The Argonauts

crowd flocking round me like friendly if over-attentive wolfhounds in the aftermath of a recital in Chicago, and had each bought a *What a Difference a Decade Made*. As well as a long letter, they'd sent a sweatshirt with my image and the words 'Claysonfest '92' printed on the front. Apparently, I have an American fan club.

The dozen or so members were twitchy with anticipation in the weeks leading up to the issue of *Soirée*, a new Clayson collection cast adrift on the CD oceans in 1997 by Havic, a company with offices in Austin, Texas — and Bracknell. The attendant press release for a forthcoming full-scale US tour has me down as a 'chansonnier', a label reinforced more recently by my contribution of two tracks to *Ne Me Quitte Pas*, a Jacques Brel tribute album, and a concert revue with five others, backed by Reading's own Knokke-le-Zoute ensemble.

Perhaps an English Brel or Aznavour is just what the world needs. Perhaps too, the world is ready for the full-scale autobiography that will result when I veil flesh on these bare bones – for there's no reason why the saga of a comparatively obscure artist and his many attempts to become rich and famous should not be at least as intrinsically interesting as those of his more celebrated brethren. In fact, I think I'll bang out a sample chapter right now…

Millennium Choice Alan Clayson

My recreational listening time is limited - so I have to really focus on a piece of music and be able to think, 'Yes, that's interesting'. Often, it's whatever I'm composing or recording at any given moment, but if there's one item I could bear hearing over again, it's John Cage's Four Minutes and Thirty-Three Seconds

Hark the Herald Angels Sing Carol singers

Many years ago a group of carol singers would entertain the people of Tilehurst in their own homes. This Christmas custom was started by Ann Lane, daughter of the Reverend Lane, Vicar of Tilehurst, and later Rector of St Michael's Church. The Lanes were a very musical family, not least Ann who, although she had quite a severe problem with her eyesight since she was a child and was never able to drive a car, passed all her music exams and, for several years, taught singing and gave music lessons at a large school.

After most of the Lane family left Tilehurst, Ann moved with her mother into a smaller house at the top of Norcot Hill, Tilehurst, and they continued with their musical interests. It was their idea to form the small group of carol singers as Christmas approached.

Rehearsals began about two weeks before the agreed date and we all met in Ann's sitting room and gathered round her large grand piano. There were 14 well-balanced voices. Besides the usual known carols, Ann always included two or three of the lesser-known ones and these had to be learned and practised. How beautiful and what a joy they were to sing. About this time, I believe Sir Malcolm Sargent was also recording these carols.

Once, I remember, as we were about to leave a particular house, and after singing one of these not so well-known carols, an elderly lady in the audience spoke up. "May we have a proper carol now?" she pleaded. Ann was not amused – in fact, she was quite incensed.

One night, after a practice, Mrs Lane, who was a much-needed and excellent alto, had observed that the weather was worsening. "Ann, dear," she said in a most kindly, but headmistressy voice, "if you wish me to sing with your choir, I must make it quite clear that I cannot stand about outside in the bitter cold and sing my best. You must arrange for us to go inside, Ann."

So that is what happened. Ann would write to people and suggest the rather strange idea of 14 extra people coming into their homes. We waited, not knowing what the result would be. Strangely enough the replies came back quite quickly. Most of the people were delighted at the idea. There would be ample refreshments and guests were to be invited in for the evening. This, indeed, would help as the charity box was passed round. There was the odd letter, enclosing a ten-shilling note and a brief message saying, "Please don't come, here is a donation. Do keep away!" We complied.

This arrangement was most satisfactory. By using our cars we were able to travel further afield, away from the smaller houses and shops and into the more residential areas where the houses were bigger.

The country lanes had no street lighting and the houses were often hidden away down long drives. Once I remember arriving at a lonely place, for these were the dark days before Christmas, and one of the cars had not turned up. This meant four of our singers were missing.

After nervous discussion and wondering how we would manage,we suddenly heard footsteps coming up the drive, crunching on the frosty gravel. Thank goodness they were here. We all sighed a great big sigh of relief. They had, in fact, had a puncture and the car was left some distance down the lane. Once, I remember, a car and its precious singers was lost altogether, at least until we were halfway through the evening.

The warmth and hospitality which awaited us were ample compensation for any disaster that befell us. Once, I remember quite clearly after being welcomed by the lady of the house and her husband, we noticed that the ladies were in evening dress and the men in dinner jackets. They were all drinking champagne. Immediately we were handed glasses in spite of Ann protesting and pointing out that we had a tight schedule, with four more houses to visit. This made very little difference and our host pointed out also that the champagne would warm us up and protect us from the bitter cold!

When the choir eventually pulled themselves together, our singing was electrified. Ann frantically tried to calm us down and bring us back to normal but the singing went like a bomb. For the rest of the evening we were about three bars ahead of her.

The long and tiring – but most enjoyable evening – always finished at Norcot Farm, on Norcot Hill, Tilehurst. This was my home for many years. Before leaving soon after 6pm to join the choir, I laid the large 9ft refectory table in the dining room with much food and drink. We seemed to need it in spite of eating and drinking most of the evening. How welcoming it was to come home into the old farmhouse, with log fires burning and the Christmas tree and holly all in their places. Everything had to be ready several days before the carollers arrived.

We began to feel the strain of singing for so long and by the end of the evening it started to show. On one occasion Ann decided to record the carols and she suggested that we made a very special effort. This would be a splendid record – indeed we might be remembered as a most unusually talented group of singers and filed into the archives for posterity. To our great disappointment the result was awful, the whole performance was flat! The audience had not noticed anything out of the ordinary, but the recording machine was particular and picked up the smallest faults which the human ears had missed. Ann was horrified. Our voices were tired and had had enough. Perhaps five calls were too much. "Oh well," someone with a keen sense of humour remarked, "we certainly shall not be included in the Guinness Book of Records."

Christmas was never quite the same again as we all moved away and the little group was no more.

All this happened a long time ago, perhaps 50 years. Ann still sings and still has perfect pitch. No tuning fork was ever necessary. In spite of her poor eyesight, she makes a journey every week to sing in a choir. She goes out, when it is dark, and catches a train, then returns to her home late at night. Denis Moriaty, who I believe has risen to greater heights, also sang in our choir. He was a much sought after tenor even in those days. Elwyn Evans, a Welshman who founded the Tilehurst Eisteddfod, is now 92 years of age.

We were indeed a very select body.

Peggy Broadhouse

A collection of conductors

Bob Russell

During the late 1940s or early 1950s, Reading Town Hall was the venue for a number of orchestral concerts given by London-based symphony orchestras under the direction of their resident or visiting conductors. As an introduction to classical music these concerts by the London Symphony or Philharmonic Orchestras were superb and gave the opportunity to listen to live performances of the great works from the classical repertoire, to watch a full orchestra in full operation and not least to note the style, control, or idiosyncracies of the conductors.

I well remember the conservative, restrained style of Nicolai Malko with the LSO in a Tchaikovsky concert. Sir Adrian Boult was always a popular visitor, a very genial man, noted for his extensive arm gestures, making maximum circular movements during Beethoven, Brahms and particularly in the dramatic emotional crescendos of the César Franck symphony.

A conductor of a quite different genre was the ebullient Joe Needham who, with the Band of the Royal Berkshire Regiment, gave well-remembered concerts in the Palace Theatre, usually on Sunday evenings. His style was extrovert, flamboyant and 'gymnastic' especially in the marches of John Philip Sousa and Kenneth Alford. The band had a wide repertoire well beyond military music. Joe Needham was noted as a disciplinarian in rehearsal but had an engaging manner with Reading audiences. The band always gave full force to the 1812 Overture. Not so well known was Joe Needham's own composition Air Raid Concerto, a full cacophony of sound effects. On leaving the service Joe Needham went north to become bandmaster of the Salford Police Band.

A conductor who, as far as is known, made only one visit to Reading, was none other than the well-known radio comedian Vic Oliver. Vic's reputation as a comedian owed much to his performances in Hi, Gang with Bebe Daniels and Ben Lyon. This American comedy show was broadcast each Sunday evening on the BBC Forces Programme live from the 'heart of London'. Vic was known to fool around from time to time with a violin, but his ability as a conductor of serious music was not so well known. His visit to Reading was with the London Concert Orchestra. His programme began with his own composition Stairway to the Stars and included Beethoven's Egmont Overture and Smetana's tone poem Ma Vlast. The concert was in aid of the Save the Children Fund and Mrs Phoebe Cusden, the fund's Reading President, spoke in the interval.

Vic's career as a serious conductor was not a long one. He did not return to comedy but turned to the repertory theatre in South Africa.

The Missing 5000 Dance bands

Experts in the study of human behaviour have no doubt kept a record of the times throughout history when there were significant changes in the style of mass-entertainment. There can be few more dramatic than the transformation which took place towards the end of the '60s, when a vast ballroom-dancing public suddenly changed its Saturday evening habits and disappeared into oblivion.

In Reading alone, upwards of 4,000 people of widely differing age groups and life styles put on their glad rags and headed for a favourite palais, club, factory canteen or church hall to dance away the night until the last waltz brought festivities to a halt just before midnight.

As a result of this hugely popular form of entertainment, the Musicians' Union slogan "Keep Music Live" had real meaning for dozens of semi-professional entertainers who made their way to venues far and wide to keep the legion of "slow, slow, quick quick slow" enthusiasts happy and on their toes – or someone else's.

The three premier attractions for Reading were the Majestic Ballroom in Caversham Road, the Olympia in London Street and the dual Oxford Ballrooms in Eaton Place, just off Oxford Road.

Seasoned regulars made sure that they arrived at their chosen destination before the 'house full' notices went up, but it was not unusual for latecomers to queue without success at the Majestic and Olympia before heading for a third option.

At the "Maj", George Watkins and his 14-piece orchestra provided the big band sound for a regular and devoted 1,500 fans on Saturday evenings – just one of the three nights each week that the band played at the ballroom between 1959 and 1967, although it had been resident there since 1948.

Crowds of around 1,000 also consistently attended the Olympia, where bands led by Don Turk and Max Seeburg dispensed the music on alternate Saturdays.

Don Turk had taken over the reins at the Olympia in 1947, when Jack Powell (not to be confused with Jack Powell of Blue Rhythm Boys fame) decided to call it a day.

Jack had led the band at the ballroom throughout the war years, entertaining vast crowds who were determined to forget rationing and the blackout.

During that time many famous musicians including Syd

There were tears at the Majestic Ballroom on 22nd October 1967, the night that the George Watkins orchestra played the last waltz after 20 years in the Caversham Road palais. There were more than 1,200 'regulars' at the final performance. Several of the musicians had been with the band throughout its long run at the ballroom. The orchestra went on to play a series of one-night bookings, starting with the opening of the new Top Rank Suite in Station Hill

photo by Reading Evening Post

Jack Powell and his Orchestra play for dancers at Reading Town Hall on VJ Night. From left to right, front row: Bob Cook (bass), Jack Powell, JImmy Knowles (guitar), May Trinder (vocals), Cyrus Chris (accordion), Harry Morgan, Cyril Harling, Jim Gudgin and Lionel Humphries (saxes). Back row: Harold Ford (piano), Denny Piercy (drums), Luther Britt (trombone), Freddie Coupe and Bill Lord (trumpets)

Lawrence, Jack Parnell and Tommy McQuater sat in with their semi-professional colleagues and in 1942 the band won the Melody Maker Home Counties Dance Band Championship.

At the Oxford, five or six-piece bands played in the two adjoining halls on a rotation basis and the 500 or so dancers who turned up on a Saturday evening were not surprised to find that groups led by Alf Grant, Bill Brannigan, Pete Forest or the immensely popular Frank Cotterell's Heralds of Swing had been booked to provide the music.

In Friar Street, dedicated ballroom enthusiasts walked beside sacks of fertiliser through the passage of Fidlers seed store before climbing the stairs to the Central Ballroom, where they performed their foxtrots and tangos on a sprung floor to the strict tempo sound of the Eric Little Trio.

As well as providing yet another venue for local talent, the old Reading Town Hall in Blagrave Street was on the visiting list of many of the country's top professional bands and news that the magnificent Ted Heath Orchestra had booked a date sparked off a rush for tickets reminiscent of today's major sporting events.

It was amusing to watch the faces of visiting musicians to the civic building because being close to the then Reading Police Station in Valpy Street, the quirkiness of the amplification system often meant that confidential radio messages were relayed throughout the hall.

At one concert performance, legendary American trumpeter Maynard Ferguson looked with amazement at a plaster figure adorning the balcony as a loudspeaker close to its mouth requested a duty constable to make his way to the corner of Chatham Street.

Venturing away from the town's main arenas, the South Reading Community Centre in Northumberland Avenue, Huntley and Palmer's canteen off King's Road and the Caversham Bridge, Great Western and Grosvenor Hotels were also the locations for regular dances.

Groups led by pianist Arthur Griffiths were a familiar sight at Caversham's Grosvenor Hotel, while at the Community Centre the music was usually provided by Jack Powell's Blue Rhythm Boys.

Here, too, the family link so often evident among the town's musicians led to another successful launch. Maurice Powell, son of saxophonist leader Jack, and Ken, the offspring of drummer Frank Bean, formed their own group, The Music Men, which was for many years resident at the Robinson Crusoe Club at California, near Wokingham.

In the days when a boot sale literally meant a reduction in the price of footwear, the accepted method of raising funds for youth groups, sports clubs and a host of charity organisations was to run a dance, usually at the local church hall or youth club.

St Luke's, in Erleigh Road, St. Giles in Southampton Street and Mary Magdalen at Tilehurst were three of the many venues hosting regular Saturday night hops.

Here, of course, the bands were smaller, but dozens of trios and quartets drew a hundred or so followers to each event, ensuring a steady supply of cash for needy causes as well as work for local musicians.

No article about Reading's dance band scene would be complete without mention of the Butcher's Arms – a public house in Hosier Street, close to St Mary's Butts. The Butcher's became the headquarters of the local Musicians' Union branch and was the regular Sunday lunchtime meeting place for the town's bandsmen.

Here, musicians were booked for forthcoming dates and promoters who quibbled over the going rate relegated to the union blacklist.

Official business, however, was more often the excuse for the like-minded to meet, enjoy a pint and generally grouse about out-of-tune pianos, the exorbitant price of reeds and the inadequate supply of free booze at the previous night's engagement.

Now, sadly, those heady days have probably gone forever, though ballroom dancing classes are surprisingly well attended. Wishful thinking perhaps, but could events turn full circle, with live music again replacing discos and a return to the dance floors by the missing thousands? Fortunately, one only has to listen to the superbly talented youngsters of today to be assured that an ample supply of first-class music-makers is waiting to take the stand should Saturday night again become "Gig Night in Reading".

Ron Pearce

Dance Bands of Yesterday
Norrie Hart and Tony Barham

Donkey's years past, the magic of ballroom reigned in Reading. One of the most popular venues was the Oxford Ballroom in Oxford Road almost opposite the Pavilion Cinema, now a snooker hall. Quite a number of bands played there, providing 'Dance Music for Genteel People', but I remember only one, the Harry Tate band (or was it orchestra; in fact, was it Harry Hale?).

Ted Smith was usually master of ceremonies but I was called in a few times when the late, great Ted was not available because I was one of the few people who had a dress suit and (a) could do the job and (b) was cheap – ten bob a night and a free drink, I think.

I remember I had to add to my attire a pair of white gloves and was provided with a chair to the left of the stage from where I issued forth on a prearranged signal to announce into the huge microphone, "Next dance please", at the end of a set. I also stepped forward dramatically when the band was ready to perform further, to announce, "Ladies and gentlemen, take your partners for …" whatever the dance was to be.

A feature of these evenings was a cabaret spot where Harry produced and played his musical saw while the players (and I) took light refreshments. **Norrie Hart**

1925 Edwards Sonata Dance Band
1927 The Jolly Quintette Dance Band
    The Bohemian Dance Band
1931 The Melody Dance Orchestra
    The Grosvenor Dance Orchestra
    Tom Smith's Jazz Band
    Mr G Whitfield's No 1 Dance Band (from Wantage)
    The Bumble Bee Orchestra
1933 Roy Rowe's Dance Band
    Piccadilly Dance Band (at McIlroys, etc)
    The Freaks Band
1936 Savannah Dance Band (played at The Cadena, etc)
    Howard Baker and his band
    Attfield's Accordion Band (played at Binfield Hall, Reading)
1937 The Utopian Band
    The Blue Star Players
    Darkie Smith's Crazy Coloured Swingers
    Ron Wood's Accordion Band (from Basingstoke)
1938 Jack Croome and his boys (popular at Caversham, etc)
1940 The Romany Dance Band
    Teddy Hale's Band
1947 Jack Powell's Orchestra and Jack Powell's sextet
    George Watkins and his No 1 Band
1948 Don Turk and his music (from Tokers Green)

Tony Barham

Music without Notes Drum 'n' Bass

AMIT KAMBOJ was born in Slough and has spent all his life there, 23 years so far. His interest in music has led him away from the traditional routes and into the world of electronic music

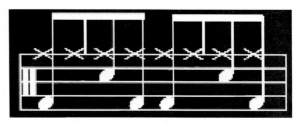

When I was at school, they told me that if I was going to be a musician, I would have to play an instrument. I always wanted to make music. It's not that I didn't want to play an instrument, I just felt it was a tedious task to learn the notes, it was the old-fashioned way of playing. So I got into computers.

What started me into making music was an old tape recorder, a really old one where if you pushed 'play' and wanted to forward into the track, you'd still hear the tape. Across the two tape decks, I could play a vocal or a beat track, record it across, pause it, record it again, keep doing it until I got a big section. Then I acquired the Amiga 500 computer, and a software package called Master Sound.

I was sampling for sounds. There was an input on the back, and you could sample any sound you wanted. It wouldn't be very clear because the sampling quality was bad – if you can imagine, 16-bit is CD quality and the Amiga was half that. I'd sample from a Walkman's output jack. When I went to my first record label, I released records from a demo from that set up. They really liked it because they felt it was raw and wasn't too clean.

I didn't know any record label in the area but there was a shop on Mill Street in Slough called Rough House Records, and I met Keith Davis there. He mentioned that he'd already got a record label up and running and showed me the first few releases that were coming out. He said, "Whenever you want to do something, bring stuff to me of this quality. I'll guarantee a release every time." I was over the moon, jumping for joy.

I gave Keith the demo and he was quite pleased. However, it was only three minutes long and it had to be five to make it a 12-inch, so I went back and finished it off.

There are so many DJs and radio stations that need vinyl to play, especially when they're mixing. Vinyl is very important for that because it's virtually impossible with CDs. Some people like the sound of vinyl – with CD there's no real harmonic content. With records, it's just an analogue track, straight from the original sound. Digital media like CDs are good for creating tracks because there might be loops and sounds that you need to send from one computer to the sequencer, digitally

rather than recording it and getting a lot of hiss.

I went back the following week and gave Keith the final piece – that was in March 1995. He arranged to book in with a company called Master Piece in Fulham. They took the digital audio tape and made a master of it so we could take it to EMI to do the main press. That was a good experience – I'd always seen the process from making the track to having it finalised on DAT, but nothing from there onwards.

While this was going on I was studying for a two-year Sound Technology HND at Ealing. There I met a lot of people who helped me, and I helped them. Just as I'm doing okay now, they're releasing records as well – people like Oliver Lomax and Justin Richardson.

Keith knew a lot of people in distributing agencies. He would give them 250 promos. They'd send one record to each shop in the London area, and from there they'd work on the pre-sales. The person who sells the records in the shop would have a good idea of how many of the records he'd sell and he'd write down the number – 50 or 70 or zero. The bigger the record label the more promos we gave them, the smaller the record label, the fewer the promos, because freebies are money out of your pocket and you don't want to make a loss.

I changed my name quite frequently. My first name was The Harlequin. The track was called *F*** You and Your Family*. Wherever you go, if you meet a DJ of that time and you mention it, they'll remember that track. I sampled the tune from a Robert de Niro film, *The Untouchables*. In a violent scene, Robert de Niro is Al Capone and he ends up swearing at Elliot Ness, the person trying to take him. There are bits where I treated it and did all sorts of things to it.

The pre-sale for that record was 900 copies. Those 900 went on sale and DJs would play it out amongst the clubs and there would be a week or two when it was alive. We'd get feedback, which was unusual, because with the style of music Drum 'n' Bass was doing, we never got any letters. But now we were getting letters from normal people who'd buy the records, saying, 'Could you please give us more of that sort of stuff, more of The Harlequin?' It was played on pirate radio but we didn't get any legitimate airplays.

For the next record, I created the track, and Keith

promoted it. We sold fewer records again, but it was played on Kiss FM and then the next day on BBC. We received no letters about this one and we made less than we had before. We just couldn't work out the picture. You get airplay but no letters and make less money.

We used to have a track out once every three months, maybe sometimes once every six months. Bear in mind it was a minor record label – Keith had to make sure the money was back in the account before starting again.

I've moved on now. I went up to see another record label in London called Renegade Hardware. There's a guy there called Clayton I met when I was at university in Ealing, and he'd say, "Do stuff for our label because we want to get a crew together and really do well. You can help us a lot." But I never recorded anything for him for some reason. Because Keith was just down the road, I stayed with him. In some ways it would have been a good thing to spark off Clayton as well. I told him I was tied up for the moment because I was working on a soundtrack for a film my brother is making. I look forward to things going well with him because I'm planning to get three or four tracks done and then I'll go and sort things out with him.

I took a break from my recording for about four months because of my brother's film. It has killed a lot of time for me since the beginning of the year. I've never done soundtracks for film before; it's a new thing. I've had to watch a lot of films, such as *Psycho*, to get to know what a typical soundtrack demands.

My heart's in music and I still just want to release records. I try to take time out to research what I'm doing and to learn more techniques, rather than just putting out one release after another each sounding the same as the one before.

The Moving Music Shop

Henry Davis and Son

The name of Henry Davis on an old envelope from Victorian times, dated 1st April 1878, is a positive reminder that Reading has always been a thriving centre for the retail music industry.

Under a multiplicity of spellings, Henry Davis and Son began trading as "Music Sellers" in the town in 1877, when they took over the premises of Mr S Witney – "Hairdresser and Toy Merchant" at 121 Broad Street.

The Davis family continued to trade from this address until 1884, when the premises were purchased by bootmakers Freeman, Hardy and Willis, remaining within the footwear trade until this day.

Meanwhile, Henry Davis and Son moved to No 10 King's Road, where the Stevens Directory for that year described their business as "Pianoforte and Music Warehouse, Teachers and Tuners".

This remained the directory entry until 1897, when it changed to Davis, Henry, Mrs and Son and then Davis, Mrs Sarah J and Son.

In 1901, it would appear that the Davis family faced opposition, for just two doors away at No 6, one Thomas Waite also opened a "Pianoforte and Music Warehouse" in premises previously owned by Allen Gordon Watson, "Outfitters".

However, apparently undeterred, Mr and Mrs Davis continued to trade unchanged until 1902, when they moved to No 14 King's Road, while adding to their description "Frederick Davis, Professor of Music".

At the same time, a directory entry shows that Mr Waite had

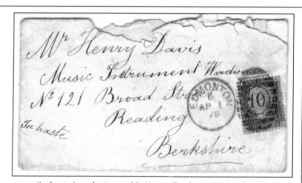

'In haste' – a letter to Mr Henry Davis on 1st April 1878

branched out to include the sale of organs to his list of wares, while with the removal of the Davis's to No 14, their old premises at No 10 became the Empire Furniture Company.

By 1908, the heading had become simply Mrs Henry Davis and Son, with mention of Professor Frederick Davis disappearing from its content.

Then in 1912 the coast apparently again became clear for the family when the Thomas Waite premises at No 6 became the headquarters for a Shipping Agency.

Around 1925, the name Arthur Davis appears to have been added to company details, but then, after continuing virtually unchanged throughout the war years, No 14 King's Road became a grocers shop called County Delicacies in 1948.

Sadly, research has failed to throw up further reference to the Davis family, but there appears little doubt that it had been a principle supplier of music and musical instruments in the town throughout more than 70 years of trading.

Ron Pearce

'Fascinating School Group steals Show' Drums

Percussionist KEN WICKENS learned to play the drums at Maiden Erlegh school and was involved from the start in the school's innovatory percussion ensemble

My introduction to live music was watching military bands with my parents. As a child I observed that the only musicians who did not have music were the drummers and presumed that you did not have to be able to read music to play the drums. (Little did I know!) I had no opportunity to test this theory until I went to secondary school.

Maiden Erlegh School Parent Teacher Association had decided to allocate a sum of money to the music department. The initial intention was to purchase a grand piano, however my father, among others, suggested a number of instruments should be bought so that the whole school could benefit and not just the chosen few.

Earlier in the year, a local percussionist, Les Lawrence,

had visited the school with a vast array of instruments. He gave a talk and demonstrated the variety of sounds that could be produced. Les finished with a mad dash around the stage playing many of the instruments, accompanied by a recording of the *William Tell Overture*. As a result of this demonstration it was decided to purchase a selection of percussion instruments.

It was somewhat of a surprise to my parents that their shy and very quiet son wished to play the drums but they supported me as, every Saturday morning, I went along with others to the school for percussion lessons. A group of about 25 pupils enjoyed these Saturday morning sessions and so, under the direction of Paul Mundy, the school's head of music, Maiden Erlegh School Percussion Ensemble was formed. It was the first school orchestral percussion ensemble in this country (as far as I know).

Our skills were developed by Les Lawrence, and other percussionists, including the professional musician Alan Graham. This gave all of us the opportunity to experience the full range of percussion instruments both tuned and untuned.

The ensemble performed at school concerts and was also called upon to do a tour of Reading primary schools, two schools a day for a week, to provide a taster of secondary

The percussion section rehearses for one of Les Lawrence's spectacular Moods in Music concerts in 1964

school music to the younger children. Another memorable performance was for a gathering of head teachers in the old restaurant in Heelas after closing time. It was quite spooky wheeling the percussion instruments through the dark and empty shop past the glass counters covered with their dust sheets.

Maiden Erlegh School percussion ensemble was to appear at a number of Moods in Music concerts in Reading and other locations including Portsmouth where the local paper was to report "Fascinating school group steals show".

Various members of the ensemble have gone on into the world of music at the highest and most respected levels and at the fun-loving. amateur level as well.

Millennium Choice Ken Wickens

As a player and a listener I admire Tchaikovsky for his ability to write such a variety of music from the 1812 to Swan Lake, and Phil Collins for his pop and big band music (very percussive!)

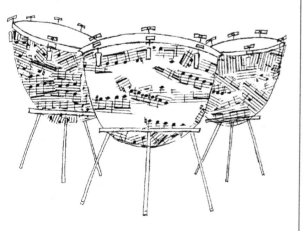

Those Music Exams

Gillian Shepheard

At 14years of age I sat my Grade 7 piano exam. In the church hall waiting-room shivered a Grade 1 violinist, a Grade 4 cellist and a battered mop 'n' bucket.

I raised my feet above the icy airstream blowing under the door and shoved my hands in my pockets. The frost ferns on the windows showed no sign of thawing. The large, unheated exam hall had uncurtained windows round three sides and the examiner sat at a folding table which squeaked every time he moved.

My footsteps drummed on the bare wooden floorboards as I crossed to the piano. The rickety bentwood chair was far too low but I did not complain. Examiners were only just second in rank to God and if he accepted the conditions, so must I.

From a distant room came sounds of toddlers' voices, mostly wailing. Nearer – through the hatch, in fact – came the clatter of washing up and chatter of the W.I.

I tried to concentrate on my scales.

The piano keys were yellow, several with their ivory veneer missing. The sound was tinny, echoing and out of tune. Bach himself could not have recognised his Partita that I had so meticulously and lovingly prepared!

I struggled on through a Sonata movement and reached the last piece, a Brahms Intermezzo, with relief. To produce the magical blend of harmonies this piece needs very careful pedalling. Alas, during the first phrase I discovered that having depressed the sustaining pedal with my right foot I had to lever it up again with my left in a sort of feet-and-pedal sandwich. Halfway through my eyes blurred. Weeping, I leapt up from my chair, sending it flying over backwards, and fled.

The examiner called me back for the sight reading and the travesty of aural tests. To my amazement he was smiling sympathetically and I realised that he too, was having a dreadful day. Now smiling back, I did my best – but how hard it is to sing a melody in tune when the example contains so many notes off key!

Even today there are too many sub-standard exam centres, but thankfully, now we have an option – the Home Visit.

Several teachers pool their candidates to make up the minimum number of hours needed for an examiner's visit. The warm waiting-room contains magazines and table games. When they go through to the studio they play on a good, familiar piano in a room where they know how the music will sound. Haven't they had their lessons on it – or, if with another teacher as least several practices?

These advantages enable today's youngsters to play their best – confirmed by the overall 10 per cent improvements in results

It is hard work for the teacher/hostess. The examiner needs regular trays of refreshments and everyone else gets cheerful encouragement but how rewarding it is to know that exams need no longer be the terrifying ordeals they were and that the examiner, too, has enjoyed his day.

The Friendly Festival Tilehurst Eisteddfod

Eisteddfod is a Welsh noun meaning 'Sitting' or 'Session', which has become widely anglicised through its application to the competitive festivals of the arts which take place annually, not only in Wales, but throughout the United Kingdom. One such festival is the Tilehurst Eisteddfod which began in 1954.

It was in 1952 that Mr Elwyn Evans, a Welshman, Churchman and gifted amateur musician, suggested to a few friends in Tilehurst the idea of a local annual festival to foster interest in the arts. A small committee was formed to explore the possibilities, the idea seemed feasible, and so it was decided to sponsor an Eisteddfod on the lines of the Welsh festivals, but with rather more emphasis on relaxed mutual enjoyment and rather less on ceremonial formality. The first competition took place in October 1954 at the Garrison Theatre, Ranikhet Camp, in Church End Lane, with classes in Vocal, Choral and Instrumental Music, and on 13th November a concert of winners took place in the Methodist Hall in Tilehurst.

From what must have been a very tentative beginning the Festival has grown in size, diversity and status over the years attracting entries from many parts of the United Kingdom. The majority come, of course, from Berkshire and the neighbouring counties.

The 30 classes in the first year were for mixed choirs, vocal quartets and duets, folk songs and solos for soprano, contralto, tenor and bass as well as for children. Instrumental classes included piano, violin, cello, double bass, flute, oboe, clarinet and trumpet.

Entry fees were two shillings (10p) and for choirs five shillings (25p) while all children's entries were 6d. Bronze medals were awarded to winners in a few classes while others received a certificate of Merit and the choirs were presented with silver-plated plaques. Set pieces were works by popular classical composers, most of which would have been readily available in musical albums. The proceeds that first year were in aid of the Tilehurst Girl Guides and Boy Scouts' Headquarters Building Fund.

Following the success of 1954 a second event was organised for the following year, but to be held in the Spring with sections also for Drama, Verse Speaking, Arts and Crafts and Dancing. The Music moved to the Village Hall and Methodist Hall as well as using Norcot School from 1958 until the closure of the school in 1977. The Music section now takes place each year in the middle of May. Concerts of festival winners which were held at Westwood Girls School, now part of Prospect Technology College, were well attended and popular from 1968 to 1974.

In 1956 the local paper reported that over 350 competitors took part in the Music sections. The 44 classes that year included those for church choirs, school choirs, madrigal groups, oratorios, Gilbert and Sullivan vocal ensembles and recorders and pianoforte accompaniment at sight, the song to be sung by the official vocalist. Records show a winner and runner-up, but the class was not included the following year.

The President wrote in 1973 that the committee had been encouraged by the way in which people had responded to the challenge which the Eisteddfod offered, the quality of the performers, the willingness to listen and to learn from the friendly advice and above all the way in which many happy relationships had been fostered and forged.

Over the years the Tilehurst Eisteddfod became known as 'The Friendly Festival' . Each competitor receives a full adjudication as well as a certificate for marks above 80 per cent, and for the highest marks one of the 20 cups.

The Eisteddfod, and the Music section in particular, has always given entrants the opportunity to perform in public under the eye of adjudicators and to learn and develop from their comments. It was reported in 1969 that two boys who had played the *Bach Double Concerto* the previous year had begun studies at the Royal Academy of Music and another competitor had won a scholarship to La Scala, Milan, attributing much of her success to participation in eisteddfods and music festivals such as Tilehurst.

Today the Music section is still open to people of all ages, offering classes similar to those of the first festival but also including Celtic harp, classical guitar and instrumental ensemble. Many classes have changed according to demand and trend in music, but the biggest change is the choice of test piece which is no longer that of the committee but of the competitor.

In 1956 the Eisteddfod was affiliated to the British Federation of Music Festivals, now the British Federation of Festivals for Music, Dance and Speech.

Every year a syllabus is produced detailing the various classes available for the Music and other sections of the Eisteddfod and since 1998 they have also been available on the Internet at the Eisteddfod's Web Site.

© **Tilehurst Eisteddfod**

An Education in Music Music teacher

TREVOR CRADDOCK, a lay clerk at St George's Chapel, Windsor, has taught in schools for some 20 years and has many private students, whose ages range from 12 to 70. He talks about his techniques in teaching music

When I am teaching, I do emphasise posture a tremendous amount – I find that many youngsters, in particular, need their posture monitoring carefully whether singing, or playing the piano. The position of the back is absolutely crucial because the ribcase is suspended from it. It is also important for the pianist to have the back in alignment because this affects the position of the shoulders and can lead to unnecessary tension.

I do use mirrors whenever possible and I try to insist on a mirror in any teaching room that I use at schools. In my own private studio I have a mirror over the piano so that people can see themselves face on and I also have an almost full-length, tilting cheval-mirror so that I can monitor them in profile and check that they are using their bodies appropriately

As much as time allows, I try to have a careful warm-up process. I think it is essential for something as delicate as the voice – an athlete or anybody playing sport tends to do limbering-up exercises first.

In musical terms, I use a combination of broken scales, triplet figures around each note of the scale, arpeggios in root and inversion forms. Then to gain more colour and dynamic variety I might make them sing up and down a scale, perhaps going up in crescendo and coming down the other side as a diminuendo and then to rectify the balance, going up to a diminuendo and coming down as a crescendo, in order to balance out the tone.

In physical terms, I use facial massage, various mnemonics for lip and tongue control; I monitor the jaw position to make sure that this is sufficiently relaxed, that the position of the neck shows no extraneous tension, and that the head is not thrust back or equally is not collapsed in any way, causing constriction of the larynx.

If the student is singing a piece in a foreign language I try to incorporate various vowel sounds for familiarity and ease of production so that they feel happy with all the range of vowel sounds and any difficult consonantal combinations, so that their singing does not sound stiff as a result. I want them to sound thoroughly at ease in their foreign language.

I am a great believer in the use of vocalise. If I feel that the pupil's vocal line is sounding rather fragmented, I will make them sing that phrase to 'ah' and release the breath evenly throughout the phrase. Then I will get them to sing the whole phrase just to the vowel sounds of the text, and then finally restore the full text. This really does encourage a sense of line and consistency of tone and also importantly, ensures that they are relating to one mouth shape rather than pulling a whole variety of shapes that look distracting and make for a rather variable tone quality.

At present I teach at Leighton Park, a mixed, Quaker secondary school where I have been for nearly 19 years, Reading School, a grant-maintained boys' school, and Luckley Oakfield School in Wokingham, a girls' private secondary school, so this really does give me a complete gamut of experience.

I occasionally take sectional rehearsals for the Berkshire Youth Choir, a splendid institution in the capable hands of Gillian Dibden who has done so much to further choral music in Berkshire, and I have administered several workshops for the Royal Schools of Church Music, principally in the Wokingham and Guildford areas.

I also hold workshops, sometimes at Leighton Park School, but more often in what is now called the Vicars' Hall within Windsor Castle, for people who might not have the chance otherwise to perform to some of their peers. I try to help them to get over nerves, to feel what the whole process of performing is about, and to project to an audience. They receive some useful criticism so that they know what is good about their performance and constructive ways in which it could be improved.

Some of my pupils have gone on to further their careers as singers and have taken their studies to quite a serious level. One or two have gone on to sing at at the English National Opera, two of my previous pupils have gained choral scholarships to Cambridge colleges, and also to the Guildhall School of Music in London, and two of my current pupils are hoping to go to Trinity College and St John's, Cambridge.

I particularly enjoy teaching adults. I have a case load of about 23 private pupils who come to me from a variety of schools – there are some very musical schools in the area like St Bernard's Convent, Slough, and Ranelagh School in Bracknell – and I also have quite a large number of adult pupils of ages up to 70, still enjoying their singing. They are very encouraging to teach, and they still show signs of improving – which proves that one can improve at any age.

An Aristocrat of Organs 'Father' Willis Town Hall Organ

Reading possesses in its now world-famous Town Hall organ an almost unique musical treasure of which its citizens should always be intensely proud. On entering the hall,, one is immediately struck by the organ's imposing grandeur. There it stands, in a magnificent carved oak case with elegant shining front pipes of almost pure tin, up to 16ft in length, its majestic presence dominating the interior of the hall without in the least overpowering it, perfectly proportioned to its surroundings, and true to all the principles of organ building. Not buried away in a recess, nor hidden behind a grille, the organ is well placed to speak clearly into an auditorium which, with its lofty coved ceiling, is ideal from a tonal point of view.

Its whole appearance proclaims that here is a very aristocrat of organs promising to sound in every way as grand as it looks. This is a real organ case, with a three-dimensional frontage measuring 25ft wide by 13ft deep and rising to an overall height of nearly 40ft, consisting of 53 pipes arranged in nine compartments shaped with all the grace of a concert harp or a grand piano, almost every pipe showing its true proportions and speaking its proper note.

And, to crown it all, at the top, and emphasised by a subtly effective piercing of the woodwork, the central feature is a shield bearing the official Arms of the Town of Reading (as existing at the time), carved in relief, asserting once and for all that this is peculiarly Reading's organ, and here it is to remain in perpetuity. This shield, if it were decked out in full heraldic colouring, would add a wonderful finishing touch to a superb composition. Also depicted in the carving are several orchestral instruments and the opening phrase of Handel's *Hallelujah Chorus*.

Beneath this sumptuous case, which contains over 2,000 pipes of all shapes and sizes, some metal, some wood, is a highly inviting uncluttered console of four manuals and 46 hand-engraved turned-ivory stop knobs – 37 different speaking-stops and nine couplers. The action is Barker-lever to Great, tracker to Swell, Choir and Solo, and pneumatic to Pedal. In 1947 the out-of-date pitch of the whole organ was lowered slightly to bring it into tune with an orchestra, and in 1964 the clumsy old trigger crescendo pedal to the Swell was converted to the more civilised central balanced pedal through the generosity of the late Harold Hartley of the Berkshire Organists' Association.

The organ does indeed sound as good as it looks, whether in solo organ recitals, accompanying choirs and choral societies, or playing with a large orchestra in organ concertos. For just over 100 years until closure of the hall In 1989 it has been greatly loved by the musical folk of Reading, and admired by the world's leading experts and recitalists.

The Berkshire Organists' Association has seen to that, by providing from its membership a succession of gifted official honorary borough organists to preside over it, and by arranging, at its own expense, public recitals and concerts by the world's leading players – including the famous Italian virtuoso Fernando Germani from St Peter's Rome, the organist of Notre Dame Paris, most of the leading English cathedral organists, an occasional theatre organist, and players from America – including Carlo Curley himself.

The organ's centenary was celebrated on 4th November 1964 by a highly successful concert jointly arranged by the Corporation and the Berkshire Association, with contributions from the Reading Symphony Orchestra and the New Elizabethan Singers, attended by the Mayor and Henry Willis III, grandson of its builder and head of the

The 'Father' Willis organ at the Town Hall

firm that has always kept it on top form. For this there was an enthusiastic capacity audience. The organ-playing was shared jointly by Laurie Warman, the borough organist, and his successor, J Eric Few.

The history of the organ goes back to the days of the mid-Victorian Industrial Revolution, when every prosperous self-respecting town built itself a prestigious town hall and made sure that it had a grand concert organ that could bring great music to the masses. Here in Reading important industries were developing under the leadership of powerful personalities who were proud of their town, and wanted to put it on the map again. Reading has greatly benefited from the generosity of men like the Palmers, the Simmonds, and the Suttons.

For the then small Georgian town hall of 1785 an organ was therefore required, and the order for it was placed with an up-and-coming organ builder who had exhibited an outstanding instrument in the great 1851 Exhibition, and who eventually built some 2,000 organs, supplying 17 of our English cathedrals – including St Paul's – and huge instruments for the Royal Albert Hall, Alexandra Palace, and St George's Hall in Liverpool. He was the greatest organ builder of his day and, being the founder of a family of five generations of organ builders, has become known as "Father" Willis.

This new organ for the Reading hall was a gift to the town from the Reading Philharmonic Society, and consisted of three manuals, 26 stops, and 1,660 pipes, at a cost of £770 including hydraulic blowing apparatus – supplemented by hand-pumping levers if that should fail. It was surmounted by two elegant winged female figures sounding golden trumpets, and over the centre "a large bust of the Immortal Handel".

Drawing by F Gordon Spriggs

At the opening concert on 16th October 1864, the famous Dr Samuel Sebastian Wesley played it to an audience of some 600 people, though it was not quite complete and did not work properly. However, this was soon made good, and Henry Willis himself (who was also a very fine organist) subsequently gave a recital on it.

To supplement this small hall, the present clock tower and council chamber were added, facing impressively towards Friar Street and the Market Place, designed by a Reading architect of national standing, Alfred Waterhouse. He also designed the Science Museum at Kensington, and the Town Hall at Manchester, and even submitted a design for rebuilding the Houses of Parliament at Westminster after the fire (but that ended up as the hotel frontage of St Pancras Station!).

By the 1880s the need was felt for a grander hall, and this was added to harmonise with the existing Waterhouse buildings by Thomas Lainson, a conscientious architect who first took the trouble to visit and study various newly-built town halls, with the result that this new hall is very efficiently designed structurally and has reverberation and acoustics well nigh perfect in every way. Here the Small Hall organ was rebuilt and enlarged by Willis to such perfection that any subsequent major alteration to hall or organ would be disastrous tonally.

The opening recital this time, on 31st May 1882, was by Dr (later Sir) Walter Parratt, shortly to be appointed to St George's Chapel, Windsor, with additional music by the Philharmonic Society Choir of 72 sopranos, 66 altos, 41 tenors, 57 basses, and the orchestra of 43 players, who also performed *Messiah* in the evening. This was conducted by W H Strickland, organist of St Mary's Minster Church, Reading (where there was already a Willis organ) who, together with a local doctor, Isaac Harrison, played a large part in all these improvements.

Sad to say, Reading has not always been very good at valuing its historical and cultural heritage, having taken little interest In what was left of its great Benedictine Abbey. This was one of the foremost in the land, where a mediaeval king was buried and another married, and parliaments held, as well as being the source of that remarkable musical Rota, *Sumer Is Icumen in*, which was written down by a monk in the early 13th century.

So, about the time that Reading's old Manor House in the Forbury was pulled down in 1962 to make way for a hideous great office block (in its turn recently mercifully demolished), and there was a scheme to run a six-lane motorway through the Forbury Gardens and part of St Laurence's churchyard, enough was enough, and the Reading Civic Society was formed under the guidance of the then Bishop of Reading, the Rt Revd Eric Knell, and Sir John Betjeman, to put a stop to all this destructive philistinism. Then in the 1970s and 1980s there was a very determined threat from a majority on the town council, who ought to have known better, to bulldoze the town hall complex and sell the site to help pay for the Civic Centre and Hexagon, getting rid of the organ for scrap.

The Berkshire Organists' Association, founded in 1921, had already foreseen the possibility of something like this happening, and by 1958 had attempted to focus the public's attention on the quality and importance of the organ. So a long fight to save it and the hall, in itself a highly significant piece of architecture, began in real earnest. They were greatly helped by the newly-formed Civic Society, and much credit is due to the late Mrs Mary Biggs and Mr Martyn Reason, leading members, for their prolonged and powerful support. Thanks to them the hall, organ and buildings were officially listed Grade II by the Department of the Environment in 1974.

In July of the previous year a massive petition for the retention of hall and organ of almost 1,000 sheets containing 6,690 signatures from far and near, including the signatures of the Diocesan Bishop (Oxford) and the President of the Royal College of Organists, was presented to the Mayor, while, unknown to the public, secret plans were afoot – unsuccessfully – to sell the organ to America. Then, in 1978 someone came up with the bright idea of giving it away (at ratepayers' expense) to a disused church somewhere in London.

In 1982 it was at last to be kept in the now saved hall – but crammed up to the roof and tonally ruined, by the insertion of a mezzanine floor right across the hall at balcony level. And now, in 1999, with hall and organ being conservatively restored, the Heritage Lottery Fund threatens to cancel its grant unless the long-suffering old Father Willis has its useful balanced crescendo pedal remade in the clumsy out-of-date trigger form, and the tuning returned to the earlier high pitch, out of tune with any orchestra. This can only add enormously to the cost, with every one of the 2,000 and more pipes having to be expertly readjusted!

The organ appears in five standard works on organs and organ building, and is the subject of a learned 70-page Symposium issued in 1972 (though no longer in print). Two fine recordings have been made of it, also now unobtainable; one in October 1973 by the French organist Monique Devernay, and the other in 1981 by Catherine Ennis. May this wonderful treasure survive without further threats to delight and uplift generations of true music lovers in the future…

F Gordon Spriggs
Berkshire Organists' Association (Past President)

Millennium Choice F Gordon Spriggs

Bach's Toccata and Fugue in D minor because it brings out the best sounds of a good organ

Friend to the Arts
Frank Schuster and The Hut

Perhaps no house in Berkshire played a more important part in the history of twentieth century music than Leo Frank Schuster's riverside dwelling, The Hut at Bray.

Frank Schuster was the well-to-do son of a Frankfurt Jewish banking family and he was a keen and discriminating patron of the arts.

Schuster had a circle of friends which included Osbert Sitwell, Siegfried Sassoon , Adrian Boult – and Edward Elgar, and it was here that Edward Elgar worked on some of his most outstanding pieces including, the First Symphony, the Violin Concerto and Falstaff. Without Schuster's help, the Elgar festival at Covent Garden in March 1904, which brought his music to the notice of a wider public, would not have been possible.

Among Schuster's other friends was Gabriel Fauré, who came to England in 1898 to conduct the music he had written for Maeterlinck's play, Pelleas et Melisande.

On 26th June 1898, Schuster gave a house-party at The Hut. Fauré was among the guests as were the actress, Mrs Patrick Campbell, and the distinguished American painter, John S Sargent. One of the drawings made by Sargent, while he was there, depicted the great actress with Fauré.

Only the previous week, there had been another party, at Schuster's London house, where Fauré met Maurice Maeterlinck, the erratic Belgian who was the author of the play The Blue Bird.

The Hut passed into the hands of Leslie George Wylde (known as "Anzey" Wylde), a New Zealand army officer who had been wounded and disabled in the 1914-18 war. The house was extended and the name altered to The Long White Cloud.

But Elgar's connection with the place did not end when it passed to Wylde. In June 1927, Schuster arranged for a performance at The Long White Cloud of Elgar's three important chamber works. (At that period Elgar's music, excepting the Enigma Variations and a number of the lighter pieces, was out of fashion and got few public performances.)

In about 1937, the house and grounds were acquired by the Moss family widely known for their achievements in show-jumping and motor-racing.

Tony Barham

The Rocky Road to Reading   Reading Festival

August Bank Holiday is traditionally that time of year when hoards of music fans grab tents, rucksacks and a steady supply of alcohol before making their way to the Reading Festival. The town's residents, on the other hand, are left reaching for their earplugs in preparation for this three-day event, where top bands play to crowds in excess of 50,000.

The festival has a colourful history which reads almost like a soap opera, with struggles over ownership, political interference and problems with drugs and violence. Nevertheless, despite its ups and downs, it remains an integral part of the summer season for many people.

The music may have changed considerably over the years but today's festival-goers still have to face the perils and pitfalls of bad weather, gruesome toilets and dubious cuisine. Problems with drugs and petty crime are encountered every year and stories abound of disgruntled fans being supplied with all manner of things ranging from Oxo to liquorice and even pasta shapes.

Some intrepid types will inevitably try to gain free entry by breaking into the festival site, though they may do well to remember the man who jumped over the security barrier and left his finger hanging behind on the fence.

The most important aspect of the festival is ,of course, the music and throughout its history Reading Festival has seen some memorable performances both onstage and off. Who could forget, for instance, the time that Meatloaf was forced to flee the stage after being bombarded with bottles of urine? Or the time that the Red Hot Chilli Peppers set fire to their hats and continued to play whilst wearing them?

The Reading Festival started out in a very different guise to the one we know today when it was first held in the grounds of the Richmond Athletic Association, in 1961. The National Jazz Festival, as it was then known, was organised by Harold Pendleton, a former accountant and avid music fan, who was inspired by the Newport Jazz Festival in America to stage his own event. Over the years the festival grew in popularity, moving to Windsor, Kempton and Plumpton, before settling in Reading in

Getting ready for Reading Rock Festival '89   *Photo by Reading Evening Post*

1971. The nature of the music changed over this time with the growing popularity of R&B and in 1964 the name was changed to the National Jazz and Blues Festival.

One of the bands to play during this time was the Rolling Stones, who happened to have a residency at the Richmond Athletic Association Clubhouse. The limited space of the clubhouse was hardly enough to contain the 1,500-strong crowd, mostly consisting of screaming girls, who turned up to see them play, so the band had to be moved to a more accommodating marquee.

At the beginning of the 1970s, rock took over as the prevailing musical genre and this was reflected in the festival line-up. In 1971, bands such as Sha Na Na and Wishbone Ash played at the festival, which was held in Richfield Avenue, Reading, for the first time. The event was staged as part of a wider festival to commemorate the 1,100th anniversary of the first mention of the town in the Anglo-Saxon chronicle and the 800th anniversary of the foundation of Reading Abbey. The bands rocked, the crowd bopped and the rain poured down in true festival style – the legend of Reading Rock was thus born.

In its formative years the festival played host to bands such as Mungo Jerry, who were then unknown, but as its popularity grew throughout the 1970s major rock bands like Status Quo and Aerosmith came to top the bill. An eclectic mix of acts could often be found during this time, ranging from George Melly to Genesis in 1973 and the following year Thin Lizzy shared the bill with Georgie Fame.

A festival to remember – Meatloaf was forced to flee the stage after being bombarded with bottles of urine

In 1978 Sham 69 were brought in to represent the growing influence of punk, which was perhaps unwise given that the Jam were also appearing that year. The mods and the punks took an instant dislike to one another and mayhem ensued as fights broke out in the crowd. After much throwing of cans and bottles the fans stormed the stage and proceeded to set upon the burly security guards. This also turned out to be the year that launched a thousand T-shirts, as amidst the fracas Bobby Sunderland, a notorious punk leader, was photographed in a triumphant pose – an image that went on to grace the chest of many a punk in years to come.

Politics reared its ugly head in 1983 when the Conservatives gained control of the local council. Harold Pendleton was told that the Richfield Avenue site would be needed for the development of a new leisure centre and as a result the festival did not take place for two years. Alternative sites around the town were suggested

and to add insult to injury a free festival was planned but eventually cancelled. For a while the future of the festival hung in the balance. However, thanks to the combination of a Labour council, which came into office in 1986, and farmer Desmond Drayton who had some spare room on his land, the festival was restored to its rightful place.

Even today the event is referred to as 'Reading Rock', a name it acquired during the 70s as the music tended more and more towards rock and heavy metal. During this time bands like Status Quo, AC/DC and Motorhead paved the way for the new wave of British heavy metal which made its hefty presence known in the early 1980s. However, by this time the preponderance of hard rock was beginning to wear thin and even John Peel refused to host the festival in 1980 because there were too many heavy metal bands.

Attendances were falling and it was becoming hard to drum up enthusiasm for a line-up featuring the likes of Bonnie Tyler and the Quireboys. This prompted the entry of the Mean Fiddler in 1989, heralding a new indie and alternative line-up with headliners The Pogues, New Order and The Mission backed up by Spacemen 3 and Gaye Bikers on Acid. John Peel was lured back as compere and for the first time in years the event was sold out. Billy Bragg also happened to play that year and many people will fondly recall how he enlisted the help of a 30,000-strong crowd to tell the Thames Valley police to F*** off. Two years later, and somewhat eerily, John Benham, the guitarist with the band Dog'ouse declared that he would like his ashes to be scattered over the festival site – which indeed they were when he died literally days later in a motorbike accident.

In 1992 things began to turn sour as the Pendletons fell out with the Mean Fiddler and the latter promptly set about organising the rival Phoenix festival which took place the following year. Nevertheless, the line-up was one to be remembered featuring Public Enemy, the Beastie Boys and Nirvana in their last ever UK appearance. Appalling weather conditions resulted in the comedy tent being blown away by fierce winds and the unfortunate Mark Arm of Mudhoney being pelted by mud balls for wearing a white suit. Bizarre happenings were a-plenty as Kurt Cobain appeared on stage in a wheelchair, wearing a wig and a dress. Perhaps the most dubious incident involved a member of the all-girl band L-7, who got her revenge on bottle-throwing fans by removing her tampon and hurling it into the crowd.

Following a long and protracted struggle with the Pendletons, the Mean Fiddler eventually acquired the Richfield Avenue site in 1993 and thus total control over the festival. At the same time, after years of complaints over noise levels, they were allowed to turn the volume up from 55 to 60 decibels when it was proved that the music was still not as loud as the traffic on the Caversham Road.

Under its new ownership, with Vince Power as promoter, the festival continued to thrive and expand with the introduction of new attractions each year. The comedy tent added an extra element to the proceedings, playing host to the likes of Denis Leary, Eddie Izzard and Mark Thomas and a late night cinema was introduced for sleep-shy festival goers.

In order to keep up with the changing face of music, dance and hip hop acts were included in the form of the Prodigy, Bentley Rhythm Ace, Tricky and Underworld. Club nights such as Fantasy Ashtray and Universe were held at the Rivermead Centre in addition to the Feet First indie disco. In 1997 three new events were held to represent a more diverse musical offering with the Sonic

Les Negresses Vertes at Reading Festival '89

Mook Experiment, the Night of the Big Drums 2 and the Vans Warped Stage featuring the UK amateur skate finals.

However, the rock element for which Reading has always been known, was still going strong with Metallica and Terrorvision pulling in the crowds in 1997 prompting an onstage war of words between Tony Wright of Terrorvision and Audioweb's Martin Merchant. The following year was something of a musical anachronism though, as seventies rockers Page and Plant were resurrected to headline the Friday night followed by New Order's eighties electropop on the Saturday.

As for the present day, it seems that the Reading Festival is slowly beginning to shake off the hard rock image it has been associated with for the past 30 years. With dance music continuing to dominate the airwaves it seems inevitable that festivals like Reading will have to make changes in order to keep up with the times. One hopes that it will stay true to its roots though and that Reading will continue to rock for years to come.

Liz Alvis

My First Rock Festival

'A weekend hippie's tale' by Sean Davis

I had been looking forward to this for months. It was to be my first rock festival and in our home town! My brother and his mates had all been to Shepton Mallet before and had regaled me with their adventures. We were going to stay the whole weekend and at the site as it would be 'uncool' to return each day. We were staying on the campsite next to the main arena.

Friday couldn't go quickly enough but we were soon meeting up and going to Richfield Avenue. We seemed to blend in with the "great unwashed" (as my parents had referred to them for months) so the decisions on what to wear had been correct. We passed through the various security checks at the gate and campsite unchallenged.

The tents were soon erected (thank God for our Scout training) and we rejoined the now growing throng in the main arena. The groups were now on their warm-up routines.

In the smaller arena were all the "shops"; the variety of available food was amazing (no fast food outlets then). You could get anything from virtually any country anywhere. It also catered for your medical needs, with a Red Cross and pharmacy tent available and even a Christian tent for your emotional requirements.

What surprised me was the mixture of teenagers not only from all over Britain but Europe and further, all united in peacefully listening to the music. It was loud but we spent the night chatting with our new-found friends long after the music had finished.

The weather turned and, as with most bank holidays, the rains came. The morning was spent mopping up and once changed into our clean 'cool' gear we ventured into town, proudly bearing our stamped hands to enable us to return to the festival.

Around early evening the bands started up again; we could actually hear them from the campsite so we didn't need to return to the arena. Suddenly a tent near us erupted with activity. It was being turned over by the security reinforcements. Nothing was found and we all had a good laugh and went back to enjoying the music.

Sunday and the last day of the festival, so I'm up with the lark – well, 10am – and a stroll to the shops is required as I've promised to meet up with Sarah, my friend from Whitley, who's only got a one-day ticket. We were strolling back along Richfield Avenue chatting and laughing when Sarah gave me back four squares of chocolate wrapped in silver foil (rum and raisin I seem to remember) which I quickly stuffed into my safari jacket as I was looking for my tickets to get back into the festival. Without warning we were propelled against the wire chain-link fence surrounding the site and somebody was demanding we produced the drugs "she was seen passing to you as you approached the gate". I handed over the package. "What is this?" They looked at each other dumbfounded. We were let off because a block of cannabis wouldn't have Cadbury's stamped on it. A red-faced constable muttered a trite apology and we were allowed to continue on our way.

The top of the bill on Sunday was the Crazy World of Arthur Brown. His rendition of Fire, standing on stage at night dressed in a white kaftan with a Viking helmet ablaze is something I will remember longer than anything I have seen at the many festivals and concerts I have attended up and down the country since that day.

The rains came down at the 1989 Reading Rock Festival and fans resorted to binliners
Photograph by Reading Evening Post

'Nice While it Lasted' Reading Festival

The Reading Festival was run for many years by Harold and Barbara Pendleton. The original idea came from Harold and famous jazz man CHRIS BARBER who were partners at the time. Chris recalls the early days of the festival

The concept of the festival came from America, although I don't think it transfers all that well. These open air festivals are not ideal in Britain because the weather system is not the same. Nevertheless, Harold and I got the idea after I played at the Monterey Festival.

I was running the Marquee Club in London at the time and Harold Pendleton was acting as manager for my band because I couldn't play the trombone and do all the business. One of the things he organised was a tour to America in 1959 and during that we played in the exhibition fairground in Monterey, California. The festival had been going a few years but this particular year was a landmark occasion and we were part of it.

Chris Barber

We thought this concept would be nice to try in Britain. They already ran a festival at Beaulieu but Edward Montagu wasn't very serious about it and there was a lot of hostility between the people going there over which types of music should be played.

Harold and I started the festival at Richmond – we were going on the pitch but they put us in the car park. It went from there to various places – one always has troubles. People who are not involved tend to say we're being noisy. I suppose you could say many people in moderate sized towns view a festival with the same sort of trepidation as when first or second division football teams play in their town and all their supporters flood in.

It started as the National Jazz Festival, although there was no marketing value in that so it became Jazz and Blues. We moved towards rock but never pop – we never had the Spice Girls. The relationship between rock music and pop music of the time was the same as between jazz and pop music in the 20s and 30s. I was never snooty about pop but, to a certain extent, pop music doesn't claim to have any artistic value.

We moved on from Richmond to Windsor and Kempton Park and Plumpton – racecourses were ideal sites because they provided wide open areas and car parking. We still had our problems though. For instance, although we got a court decision at Windsor saying we were not making an unacceptable noise and upsetting the people opposite the festival site on the other side of the river, it didn't help us in th end. Unfortunately the site was owned privately and certain people on the town council then told the owners of the land that if they wanted to get permission for gravel pits, they should not rent the land to the festival. This happened a lot.

The original site at Reading was a council site which was reached from Cow Lane and we were there for quite a long time. At every council election, the people not in power said it would be a good idea to get rid of the festival, and they said it in order get themselves into power. Then when they did get into power, they had to get rid of us! Luckily we got an agreement with the farm who owned land at the back which we used for car parking so we were able to get on that site.

In the meantime, we had improved the site, laying underground pipes for proper toilets. We could have got away with more temporary stuff. Anybody who has ever been to Glastonbury will know what toilets should be like. Also at Glastonbury you walk along half a mile of drug dealers which we never had at the festival. Thames Valley Police used the festival for training to see if they could spot a dealer. There would be about 10 or so arrests at the railway station on the first day and really you could do that anywhere in Britain.

We always took trouble to get on with Thames Valley

Billy Bragg at the 1989 festival, run jointly with the Mean Fiddler

Police and we took notice of the environmental officers, making sure we weren't too loud.

In the early 90s we came to a temporary arrangement with Vince Power of the Mean Fiddler . We ran it jointly as partners for three years and he brought in his ideas. We didn't see any reason to continue after that, but he was very angry about this and ran the Phoenix jazz festival at Stratford-upon-Avon at the same time as Reading Rock – the phoenix rising from the ashes of Reading Festival. It didn't do very well.

Eventually he offered the owner of the land a certain amount of money, and of course the owner thought five times the rent sounded very acceptable. He took it over and since then we have had no real connection. But it is still profitable and still pleases a lot of people.

I played in the first two festivals at Windsor and Plumpton and at Reading a couple of times. I would always try to go along though because it was a chance to meet my friends and other musicians. When you are a touring musician you don't meet other musicians very much. A lot of the rock musicians started out as jazz musicians; for instance Rod Stewart played banjo in a jazz band.

We always had a double stage at the festival so it was amusing to read later that Vince Power was providing a double stage to prevent that inevitable changeover between acts. We wondered what he was talking about because we had had two big stages side by side so you didn't have the delay of getting the stage ready for the next act. It worked very well when we ran it.

We took everything in our stride. If you have famous rock stars, they want special tents so that they don't have fans mobbing them – although I don't think we had the kind of fans at a rock festival who would do that. So we provided back access for the stars separate from the front where the public went in. One of the groups came in a hired Rolls Royce and I don't think anyone saw them except the staff. They were not impressed. They would have been more impressed if they had turned up in an old MG with a starting handle. Typical rock, flashy! You get folk singers coming in a Rolls, dressed in suits and changing into dungarees to go on stage.

One of the problems ywith a big festival is letting people out and then letting them back in again. You need a pass out ticket. Harold had a bright idea of issuing bands like the ones they use on new-born babies. One firm in the US made them so we ordered 50,000 bands with 'Reading Rock 79' (or whatever the year was) They came back with Rock 79 – they thought it said 'bands reading Rock 79'!

I can hardly remember any particularly memorable occasion, it's all a mass of past events. I can probably find something to enjoy in almost anything. I always liked Status Quo and enjoyed the Faces – but not a lot of things stand out like the Rolling Stones concert in Hyde Park or Live Aid. I don't really miss it that much. It was an era that has passed and it doesn't bother me a great deal. But Harold put everything into those festivals. We would talk about it as partners but he was responsible for all the day-to-day running.

It was great while it lasted. The festival still has a good reputation, is still going on and will continue while people enjoy it.

A New Adventure into Music Reading Festival

Local journalist ALAN PORTON has fond memories of the old rock festivals and some of the stars

Brought up to the swing sounds of Bobby Darin and Frank Sinatra, my first adventure into rock music came courtesy of Rod Stewart and Maggie May. It was the record which opened up a completely new adventure into music – I was hooked on rock 'n' roll.

Living less than ten minutes from the site of the Reading Rock festival, the sound of the August Bank Holiday music bonanza was never further than an open patio door away. So when given the chance to attend the event as a news reporter I snatched the ticket – Yes, Thin Lizzie, Rod Stewart, The Kinks and Black Sabbath. I rocked along to them all.

I was a regular until the promoters decided that rock music was dead and a new generation of bands took to the stage.

There were many highs and a few lows but the performances I will always recall with fond memories are probably not the same as others. The set by American rockers Starship was special, particularly as minutes before they arrived on stage Meat Loaf had been bottled off. Phil Lynott and Thin Lizzy were superb and it transpired it was to be one of his last gigs before his tragic death. Gary Moore of Thin Lizzy and Greg Lake of ELP joined forces for a superb set while Yes never failed to please – in spite of the line-up changes they remain as good today as they were all those years ago.

I have been fortunate enough to meet quite a few musicians during my time as a journalist and most have left a lasting memory. The members of Saxon once arrived unannounced in my office brandishing copies of their new album. A photoshoot followed in the Forbury Gardens but little did I realise that 20 years on I would be helping to promote a gig with the same band at Rivermead Leisure Complex.

One musician I got to know was former Uriah Heep front-man Dave Baron – he lived locally and I remember visiting him at his home in Sonning one afternoon for an interview and getting home eight hours and four bottles of wine later. Dave was a great musician and a perfect gent. His sudden death was hard to comprehend. He had been a member of a legendary band and still had so much to offer.

Another musician I came to know really well was rock legend Ian Gillan. I first met him at a charity cricket match

Ian Gillan – hectic but interesting

and later through Reading Football Club.

A proposal was put forward to merge Reading and Oxford United Football Clubs by the then chairmen of the two clubs, Frank Waller and Robert Maxwell, both now dead. The proposal almost resulted in riots in both towns. Step forward Ian Gillan who at the time lived in Purley-on-Thames and played park football for the local police team. He rang me on the sports desk and said he, along with others, was interested in buying Reading FC. The next few days were to say the least hectic but interesting. At the time Ian was recording a new album in London and would think nothing of ringing me at 3am to exchange notes on any progress.

One Saturday morning he rang me to say he wanted to accompany me to Elm Park to watch Reading in action. He parked up at my house at around midday and we walked to the ground – ten hours later we returned having visited a nearby public house – I had experienced the habits of rock musicians first hand. To make matters even worse he purchased a large bottle of Scotch to take home and duly walked into my dining room, dropped it on the floor and ruined a carpet which I had fitted only days earlier -- how could you explain that to an insurance company?

The next time Ian called he was accompanied by two other gentlemen. They had been to Adwest to meet Frank Waller to discuss a deal, only to be refused entry because they were late. They returned to my house hoping that I could persuade the Reading chairman to change his mind. One of those two gentlemen was a certain Richard Branson, and in fact it was he who would have purchased the club had not former Reading player Roger Smee stepped in and bought it ahead of Ian Gillan and co.

Taking a Bow Reading Scottish Fiddlers

STUART FORBES has long been intent on keeping Scottish music alive. He has achieved his purpose and in a corner of southern England fiddles still flourish

When I was 16 I had a real nightmare which has influenced me ever since. My nightmare was that Scottish traditional music would die out and all these guitars and pop music would totally swamp it. At that time, the '60s, Scottish music was dying. If you wore a kilt you'd be laughed at. Nowadays, partly due to a resurgence in nationalism, you'd be laughed at if you didn't wear a kilt at a wedding. In the mid '60s you had flared trousers, long hair and flower power and if you played the fiddle you were "square, man". It was difficult in my teenage years because there were very few school orchestras and people who played the fiddle were made fun of. Nowadays you are proud to say you play in an orchestra.

In those days, people would not turn out for a concert or a local dance because they would all be watching the television. This killed a lot of live music long before discos. All you needed was a couple of guys with guitars who sang a few songs but once they went and discos arrived there was a whole generation who lost the art of performing with a band.

I'm from Buckie, in Banffshire, on the Moray Firth coast, and ever since I can remember I always wanted to play the fiddle. I started when I was 12 and had a very good teacher in Elgin who taught classic and Scottish music in parallel. But by the time I came to England in 1972, my fiddle playing had totally disappeared. I was in banking and studying for my exams. However, in Scotland there was a resurgence of accordion and fiddle clubs, as well as strathspey and reel societies and you had massive fiddle rallies with anything from 50 to 500 fiddlers. The Scottish Fiddle Orchestra under John Mason even performed at the Albert Hall.

By the end of the '70s, my studies had come to an end and I felt a huge gap in my life. I went to St Albans early in 1981 to a fiddle rally, which was totally new in this area, and on the way back I said to my wife: "We could run one of those." A few weeks later I went to a concert in aid of the Ken Thomas Body Scanner Appeal and I knew I'd found a cause. That's when we started to collect the first group of fiddlers. I didn't know any other players in the area so I put an advert in the paper and from that I got a couple of names. One was a Scot, Roy Laing, a well-known fiddle teacher in Caversham, who had played with virtually every orchestra in London and conducted the first fiddle rally in 1981; the other was Richard Smith,

There were several musicians in the 18th century in Scotland who influenced fiddle playing. There was a famous family of musicians called the Gows, one of whom was Nathaniel Gow, who was leader of the Edinburgh Assembly orchestra and published collections of dance music. There was also Marshall from Fochabers, who worked for the Duke of Gordon, and wrote hundreds of fiddle tunes, very difficult pieces which weren't user friendly for fiddles in those days. Somebody charged him with this and he said: "I didna' write music for bunglers."

In the latter part of last century the first of classically trained fiddle players, James Scott Skinner, who called himself the Strathspey king, wrote about 600 tunes. He had fiddle lessons from Rougier, the principal violinist of the Halle Orchestra, and in later life his concert programmes always ended with the strathspey and reel. The Strathspey (Valley Spey) is the slow dance of Scotland as the reel is the quick dance. Like the reel it is in simple quadruple time but it has many dotted notes.

who was very much into the English folk scene. Getting Roy, who came from the classical tradition, together with Richard from the English folk tradition was my main achievement. After that it was a question of keeping your ear to the ground, "Does sanybody play the fiddle, ah you, how about doing this?" They didn't have to audition, anyone who could hold a fiddle could take part. Some of the music is quite simple but some is more challenging, particularly the fast reels – you have to be a reasonable player to get round it at that speed. A lot of the problem is that the music is 32 or 64 bars and it is hard to get the hang of it.

We didn't have many rehearsals and the first one might be described as shambolic, but the atmosphere at that first rally was totally electric – I still have a recording of it. People had never been to one of these rallies before but they spontaneously started dancing. It was wonderful.

Fiddles groups are predominantly violins, but if you have only fiddles you have all top and no middle or bottom. It's nice to have some 'cellos, and accordions playing, then it's not just a free for all. At that first rally we had six 'cellos, a viola, a double bass, a drum and a couple of accordions as well as the fiddles. There were about 60 altogether and they came from as far afield as Southampton and Cambridge.

Some of the more well-known names at that first rally were people like Elizabeth Copperwheat, a fiddle teacher who was conductor of Woodley String Orchestra, David Shirt, who owned The Viola Gallery at the time and was a well-known string teacher, and Roy Laing. And there was me with very modest ability. My achievement was to get these people together.

We held the rally at Bulmershe School, which was our

resident home for these rallies until they came to halt about six or seven years ago, and we raised a couple of hundred pounds for the Ken Thomas Appeal which, in 1981, was a considerable chunk of money. That first rally took six months of my spare time to organise and you get to the point of saying, "That's it, never again." But we're still around.

We've changed slightly and now do things like ceilidhs, where we have a group of maybe 30 fiddles and accordions, a well-organised concert and some ceilidh dancing afterwards. We've also moved to the Piggott School in Wargrave.

After the first rally, we said we would meet on a regular basis, once a month, which we did, starting in the autumn of 1981 and we still meet at Willowbank School on a Wednesday. In 1988 we felt we needed someone special to give the group a bit of life. A leading accordionist from Scotland called Iain MacPhail came down and presented the rehearsal as a wee concert. That was absolutely phenomenal and it was the first time we had seen a standing ovation for a long time. It was also the start of my friendship with Iain. Ten years later I have ended up doing tours of South America with him and even released one of his records, so it was a significant point in my life.

Rather than rehearse every month and have one concert, we now have a rehearsal one month, and the next month we have a box and fiddle evening with one or two soloists. These have been very successful. They're an awful lot of fun because the standard is good, but it's not a competition and it's about us making our own entertainment as well as entertaining the public. We have had many other well-known Scottish people including Nicol McLaren's band and Ron Gonella, the best of the Scottish fiddle players.

The first time I met Ron was when he adjudicated me at a competition 30 years before, and the first thing I said to him when we met again was, "You marked me down." I had a great time with him, and managed to arrange a meeting with his cousin Bert Gonella, who lives in Tilehurst. Bert is a former singer at Glyndebourne who had become a teacher and was music critic for the Reading Chronicle under the name of Cantabile. The two of them hadn't met for about 15 years. The sad thing was that four months after they met Ron had died of a brain tumour. You know how sometimes you feel in your lifetime you have done things that were right and good? I'm so glad that I managed to get those two together.

This goes back to my experience when I was 16 thinking Scottish music was going to die. Thirty years later I feel I didn't let it die and, better still, I have managed to keep a little corner of it alive in the south of England. My own 16-year-old son plays double bass with us now and he

Reading Scottish Fiddlers in the early '80s

wasn't even thought of at the time of the first rally.

Our members come from three categories: exiled Scots or ex-pats; or good fiddle players who either come from a classical background or an English folk or country dance background. I think the consensus is that if you have a good classical technique you will find Scottish music is quite reasonable. Irish players may find it quite a lot different because of the bowing: the Irish tend to play a whole pile of notes in one bow, the Scots tend to prefer a lot of separate bows.

Some members have been with us since 1981 and our resident accompanist joined us on day one. If you put 18 years on to anyone's life they are not quite as young as they are. It is getting hard to get new members because people work such long hours now, tending not to want to turn out again in the evenings.

Apart from the Reading Scottish Fiddlers, I play with a couple of Scottish country dance bands, The Craigellachie band, in Basingstoke, and the Craigievar ceilidh band run by my brother. I've also got into producing Scottish recordings largely by accident. My uncle Bill Forbes, from Tilehurst, devised Scottish country dances, and wanted to get them recorded. Nicol McLaren and I put our heads together and we recorded the first one with his Glencraig Scottish Dance band. Others have followed.

I play mainly because I enjoy it and make recordings because I want to do them not because I have to; they are not a chore. It's as though I am still trying to whip that nightmare I had years ago out of my system.

 Millennium Choice Stuart Forbes

Heroes of Longhope by W R Aim, a slow Scottish air that is very evocative

A Place for Music   Free festivals and after

SIMON CHATTERTON, who is now arts officer at South Hill Park, says that the musical history of Reading over the past three decades can be traced through its venues

Reading's recent musical history can be traced through its venues, occasionally, like the Paradise Club (now the After Dark) in London Street, surviving every change of musical fashion thrown at them, others mostly alive and kicking one minute and seemingly off the musical map the next – the Trade Union Club, the RBH Social Club, the Bones Club, St David's Hall, Alleycat and the soon-to-be refurbished Town Hall, the latter home to punk and reggae bands as well as choirs and orchestras.

When the venues haven't been there, people have created their own – often in the most unlikely places. Reading has always had a wonderful tradition of musicians, performers and artists coming together to create their own events.

Free concerts in the Abbey Ruins in the early 1970s led on to punks taking over the old Granby Cinema in Cemetery Junction for a music festival. In the 1980s, groups of community artists and musicians squatted the old dole office at 21 South Street, the former Huntley & Palmer building and later the Rising Sun in Silver Street in a bid to create arts spaces for local people.

When I arrived in Reading in the 1980s, at the age of 16, I was swept up in organising the first of a number of large free festivals that took place on old wasteland and in deserted buildings in and around Reading. In the '80s. Doris's Birthday Party, as the event was cryptically called, took place on the site of the old coal yards,where Tesco?s is now.

Over the next five years as the free festival scene bloomed nationally; these events would attract several thousand people and became the precursors of the '90s raves and free parties.

We used to advertise a free festival to be held in one place and then right at the last minute switch the venue. Bands played for free and to raise money we held benefit concerts for staging and PA equipment.

Out of these gigs grew The Conspiracy, a voluntary organisation set up to promote local music, raise money for community groups like the Women's Information Centre and Red Rag, and to share the skills and resources that people needed to put on their own events. The Conspiracy also secured funding to produce a DIY

Promoters' Pack which we distributed nationally and to set up a PA system for local groups to use.

Since the days of Conspiracy, the local music scene has changed, largely due to the rise in club and bar culture. Although these developments have seen scores of new pubs open and have brought hordes of young people into the town centre, Reading still lacks a proper live music venue.

The Rising Sun in Silver Street was set up to provide an alternative to the pubs and a focal point for local artists and musicians. It had been empty for three years when a group of us moved in November 1990. We put down flooring, connected electricity and fixed the plumbing and toilets. After six days the landlord came with some builders to throw us out but later he asked us if we wanted to lease the building for a peppercorn rent.

Almost 10 years on the centre survives, still reliant on the energy of its volunteers, providing a venue and recording studio for local music as well as an artists' studio, workshop and rehearsal space.

Reading's music scene has always been resilient and has always had to make its own way, largely without support or funding. Against the prevalence of mainstream bars and clubs, organisations like Readipop and events like Tim Hill's Pandaemonium nights have flown the flag for Reading's individuality and variety.

Local hip hop night, the Breaks, has recently been listed as one of the world's best clubs by a nationwide music magazine and we may yet even see the day when Reading bands made good no longer have to pretend to be from London.

Much of Reading's cultural life has been made possible by the passion and energy of local musicians. Unfunded and unrecognised, save for grateful audiences, many have also remained unemployed in order to keep their music afloat.

Maybe, the next time that a Government minister holds forth on the topic of benefit scroungers, they might remember that the single biggest source of arts funding in the last 30 years has been the dole and that without it our home town might have been a far less lively place in which to live.

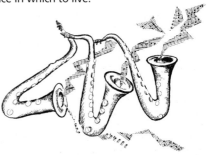

Moving People's Hearts   Alternative folk music

DAMIAN CLARKE and his group Press Gang have been playing folk music at home and abroad for many years. He writes about Reading as a major centre for folk music and has a strong heritage of 'mixing it'

There's folk music – and there's alternative folk music, aka roots music, rogue folk, celtic rock, punk folk, cowpunk, speedfolk. These are but a few of the attempts to describe a music genre that embraces the tradition of folk music without wishing to align itself with the debatably more 'traditional' folk music attitude that had arisen out of the last revival of the late sixties. Reading is a major centre for folk music, both traditional and alternative and even spawned a band that managed to take traditional folk songs into the alternative music scene.

I've been fortunate to work within the gamut of folk tastes. I can remember the heady days of the rise of punk folk when suddenly playing a traditional song didn't mean that the audience had to sit in rows, keeping absolute hush during an interminable sea shanty, and instead meant a packed-out Hexagon swirling around like a maelstrom to the Pogues at their height.

I can remember the cosy but anarchic attitudes of the student folk club, the place where I first began to experiment my punk folk ideas on a bemused audience. This club rejoiced in the name The Turk's Bottom which then made complete sense as the Turk's Head, now rejoicing in the name Fez and Firkin, was then a very popular student pub. Characters, ideas, poetry, songs and dance all spring to my mind when I remember that back room. But I also thought that it was too exclusive, secluded, that folk music had to reach out more. So it was off to the pubs and clubs with a band.

I can remember being told at an early concert at a local folk club, 'how to do it' by various well-meaning members of the audience – all of whom had worked with Steeleye Span or Fairport Convention in their early days when those chart-topping bands likewise had got it wrong! Fortunately the advice from the bands concerned was always, 'do it your way, enjoy the music'. So I did and now the band and I have played internationally. But Reading played a big part in getting us there.

Reading is a melting pot. It is full of people from many different cultures and if you look hard enough you'll find a wealth of influences and ideas for songs and if you listen, you'll hear music from all over the world floating out of the windows and being played in the streets, schools, festivals and clubs.

There was a time, about 12 years ago, when Reading was a bit of a centre for young musicians looking for new ideas that had more substance than purely commercial music. Politics were high on the agenda, there was the Poll Tax, the widening economic gap, the Criminal Justice Bill and other social issues of the like that have always been a part of folk song material. My band discovered that singing about similar events from hundreds of years ago was still relevant to people who had no love of folk music or folk clubs. The folk-punk days died out but there was this new exciting scene of bands singing about revolution and real life but all using some kind of roots music. There was reggae, dub, celtic, east European, Asian and still it goes on. Sadly, few of the bands remain in Reading, musicians always move on.

We did look for traditional folk songs from Reading that we could bring up to date. Of course there is the famous *Sumer is icumen in* and there was a song called *The Berkshire Ballad* but neither of them quite fitted the bill. George Whitfield managed to squeeze in some words written by the poet Mary Russell Mitford about a pub at Three Mile Cross to a song called *The Brandy of the Damned* that we were writing at the time and that was a start.

Damian Clarke

But then George wrote a round, a repeating song like *London's Burning*, called *Scarlet Town*. This explores the idea that the red stones from the old abbey were eventually taken away and used in buildings and bridges around the town and can still be found today, if you look hard enough. We've performed this in schools in the town and elsewhere and maybe one day it too will become a playground song, perhaps in 100 years time it will even be known as a traditional song!

In Scarlet Town, there's a stolen stone
And it's hidden in a house by the Holybrook
It's from the Abbey, the Abbey
And there's hundreds more if you know where to look
(Words and music: George Whitfield)

I think we must have played folk music in every venue in town by now and quite a few of the streets, but there is one place that will always remain in my memory. Opposite the original Reading Tech College on the Kings Road there is a grey office building which used to have pub on the ground floor called the Cap and Gown (I don't know if it still does). They had a cellar bar where we were allowed to run our own club which tried to host some of the current names from the alternative folk scene.

The first week we played our then mega-speed-thrash-folk to a motley audience of curious friends, one or two cognoscenti and several folkies. All I can remember is looking through the sweat and mayhem to see someone knitting in the front row! But they seemed quite happy.

The highlight had to be the night we booked anunknown American singer, courtesy of an ex-Reading musician, Pete Lawrence, who had gone on to start his own record label, Cooking Vinyl. She was Michelle Shocked but we had no idea just how big she would become.We had supported her on her second ever date in the UK at a London pub and, yes, I was blown away by the very first song. I vowed there and then that I wanted to be able to learn how to entrance an audience with just a powerful song and my voice.

Anyway the day before she was due to play, with only a couple of tickets sold, she appeared on Woman's Hour. Suddenly, it was out that people could see her at our little club and all the tickets went within hours. We wondered if we should find a bigger venue but thankfully we didn't as the loss of intimacy would have prevented the special night she gave us. She played the first number at about 8.30pm having been booked to

play a standard two sets, finishing with the bar at 11 o'clock. The audience, which had been buzzing anyway, wildly applauded. She played another and the audience became even more ecstatic. Michelle sat there beaming a huge Texan smile.

"This is too easy!" she said. "I guess I'm going to just have to play here all night until I tire you out." I couldn't believe she was saying this. What would happen, when would it end, could we go on all night, would she run out of songs? In the end, people began drifting out saying personal thank yous around midnight but some of us stayed there till gone 3am when we were finally kicked out by the landlord! She had begun playing requests, blues, gospel but the energy and spirit never left her.

As a musician I left that room with a very different set of personal goals. Michelle is just one of that rare brand of folk musicians who manage to combine a down-to-earth approach with the ability and talent to create magic when they entertain. Something that moves people's hearts through powerful meaningful songs about people, places and their lives. That's folk music for you, and some of that magic takes place in Reading.

Let's hope new musicians will read this and realise there is a strong heritage of 'mixing-it' in Reading and will carry on where others began. Some would call that the living tradition of folk music.

Riverboat shuffles were a popular pastime in the late '40s and throughout the '50s. This picture shows musicians including John Palmer and Ken Turton (saxes), Harvey Bard (drums), Denny Strudwick (piano), Ron Pearce (bass), and Ken Bowsher (clarinet). The occasion was a Thames steamer trip organised by SLy (Society for Local Yokels)

Steve The Flute Flautist

Flute-player STEVE SEATON is well-known in Slough. He started his musical career in the Army but now his trade is plumbing and he plays mainly for the love of it

I'm always dealing with pipes – with holes or without. One type is copper coated, the others silver coated. I'm a plumber by trade but I'd rather be a flute player, any day of the week. My flute is my best friend. I've been through a divorce and things like that and the only thing that's been good to me is my flute. I've made friends through the music.

I need a new flute though, that's the problem. Mine's battered, 20 years old, and has been all round the world. It's got big dents in it where it's been stood on by high-heeled shoes. Poor old flute, it's on its last legs, I don't know how it plays. You look along it and it's bent, like a half moon. It cost me 70 quid to get it serviced.

I went to Dawkes, the music shop in Bath Road the other day and they're hitting me with prices like four grand for a new flute. Yeah, all right, I'll see you next year or two.

The thing is with a flute you're playing with all your senses. You're playing with your mind, playing with your hands, with your lips, even your eyes take some part in it. If you're nervous, your knees go. When young musicians start to play they get the jitters and when you're standing it's usually the knees that start to go, jerking in panic. You've got to get over that first, whatever you do. You can mess it right up if you let it get to you.

I used to let it get to me sometimes and I'd be a bit twitchy on my notes. You get over it, you get a bit bolder. But you should never be complacent. The day you go up and don't have some fear in you, you are not playing very well. Confidence and nervousness combined is a good thing. But not to be too nervous. The worst thing is if you don't get feedback from the crowd. It makes you anxious.

My music is quite diverse; I can play most things. I started off playing music in the Army when I was 15 years old as a fife player in the Corps of Drums. I wasn't what you might term a bandsman, I just taught myself up to Grade 5 music. I used to teach the young lads to play the flute. I led by example, so it always put me under pressure to play that part perfectly so they could follow me. I didn't join the Army to play, I just joined. I wasn't sure what I wanted to do. I just had this feeling to do it, that was my channel in life. I started with very simple tunes and before I knew it I was playing very complicated parts including Bizet, a lot of regimental and classical music,

Blue Danube Waltz and a bit of Tchaikovsky.

The highlight in my life in the Army was to help to arrange some music for the Trooping of the Colour at Horse Guards Parade, in front of the Queen, the Duke of Edinburgh, and all the royal family. I arranged some parts which included signature tunes of soap operas like *EastEnders* and *Take the High Road* – that was a very good Beat the Retreat tune.

The worst thing is sitting on your flute before you go out on parade or leaving it behind. I used to have nightmares about leaving an instrument or piece of equipment behind or breaking flutes before going on parade. The other paranoia was being late for the Queen's birthday parade. The paranoia is still there because you don't want anything to go wrong and things do go wrong.

In the end, the Army was taking me in one direction and I wanted to go in another; they wanted to promote me and I just wanted to get out, not be in uniform any more. I was 37 when I got out of the Army. You can't stay in the Army for ever, you have to get out and do something– that was my philosophy. I lost some pension money but I thought if I don't get out now I'll never get out. I was one of those people destined to stay in for 22 years and you come out and just go into the police or a security company because you can't change. I got out when I was agile enough mentally to do something else. I just wanted to play the flute, which I do. I'm still the same person as I was then. I haven't changed.

It's been quite an interesting career/interest/hobby. I've done everything from busking to playing Jamaican Farewell at the Shaping Slough concert in the Kings Centre when Slough became a unitary authority. I generally play with a drummer.

My present drummer is Gary Jeffries. He's primarily a Latin-American drummer, a percussionist not a bongo player, but he plays anything, like me. He can play timpani, the bodhrun, congas, bongos, and he's very articulate. We met when we lived next door to each other in Windsor. I was getting divorced so we just went out busking, not to earn any money, just to have a laugh on Eton bridge.

Most of my music is military but you can't play it to a civilian population. It's okay if you're dressed in uniform. I play stuff they can relate to: rock, pop, folk, Irish, Latin-American. We play at Windsor Arts Centre, the Sound Hole, Slough Festival, the Herschel Arms, Slough Working Men's Club – wherever and whenever required really. It takes a lot of practice because if you don't get it right on the day why bother in the first place? The money you get is nothing for the pressure, the hours you put in, but it's not for the money, it's for the sheer enjoyment of playing. If it's 'Steve the Flute and Friends' obviously friends cost money. I don't want them to come and play for nothing, it's unfair. For instance my guitarist at Slough Festival was Pat Alford, a well-known guitar player throughout the area. He used to play in lots of pubs and clubs and every opportunity he gets he will play. He had what they called Pat's Music Machine on a Sunday night in the Wheatsheaf Pub in Albert Street. A lot of local musicians used to play down there and it was lovely; it finished off the week and started a new week. It didn't matter what you played. At the moment we've got nowhere like that except the Sound Hole, where you can actually go down and play something.

I played with the Grand Union Orchestra in the Wheatsheaf pub last year and the year before that, which was absolutely great. They all piled into the pub, amplifiers, guitars, drum sets all over the place. Half the pub was full of musicians but what a night. It was amazing. I played *Summertime* on the flute and a girl vocalist joined in with it. I wish I'd have taped and videoed the occasion because it was absolutely brilliant. Best I've ever played I think. You have all those musicians around who are playing with you and relating to what you play and you're the focus of their attention; they're there for you.

I'll play the flute wherever I am. I've played in the Sudan, Kenya, all the hotels down the beach at Mombasa, the beaches of Brazil – just for a laugh. I was in Philadelphia when Sarah Ferguson got married and we did a mini Royal wedding over there. There were only two of us – me and a drummer who was a Scots Guard, and we played outside this hotel for hours and hours and hours. Every time I go on holiday I always make a prat of myself and go up to the mike.

My flute can break the ice meeting people. In Germany for instance, I was at a Bierfest in Ronnenberg, just south of Hanover. There must have been about 2,000 people in this big marquee. I got up on stage to play in the intermission and I got them all doing the Conga – all these people dancing together. It created some sort of atmosphere. The local fire brigade band, called the Flute-Players, presented me with this big badge and I was made an honorary member.

I play more flowingly now, I suppose. It took a lot of years to do that. I used to be too jerky, trying to be too articulate with it, every note had to be perfect. I was trying to lip every note as opposed to binding it in. When you try and do that, it sounds too staccato. I wouldn't say I'm the best musician on the planet. I am not, nowhere near it. I don't believe anybody should think that. You start down that path and you get complacent. I don't want to be complacent, I just want to keep doing what I'm doing. There's a philosophy there, somewhere or other. I don't see myself as being a star.

At the moment I'm just playing what I need to play. I've

Steve Seaton

got about 200 to 300 tunes written down somewhere and that's nowhere near what I can play – at least 400 tunes, 500, I don't know. Most of them I can play with a bit of practice – probably as well as I used to years ago. For instance, at the Slough Festival, I must have played 20,000 notes. I had to remember all these notes in sequence.

That's the thing about being a musician. There is a knack of doing it, and you are not reading off the music. The most important thing is to go on stage and commit it all to memory. Professional musicians are absolutely brilliant, but they read off sheet music. They are a different type of musician. For me, being a musician of a different category, I commit it to memory.

The stuff I play I keep playing because it is a challenge, like that Rolling Stones number, *Paint It Black*. That is very difficult and I play it a completely different way from the Stones. With a flute and drum you're limited, so you repeat it, you build it up, you build it up, and then you go bang. I arranged it myself, with a drum part, and I give Gary a slap now and again for playing it wrong.

Gary's a very good musician, that's all his life is about. He just wants to be a good musician, it's all he wants. For me, I want to be a tradesman as well, earn a living. For him, music is the be-all and end-all. If I was going to get into the music industry at all, it would have to be very passively, slowly. Like I am, maybe.

Millennium Choice Steve Seaton

Bizet's Carmen – a very sad and moving story

Stille Nacht, Heilige Nacht German carol singers

PAT ROLT remembers a magical Christmas in Whitley half a century ago when German prisoners of war were welcomed into the homes of local people

It was in 1946 and the Roman Catholic community in Whitley had just welcomed their own parish priest Father Patrick Collins (RIP). Our first Mass centre in Whitley was the Scout hut in Callington Road but we soon outgrew this and had our Sunday Mass in South Reading Community Centre.

It was then that the German prisoners of war, who were detained in what was to become Shinfield Park Air Force Station, were allowed to march from Whitley Wood Road and along Northumberland Avenue to attend Mass at the Centre.

They came on trust with just one German officer in charge. I remember that they stood at ease at the side of the building waiting until all the families had taken their places before filing in to sit at the back of the hall.

I must say that these men were received kindly by the people of Whitley. Bearing in mind that the Second World War had only just come to a very welcome end and most local men were still serving in the Armed Services, people could have reacted so differently. There were very few who were abusive. Somehow the POWs' sadness and dejection came through. These men were after all someone's son, husband or brother a long way from home.

My sisters, brother and I were young children ranging in age from three to 12 years of age and we all have memories of these men. Soon we were being given small gifts – but only after the officer had checked out if it was all right with our mother – just an apple, orange, box of cough sweets. Obviously they had saved these items especially for us. They had so little and in these austere post-war days we did not have much more.

I remember particularly Christmas 1946. Father Collins made a request from the pulpit and it was to see if any of our families felt that they could invite POWs to their homes for Christmas lunch. Our family felt we could and we had Andreas Bauer, who was a young man conscripted from his seminary to serve with the German Army, and Toni Bedeuker, a tailor by trade, who had three daughters and a son, the same as our own family at the time. Toni's young son was later to die from malnutrition.

We gathered with a sense of new hope for our Christmas Mass in 1946. The war in Europe was over and also the war in the Pacific and those fathers who had not yet been demobilised would soon be coming home. The grown-ups kept saying "everything would return to normal" but those of us who were children during the war did not know what 'normal' was. We also did not know how special our Christmas celebration was going to be.

The POWs had formed themselves into a choir and had spent long hours practising. I remember being spellbound by their rendering of the Latin Mass sung in plain chant, as was the custom at the time. They also sang a selection of Christmas carols in their native tongue and for me *Silent Night*, in parts, was so beautiful that no professional choir could have impressed me more.

These men, far from home, dressed in black boiler suits with huge POW stamped on their backs, sang their hearts out for us, to thank the Catholic community of Whitley for their kindness to them.

Father Collins asked if they would sing an encore and *Silent Night* was sung again for us. A poignant memory for me was seeing the emotion on everyone's face, grown-ups weeping openly and the spontaneous applause.

For us children the 'specialness' of Christmas was not yet over. Andreas and Toni had not come to our home empty handed. They had made out of scraps of wood and material a wheelbarrow for my brother, a rocking cradle with blankets, pillows and sheets for my younger sister, and my older sister and me a doll's house furnished completely with curtains and covers and even an electric light operated by battery and a switch.

The workmanship was superb, everything beautifully finished and painted and Toni had employed his skills as a tailor making the minute soft furnishings. These gifts were well received, totally unexpected. Toys were difficult to come by and we felt we were indeed fortunate.

Our friendship with the POWs continued until they were repatriated and as one returned home another took his place and came to our home for Sunday lunch and tea until Christmas 1947.

The memories of these events are still vivid to me even though they took place 52 years ago and I think a lesson was to be learnt at that time which still holds good in today's world; that we can come together in prayer, whatever colour, race, creed or culture, that to God we are all his children.

Perfect Pitch Harmonica player

The sound of HARRY PITCH on the harmonica is familiar to the millions of fans of Last of the Summer Wine. He talks about his long musical career

What's the appeal of the harmonica? Easy. There is no other instrument that anybody can get a note out of simply by blowing it. With a flute, or a trumpet, or a guitar you've got to know what you are doing, but with a harmonica you just blow. Of course you can get a note out of a piano but a harmonica is portable. You can just put it in your pocket.

Thousands of guys had harmonicas during the war and I do believe that one of the astronauts took a harmonica with him to the moon – talk about *Fly Me To The Moon*.

I discovered the harmonica when I was eight. Before the war, kids used to walk about playing tunes on the old-fashioned mouth-organ and I was just one of those kids. I said, "I can see how this works", and I started picking up tunes and it just came naturally. We weren't a musical family. All my brothers and sisters have got tin ears and can't even hum a tune. I was completely self-taught.

There were harmonica bands in those days, with bass harmonicas and chord harmonicas, playing in big dance halls all over the place, and that's how I started, playing in specialist groups as a concert soloist.

I taught myself the trumpet also in my teens. I played that during the war when harmonicas were very difficult to obtain because they were all made in Germany. It was a sort of cottage industry in the Black Forest in the early 19th century. They made different parts of the harmonica and sent them to the factory where they were assembled. These were just blow and suck things and very simple.

Then the chromatic harmonica came along and everything changed. A chromatic is like the piano. You have the ordinary notes and with the button pushed in you have the chromatic scale. You could now change key and of course it became a completely different animal. The ordinary blues harp – the one that blues singers play – are in a set key and you can't deviate, whereas with the chromatic you can play in any key.

Larry Adler was the first harmonica player to bring the instrument on to the concert platform and also the film and recording studio. He has always been my idol and is the doyen of all other harmonica players.

Larry Adler learned to read music after he started to play but he told me that he'd got a good ear and if he hears something, he can play it. He can learn it very quickly. I'm the same. As a matter of fact, for some of the operas I've done, I couldn't read the music because it was so ridiculously hard. To do me a favour, the conductor recorded the harmonica part on the piano and I would play it in my car, listen to it all the time and by so doing I soon was able to play it.

Harry Pitch

There are players who, if you give them an instrument, cannot play a note without music. I once said to a musical director, "You know, if a fly crawled over a piece of music and its feet had ink on them, some of you guys would play it." Take the music away and they would be blind, but if you gave me a set of chord symbols I could play an ad lib solo based on these.

I do a lot of playing in places like the Pizza Express and Pizza on the Park, and in one of the big Pizza Expresses in North London, in Kentish Town, near Camden Lock. Larry Adler, who is now 85 and still going strong, lives just up the road from there and he always comes to see me.

The last time I saw him he said, "It's nice to see you, keeping busy at work. I always come to hear you because you are one of the finest harmonica players in the world." What can I say? He said that I'm doing the sort of things that he could never do.

It wasn't until I went from the old-fashioned mouth-organ to the chromatic that I thought "This is it." The first chromatic harmonica I had, I'll never forget it. I bought it in London for 10 shillings. The same thing today would cost about 100 quid. 50p – that's the way things have gone.

I became a Carrol Levis Discovery, started playing the trumpet with the big dance bands and eventually led my own band. At the time I was living in London and playing in bands – Friday, Saturday and Sunday – I was always out playing.

During the week, I was playing with bands and doing a job. Luckily I was a salesman of machine tools to the engineering industry and I was able to skive off and do what I wanted to do because I was pretty good at it. I was able to work the oracle until I got so busy during the mid-'60s that I had to give the job up. It really snowballed. I was doing so much stuff. I've got no complaints. It bought us a boat, Harmonica Harry, and all that sort of stuff.

I first started recording because I had been playing trumpet in a band with Ron Goodwin and another guy, and Geoff Love on trombone. We were all ordinary band musicians at the time. Of course, they all went off into the wild blue yonder, doing marvellous things in studios. They knew I played the harmonica, and when Ron Goodwin was making a record with Malcolm Arnold, Ron mentioned me and I did a bit on *The Bridge Over the River Kwai* for him. That was one of the first records I ever made in the middle '50s.

I was also the harmonica player whenever they wanted one at the Abbey Road studios and one day they called me in to a recording session. It was Frank Ifield and he was recording *I Remember You.* I used to play that with a big band – it was a nice tune – but Frank put in all this yodelling and I said to my wife, "This is bloody awful!" After that it went into the hit parade and was in the charts for about six months.

From then on, Frank Ifield insisted that any time he was on the radio, or on television, singing I Remember You, I was with him. It was the same with Gilbert O'Sullivan when he did *Clare*. If he was guesting on a programme and singing *Clare*, I would be there just to do my little backing piece.

I Remember You was a watershed, because anybody who was anybody then said, "We've got to have a harmonica – just little bits, eight bars here and there. Val Doonican had a big hit with Walk Tall and I did lots of broadcasts with him, Dusty Springfield, Cliff Richard, Petula Clark, Anita Harris – *I Remember You* started it and it just went on and on.

In the early '70s, Ronnie Hazlehurst, a musical director at the BBC Television Centre, recommended me to play the theme and incidental music to *Anne of Green Gables*. Shortly after that, he called me up and said: "We have a piece in the Comedy Playhouse series."

This was a vehicle for one-off comedy shows like *Steptoe* and *Open All Hours*. Some just disappeared, but others became part of comedy history. One of them was *Last of the Summer Wine* and it's been going regularly since 1972.

The late Bill Owen – Compo in *Last of the Summer Wine.*

Ronnie Hazlehurst wrote the music for the main characters, three old guys – delinquents — who were kids together and who, after going their own separate ways, retired and came back together. They are each represented by instruments; one was the penny whistle now a flute, another is a concertina or accordion, and the third is the harmonica – that's Compo, Bill Owen, who recently passed away. He was a lovely guy.

It started out like that but after a while it got much more melodic and the music is specially recorded for each single episode. Of course, a lot of the exteriors are shot in Holmfirth in Yorkshire, but all the interior scenes are done at Shepperton Studios. When everything is finished and the music has been added, they show three half-hour episodes to a seated audience and then record the audience reaction. They warn them not to crinkle sweet papers and make a noise because they've got microphones up in the roof.

They turn it into a concert and all of a sudden, Robert Fife – Howard – comes on, then Pearl and Marina, and they're all dressed in costume and sing a song. Then Cathie comes on and says, "Ladies and Gentlemen, Ronnie Hazlehurst, who writes the music can't be with us today but we've got the man who actually plays it and he's going to play it for you."

Then I come on – there are about 500 people sitting there, no piano, nothing, and I just play the tune. You could hear a pin drop, and when I've finished, you would think that Spurs had won the Cup.

My forte is playing ballads – things like T*he Shadow of Your Smile, Stardust, Over the Rainbow*. At a recording session once a guy said to me, "Who is your favourite singer?" I said, "Jack Jones, Frank Sinatra, Tony Bennett." He said: "We want you to play some solos and what we want you to do is sing through your harmonica. Nothing flash, just interpret how you would sing if you were a famous singer – and that is the answer." The fewer the notes the better, but a nice tone and warmth.

When we do big concerts I listen to the audience and they are absolutely dead quiet and that's the way it should be. Keep it simple – the *Skye Boat Song, Danny Boy, Amazing Grace*. Not masses of notes.

There's a musician called Toots Theilemann who is a fabulous guitar and harmonica player. There is a very important similarity between us because I play trumpet and he plays guitar so our approach to playing the harmonica is the same; he's got the wonderful knowledge of playing chords and my style of playing jazz on harmonica is similar to my style of playing trumpet. There are certain phrases and lines of playing on a guitar completely different to styles on a trumpet – a trumpet is much more spiky.

I'm probably the only harmonica player in the world who's played jazz and then classical music on the same day. I've played with jazz greats like Ronnie Scott and John Dankworth and also played at the Royal Opera House, Sadlers Wells, the Barbican and Festival Hall. I was the ad hoc harmonica player, when they needed one, at the London Symphony Orchestra.

When we moved to Maidenhead in 1977, that coincided with the birth – if I can use that word – of the disco and everything went like a lead balloon. Live music has eventually started building up again.

I've got a jazz group called Rhythm and Reeds which is always busy with broadcasts and club dates. The rhythm section is Alan Ganley on drums, Peter Morgan on bass, Bill Le Sage (piano) and the reeds are myself on harmonica and a marvellous accordion player – I think the best in the world – called Jack Emblow. I like playing with Rhythm and Reeds. I also run a dance band and a traditional jazz band called Thames Valley Jazz Men.

Musicians never retire. They just keep going while people still want to give them money.

Millennium Choice Harry Pitch

Aaron Copland's Suite for Appalachian Spring – you can hear the dawn breaking. Also very much influenced by Copland is Ferde Grofé who wrote Grand Canyon Suite

Holst's Benefactor
Music in Hermitage

The Berkshire village of Hermitage is remembered as the place where the novelist DH Lawrence lived for a time before leaving England to live in Italy. Here too, was the home of Robin Milford who taught music at nearby Downe House School. Milford was a composer and is now remembered mainly for his songs, which are said to bear comparison with the works of Peter Warlock and Ivor Gurney.

Among Milford's friends was Gerald Finzi who lived just over the Hampshire border, and it was at Milford's house in 1940, that Finzi met a composer from an earlier generation, Henry Balfour Gardiner. In former years Gardiner had lived at Ashampstead Common, a few miles away, but had left Berkshire to live in North Dorset where he became involved in forest re-generation and pioneer conservation work long before this became a popular movement.

Finzi was then in his late thirties and had already written some important musical works. Gardiner had composed some fairly ambitious works including A Berkshire Idyll and an opera based on a Thomas Hardy story. The opera never became an artistic or commercial success but a piece taken from it called Shepherd Fennel's Dance became very popular as a light orchestral item and is still played, occasionally, today.

Gardiner was a friend of Arnold Bax, who had often been a visitor at Ashampstead, but Gardiner will be remembered, in particular, for the financial and promotional help he gave to important composers who could not get a substantial income from their work. Delius stayed at Ashampstead for a week in 1910 and was there again for a time in 1920.

Gustav Holst, disadvantaged by poverty and ill-health, despaired of getting The Planets performed by a professional orchestra. Henry Balfour Gardiner hired the Queen's Hall and obtained the services of a good orchestra. The Planets Suite was performed and was an instant success.

Tony Barham

The Worst Reason For Not Singing Reading Haydn Choir

In the 30 years since it was formed, Reading Haydn Choir has broadened its repertoire from the purely religious to the frequently secular. It is unlikely that this includes Money, Money, Money, but finances are never far from the choir's minds writes BOB KNOWLES

Every Thursday evening, the rehearsal room at Leighton Park School is full of amateurs – that is, people who love what they do, and do it for love (supplemented, in our case, by a membership fee that varies but in most cases compares roughly with the fee for an evening class). What we do is sing, rehearsing about 30 times a year, with three or four concerts a year – sometimes (as in the '98–'99 season) more, rarely fewer.

The Reading Haydn Choir was formed nearly 30 years ago, initially to sing strictly religious works in a liturgical setting; but now but now the repertoire often includes works that are secular – anything choral. Much of the choral repertoire happens to be religious, but we're not a church choir. We often sing in churches though, for obvious reasons: churches have enough room to seat an orchestra (when we can afford one) and a choir, an audience of around 100, an organ, a reasonable acoustic (sometimes), heating (occasionally)… We are about 35 strong, and always looking for new members (who, at the 'audition', which is gentle and sympathetic, simply have to convince Mandy that they can sing largely in tune and are not totally phased by the sight of written music).

I joined the choir in the late 1980s, when the finances were in turmoil. They had hit rock bottom in the previous season. Members of the committee had resigned, and there was a lot of ill feeling about things I have never got to the bottom of. I think the main feeling was one of exploitation by a conductor who was felt to have been using the choir and its (meagre) resources as a stepping stone for career advancement in the London music scene. So, in my first season, the choir was subsidised by a member who didn't want to see the choir go under (a possibility raised in the summer of the previous year, after several members had already bailed the cash–strapped choir out by paying their subscriptions several months in advance).

With funds so tight, raising money was even higher on the agenda than usual, with elderly members risking turned ankles in slippery wastepaper containers – anything to help to defray the costs of the next concert. Soloists cost us amounts that vary, but are usually in three

figures; orchestral instrumentalists usually cost a bit less; venues and music have to be hired, both for concerts and for rehearsal; tickets, flyers, posters, and programmes need printing for each concert. In sum, a concert can cost less than £1,000 (at the cheapest) or several times that. Three concerts a year at £x000, 35 choir members at £x per year – as they say in some parts of the world, 'Do the math'.

We can and do cut some corners – say, a small string ensemble rather than a full orchestra, or one instrument playing the part of another one that (according to the score) plays a few bars and then sits counting – but there are limits. In the year I joined, we sang Mozart's *Requiem*. As the choir had no money at the time there was to be a keyboard accompaniment. Luckily for me if not for the choir, we received an anonymous donation of £200 that was conditional on our having a small orchestra; if not, my first year might well have been my last. The Requiem is a marvellous piece and widely known (if subliminally – I bet most people who don't know it could hum the opening trombone solo of *Tuba Mirum*, even if they couldn't place it). To hear that theme, for example, plonked out on a keyboard would have been indescribable. Or the *Lachrymosa* – you know, the bit of the *Amadeus* soundtrack that plays when the funeral carriage is trundling by – given the Winifred Atwell treatment… we are talking tragedy here, not farce.

There is (financial) hope, in three forms. There are grants and other donations, subscriptions, covenants, fees for occasional performances; there are collaborations of various kinds; and there are ticket sales. We sing regularly (for the last three years, that is) at Waterstone's bookshop in Reading at Christmas. Long may the arrangement continue, as half the proceeds go to charity. And at our first Waterstone's date in 1998 (we sang there twice last year) we were approached out of the blue by a passer-by who engaged us to sing carols at a corporate function before the Waterstone's recital the following week.

We have sung twice with the South Chiltern Choral Society under Gwyn Arch – which gives us a chance to sing works the scale of which would otherwise be completely beyond us. I didn't count, but at our last performance – with South Chiltern Choral Society and Parenthesis, another choir (formed originally by parents of children taught under the auspices of the Berkshire Young Musicians Trust), I think the orchestra alone probably outnumbered the Reading Haydn Choir. There is a price to be paid for singing with so big a massed choir. Some members would prefer that their choir and their contribution to it should be valued separately; and each of the contributing choirs did, at that performance, have their own freestanding section of the programme, in the first half. But collaborating with other choirs certainly spreads the financial risks of music-making.

Sometimes I think choral singing is a dying tradition. When I joined the Reading Haydn Choir I was, in my late thirties, one of the younger members. Even now, ten years later, I am far from being one of the older members. But I hope I'm wrong. Both my children sing in Berkshire Young Musicians Trust choirs, in spite of Wokingham District Council's insistence that I should pay more than most other Berkshire parents. Perhaps our children will bring new blood to the many ageing choirs out there, and start younger than I did (as I sang in choirs at college but was a solo folk singer for much of my twenties and early thirties before returning to the choral tradition).

Money (that is, bums on seats) is ultimately the price that has to be paid for live music, certainly for music that involves ensembles of more than a dozen or so performers. A combo of a dozen or so can busk, but that's the limit beyond which big money has to be involved – a subsidy or ticket sales. Some amateur choirs have a statutory minimum of tickets to sell – three or four per member – on top of a subscription, music to buy, travel… But our choir has resisted enforcing any minimum ticket sales – the fear is that any arrangement like that might make people stop singing. And not having the money – as the MD of my son's choir said – is the worst reason for not singing. I can't think what the best reason is, but I can see her point.

Millennium Choice Bob Knowles

Mozart's Requiem

Serenade to Glenn

Gerald Bradford recalls a strange incident

A well-remembered event in Newbury is the visit of Glenn Miller and band of the USAAF in August 1944. They played in the Corn Exchange. It was the last chance for all those local girls to see and hear this celebrated band. The hall was filled to capacity so several hundreds sang and jived in the Market Place. A few months later, on 14th December, the small aircraft taking Glenn from Bedford to Paris vanished without trace over the Channel.

Gerald Bradford, a young local musician and a discharged soldier, recalls the occasion: "I was playing in a village hall somewhere locally at the time of the concert, but my wife Gladys went and saw this great orchestra playing. Sadly, she never got his autograph and I missed the Market Place 'relay'.

"About a dozen years ago we went to see the new Glenn Miller Band playing at Greenham Lodge, which was used as the officers' mess by the First Canadian Regiment stationed in Newbury during the war. It was an American Air Force Band and they wore Second World War uniforms and played all the old Glenn Miller music. The following year they played in the Market Place, Newbury, and of course we went again. I walked towards the band and noticed the same leader with an officer ,who introduced himself as 'Entertainments' and said, "I understand you have a band that plays this music. Could you deputise for us in two weeks time at Welford airbase for a 40s night? We are returning to Germany." I quickly contacted the leader of our own 'big band' and confirmed this unexpected musical honour. We then got down to 'tough' rehearsals.

Just before the night the officer took us to see the canteen and afterwards said: "Now I will take you to a very historical site, an old timber farm gate where Churchill, Eisenhower, Montgomery, Tedder, the Allied Chiefs of Staff and De Gaulle met in top secret before D-Day.

That evening we played on a semi-circular stage. As we entered the canteen it was like the past meeting the present. About 120 people were dressed in WW2 military uniforms, GIs, British, 'Dad's Army' and war utility clothes. etc. Very nostalgic to eight of us in theband. We seemed to sense success despite some apprehension at first. After the end of our opening Moonlight Serenade we felt the audience were with us. Geoff Millsom's clarinet ending never sounded better.

During the interval, Gladys came over, quite excited, saying: "It's incredible. I've never heard the band sound better." Later the colonel told us that Glenn Miller had played on the same stage soon after he came to the UK.

I will always remember that night. Were we really that much better? Gladys is a very good critic after nearly 60 years as an orchestra wife. She should know.

The Glenn Miller tribute band

From 78s To CDs Hickie and Hickie

ROBERT ELPHICK, son of Frank William Elphick who bought Hickie and Hickie's music shop in Reading in 1913, worked with his brothers in the family business. He was a Saturday boy during the war and became company secretary in about 1953. He started working full-time in 1955 and later became managing director. He is retired but still maintains a keen interest and close contact with the business

I suppose we were the first firm in Reading to sell records because they came in immediately after the 1914-18 war. There were records before then but not many. They began to be popular in the '20s and we did a lot of business in 78 records.

In those days, when you came into our shop from Friar Street, immediately on the left hand side was the counter for sheet music which was kept in folios in boxes behind the counter, and then behind that was the record counter with all the records in paper sleeves in racks. You didn't have any out on display. The customers would either look at catalogues or say, "Have you Bing Crosby's *White Christmas*?"

> **My earliest memories were coming into the shop from school. We lived in Spencers Wood and I used to wait for my father to take me home. I can remember going to Lyons in Broad Street and I would have a cup of tea, a poached egg on toast and a roll and butter, waited on by a nippie and it was 6d. My main memory is war time. There was blackout and you came in through the front door in Friar Street where there were black curtains you had to part to get in. We had a skylight with great big curtains over it.**

At the beginning of the Second World War I used to be a Saturday boy and sell records. They were in numerical order and you had to get the number from the catalogue

Members of the Elphick family and staff at Bournemouth in 1954

and then find the record. Decca was F and Harry James was on Parlophone, I remember. We were very busy and did a lot of record sales. A 78 cost two shillings then. We had three audition rooms round the corner and people used to go and try out the records and the young' so-and-so's of the day were a pain – I was one of them – they used to play all the records and then go out. I have still got all my 78s – they sound terrible now. Incidentally, Hickies can still sell you steel needles for 78s.

Vinyl came in in the late '50s or early '60s and the main thing was the 45 single. The charts started and you got The Beatles on singles. Then there were the 10in LPs – Mozart's *Eine kleine Nachtmusik* was on a 10in LP – and then the 12in LPs. This was a great improvement because if you had a symphony on 78s, you needed about six records.

There were still records during the war, in fact we had some very good ones because that was when we got American imports like Glenn Miller. It was a lot easier during the war than pre-war when American bands were prohibited from playing in Britain and there had to a be a mutual exchange – 20 American musicians for 20 British musicians.

Vinyl lasted a long time; we sold them until five years ago. The last time we updated the record department we still had to fit it out to take vinyl and we had browsers we could adapt from vinyl to CD. Then it was all CD and cassettes.

> **We used to promote concerts at the Town Hall about every three months and my father attended wearing his tail suit. There was a performance of The Messiah with Isobel Baillie and Katherine Ferrier, and we had the London Philharmonic several times. That was quite a business. We had a big chart and did the booking in the shop and also had to arrange the seating at the Town Hall. The seats were all movable in blocks of six, and our staff had to place them round the hall and put numbers on the back of the seats. When there was a concert with a pianist, the balcony on the left hand side was always in demand because that's where you could see best. The concerts went on until the '60s.**

Our prime time was in the '60s. We had pop records on the mezzanine gallery. On a Saturday this department was absolutely heaving. You could not get through there were so many people. We had six or eight serving and going full belt. On the pop record gallery there were listening booths down each side and then you came up into the hi-fi department, which was all very plush with red carpets on the floor and red velvet curtains – they didn't draw, they just dangled.

> **The guitar became very popular in the '60s because of the new groups like Bill Haley and the Comets and the Beatles. But then the young people have always had their music.**

There was about 80 staff then. We had eight tuners and 10 or 12 workmen in the piano workshop, and another 10 or 12 in the radio and television service department. The electrical service department had three electricians. We employed a lot more shop staff because we had the corner shop for radio and television with probably four assistants working in there, and about three in the electrical showroom. We employed about six people in the record department, three for classical, three for popular music, with additional Saturday help. It was very much personal service and customers had to be served for everything.

The office staff was quite big because with all of the work – if you serviced a set or tuned a piano – nobody ever paid at the time. You'd send out an invoice and with any luck you got paid. Usually you sent a statement but, if not, then you would send a reminder. We had an enormous sales ledge;, it went to thousands of entries. There were ledger cards on trays and it was a terrific business keeping them in alphabetical order – we had an enormous number of Smiths.

Stan Taylor, a blind tuner, worked for Hickie's for more than 50 years. He mainly tuned stock and hire pianos, because he didn't have a guide dog and if he went anywhere one of the shop girls or an apprentice took him. Another blind tuner, Edward Wilkinson, went from us to the Royal Normal College, a college for the blind in the Midlands, and became a principal tutor. He was a pianist and my father put on a concert for him in Palmer Hall.

Leonard Heeks was the mainstay of the classical record department. He came originally to the Slough branch, and when the manager Mr Haines engaged him during the war he told Leonard: "It's unusual to have a chap, we always have girls." After the war he moved to Boscombe branch, where he met his wife, and then moved back to Reading and lived in the flat above the shop.

> We used to have a football team, which played fixtures with other local businesses, and a cricket team. I remember my father used to organise swimming at the local baths. We had a lot of apprentices in those days.

Keeping It In The family
Hickie and Hickie

It was in 1864 that a name synonymous with the Berkshire music scene for more than a century first made its appearance in the town of Reading. Trading from a residential address in Great Knollys Street, probably as tuners and repairers, the Hickie brothers made steady progress leading to a move in 1908 to 153 Friar Street – premises that continue to carry the family name to this day.

At that time, just a few doors away at 159 Friar Street, a music shop run by Miss Binfield (later to become Attwells and Binfield) was managed by JE Hickie who, one assumes, later moved to 153 with his brother, William.

Although continuing to deal under the name of Hickie and Hickie, the business took a step forward in 1913 when it was purchased by Frank William Elphick, who was instrumental (no pun intended) in adding a piano repair workshop at 20 London Street and a radio and television workshop in Chatham Street.

Both of these operated successfully from their respective addresses until the late 1950s, then moving to Queen's Road premises formerly owned by Fowler Lee before finally opening at their present address in Livery Close, South Street, when the Queen's Road building was redeveloped as offices.

More important than bricks and mortar, the company remains firmly in local ownership, for when Frank William Elphick retired from his position as managing director in 1958, he was succeeded by his eldest son, Jim, assisted by brothers Frank and Robert.

Then, through a transitional period during which Robert became managing director, responsibilities for the running of the company were invested in Robert's son, James, and brother Jim's son, John Michael, in whose capable hands Hickie and Hickie continues to dispense its musical merchandise into a second century.

However, it is not only in musical retailing that Reading owes so much to Hickie and Hickie, for the directors have always encouraged music making among their staff.

Two names that spring to mind are those of Fred Tull and Norman Lambden who, in their day, were prominent among the town's dance band personalities. For many years a saxophonist with the Dcn Turk Band at the Olympia Ballroom, Fred joined Hickie's as an apprentice piano technician in 1924, earning two shillings and sixpence a week. Trumpeter Norman Lambden – also a piano technician – played alongside Fred Tull at the Olympia before joining the George Watkins Orchestra at the Majestic, where he remained until its closure in 1967.

Ron Pearce

"I'm Interested In Metronomes"

JOHN ELPHICK reveals a bizarre side to life in a music shop

Ever thought that you'd like to work in a music shop? If you appreciate music and instruments it can be a rewarding job. Your customers are often of a like mind and usually have a more relaxed attitude to you than if, for example, you worked in the complaints department of British Gas. But beware! Pitfalls await the unwary salesperson, so here are a few tips on coping with the difficult customer.

No 1: The drunk who wanders in and tries to play Chopsticks on the nearest piano. Your immediate reaction will be to slam the lid down on his fingers and then throw him into the street. However, as he will undoubtedly be bigger and more aggressive than you, a degree of caution should be used with this approach. Heavy sarcasm – express your wonder and surprise at his skill and congratulate him on his mastery of the piano. This may be enough to persuade him to go to the nearest pub to celebrate his newly discovered talent.

No 2: Family with small child who plays Chopsticks (or Für Elise) – same advice as above.

No 3: Anyone playing: Chopsticks (piano), Girl from Ipanema (sax), Smoke on the Water (guitar), Stranger on the Shore (clarinet). An expression of bored indifference can usually communicate to the more sensitive that you've heard it all before and their playing is not impressing you. After all you're in charge and quite within your rights to grab the instrument and escort the person to the door.

No 4: Anyone inquiring about violins or cellos. These people do not usually come within the category of relaxed music lovers – treat them with suspicion. Don't forget that if they succeed in buying anything from you, they'll bring it back the next day.

No 5: Beware the harmonica buyer, 90 per cent of whom are drunk. The exception here would be the occasional request for "Blues harp in A, please", but usually the sale involves a long explanation from you on the different types of harmonica and will end with the purchaser opting for a £4.95 Chinese harp in C. If he doesn't lose it in the pub that evening, he will return it for a refund the next day.

No 6: The anorak. You will soon be aware that you have a new friend. He knows more about his particular subject (drums maybe) than you do. He will visit your store most days to inspect the stock and tell you what you should have, and why what you have is not what he would have. There is no cure for the anorak; he is unlikely to go away no matter how he is treated. Try ridicule, try ignoring him, try running out of the back door – nothing works, he'll always be there to bore the pants off you (figuratively speaking).

No 7: "I'm interested in metronomes." No one can be interested in metronomes – this indicates a disturbed mind and, as such, this person should be treated with caution. Suggest that he/she seeks help (same advice would apply to "I'm interested in music stands/music cases/clarinet pull-throughs", etc).

Next. "No, I'm sorry we don't sell vacuum cleaner bags/TV aerials/turntable drive belts/mobile phone chargers – but okay, we do sell metronomes."

Now we have 15 staff and some of those are part-time. The workshop is down to two, one workshop man and one part-time polisher, and the radio and television service has gone. It has changed quite a bit in the last 30 years, but then, everything has.

The main business in the '20s and '30s was pianos. Stringed instruments like guitars, banjos and ukuleles were lumped together under instrumental small goods and sundries and it was not a big part of business. The major items were pianos and student instruments, such as violins, clarinets and flutes, and we have expanded more on these in recent years. Usually if you wanted a specialist musical instrument you tended to go to London. We never got into brass instruments.

> We've never had a piano pinched but we have had TVs stolen. We have also had amplifiers, a saxophone, and two silver flutes taken.

The '30s was a very good time for piano business. In the post-war years, it gradually tailed off. There is more interest now, generally, in playing music but the actual sale of pianos is quite low. There are only something like 5,000 pianos sold nationwide; it used to be 100,000 before the war. There are so many other conflicting things, like keyboards, which are portable. A piano is a big item; it's a piece of furniture. To get a reasonable instrument you have to pay £2,500 and that is still quite a lot of money. At one stage we did a piano for 18 guineas. If you relate that price forward, it would be about £1,000 now.

> Harry Harris, the vanman, told a story some time ago about delivering a piano to Theale at Christmas time. They had promised to get it there but had no form of transport and so they delivered it by handcart to the Rifle Volunteer in Theale. The landlord was grateful, gave them plenty of liqueur and Harry doesn't remember going back home.

We were the first business in Reading to have television. When it first started we did a lot of business part exchanging pianos for television sets. I remember going to watch one of the earliest televisions at our radio workshop in Chatham Street. It was a test match. You had this tiny screen – there was no zoom lens – so all you saw were little white figures. Reading was on the outer fringe of the signal from Alexandra Palace and to receive a signal we needed a very high mast . We had a wooden mast delivered and it had to come by river because it was too long to travel by rail or road.

In those early days we probably sold one or two sets to wealthy people but you almost had to put an engineer in with a set. Then it took off and we had a good radio and television business which kept going until about ten years ago. We stopped because we were losing money. Customers could buy the sets cheaper in discount warehouses, although our prices were comparable when you consider we used to deliver, service and give maintenance as well as sell them.

We are one of the few independent businesses still going in the town centre: Jackson's, Butlers and us. All the rest have gone. Our competitors Barnes and Avis were taken over by Rumbelows and even Rumbelows has gone. At one time we had branches in Basingstoke, Boscombe, Gloucester, Luton, Slough Reading, and for a very short time in Henley and Pangbourne. Slough opened in about 1932 and closed when the town was redeveloped. Boscombe was also opened in the 1930s and closed about 20 years ago. The Gloucester shop opened in 1927 and was closed 15 years ago.

How did we survive? Bloody-mindedness! The main thing was we owned the property. I think if we had to pay a market rent we wouldn't be here. The property keeps the business going. We've developed the properties we have owned in the past, condensed our shop operation and let off offices. We'd make more money if we ceased trading and let the property off but we have family to keep the business going and there are other children we hope will continue. If we can keep going, we will. I'm not going to be the one who closes it.

Frank William Elphick (standing) with the staff of Hickie and Hickie during their annual charabanc outing to the seaside in the '20s

Hitler's Opera

During the 1939-45 war, an American visitor told people who lived in Kingston Lisle (then in Berkshire) that the district would not be bombed because of the nearby ancient monument known as Wayland's Smithy.

The American told them that, as a young man in Vienna, Adolf Hitler had set out to write an opera, probably in a rather Wagnerian style, called Wayland the Smith. The young Adolf could play the piano to a certain extent but when it came to writing music he had to rely upon the help of a student friend who patiently wrote down each section as Hitler composed it.

Before the composition was complete other matters came to occupy young Hitler's mind and it seems no further work was done on the score.

As the district is largely rural, one would not have expected much bombing anyway, though, at one time, there were fears that the military base at Shrivenham, a few miles away, might attract Luftwaffe bombers.

I have been told that the local people treated the matter with a proper scepticism but, about 25 years after the war, a party of Oxford undergraduates visiting nearby Uffington brought two young German visitors with them. They were told about Wayland's Smithy and the opera.

Not only did they confirm that Hitler had written an opera with this title but they also mentioned that Friedrich Wilhelm Nietzsche (1844-1900), the philosopher whose writings were admired by Hitler and by his National Socialist Party, also wrote music and, as it happened, nine songs written by him had lately been performed in a recital at Oxford.

Tony Barham

Suite: Memories of Highdown 1970-78

Prelude

This 'musical offering' sketches the beginnings of music at Highdown School, summarises briefly a number of outstanding events in the first eight years, then focuses in some detail on a memorable specific occasion – the school's first Old Town Hall concert in July 1978. These recollections are purely personal and I apologise in advance to any people who feel that their names should have been included and likewise to those who feel that theirs should have been left out.

Theme: Andante historico

Highdown School opened in September 1970 at The Grove, in Caversham, a stately Georgian house with newly added single storey complex surrounded by 32 acres of parkland. This was Reading's first 'comprehensive' school. The 1,050 pupils initially on roll were the result of combining two smaller schools, The Grove School (already on site) and E P Collier School (from Lower Caversham) and adding a new eight-form first year intake.

Music was (and still is) taught in the medieval tithe barn and adjacent 'temporary' accommodation. The Barn is situated next to the Victorian walled garden – then part of the Rural Science area – the domain of an over diligent cockerel whose daily demands were voiced loudly and frequently, an intrusive obligato to many musical activities. The music department consisted of three staff: Margaret Price (succeeded in 1974 by Pamela Chilvers who was in turn succeeded in 1976 by Ann Armour), Sylvia Newton (part-time when not wearing her senior mistress's hat) and myself. A team of eight peripatetic instrumental teachers visited the school regularly, supported generously by the Authority (Reading at that time) in the person of Noel Hale, the music adviser. The school inherited a useful brass band from the Grove School, trained under the disciplined baton of the much respected George Watkins, a septugenarian who, with his son Ted, ran Reading's long-established Spring Gardens Band.

Variations

Outstanding musical occasions during the first seven years were:

1971 St Lawrence's Church – Mendelssohn's *Hymn of Praise* performed by pupils and staff with a part professional orchestra led by Susan Greenwood.

1972 Highdown School – Gilbert and Sullivan's *Trial By*

Jury – senior pupils and staff with orchestra. Produced by Desmond Saunders

1974 Highdown School – Menotti's Christmas opera *Amahl and the Night Visitors* – pupils and staff. Produced by Sylvia Newton.

1975 St Mary's Church – Benjamin Britten's *Noyes Fludde* – 150 pupils and staff. Production was by Tony Gilbert, and the professional accompaniment was provided by Roy Goodman and his Brandenburg Consort.

1976 Highdown School – Gilbert and Sullivan's *The Pirates of Penzance* – staff and senior pupils. No less than 20 members of staff agreed to make fools of themselves as 'brave and dedicated policemen', 'fierce bloodthirsty pirates' and 'beautiful young maidens'. Again the production was by Tony Gilbert. The part professional orchestra was led by Roy Laing.

All staged presentations were made possible by the invaluable co-operation of staff from the Creative Arts and Technical Departments headed by John Paris and John Bailey.

Interspersed with the above were regular North House Room Christmas and Summer concerts. Particularly notable were the performances of Bach's *Concerto in D minor for Two Violins* by Amanda Vincent and David Lewis; and of the first movement of Beethoven's *Piano Concerto No.3 in C minor* by Neil Sissons, both accompanied by the developing school orchestra. No annual summer fete was complete without the school brass band dispensing a stream of marches and novelty numbers from under a nearby shady tree.

Although generally adequate for school concert purposes, North House Room (the largest 'hall' on campus) was limited for space, restricting movement of performing groups and allowing a maximum of only 230 in the audience. In 1978 therefore, it was decided to take the bold step of hiring the Old Town Hall for the summer concert to accommodate the now large numbers of children keen to display their musical skills and a much larger audience. This is what happened.

Ancient Ayres and Dances

During the day of the concert, strategic bussing was necessary to convey the 200 performers to the Old Town Hall to meet planned rehearsal schedules – 7.30 pm signalled the beginning of proceedings. The first half of the concert consisted of music composed largely before 1800. It featured the Thursday Orchestra (woodwind dominated), two recorder groups (one trained by Jane Hodges), the Senior Madrigal Singers (organised by Elaine Jones), a Baroque Brass Quintet (trained by James Hall) and the Monday Orchestra which played music by Handel and (after a false start) accompanied James Hall (Grade 8) in the *Andante and Rondo* from Haydn's

Trumpet Concerto. Kevin Potton, the first of our four Grade 8 pianists on display, played a crisp and busy piece of Bach. All performers aquitted themselves creditably in these pleasant and predictable idioms and there were few surprises for the audience of 500 until the closing item of the first half that is – Neil's organ solo. Perhaps I had better explain.

Scherzo – Lisztmania

Neil Sissons arrived at Highdown in 1972 from Reading School to study Music (and English – and French) for A-levels. He was already an accomplished keyboard player and bent on a professional career. From Highdown he had gone to study at the Royal College of Music and thence to Oxford where at the time of the concert in question he was Organ Scholar at Worcester College. Some weeks before the concert, Highdown headmaster Andy Clarke and I visited the Old Town Hall to assess the possibilities for a concert there. We stood on the balcony and surveyed the scene. The feature which commanded our attention was of course the 'Father' Willis Organ. We looked at each other and exclaimed "Neil!" And so it was that Neil was invited and readily consented to perform at the 1978 concert. He said he would play Liszt's *Fantasia and Fugue on B.A.C.H.* – one of the most spectacular works in the organ repertory. (Well, wouldn't you?)

He began to play and as the great organ came to life, hoards of demonic semiquavers rampaged up and down the manuals as if in some Gothic nightmare. Gasps and cries of astonishment and admiration arose quite spontaneously from the girls of the third and fourth year choir who were sitting near the organ. By the conclusion of the final peroration the whole audience had become enthralled by the spell cast by the three contributing magicians: N Sissons, F Liszt and H Willis.

Intermezzo – piano e cantabile

The second half of the concert was concerned with music composed after 1800. Items were by two choirs, three more Grade 8 pianists, the Monday Orchestra and the brass band. In contrast to the flamboyant and exciting organ work the pianists, taken collectively were in more mellow mood. David Goodworth played John Field's *Nocturne in B flat*, Jane Hodges Chopin's *Raindrop Prelude* and Cameron Spence more Liszt – the *Sposalizio* from the Italian Book of the *Annees de Pelerinage*. The Monday Orchestra led by Edward Morton mustered a lively account of Vaughan Williams's *English Folksong Suite*. Both choirs benefited from the rich spacious acoustic of the hall, the first and second years beginning with *Swing Low Sweet Chariot* – then *Rio Rio* and ending with a sparkling *Star of the County Down*. The third and fourth year girls (40 potential Janet Bakers!) began with Harpers Bizarre's *Feeling Groovy*, perhaps appropriate after their earlier 'Gothic' experience, followed by *The*

Highdown School

Rivers of Babylon and an unforgettable *Tola Tola Lol*. Enid Coles was at the piano for these choral items.

Alla marcia – allegro con gusto

Finally we come to the Brass Band led by James Hall. The year 1978 marked the retirement from schools' bandwork of George Watkins (mentioned above) and a short speech of appreciation preceded the first number. George would declare that any band that he trained would be so well prepared that it could be conducted by anyone. It was my lot on that evening to put his claim to the test! We began with a piece called *Maryland* which I well recall attempting to conduct some years before with the band on the back of a *Big Wheeler* going up Rotherfield Way (very steep!) in a carnival parade. (No, nobody fell off.) Variations on *My Grandfather's Clock* was the second piece, a showcase for another Grade 8 pupil, Linda Johnson on solo euphonium.

The concert ended at 10.40pm after a Fantasia called *The Black Knight* which dated appropriately from Victorian times and which would doubtless have received the silent approval of the ghosts of thousands of bandsmen from the area for whom, over the years, the Old Town Hall had been the focal point of their highest competitive aspirations.

Coda

Around 1980 Highdown School had increased to a maximum 1,450 pupils. Two further equally successful Old Town Hall concerts followed but with a subsequent declining school roll, musical events on the scale remembered above were from that time no longer possible.

Raymond Jones, ex Head of Music

Counter Points Heelas customer concerts

Ever wanted to hire musicians to perform just for you? What about the Empire Brass Quintet, from America, or the Norwegian Chamber Orchestra? No matter if your house isn't big enough, hire the Hexagon and ask your friends. You like the clarinet? Of course – get Gervase de Peyer. You like accordion music? Get Howard Skempton. After all, the Archduke of Austria hired Mozart.

It's easy to be a patron of the arts and encourage excellent players to give their best to a willing audience. Easy, but few true patrons are about these days. Concert tickets cost a great deal to music-lovers. Into the account come venue hire, equipment, performers' fees, advertising, forward booking arrangements and the other thousand and one hazards of putting on an event. It's a high risk business, with high costs and a high level of enjoyment possible for all participants if it all comes together on the night. But because of the high costs, subsidies must come from somewhere if musicians are to be paid properly and concertgoers' ticket prices kept affordable.

For Berkshire music lovers however, the occasional treat is free. Really. Who heard the Georgian State Chamber Orchestra a few years ago under their artistic director, the wonderful Liana Issakadze? One of the top ensembles of the former Soviet Union, they would not have been locally available but for patronage. Let us now reveal the secret – you are most likely to hear of these splendid free events if you are a regular customer at Heelas, or anywhere else in the John Lewis Partnership. And who has never shopped at Heelas, Waitrose or Caleys – roses by any other name?

Since 1951 the Partnership has provided regular opportunities for performance of great music by great artists and all because John Spedan Lewis, the Partnership's founder, met by chance – at a musical event of course – Boyd Neel, whose orchestra was becoming well-known. The notion of putting on "gift concerts" for customers was established in London, with the object of encouraging musicians and providing a new opportunity for them to be heard. Over the years the focus has refined and developed.

Today the policy is to hold the events outside London, on the basis that Londoners have more than enough choice of musical goodies anyway! Every three or four years your local JLP store is likely to be organising a free concert, the programme chosen so as to provide contrast with any other that may be available. Berkshire has been given good music by famous soloists and groups ranging from the John Aldiss Choir, the Allegri String Quartet, through to the Nash Ensemble and a host of others, since concerts are arranged right in the community where trading is done. The benefit is enormous: concerts are presented which would not otherwise take place, with musicians of international recognition whose fees would be unaffordable to the local community.

Favourable publicity for JLP has never been the primary aim. Rather, they wish to be useful, providing arts patronage in the best – and almost lost – sense. Thus we have a public good that tingles our ears and touches our spirit. Children's concerts are a recent new feature. In all areas, audiences of all ages applaud and stamp their feet to show approval and appreciation of a truly great event. And it's free, to you. You'll get advance notice of the next concert if you are an account customer, but you don't have to be – just watch out for the notices and then take every opportunity of enjoying yourself. Bravo! Encore!

Christine Taylor

Everybody wants to be a Star Berkshire School of Popular Music

Singer and teacher TINA REIBL founded the Berkshire School of Popular Music in the '80s. Although she has now sold it, she is still singing and teaching potential stars with her own highly individual methods with which she helps music students to prepare themselves internally as well as externally

Singing is my first musical instrument.

I'm from Germany originally. I used to be a social worker with youngsters and I worked quite closely in the creative field, teaching people to play the guitar and singing with them. When I came over to England, I thought, let's take my hobby and make it into a profession. It doesn't really matter what it is you want to do; you can achieve anything. I honestly and truly believe that. There's no stopping me.

So I auditioned for a place on the jazz and rock course at the Guildhall School of Music and Drama and was accepted as the first vocalist on the course. After finishing my studies, I worked as a professional singer for a year but I felt that I really wanted to go into music education. I'm a definite 'edu-tainer'. I really believe that unless you are having a great amount of fun you're not learning anything and I pride myself on the fact that what I'm doing is real big fun. I thought it would be brilliant to set something up that was different from the one-to-one lessons that everybody does. People should have the chance to play in ensembles and work with others in a group.

We set up the Berkshire School of Pop Music in 1985. We hired the Sheephouse Farm, in Maidenhead, a set of stables that weren't in use. We painted them white and put a cupboard in and a few chairs and started from there. We taught guitar, bass, drums, keyboards and singing – the normal line-up of a rock band. The school grew very quickly, having it's own band and choir. Every Saturday morning we'd come together to do band coaching, and we'd do big end-of-term concerts twice a year.

We started to bring in other people because we wanted to give the students the experience of working with top-class professionals. We ran a workshop with the London School of Samba, spending a whole Sunday playing Salsa and Bosa Nova and other Latin music. We did a wide variety of workshops: composition, song writing, how to work with an accompanist, how to go for auditions for singers, things like that. We would also study music theory and technology.

Tina Reibl

Most students would stay with us for years rather than weeks. I have a number of students who are now professional musicians and are doing really well . At the time, the Arts Council of Great Britain had set up a scheme for people doing music education projects. If you got company sponsorship they would match the amount; like-for-like funding. I went to ABC Music and they sponsored me, and I sent all of it to the Arts Council. They wrote back saying that popular music was not considered a part of real music and that they couldn't match the funding.

It was hard going because there was nobody who would support the seven of us. We did all the advertising ourselves. We did get some funding from people like Jazz South and the Musicians' Union but with the hours that go into raising sponsorship, it's not really worth it. However, we scraped through, something of which I'm very proud.

The seven teachers at the school had a travelling show called the Rock School Road Show. We wrote a programme about how popular music developed: the beginnings of rhythm and blues and gospel up till now. We played little examples of each style, explained about the instruments and took it round the schools in Berkshire and Hampshire. It was very successful. We also did some peripatetic teaching, going into schools to teach guitar, bass and drums. The pupils could then come to our ensembles on Saturday mornings to join in the group activities.

I ran the pop school for seven years but I eventually sold it to a keyboard player and his singer wife and they're still running it. It's so nice that it still lives because it was my baby.

I then went on to Langley College as a lecturer in performing arts on the BTech Performing Arts course. I was teaching the singing side of the course and also vocational evening classes called Voice Workshop. I must have seen hundreds of people come and go, some of whom are actually quite successful. I had a couple of students who went into West End shows, another who got a recording contract, people working at the Running Frog recording studio in Windsor. The amount of people who achieve their aim to make music their living, become singers, have a band, do gigs, is amazing. Somebody came up to me once and said: "In the old days, every boy wanted to be a train driver, and every girl wanted to have children, have a nice house, nice husband. Nowadays, everybody wants to be a star."

It's true. People have got these amazing ambitions and yet so few actually achieving them. I asked myself, what quality do you need, apart from obvious musical skill, to make that happen? Often the people who had the nicest voice or were the most talented were not the ones who made it. The people who made it had quite different qualities.

So I went and studied abroad for a Practitioner's and Master's degree in Neuro Linguistic Programming (NLP). NLP asks the question: "What makes a successful person, in any field, singer or business person? What is it you need to succeed?" The answer has to do not only with the ability to withstand pressure, to work under stress, but as importantly how people talk to themselves internally. You can make yourself really nervous before going out by telling yourself: I won't be able to hit the high note and I'm sure I'm going to trip over my microphone cable. People look at the audience, wrinkle their brows and say, "Oh they don't like me." It's the way you prepare yourself, internally, that makes the great difference.

I started to incorporate what I had been learning in my classes and had tremendous success with people who finally got around to doing something they had always wanted to do. In using the technique, visualising successful experience, people were audibly so much better, quite miraculously sometimes.

One technique is called modelling: Who's your hero? Who would you like to emulate in real life? It might be Frank Sinatra or Barbra Streisand. What can you take from him or her? The difference is the students are not seeing me as the master but modelling total excellence, whoever the pupil's master is, in their minds. Although they haven't learnt to sing any better physically , the difference in their performance is surprising.

When we watch masters, we take in a lot more subconsciously than we do consciously. We're drawing on their results, all the little observations we've made and stuck away somewhere at the back of our minds which we usually can't access. By doing things like visualisation, we access lots of observations we've made in the past, bringing them back to the forefront of the mind. We can

then overcome a lot of barriers, extending the comfort zone, focusing on what it is we want. We develop this really strong focus, saying there is no failure, only feedback and being positive about failure – what can we take out of that, how can we make it better next time; creating a positive frame of expectancy.

Singing can be so frightening. I spent lots of time at the Guildhall School crying in the toilets. I was not alone. It was a petrifying experience. At the school it was very pressurised; the best people were there and they made you feel competitive. You had to be better than the next person. I have never treated my pupils like that; it is always better to work together and to pull together than work against one another. I remember singing with a big band, coming out, just looking at them and feeling I was going to faint: "I can't do this." That's not a good place to be internally, scared, if you want to be successful.

As for now, once a singer, always a singer. I teach singing on a Musical Theatre course at Redroofs alongside my private coaching at home – my students at present include a magician, a songwriter and some actors. This summer I ran a Rock Week for young players at Windsor Arts Centre in conjunction with the Running Frog, and I do the occasional session work and rehearse with a guitar player, learning new repertoire for performing.

I also hold hypnosis classes. NLP works a lot with language patterns; if I talk to you in a certain way, I will entrance you. When I work with singing students in visualisation, I say to them, take a deep breath, relax, close your eyes and imagine you're on the stage in two weeks when you become Frank Sinatras. I'm not hypnotising my singing pupils, I have to say, though some of the techniques – visualisation, relaxation – that you need to learn to get on top of stage fright are probably trance techniques. But the students are in control of the trance themselves.

NLP is such a powerful tool that I thought it could benefit others outside of singing. I have other clients with whom I use it to help them overcome depression or phobia, and to be more successful, assertive, and creative.

I see myself much more now as a facilitator. I'm happiest, if I see my students do well. I went into the Running Frog studios the other day to do a session and every single person in that place had been taught by me. I felt like 'The Mother of Rock 'n' Roll'. Absolutely amazing.

Millennium Choice Tina Reibl

I think Manhatten Transfer's version of A Nightingale Sang in Berkeley Square (Maschwitz and Sherwin) is gorgeous. I love what they are doing with their harmonies. I also love the song, the lyrics are so romantic and descriptive

Two Worlds of Music Indian Music

In the '80s ARATI BASU ran one of the first groups for Indian children in Reading which taught them the music and dance of their own culture. Now she has gone back to school herself to study for a degree in Western music and to trying to close the gap between Indian and Western music

India is a very musical country. Music is natural to us and there is singing or dancing in almost every household. My father's sister was a very good singer and would travel around India singing. She worked for films as well, singing for the actors who would mime to her. I learnt singing when I was young and later I used to sing as a semi-professional.

I started learning the harmonium when I was five years old, sitting on my folded legs so that I could reach the bellows at the back. I began with my auntie's teacher who was very very old, at the end of his time then. With my father's transferable job we travelled round the country. Wherever we went my sisters and I had a music teacher coming to teach us. I used to play harmonium and sing and play guitar; my next sister used to learn sitar and singing; and my third one went for classical singing and played the tambura. I was an all-rounder – perhaps I was a bit lazy. I didn't want to devote that much time to practising and you have got to be dedicated to be a classical musician, especially in India. I used to get the tune quickly in my head and play it from there on the harmonium.

There are different types of music in India as anywhere – classical, semi-classical, folk, and in that folk music there are so many different varieties, songs for fisherman, people who work in the fields, people who drive the carts. They each sing a different type of song. India is such a vast country; you go to different regions and get different types of music.

Classical Indian singing is mainly divided into two, North and South – I am from the North. The whole classical genre is more or less the same and as you go to different districts only the decoration and presentation will be varied. But whether it is North or South, there is always drumming or some kind of percussion, you cannot think of a song without it. Now I'm studying western music I realise there can be instrumental music without any drum kit. There is a rhythm, musical rhythm but no drumming, no percussion with it at all.

In Indian singing, whether it is classical or folk or semi-classical, always there should be percussion. There are parts which haven't got percussion which is the introduction in the classical music, when you are unfolding the Raga. At that time the percussionist will be sitting with the singer next to him or her with the tabla, but not playing it. After the artist has finished unfolding the Raga, then he or she will start a rhythmic portion and at that time the percussionist will play and join the performer. You have to have at least two parts in the classical singing, the introduction or the unfolding of a Raga, and a rhythmic section, called Khyal. In non-classical singing you may or may not get that part without percussion, you'll get just the part with percussion. When you are singing something which is not classical you don't have to stick to any Raga; there is no need to unfold the Raga, you are using just melody which could be a mixture of two or three different Ragas.

A Raga is just sets of notes which you improvise around. It is a group of notes from an octave. In Raga you can have maybe five notes, maybe six notes, maybe seven notes depending on which Raga you are singing, just those few notes. If you have chosen a Raga with five notes for example, then you will be improvising around only those five notes mentioned in the Raga. Exactly like that, if you choose a Raga with six notes, then you are limited to those six notes to do your improvisation, and so on. You will not touch any other notes in the octave unless it is mentioned in the Raga.

Every Raga has got a fixed number of tones and semitones and a prominent note, second prominent note, and there is a catchphrase of a few notes. As soon as someone starts a Raga they slip in that catchphrase, and people will know that he or she is singing Raga because of that catchphrase. Only these forms are written down but it is the embellishment and improvisation that vary from place to place. Sometimes somebody follows the classical singers with the harmonium. They play tambura which has only four notes, tonic, dominant and two tonics again in two lower octaves, and all these middle notes have got to be provided from your voice.

They used to say that you had to be taught for six or seven years to learn a Raga. In those days most people had time, not these days. These days you have preliminary education for three or four years and learn a Raga a year, something like that. People haven't got that much patience and haven't got that much time to devote to music only. Nowadays people have to study while they are learning music. Once you are established, you can earn your living from full-time music but until that happens, you need to leave your options open to get a job.

I married and had a son before I came to England. I kept my music up to a certain extent; I brought my books with me and used to sing at home but on my own because I didn't have an harmonium. I didn't bring it with me. Only 20 kilos of luggage were allowed and an harmonium weighs about 17 or 18 kilos so I couldn't bring that. It wasn't until I started my children's music group in Reading that I bought a harmonium for them.

It was in the early '80s. My son was grown up and I had some time on my hands. I had a few friends who talked about having a school for their children which taught them something of their music and culture because there was nothing like it at the time. I met John Sherman, the headteacher of E P Collier School, and he was willing to give me the use of his school on Saturday mornings.

So I had the school and a little bit of money, about £50 from Youth and Community, and with that I started Saturday school, with some instruments and a few costumes – I made the costumes myself because I didn't have enough money to buy them. I started teaching the children some singing and asked my friend Nina Dutt from Slough to come and teach them dancing. We used to meet on Saturdays, and sometimes during the week, after school or in the evenings as well.

We had about 14 or 15 children, aged between seven and 14, mainly girls including John Sherman's two daughters. I taught them singing while I played the harmonium which I bought from Southall. I taught them Rabindera Sangeet – the first word is the composer's name and the second means songs. Lots of people know them as Tagore songs. Music for all his songs are written up so it is easy to teach them with young people. It's considered not quite folk because it has got Ragas in it, but it's not quite classical singing because you cannot improvise on it.

> Rabindranath Tagore (1861-1941) was famous in every field of Bengali literature. He was a poet, an artist, and composed more than 2,000 songs. The largest number are devotional songs but he also wrote about nature, about people, about different celebrations. Now people have started to research his work, he is considered a combination of Shakespeare and Beethoven. He wrote the words and the tunes, and would sing the songs to his nephew who used to write down the notations. He also wrote musical drama, dance drama, short stories, novels. He produced a tremendous amount.
>
> He was an educationalist as well and there are now two Tagore universities in Bengal, one which he himself established as a school for children, and people come from all over the world to those universities. He won the Nobel Prize, was knighted by Queen Victoria, and was awarded an

Mrs Arati Basu with some of her young pupils

> honorary degree by Oxford University at a ceremony in India. Rabindranath Tagore wrote India's national anthem. Later on Bangladesh chose one of his songs as their national anthem. So he is the only composer in the world to have two national anthems to his credit.

The children I taught didn't know about Tagore or any of his songs, so I talked about him a little bit and then started teaching them. I felt it was important that they should know about their own music and culture. There wasn't anything like this in schools at that time although it's better now. However, some of them were from Hindi-speaking families and their parents began saying: "Oh, why do you teach Bengali songs all the time?" So then I started teaching them one of these Tagore songs, which is Bengali, and one folk song or film song in Hindi, and they were happy then.

The school ran from 1982 until 1989. When the Indian Community Centre was established, they said they would start a school too and since there was no point in running two schools for about 20 pupils I gave up mine and joined them for a while. Then I was made redundant from my full-time job with British Rail so I took the opportunity of going to Dartington College of Arts for a couple of years on an Indian music teachers' training course. Dartington has got connections with Tagore as well because Leonard Elmhirst who founded the college, worked for Rabindranath Tagore as the head of the agriculture department in his university for several years.

I pent most of my time in the college. I thought I must learn whatever I could in those two years and make the most of it. I can remember my tutor saying, "What is it you are doing? You are going to all these different classes." I said, "I want to learn whatever I can, so I just go to any class I am allowed to."

When I finished, I worked in schools and universities, running workshops on Indian culture and music, promoting Indian musicians, lecturing around the country, and performing. I ran an after-school club at

South Street Arts Centre in Reading and at the end we put on a show. That's when I came to know Doctor Kent who is my tutor at the University of Reading. He came to see my show and I got the idea of doing a degree in Western music.

So I sent a letter and my CV and got a letter back saying 'yes, with your past experience you can join us in the second year'. I was over the moon. But in the end, because I didn't know much about western music, he suggested I start in the first year. I am glad I did, because it was just like starting from scratch. I even had to learn to play the piano, but I was allowed to do my sight-reading on the harmonium.

The music is very, very different. In Indian music you are taught to listen to it then sing it, there is no sign of notation unless you do Tagore songs. But even then the notation is written quite differently from western music; where you get a stave, and you write down dots or dots with a tail. In Indian music you write the words of the Sol-Fa. So there are only two lines of music, with words of the Sol-Fa written and words of the song written, there are no lines or signs. Flats have a line underneath the note to denote they are flat, and a line on the top to denote sharps. In western music the same note can be flattened or sharpened so it has got two names.

In Indian Sol-Fa, it hasn't. Only four notes (2nd, 3rd, 6th and 7th) can be flattened and one (4th) can be sharpened; that's your five notes making ten notes in the octave. Two notes (1st and 5th) are fixed notes; they cannot be flattened or sharpened – they are the tonic and the dominant, which makes twelve notes of the octave. There are also three different types of notations in India.

My musical project is transcribing Indian music into staff notations, then I'd like to see western musicians playing it. When I was in Dartington I ran an ensemble with western musicians, flute, guitar, violin. I used to say to them, "A, B, C, D, like that" and they played with me. Now I have transcribed a couple of the Tagore songs because the notation is already there and I hope in my recital I'll have two English people who can play with me. We do a recital every year. In the first year I sang one Italian song and one Tagore song; in the second year I'm doing one German song and two Tagore songs. The singing is different too because in western singing you use your whole body, your stomach, your chest and throat. In Indian singing you are using your voice and vocal chords. It's a different sound.

When I finish my degree, I'd like to do a bit of research, particularly at the Tagore university, looking at Indian music from my western music base. Most modern composer in this country are now very interested in Indian music.

Millennium Choice Arati Basu

I enjoy learning and I enjoy most music except when it is just banging tins and tearing up newspaper. That's the only music I don't like. I was quite happy listening to Messiaen's birdsong until somebody said, "Oh that's not the proper music, you should be listening to Beethoven or Mozart."

Juke Box Memories
Growing up with the pops

My first recollection of music was as a small child in the front room of my aunt's house in Maidenhead playing a gramophone, winding it up and listening to Caruso and Any Umbrellas. I remember the records were kept in a pouffe with a lid.

At the age of about 12, I stood under the greengage tree in the garden (we have an offshoot in our garden because we now live in the house next door) and sang Cherry Pink and Apple Blossom White and Unchained Melody – "Oh, my love, my darling…" – like a pop star.

At school, we learned Men of Harlech and There'll Always Be An England. Why don't the children learn them now?

In my teenage years, at the start of the swinging sixties, I frequented a coffee house in Bridge Street, Maidenhead, where I listened to the juke box. I was not smitten by the looks or gyrations of Elvis Presley or Cliff Richard, although I later became a fan of both, but preferred Gene Pitney, Roy Orbison, and Neil Sedaka. My favourite song was Del Shannon's Runaway. Oh, the jiving we did.

I have always been, and still am, a romantic at heart so I Can't Live, If Living Is Without You and As Long As He Needs Me are firm favourites, along with For I Am His Woman And He Is My Man.

When my elder daughter was a teenager, we enjoyed Top of the Pops as well as Country and Western, popular classics, folk songs (and I've kept all of the records) as well as movie themes. Some music gives me goose bumps especially the theme from Bilitis (never did find out what that was) as well as reducing me to tears of sorrow or joy as the mood predicted.

I now watch TOTP2 and am again a teenager dancing, which plays havoc with my ME (Viral Fatigue Syndrome). The following day I can hardly walk and have to come downstairs on my rear end. It's worth it.

Margaret Hnatiuk

Rural Hams or Quality Theatre? Kintbury panto

There must be something about the air in Kintbury which nourishes dramatic talent. Few rural communties could boast a thriving group like St Mary's Drama Group, with members of all ages as well as a subsidiary company called the Benchmark Theatre Company, not to mention The Kintbury Players. But the highlight of Kintbury's dramatic year is the annual pantomime, writes GERRY HEATON

When the Coronation Hall rings with song and the sounds of "Oh yes you are!" and "Behind you!" the people of Kintbury in West Berkshire know that it is the pantomime season again. This does not take place during the festive season as you might imagine, but in February, and marks the culmination of many weeks work for the members of St Mary's Drama Group.

But why not Christmas? It used to be Christmas – a nightmare at Christmas! The pantomime involves six performances during its production week as well as two dress rehearsals and a technical rehearsal. This meant that everyone involved gave up much of their Christmas time and New Year and returned to work or school extremely tired. Something had to change and so the much-discussed move to February finally took place.

Why February? In order to encourage a truly community-based society, St Mary's Drama Group's performances are usually held during half terms. This means that the talented children of Kintbury can take part without encroaching on school time. February half term was the closest holiday to Christmas.

St Mary's Drama Group has always valued its young members and it was mainly for the children of the village that the society was set up by Christine Millard in 1972. Christine is the much-loved wife of Albert Millard who was the vicar of Kintbury at that time. It was during Christine's time that the group won many prizes at the now disbanded Maidenhead Arts Festival. Since then it has expanded to take in all ages and has developed through the many talents of its varied membership.

What is particularly exciting is that many of the children who have joined over the years are still members and some have gone on to direct productions, or help to 'run' the group. In fact, some of the younger members are the children of children who helped to form the group.

The pantomime is the main production of the year and takes up the most rehearsal time. Recent productions have included old favourites such as *Cinderella* and

Sleeping Beauty, as well as the 'newer' titles of *Robin Hood* and *The Grand Old Duke of York*. The extravaganza in 1999 was *The Snow Queen* and was thoroughly enjoyed by cast and audience alike. The review in the Newbury Weekly News summed up what St Mary's Drama Group is all about: "There is something about village life that produces the best of team spirit."

Forward planning is the key to success and this is already under way for the pantomime in February 2000 – *Jack and the Beanstalk* – with rumours already circulating that the 2001 performance will be *Ali Baba and the Forty Thieves*.

Many of St Mary's Drama Group pantomimes are written by members and this may well be why the pantomime has built up such loyal audiences over the years. People eagerly arrive at the Coronation Hall dying to see what outrageous characters many of the old familiars will appear as and secretly hoping they will get a mention.

There is the inevitable type casting with some of the older members having crafted a definitive persona after many years in the same sort of role. The pantomime is certainly about ham acting, but only in the finest traditions of one of England's oldest art forms and it's all done in the best possible taste!

The arrival of autumn heralds the 'dreaded' auditions! Not so much dreaded by the actors who only have to read the script to be cast, but dreaded by the poor director who has to cast the beast and be fair, try not to disappoint, or reject and who is often painted as 'the baddie' by those few who don't end up with what they wanted. Not an enviable position.

Rehearsals then begin in earnest, only pausing for the Christmas break before moving up a gear as the performance deadline approaches. During this period the costume-makers are fiercely measuring, cutting and sewing; set designs and production plans are put in place; and finally the publicity team gets going to ensure people come to watch. The final stages are taken up with set building and dressing and the last, but all important, frantic rehearsals.

As the curtains are drawn and the opening song is sung by the citizens of Kinterania or Kintesburg (or whatever Ruritania happens to be called that year) the poor wreck of a director can breath a sigh of relief and relax. All those weeks of saying "Never again!" give way to "When I do my next production…" and so the cycle starts again.

'It's a Great Craic all the Way' Irish Traditional music

Irish traditional music is alive and well in Reading thanks to a group of dedicated musicians, not least Les and Sara Daniels of Sonning Common. Les plays tin whistle and flute and Sara sings traditional and self-penned songs and plays anglo concertina. SARA DANIELS writes about Irish music with help from Les Daniels, John Ryall, Lennie Attrill, Paul Hancock and Ian McGirr

In the early days of our interest in Irish traditional music, we were fortunate in Reading to have Paddy Coyne, an accordion player from Connemara, who introduced us to many great talented Irish musicians old and young. Irish music sessions at his pub The Claddagh Ring, or the Kennet Arms as it was 20 years ago when we first started going there, set the scene for many a long night and early morning. Some memorable evenings stand out: Cathal Haydn, a fiddle player from Tyrone, and the flute player Marcus Hernon from Connemara with his brother PJ, also Martin McMahon, a great friend of Paddy's and a wonderful accordion player, for the dancers and the sessions. Before that time I had never witnessed such great playing.

Sometimes musicians passing through from Ireland on tour in the UK would stop over and a session would be called, or a late drink after a gig. Singer Delores Keane and members of her family Christina and Matt, and Tom and Dick Joyce from Headford, Co Galway – as newcomers we learned so much from these generous musicians.

Occasionally the hit and miss publicity for gigs could cause trouble, as with Eddie Corcoran. A mis-spelling in his name and not mentioning that he was a whistle

player from Sligo brought two ageing female rockers to the pub. They were incensed not to find the long dead rock legend Eddie Cochrane.

Later the sessions were filled with the surge of young players from far and near. London brought Teresa Heanue (fiddle), Mick Conneely (fiddle), Jason O'Rourke, a concertina player living in Oxford at the time, now in Belfast, and musicians from Leeds and Birmingham like Kevin Crawford, a flute player, now living in Ennis, Co Clare, and Teresa Moran (whistle).

Many talented youngsters from Slough, High Wycombe and London, taught by Brendan Mulkere in Sunday morning classes, put our early feeble efforts to shame, but we kept at it, as they say. Not to be forgotten were the tireless efforts of people like Doug Lang, bodhran player and catalyst. Many a good night was brought together by his enthusiasm for Irish music and his knowledge of the people who played it. He still hosts sessions in Oxford at the Elm Tree, on the Cowley Road.

Folk clubs in and around the Reading area are long-suffering when it comes to singers. Many a folk club audience will endure the ramblings of a 40-verse ballad, or the two or three false starts to a forgotten song. But pub sessions are noisy affairs and often not so forgiving. A crowd will always quieten down for a singer, but if you are not up to scratch they will quickly return to their pint and chat!

Old style or sean nos singing is sometimes lengthy and vocally ornamented and sung unaccompanied. It is an experience shared by the company and requires some effort on the part of the listener. Favourable comments are occasionally given to the singer during the song as encouragement or, as with the tunes, when a phrase is turned in a particularly pleasant way. Thus the song becomes part of both the singer and the listener.

Just as the music and song is a fluid, ever-moving entity, so the sessions peak and trough. The musicians move away in the course of their lives and occupations. Other musicians come to Reading and new sessions start up. A long-running session in The Dove, Orts Road, ended in 1998 when Rose the landlady called 'time' and retired from the pub trade.

One way to locate the current Irish session in Reading is to find the dancers. A regular ceilidh club meets at the Reading Irish Centre in Chatham Street, which was built with the help and co-operation of the Irish community in Reading.

The occasional visitor to Reading would be fortunate to find the impromptu session. They are gatherings brought together by word of mouth at short notice, maybe for a particular celebration or an unexpected visiting musician looking for a few tunes. The atmosphere is deceptively casual. The musicians are infinitely serious about their

Ian McGirr (banjo), Pippa Jones (guitar), and John Ryall (fiddle) at the Claddagh Ring 1994

playing. As the night moves on, more and more favourite and unusual reels are dug from the depths of their memories, fellow memories are jogged, and a tune taken up by the first few bars of a long-remembered set.

Those new to Irish music often say, "It all sounds the same, diddley, diddley". But of course, it's not. There are thousands of tunes, jigs, reels, hornpipes, polkas, slip-jigs and more. Each tune is different. A 'trained' ear will notice where the tunes change in a set of two, three or more, and where a musician will put in a variation of their own choosing, or if the tune is a different version of the same tune played by another well-known musician, even who played this particular tune, and at what venue! And so it goes on. The more you know, the less you know. But it's a great craic all the way!

Les took to playing the tin whistle in 1973, about the time the Chieftains were becoming popular in the UK. He met Jack Armstrong, a whistle and flute player, at that time living in Tilehurst. Jack had come over from Sligo to England in the fifties. He hadn't played a note for 20 years but Les coaxed tunes from him. His stories of playing back home for the dances and kitchen sessions were as valuable as his tunes. Sadly Jack died in 1995 at the age of 76.

Lucy Farr, a fiddle player from Galway, now living in West Berkshire, is our most treasured link with the 'old' players. She joined Reg Hall in the '60s and became part of the famous dance band The Rakes. Lucy recorded an album to celebrate her 80th birthday and at 87 she is still playing. The *Paddy in the Smoke* album recorded in 1968, on which she plays alongside the great musicians of that time in London, has been re-released on CD featuring more of Lucy's own tunes. .

We will forever need these wonderful musicians to remind us of the ways of tunes and the manners of playing them. New bands will undoubtedly push the boundaries of Irish music, bring fresh ideas and mixing musical cultures which are sometimes exciting and always welcome. But the strength of the old tunes and the way

Les and Sara Daniels at the Claddagh Ring 1994

of playing for the feet of the dancers will live on long after the hybrid bands have come and gone.

Twenty-five years ago the Chieftains brought to my untrained ear an 'acceptable' sound. By acceptable, I mean a recording quality and production comparable to the mainstream music we were used to. I found it difficult to listen to recordings like The Russell Family from Clare. The wonderful whistle playing of Micho Russell and the sharp clear tone of the concertina were too 'raw' for my ears at that time. It was a few years before I learned to appreciate their astonishing power as musicians and to hear the intricacies of a seemingly simple tune or the humour in the voice of a gravel-throated singer. The Bothy Band, De Dannan and Planxty albums followed and, in the absence of local teachers in Reading, became the 'bibles' any aspiring musician had to own and learn from.

But no album can better hearing good musicians in person. The Willie Clancy Summer School in Co Clare is a wonderful week of morning classes and endless sessions, or you could say, early morning sessions and endless classes depending on the quality of the music and your hangover! Named after the famous uillean piper, it is a week well worth the pain! Both Les and I remember our numerous visits with gratitude and affection, not least to our friends who suffered our blatant name-dropping when we got home.

Arda Berkshire was a band put together in 1982 by Len Attrill, an accordion player, originally from the Isle of Wight and at that time living in Reading. He had been playing tunes in The Greyhound pub, Silver Street, with Pippa Jones, guitar, John Ryall, fiddle, and Paul Hancock, whistle. Later Les joined them on whistle. When ceilidh bookings started coming in from local Irish Centres they needed someone to sing the waltzes and song spots. As I had been singing round the folk clubs, I willingly obliged. I took up the anglo concertina in 1985 so it was a while before I could join them on the tunes.

Paddy Coyne (accordion), Dick Shanks (fiddle) and Luke Daniels (bodhran) at the Kennet Arms 1983

The band grew like Topsy, with musicians like Ian McGirr, a talented young banjo player from Bracknell, and Terry Clarke, guitarist singer/songwriter. Luke, our son, then aged eight, started on bodhran. He took up the accordion and went on to win Radio 2's 1992 Young Tradition Award and now plays with the Riverdance Show touring America. Later Dick Shanks, a fiddle player, joined us. He could raise the rafters with his lyrical Irish songs and 12-string guitar. The Arda Berkshire played at a wide range of venues from London to Cornwall and supported acts such as The Dubliners.

A liaison between the band and a play written by Julia Feeney resulted in a successful production at the Progress Theatre in Reading. *The Homecoming* was the result of sheer enthusiasm and the hard work and talent of all those involved. In 1986 I recorded an album, *Bushes and Briars*, featuring Arda Berkshire and in '93, after a flush of songwriting, recorded *Celtic Clasp* with Pippa Jones. The band being 10-strong at times brought forth a few wisecracks – 'alfa Berkshire, or one I particularly liked, 'arda Hearing, prompted by the confused expression on our faces when Lennie shouted something incoherent at a key or tune change.

Julia Feeney and Linda Heneghan both ran Irish dancing schools in Reading. Many of the best nights were enhanced by the feet of young dancers and I know that for musicians to play for a good dancer is a joy. Linda still teaches dancing at the Reading Irish Centre. We had great fun at that time and although Arda Berkshire split up amicably some years ago, all the musicians still play, with a number of them appearing under the name Mighty Craic, while Terry Clarke has recorded a number of CDs.

Local Folk Clubs, Readifolk, Maidenhead, Bracknell, Slough and Nettlebed all have Irish bands and musicians on their guest lists from time to time. The folk music circuit today provides a living for a lot of 'professional' musicians and singers. They justly deserve the monetary rewards and acclaim for bringing their art to the point of group or solo entertainment, holding an audience for two hours or more. For many of us regular session players, or 'pot boilers' as Dick Joyce calls them, Irish Traditional music will always essentially be a very social affair. It lives and breathes in the heart and minds of the people and no amount of money will make a good musician play better in front of a thousand-strong audience, than if they were sitting in a kitchen with friends and a few beers.

Millennium Choice Sara Daniels

Stór Mo Chroí (Treasure of My Heart), sung by Sean Keane, for me epitomises all that folk music and tradition is about. No matter how the emigrant prospered abroad, Erin's soil was always home. Loved ones kept the door open, constant in the hope of their safe return. In today's climate of transience and insecurity the need for roots and someone who cares is as important as ever.

Memories of Moss
Arthur Moss and his choirs

Early in the 20th century, a dominant figure in the musical life of Reading was choirmaster Arthur Moss. He was the moving spirit behind many important concerts and also distinguished himself as composer and arranger.

A number of stories are told about the local choirs of his day. At one time, it seems, whenever rehearsals were in progress at the (old) Town Hall, sandwiches, pies, and other choice morsels, were sent in for the singers from a nearby hotel. As a misguided measure of economy, another caterer was awarded the contract to supply refreshments but these were soon found to be dried-up sandwiches and stale cakes.

The chorus and orchestra hit upon a way of underlining their grievance. As the boy brought in the basket of food they struck up Elgar's 'It comes from the misty ages'. Arthur Moss took the point and made arrangements for the original supplier to provide all future refreshments.

About the same period, the music critic of a local paper wrote with enthusiasm about their performance of the Brahms Requiem, likening it to "A draught of Lutheran beer". This gave rise to some disquiet as many of the singers were drawn from the Temperance Choirs of the borough.

A performance at Reading Town Hall in 1905 of Mendelssohn's 'Hymn of Praise' is thought to be the fastest ever achieved. In those days it was usual to hire professional singers to come down from London for some of the more demanding solo parts. On this occasion, a long work by Elgar occupied most of the concert and the Mendelssohn piece was to end the performance.

Arthur Moss was insistent that the duet, 'I waited for the Lord', should be taken slowly and then it was found that the rest had to be sung at breakneck speed in order that the soloists from London could catch their train.

Tony Barham

The Complete Professional   Laurie Holloway

Although he comes from Lancashire, **LAURIE HOLLOWAY,** the pianist, composer, arranger, and musical director, has lived for more than 30 years in Bray with his wife the jazz singer Marion Montgomery. Playing for artists as disparate as Dame Kiri Te Kanawa and Dame Edna Everage, Laurie has been a professional musician since he was 16. Highlights of his long and distinguished career, which encompasses television, radio, concert performances and recordings, includ playing for royalty and performing as a soloist with the London Symphony Orchestra as well as being their guest conductor for a Summer Pops series at the Barbican. In 1993 the British Academy of Songwriters, Composers and Authors (BASCA) awarded him the Gold Badge of Merit for his services to the music industry

When they asked songwriter Sammy Cahn where he got his inspiration from, he'd say, "First the phone rings." I like the phone to ring and somebody to say, "We've got this big show with a lot of music. How many musicians would you like?" And I'll say, "Well, I'd like a big band with strings, in fact let's have the LSO or something like that." If it's with Kiri Te Kanawa or Elaine Paige, I go to them and routine the tunes they want to do, key and length and everything else, and then come back here and sit down and write it. That's hard work. The first note's hardest and then it's OK, it flows after that, but to write about three minutes of music for a big orchestra like that takes a day, and you've had enough at the end of it. Then I give the score to my copyist and he writes out all the individual parts, and the day comes that you're performing. You go to somewhere like the Barbican and you stand in front of this band and you make a downbeat, and they're playing your arrangement. That's great, just to do it from scratch. And it usually works out all right.

Fortunately for me there aren't that many about who can play piano, do the arrangement, conduct, take care of business professionally, deliver when they want it and do it well, and make sure that anybody working for me does it well – like the copyist producing something legible with no mistakes. They know they can trust me to do that.

I've been sort of rediscovered recently because they're doing some TV variety shows again. I'm working on Michael Parkinson's new BBC TV talk show – we've been friends for years but I've never worked with him before.

When Lenny Henry was a guest, he sang a number on the show – I didn't know he could sing but he was great. He and I didn't actually meet until five o'clock on the afternoon of the show. I had done the arrangement for him before we met. I'd heard what key he did it in and he left the routine up to me. We'd been trying to contact each other on our mobiles but we kept missing each other so when I was having a haircut on the Wednesday morning before the show on Thursday, I sang the arrangement over to him from the hairdresser's. I did it without a piano actually. I arranged it in a dressing room at the BBC on the Monday and Tuesday and I found something quite interesting. I did it quicker without a piano because I didn't go off on any tangents. I didn't have any options. I just had it in my head, and that was the way to do it. If you're sitting at the piano you can get too involved, so I think I'll throw the piano out! So that's really what I like to do.

We were a musical family back in Oldham – we all sang, my dad and my brother played piano, and we were involved in the Mission – but I was the odd one out because I turned pro. I played from about four years old and remember playing *Drink To Me Only With Thine Eyes* in the blackout. At seven I went to a Mr Emmett round the corner for weekly lessons. The great thing about him was that he made me learn the theory of music parrot

Laurie Holloway and Marion Montgomery

fashion before he let me play anything. It helped a lot with sight reading because it gave me the groundwork. Music is mainly mathematics. They often say maths and music go together so if you're good at maths you're good at music.

When I was 11 Mr Emmett said: "That's it, I can't teach you any more", and I went to a classical teacher from 11 to 16. I was always playing piano. Sunday night was Top Twenty night and I used to listen to that and collect all the music. I was playing sport as well, so it was a good time. When I was about 11, I became organist and choirmaster of the Mission, and later started playing for dances. I would go in the music shop all the time but couldn't afford to buy all the music so they let me play in the shop. Then one day, a knock on the door, Monday afternoon, just got home from school, this chap has been to the music shop and asked if they knew a piano player. So they sent him to me. He was a chap called Eddie Mendoza and he was doing the Theatre Royal, Oldham, that week. His piano player hadn't turned up, so I did the week. I was about 14 and terrified, I really was – and I still am relatively but you've got to be a bit nervous. Still it was great playing on that white piano, I'll never forget it. I got £5 for it, a cheque, and it bounced!

At 16, my dad said I should get a proper job, so I became an apprentice draughtsman, but I was earning more money playing for dances than I was at draughtsmanship. I had a good friend who was a singer in a local ballroom, and he'd heard that a chap wanted a piano player so I said, "Right that's it, I'm off." My dad was upset but I called my boss up at work and said I'd like to finish, and he replied, "When?" I said, "Last night", so that was me turning pro at 16. I didn't have any doubts.

That was a good time. We played six nights a week, 7.30pm to 11pm for dancing; you could lie in bed in the morning, go to the pictures in the afternoon; it was tremendous. It was one of the happiest times because once you get successful it gets hard again. I was learning tunes – I could play by ear so if I heard something I could pick it up fairly quickly – and learning to improvise. You'd play the tune through once and then the band leader would say, " Right, you take 16 bars", and then you'd play the melody for a while and then start improvising and that's how jazz starts really.

So that was the beginning of a long, happy musical journey. I played with various bands and then spent two years on the Cunard line, crossing the Atlantic and playing everything from church music and tea music to bingo music and dance music. It was a great experience and during that time I learned to arrange music. Strangely enough, I've since discovered one of my very good friends, John Prescott was on the same ship as a steward at the same time, and we never met. He's done all right, hasn't he?

When I came off the boats I went down to London. There's a street behind the Windmill Theatre called Archer Street, and every Monday afternoon it was packed with musicians, like a labour exchange. I got an audition at the Astoria, Charing Cross Road, with Ronny Round and his Blue Rockets, and I got a job there and also in a strip club called the Gargoyle round the corner. From Monday to Saturday I played 2.30 to 6pm and 7.30 to 10.25pm at the Astoria, and then 10.30pm till 3.15am at the Gargoyle. It was wonderful, you didn't think about hard work then. On Sundays I used to play in a pub at Manor House with a really swinging band. The drummer played with Cyril Stapleton's band, and when Cyril suddenly needed a piano player I went with him for two or three years. Cyril's was a recording band, so through him I met studio musicians and contractors and eventually left to became a freelance. That was the end of that period of being in regular employment. I've always been in work but you never stop worrying when you're a freelance, you look in your diary… and you probably do more because you worry.

A platform for musicians

Marion Montgomery and Laurie Hollway have set up the Montgomery/Holloway Music Trust, as a charity which affords young musical talent (pop, jazz and classical) from the Berkshire area the opportunity to study and perform.

The main aim is to provide platforms for public performance by aspiring singers and musicians to give them insight into the standards required of a professional peformance.

The Trust holds an annual seminar of about five days at which students are tutored in performance craft and the art of accompaniment. Professional performers like Rolf Harris and Jacqueline Dankworth pass on their expertise and there are lectures on subjects ranging from broadcasting techniques and stage management to acting and writing. The students then get an opportunity to perform at three concerts under the headings, Jazz, Classical and Inspirational, the last reflecting Marion and Laurie's Christian beliefs.

Laurie said: "It was Marion's idea and she tends to be more involved in it than I am because I'm pretty busy. Marion gives master classes on performance, and tells students how to walk on stage, how to dress, what to do if something goes wrong. What I like to do is play and hope that they can pick something up from my playing. I can show them little physical tricks you can play – I call them Hot Licks and Funky Tricks. I'm more heavily involved accompanying students. It's very satisfying for us to put something back in the music business."

My aim was to get into studio work because there were only five or six piano players who could do it . I would work three hour sessions – 10am to 1pm, 2 to 5pm, 7-10pm – most days and we used to do jingles before 10am and then after 10pm I'd go and do a jazz club. I was young and healthy.

I started doing theatre work – like Lionel Bart's Blitz at the Adelphi – and television work and I went on the road with Cleo Laine when she left John Dankworth's band and became a solo artist. So I was building up contacts and it went on from there. I became Harry Rabinowitz's right hand man for London Weekend in the 60s and we did lots of live television – Frost on Friday, Frost on Saturday, Frost on Sunday, David Jacobs – all kinds of good variety that's not on television now. Harry didn't play piano or do arrangements, so I did all that for him, and I used to dep for him when he had too much work.

I met my wife, Marion Montgomery, at a club in London. I was working with John Dankworth and the other group was The Dudley Moore Trio, and Dudley and I both fancied Marion. I got in first and we married in 1965.

In 1969 I got a call to do some arranging for the singer Englebert Humperdinck because his arranger had been found mentally exhausted in a car park. They asked me to go on the road with Englebert, and it seemed the right thing to do at the time. I travelled round the world with him as his musical director. Abigail, our daughter, was only three and if I'd been a bit wiser I wouldn't have done it, but I wasn't, so I did. Marion and Abigail came to visit us wherever we were playing and Abigail had a great time but I missed a lot of her growing up.

Financially it was very advantageous. In a way they bought me; it wasn't educational by any means. We'd go out on the road in April with 14 songs and we were still doing the same 14 songs at Christmas time. We went a bit mad actually, that's what happens on the road. There was a group of guys, me conducting, a bass player, a drummer, a guitar player, a road manager, a valet, the tour manager, a representative from Gordon Mills, and Englebert. He and I were mates. We travelled first class while everyone else went economy; we played a lot of golf, we drank too much, and we had a great time. But after five years I'd had enough so I came home and picked up where I'd left off.

I got back with Harry Rabinowitz straight away and worked for London Weekend TV on a freelance basis – it was the good years of music on television. I wrote the signature tunes for shows like *Game For A Laugh*, *Childsplay*, *Punchline*, *Beadle's About*, *Blind Date* – that's been going since 1984 so the royalties are very nice. I've started writing now with Barry Mason, who wrote Englebert's hit, *The Last Waltz*, and *Delilah* for Tom Jones. I always did compose bits and pieces, mainly for

television, but only a song or two. I always figure that a lot of my friends are composers but failed musicians. Tony Hatch was an unsuccessful clarinet player, so he had to do something else. If he'd been successful he wouldn't have been a composer, and if I hadn't been as successful at what I was doing I might have been a composer. You have to make a living in music, so what do you do?

Stephane Grappelli

I've enjoyed playing and writing for great artists like Dame Cleo Laine, Judy Garland, Liza Minnelli, Dusty Springfield, Anthony Newley and Sammy Davis Jr, and one of my more memorable tasks was teaching Elizabeth Taylor to sing *Send in the Clowns*.

One of the greatest musicians was the legendary jazz violinist Stephane Grappelli who was a big friend of mine from 1962. I worked with him when he came over here whenever he used the piano. He had a birthday concert at the Barbican every five years with the LSO. I had the LSO as a band with Stephane playing and me conducting from the piano, and that was a great satisfaction.

I worked with Yehudi Menuhin and Stephane together and I wasn't impressed at all because Menuhin couldn't do what we were doing. Everything was written down, and he was very cold and mechanical. Stephane was just floating loosely – but a brilliant musician. He was wonderful, a one-off.

I think a great person is someone who is a one-off, like Marion is a one-off. There's nobody like her. She doesn't know a lot about music but she's just natural. I like people like Brian Lemon, the piano player in Best of British, he's a natural, and John Dankworth is excellent. He and I are going to do an album , just the two of us, piano and sax. We've been threatening for years. Dame Kiri Te Kanawa and Elaine Page are wonderful to work with. I play on Kiri's popular music albums and appear with her in concert, and I've been Elaine Paige's musical director for years. Anybody who's a big star and who's lasted a long time has got validity; there's something special about them.

Millennium Choice Laurie Holloway

I like all music of quality BUT if you want to be slightly jocular, I am extremely fond of the Blind Date theme as it has improved my standard of living!

Music Among Friends Leighton Park School

Leighton Park, then within the belt of countryside to the South of Reading, was opened in 1890 by a small group of Quakers as a boarding school for boys only. Its standards were to be as good as the best of the public schools, but music was rather a problem. During the pietistic days of Quakerism in the middle years of the 18th century, all the arts were regarded as a forbidden spiritual distraction. Gradually these fears and suspicions had been eroded.

At Leighton Park, while drama remained banned at first, there was a strong Evangelical influence among the school governors, and so it was that a hymn was sung by the whole school at each morning assembly. Hymns were sung in unison: harmony was still felt to offend Quaker insistence on simplicity. Any further reservations about music, however, were swept aside by the boys, nearly all from the homes of the new affluent class of liberalised Quakers.

From the outset, occasional social evenings, held alternately in the two Boarding Houses, were one opportunity for performance. Another was meetings of the Music Society with its committee of boys under adult guidance.

The Music Society with a termly subscription of six (old) pence, developed a varied programme. It included lectures by outside visitors as well as those by the boys. It held informal concerts of its own as well as those for the school and for visitors. It also arranged visits to the many and varied concerts in Reading Town Hall.

The orchestra remained small, until numbers in the school exceeded 200 in the 1950s. By the 1930s, there was "a considerable body of strings (including a double bass), two flutes, two clarinets, one oboe, one bassoon". By the 1950s there were two orchestras in being and a jazz band initiated by the boys was flourishing. There were always fashionable crazes. In the 1960s it was as difficult to escape the noise of aspiring guitarists as it was from novice ukelele players in the 1920s.

Gradually singing gathered support. Small House Choirs became a feature in the general hobbies competitions. Hobbies at times ranked as important as classroom lessons. Each of the House Choirs was conducted by the boys and the fact that singing in harmony was encouraged (in contrast to the unison singing of hymns) added extra interest and excitement.

A Choral Group gradually developed into the Choral Society and was at first independent from the Music Society. In 1947, Fauré's *Requiem* was performed. This was thought to be the first performance of the work by a school in this country. The biennial production of operas (often by Gilbert and Sullivan) alternated with a school play, both under the aegis of the Literary, Historical and Archaeological Society. Once every three years all the Quaker Schools have joined forces for a major singing event. The most recent one (in 1998) was Verdi's *Requiem* in Thaxted Church, organised by The Friends' School, Saffron Walden.

It took nearly 30 years before a small suite of music rooms was built and these soon proved inadequate for the numbers involved. Eventually the hexagonal New Hall was opened in 1972. Beside the hall, a Music School was attached backstage, including a recital room, also hexagonal, and ten individual practice rooms. The New Hall with its large area of movable rostra has allowed imaginatively varied presentations of music and drama, enjoyed over the years not only by the school but by thousands of visitors.

Edward Ballard (1895-1918) was the first 'serious musician' on the staff. Between his time and now the

Leighton Park School orchestra in 1912

The Chamber choir performs at the Society of Heads of Independent Schools conference, Chester, in 1999

The Leighton Park Big Band plays at the Madejski Stadium, 1999. Richmond Rugby Club waas playing Northampton

school has grown from fifty strong to around 360 pupils. Leighton Park welcomed girls into the sixth form in 1975 and became fully mixed in the 1990s. It is not unfair to claim that music and drama have drawn particular benefit from this transformation.

It was not until Humphrey Hare's time (1934-1950) that a solid tradition of music learning and performance was established, such that since his day more than half of Leighton Park pupils learn one or more musical instruments. Humphrey Hare was a remarkable man. His appointment was as the teacher of chemistry. Gifted as a musician – conductor, composer, singer (bass), pianist and cellist – he is remembered as having 'a flair for dramatic interpretations'. Regarding the wider fields of Berkshire music, he established and conducted the Reading Youth Orchestra; and there are many accomplished amateur musicians in Berkshire today who owe their discovery of a flair for music to the guidance and inspiration of Humphrey Hare. He would certainly have been amazed and gratified to have known that, in time, at least two of those in his first orchestra 'came back' to teach their instruments at Leighton Park.

Donald Pitcher (1949-63) was of a different mould, having a great enthusiasm for opera. He revived, adapted and directed A Quaker Opera and also Sheridan-Linley's Duenna; both performances received major appreciative reviews in the national press. Peter Allwood (1975-1979), now the Head of Music at Christ's Hospital, Horsham, brought the Jazz Band, Big Band, and Brass Groups to the fore, whilst Nicholas Houghton (1980-1988) started a series of subscription concerts which were also open to a public mailing list. 1986 saw the first of a number of major overseas music tours when the Big Band went to Kuwait. Since then with Andrew Forbes (1988-97) choirs and orchestral groups have been to France, Italy, and elsewhere in Europe.

If you step through the corridors of the music department today, you will be assailed by a great medley of sounds. Under the direction of Stuart Beer, who came to Leighton Park from Chetham's School of Music in Manchester in 1997, the practice, teaching and recital rooms are in constant use from early morning until well into the evening. More than 200 instrumental lessons are taught each week by 24 visiting teachers, and with individual and ensemble practice as well as the usual class and examination teaching, there are times when it is hard to know where and when to fit everything in!

Young musicians range from beginner brass groups feeling the way on their shiny new instruments to many pupils playing or singing at Grade VIII standard or above. Group activities encompass instrumental and singing ensembles of all standards, including Leighton Park's award-winning Big Band and Jazz Band and the annual staged musical production. Life as a musician at Leighton Park is never dull, often demanding, very diverse and, above all, rich, rewarding and great fun.

How many Old Leightonians have "played for England", you might ask. Sir Richard Rodney Bennett is probably the only name that would be recognised among the nation's composers. At school he was an accomplished pianist, organist and percussionist, and he had already started composing. At the speech day concert in 1950 the orchestra played his variations on Lillliburlero, "which brought the day to an end in a riot of home-produced fun". He also gave the opening recital for the inauguration of the New Hall in 1972.

Such has been the history of music at Leighton Park School. The oak leaf is the symbol of the school. From small acorns large trees grow and 'the school oak' (probably well over 400 years old) still stands proudly next to the music department; and music, after a hesitant start, and without the background of a school chapel, grew and developed with the school, to become a major feature of its life, and to make a significant contribution to the cultural life of Berkshire.

Tim Newell Price

Friends of Mendelssohn The National Authority based in Reading

The great champions of Mendelssohn in this country are Pam and Bill Gulliver who, determined to dispel the many misconceptions about the composer and his work, have founded the Friends of Mendelssohn which they run from their home in Reading. Undeterred by the fact that they are both visually impaired, the couple have become the national authority for information on all aspects of Mendelssohn's life and work. Pam, who has become a recognised expert on Mendelssohn, has written her own book on the composer under her pen name of Mary Allerton-North (a variation on her Northallerton birthplace) and Bill is well-known as a marathon runner raising funds for charity.

Pam founded Friends of Mendelssohn in 1994 after she heard an interval talk about Mendelssohn during a concert on Radio Three. The presenter mentioned a British branch of the International Mendelssohn Foundation but despite her efforts Pam could find nothing about it. Eventually she heard from the headquarters of the Foundation in Leipzig, where Mendelssohn lived in the final part of his life, that the person who had run the British branch had pulled out. As a great admirer of Mendelssohn's music, Pam decided she would research his life and get to know more about him.

She said: "I read one book and I was so angry with the rubbish that the author wrote, so many discrepancies and inaccuracies, that rather than grumble about that particular author I decided to write a book myself exploding some of the myths about him. There were so many and the more I researched the more inaccuracies and discrepancies I found.

"Mendelssohn was always attacked because he came from a wealthy family and therefore by definition his life must have been easy. There was a myth that his father, who was a banker, gave him a great deal of help and quite honestly it was not true. It was Mendelssohn's own determination and personality that got him where he was.

"Mendelssohn's music has never been very popular because critics have always said it was lightweight and frivolous, fit only for drawing rooms, until they tried to play his piano works and then probably found it more difficult. Wagner did a lot of damage by having a phobia about Jews although Mendelssohn's family did become Christian. Bernard Shaw jumped on Wagner's bandwagon and he had a lot of influence. Of course the Nazis banned his music, and banned anything to do with Mendelssohn, even excising anything about him from

Felix Mendelssohn
1809 ~ 1847

studies on music because his family was Jewish."

Pam became his champion and founded Friends of Mendelssohn, a music appreciation society, in order to share her love of the composer and his music. With Bill as chairman, the society met for the first time in 1997 on Mendelssohn's birthday, 3rd February. The first AGM set the pattern for future meetings – business for about an hour and than "a good tuck-in" at an hotel.

Pam said: "We go right through the menu, it's a way of saying thank you. At our first meeting we had Veuve Clicquot champagne, because Mme Clicquot herself gave Mendelssohn 24 bottles of her champagne and intended to do so every subsequent year. However, it was the year before he died so she wasn't able to render that service for very long."

It is a most unusual musical group which reflects the many interests of its hero. Pam said: "We expect our members to work hard. We adopt a Mendelssohnian phrase: 'While I rest, I rust.' I've got a little rhyme:

"Join Friends of Mendelssohn,
Have lots of fun
But there'll always be plenty
Of work to be done."

They advertised in various journals for members and gradually picked up people who shared their interests.

Pam said: "We rely on quality rather than quantity. We have one person from Blackpool who chose Mendelssohn as her special subject on Mastermind; there's someone from Northern Ireland; I was going to say we are negotiating with the Martians at the moment! We are a national organisation and just happen to be living in Reading. We do have quite a few members from the town; they seem to be our working executive and are very keen."

The group meets when there is a particular project in mind. It is planning a holiday in the footsteps of Mendelssohn, visiting various parts of Germany in which he was involved or associated. Team Mendelssohn runs regularly in marathons. Bill has taken part in almost 100 marathons to raise funds for various charities. At the 1999 London marathon he ran in the Friends of Mendelssohn T-shirt in aid of Bobby Moore's bowel cancer fund.

The Team Mendelssohn project for 2000 is to cycle from Reading to Clonmel via Bristol, Swansea, and Düsseldorf, Reading's twin towns, and bring greetings from the Mayor of Reading to promote business, culture and sport in these towns.

Pam explained: "Because Mendelssohn himself was so eclectic we do many different things. He was a tremendous athlete, in fact if the Olympic movement had existed he may well have gone in for the pentathlon if not the decathlon. He was a horseman, oarsman, a marvellous swimmer, always hiking, mountaineering, you name it, he managed it. He found skating too cold, that was the only blot on his sporting copybook.

"In fact, it is because he was such a versatile personality that he is so fascinating. He was a very keen artist as well as an athlete and music seemed to be just one facet of his life."

Bill trained as a violinist under Menuhin and Pam was taught to play the piano reading Braille music and memorising it. Both academics, they set up courses for the Open University and now run a free therapy service from their home.

Pam said: "We live in a purely sighted world, which can be a nuisance but we think our way round it. In our line of work we meet everyone from royalty to dustmen and treat them all the same, as Mendelssohn would. He is our role model."

Bill is convinced of the lasting influence of Mendelssohn. "He gave Wagner his broad sweeps of musical ideas. Wagner 'went fishing' and developed Mendelssohn's music thematically, and then criticised Mendelssohn as a form of smokescreen because he had borrowed from him. You listen to The Ring and you immediately pick up the opening of the first movement of the Symphony No

5, the Reformation, and the Fair Melusine Overture.

"Mendelssohn is the bridge between the classical and romantic periods not only in direct compositional styles but philosophically as well. He was generous to other musicians and singlehandedly raised the standards of singing and musicianship.

"What is so easily overlooked is that without Mendelssohn, Bach would be a minor composer today. It was Mendelssohn who, on being given the score of the St Matthew Passion as a Christmas present, recognised the untapped marvel of this score in 1829. Bach died in 1750 and the last previous performance of the St Matthew Passion had taken place in 1729. He had been quite forgotten. So Mendelssohn revised it and resurrected it for that centenary of that performance in Berlin. It was so popular Mendelssohn was forced to put on another performance by public demand which was sold out. When the third performance took place, Mendelssohn was making his first visit to London.

"He was much more popular in England than he was in his own land, and so much loved that whenever he appeared to conduct a concert or even as a member of an audience, a whisper went round. Yet Mendelssohn was so modest, he was probably his own worst enemy. He would never criticise anybody in public, never write about music, never enter competitions nor judge them."

Pam and Bill, who pride themselves on being 'non-establishment', have made their home into the national headquarters for Mendelssohn research, with a comprehensive Mendelssohn library. They are increasingly used by libraries, students and researchers; Pam has written programme notes for concerts, sleeve notes for a CD by the concert pianist Vanessa Letarche, and continues her campaign to correct the mistakes and misconceptions about Mendelssohn made by broadcasters.

Pam fulminated: "I was so insulted once when a know-all from the Mendelssohn Foundation visited us. He said: 'You are very emotional but you're not focused.' I thought well, I don't care about being emotional but I am certainly focused."

Something a Shade Macho? Reading Male Voice choir

A terrible début did nothing to deter Reading Male Voice Choir. Since then things have looked up, writes GWYN ARCH

I suppose it all really began on a Saturday in June, 1971. There I was, conducting the summer concert of my village mixed voice choir, the South Chiltern Choral Society. It was the usual ragbag of part songs and madrigals relieved by the occasional guitar solo, soprano aria or whatever in those days characterised the final concert of the season. Looking back, I guess it was pretty indifferently performed because there never was enough preparation time. The 'big' event of the year always took place around Easter and at the end of March that year we had performed Beethoven's *Mass in C* and a Byrd unaccompanied Mass, leaving about eight or nine rehearsal opportunities to assemble the ingredients of the summer event.

So I thought I would cheat a little and deviously devise a way of squeezing a bit more rehearsal time. I suggested to the tenors and basses that as a contrast to all the (rather precious) madrigals we were learning they might like to do a couple of male voice items to fill out the concert. Something a shade macho with maybe a hint of sexual prowess? They fell for it, of course, and it was a simple matter to persuade them to come to my house for extra rehearsals. So there we were, 20 men, a more informal environment, hearty, swaggering repertoire, glasses of beer, male banter, etc, and they liked it. They loved it. They couldn't get enough of it. "In the autumn," they said, "why don't you form a male voice choir

separate from the choral society? There hasn't been one in this area since the Reading Police choir disbanded years ago. We'll all join. Please."

"OK," I said. "If you promise to support me, I'll get an article organised for the local paper, backed up with an advert, and we'll give it a go."

The first rehearsal of RMVC (*you* work it out!) took place in Caversham Further Education Centre on 15th October. It attracted eight men, and of these I recognised one. One solitary member from SCCS. Nineteen defectors already. We launched ourselves into a simple arrangement of the spiritual *Steal Away*. After all, we were booked to do a ten-minute cabaret spot for some kind of social/dance at Alfred Sutton school five weeks later. I thought a reasonably good start had been made.

The following week, numbers fell to six (1.5 men per part!) and I wondered, "Where did I go wrong?" but it turned out to be the nadir, and to this day holds the record for lowest attendance at any rehearsal. By the time our cabaret spot came along I think there were about 12 men who braved the curiosity and incredulity of the Alfred Sutton crowd. We managed to get through S*teal Away* and made uncertain inroads into some other little ditty. I *can* recall making a surreptitious escape through a side door. It was a truly terrible début.

After that, it would be fair to say that things looked up a bit. We entered our first competitive festival and the Chronicle printed the joyous news that the newly-formed RMVC had come second in this prestigious event (held at Brent Town Hall). If you come in the first three the contest is invariably described as prestigious. Anyway, it was jolly decent of the paper not to point out that there were only two choirs in this competition, and the one that won was streets better. Possibly we had forgotten to give them this information?

Reading Male Voice choir at Huddersfield Town Hall in 1986

Anyway, our rehearsal facilities certainly became more prestigious – the 18th (?) century barn that served as the main music studio at Highdown School, and a few years later the chapel in Broad Street (the one that has now been converted into a branch of Waterstone's). It had a flattering acoustic, but unfortunately this leads a choir towards a belief that they are a lot better than they really are, so a move was made to the main music studio of Bulmershe College, where I happened to be head of the music department, where parking was much better, and where choir members could pretend to be academically-minded in order to take advantage of student-union bar prices. When I left the college in 1985 this ideal rehearsal facility had to be abandoned, and for the last 15 years the men have met every Friday evening in a primary school hall in Woodley, where the parking is still fine, but the coffee brew not quite so heady.

Over the years the choir has grown, of course, usually in inexplicable spurts, but today (1999) hovers in the low seventies. I don't believe in auditions – this is a community activity. In fact, the men audition themselves. They either stick with it (often finding the act of memorising the words much harder than the notes), or melt away after a few weeks. There can't be many other choirs in the district with 39 tenors!

The standard has improved along with morale and application, and we no longer sidle away. Indeed, it's often a case of staying a little longer to sing an encore. Competitions don't attract us much, but having been auditioned by the BBC in 1977 in Reading Town Hall (the finest building in Reading for singing and unbelievably closed for the last 20 years!) we won through to represent the United Kingdom in the international rounds of the radio contest Let the Peoples Sing in 1978, eventually succumbing to the superior artillery of a male voice choir from Bulgaria. There have been other competitions, too. It turns out that there are two Cheltenham Gold Cups, one for horses and the other for voices. We won the latter some years ago.

I suppose that the best things about the choir are: a) the rapport, b) the concerts, c) the music and d) the tours. A few sentences about each and my meanderings are over. The rapport, the sense of belonging/identifying, the companionship, is amazing. Here we have a huge cross section of society. Very few jobs, trades and professions go unrepresented. I need advice on plumbing, electrics, building an extension? – all obtainable in the interval on Friday evening. Life from the point of view of a customs officer, computer systems installer, teacher, railway engineer, sports journalist, trade union officer, Formula I racing team engineer, managing director, classic car restorer, prison governor, engineer, air traffic controller, health centre administrator, hearse driver, TV reporter?

The concerts are at the heart of it all; trying to persuade others that this song that we enjoy so much is worth listening to; the attempt to communicate enthusiasms. On average, the choir performs once a month. In 28 years this is well over 300 concerts in churches, school halls, community centres, concert halls – and chapels! They are all different, environmentally, atmospherically, and in the effect on the listeners (even though the audience is invariably laced with our supporters).

However, on the whole we seem to be winning over our audiences more readily than in earlier years. It's quite an operation, too, these days. The choir has its own liveried trailer, (courtesy of our current sponsor, the Head Partnership, solicitors in Lower Earley), and it's cram full of portable, purpose-made staging, amplifiers, microphones, (we provide our own comperes for the concerts), loudspeakers, and the sometimes reluctantly necessary electric piano for venues that don't have their own. The trailer goes on ahead and everything is set up before the main body of singers arrive. Pretty well all the concerts are for charities and fund-raising of all types. Raising £1,000 or so is frequent, not that we feel goody-goody about it – we need outlets for all that rehearsing!

Then there's the repertoire. The librarian tells me that he has just under 300 sets of songs, every single one learned by heart at some stage or other. At any one time the choir is ready to perform about 20 items at the drop of a hat. When a new song has been rehearsed and committed to memory it is then incorporated into the programme for the next concert, and the one that has been in the repertoire longest is dropped.

There is thus a process of continuous evolution of the material – it takes about two years to turn round completely. I am able to indulge one of my hobbies, too, so my own choral arrangements feature regularly and their effect on audiences gauged. Some of them have even lasted the full two years, and have been published and sung by other choirs, so in a small way I think we are beginning to influence the somewhat old-fashioned repertoire of the average male choir.

I'm very fortunate to have had the same accompanist and deputy from the beginning. He is Clive Waterman, the headmaster of (could it be?) the very Woodley primary school where we rehearse. Now there's a coincidence! Clive always conducts one or two items in the concerts, and I play for him. It's a great partnership, and maybe, when I go, the committee will be able to save money on advertising for a new conductor.

Finally, the tours. Here I can be truly succinct. We have given concerts in Ireland, Germany, Italy, Holland, Norway, Majorca, France, Switzerland, Spain, Wales, Leicestershire, Oxford, Thatcham, Tilehurst… Am I beginning to ramble?

Still in the Mood The MillsTones Dance Band

MALCOLM LEE tells the story of the The MillsTones Dance Band and dedicates it to the memory of the band's founder Frank Mills

"It's because we are dinosaurs," came the reply after I had taken the opportunity during a break in rehearsal to find out from the members of the band why we hadn't been getting many gigs recently. Our rehearsal that night at the Scout hut in Evendon's Lane, Wokingham, took on a different tone as the possible death knell had been sounded. Or was it being sounded prematurely?

The MillsTones is a Big Band playing the music of the Glenn Miller, Count Basie, Stan Kenton, Duke Ellington era and has amongst its members some truly talented players. I may not be in that class but having been lead trumpeter of the band for over 25 years I certainly have had the privilege of sitting amongst so many excellent players at rehearsals and at gigs. Blowing my own trumpet I have to say that I must have something after all these years, or is it just because I am secretary, treasurer, gig finder, letter writer, gig pad 'looker-after', stage-setter-upper and clearer-upper, gig psychic "where's the toilets?", that the rest of the band put up with me?

I don't do it all though, oh no. Where would I be without the MillsTones – Paul Tungay, second trumpet, who has played his silky solos with such greats as Frank Sinatra and Syd Lawrence, Geoff Hartnell, third trumpet, who gives me moral support as he calmly gets on with the electrics at gigs and keeps my tensions in check as I faff about waiting for the last player to arrive at the gig with only minutes to spare, Steve Kerry, first trombone, Malcolm Stewart, second trombone, and Len Pibworth, third trombone, all who help provide that distinctive Glenn Miller sound. Then there's Lol Simmons, baritone sax/clarinet and founder member, Clive Downs, second alto sax/oboe, Alan King, first alto sax/soprano sax/clarinet, who often comes to my rescue with names of deps who can help us out at short notice, Trevor Hayward, first tenor and the band's best supplier of jokes, Dave Thomson, bass player and weather man, Ernie Cox, percussionist with so many cases, David Jones, piano and trumpet, Lynn Harrison, vocalist ,and last but not least, Stuart Cawthorne, second tenor and the present leader.

Since I became secretary of the band in 1980, 1 have noted that on the 220 gigs we have played, we have used 105 different musicians from the Berkshire area. Some have been professional players and others learners, but all have shown an equal enjoyment and love of playing our style of music.

In 1973 I was invited to fill the vacant first trumpet position by the founder and leader of the band, Frank Mills. (The name of the band, when it was started by Frank several years before, was made up of Frank's surname and the word Tones.) I had known Frank for some time as both he and I were members of the Sandhurst Silver Band. The previous first trumpet player had also been a member of Sandhurst and my bumper-up player on solo cornet at the time was also the MillsTones' drummer. Nigel Simmons, son of Lol Simmons, the baritone player in the present Millstones line-up, also played at Sandhurst and later with the MillsTones. Frank had a long history of music, in particular brass bands having hailed, proudly, from Oldham in Lancashire. It should be noted that they are brass bands oop north, not yer softy southerner silver bands.

Frank didn't mince words, he told it as it was and we all admired him for it. He was a leader you respected for his knowledge and belief in helping others to enjoy music whether it was the players who "didn't do it for the money" or the many different types of audiences. Frank always had them eating out of the palm of his hand with his cheeky asides and wishes for a "safe journey home" and "look out for the bogey men."

"We've had a request for this number," Frank used to say to the audience and the trumpet section then imitated Pinocchio's long wooden nose as we questioned among ourselves the non-appearance of anyone who could have possibly requested such a piece of music. It was Frank's enthusiasm that generated such a warm feeling amongst

The MillsTones

band members and audiences alike and was dashed so sadly as his life ended in 1995 at the age of 71 following a heart attack at the wheel of his car. To Maureen, his widow, I dedicate the following stories in Frank's memory.

Lol Simmons and his son Nigel have more in common than the fact they have both played in the band. Both have found unexpected ways to get off the stage, Nigel's route being rather more spectacular than his father's. One evening in Camberley the MillsTones were playing a concert to a packed hall. During the playing of *Little Brown Jug* the person in charge of the spotlight wanted to show his knowledge of Glenn Miller's classic by throwing the switches to the stage lighting, leaving one spotlight on Nigel as he stood to play the famous second trumpet solo. Nigel's performance was rock steady; unfortunately the return to his seat was far from that for as he was sitting down he moved the chair backwards and fell over the back of the stage. To his credit Nigel still held on to his trumpet although all that could be seen by the audience, thanks to the skill of the spotlight technician, was his legs pointing to the ceiling.

At the next gig in Arborfield a few weeks later, not to be outdone, his father Lol, playing baritone, fell off the side of a raised platform as he moved his chair sideways. There may be no connection between their surname Simmons and the past local brewery, but the drinks were certainly on these two!

We have played in village halls, town halls, concert halls, tents, barns and boats and, thanks to a double booking, the MillsTones once found themselves travelling up to the West End to play at a dinner dance at the famous Savoy Hotel. Our pianist was expected to play background music during the meal that evening, with the band to follow, but just before the night of the gig, our pianist fell ill and after many frantic phone calls and thoughts of "let's call the whole thing off", a young pianist, a student at The University of Reading, recommended by a friend of a friend of one of the band members, was found. This was one of those occasions when a gamble paid off as our young pianist, unknown and unrehearsed, wowed his audience with some superb playing and contributed to a memorable evening. So delighted was the audience that we were invited back and we have dined out on that story more than once, but not on the Savoy's sandwiches which, it has to be said, were the soggiest we have ever eaten.

The Savoy, where stars appear, is not the only exotic location we have played at. Hartland, North Devon, can also display some wonderful stars. Having performed for the gentry in London we were invited to play at the Hartland Cricket Club's annual dinner and dance. This was one gig we were not going to be able to drive down

to and back on the same night, so the local people of Hartland kindly found places overnight for band members and, to make a proper weekend of it, our partners too. I can tell you that away from the light pollution of the big towns the stars shine very brightly in deep and darkest Devon. I looked at them for quite a few hours after our gig, having sampled a few jars of cider. They also make better sandwiches in the West Country to which my dog Jamie could testify when he went into the village hall at the end of the gig to help finish them off.

Not only the stars in the sky come out at night, so do the stars of stage and screen to hear the MillsTones play *Moonlight Serenade*, etc. Around Maidenhead and in particular, Bray, you could be mistaken for thinking you were in Berkshire's equivalent of Beverly Hills and on several gigs when the local celebs are asked to assist with charity money-raising functions we have found those stars dancing to our music. Marion Montgomery, Laurie Holloway, Dorothy Squires, Mary Parkinson, Rolf Harris, and Susan George's mum are a few I can remember who have tripped the light fantastic with the MillsTones. Local Wokingham MP John Redwood has also been able to help out his local party members at their fundraising dances and has shown that he can dance better than he can sing, but only just. Just for the record John Redwood always sees red when we play. The band wears red shirts.

None of this could have been possible without Frank Mills. He was always there to guide us and I know that he would not let the recent lack of gigs get in the way of the band members enjoying rehearsing this style of music. I'm not sure he would agree with the 'dinosaurs' theory. Even now beginners turn up at the Scout hut in Wokingham to learn to play big band music – a sign that we have a future. Frank would be pleased. So are we.

Let us hope that with the new millennium, people will be in the mood again for *In The Mood* and that the MillsTones will have many more "safe journeys home" to come.

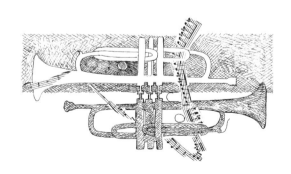

Playing the Pans Meadway Fiesta Steel Band

Over the years the fame of the steel band at Meadway School in Tilehurst has spread far and wide. It was the brainchild of a teacher there, LEONORA JONES

I knew nothing about steel bands and pan playing when I started the Meadway Fiesta Steel Band in 1976 but I had appreciated the wonderful sounds made by some of the local bands already established in Reading – especially at Carnival time. At that time Meadway School was on two sites, with the lower school at the old Wilson Road School site and the senior school at the present Meadway site. We had a large number of West Indian children on roll, so I started a steel band for them with the help of a member of staff, Horace Seegobin. We purchased some instruments from a school which was renewing its 'pans' (they are *not* called drums!) and we were guided into the skills of pan playing by a helpful parent, Percy McCleod – known as Mac – who had his own adult steel band. He continued to help with the music training from those first days until his retirement in 1999. He will be greatly missed and we would like to express our thanks to him.

I discovered that although the pans start their lives as discarded oil drums, many highly skilled stages of workmanship are expended upon them before they reach the level of being musical instruments. They vary in quality of course – as do all musical instruments – and though our original starter purchases were of modest value, our chromed pans which we use currently were £500 each and they are even more expensive to buy now.

I also learned that the world of pan playing is full of paradoxes. For example, the 'sticks' used to play these £500 pans are merely pieces of dowelling or bamboo, with strips of rubber wrapped around the tops where they contact the pan surface and all are of varying weight, thickness and length of 'lapping' to suit the size of the pan and the players' preferences. The basses are played with two halves of a rubber ball mounted onto the ends of two wooden sticks. The expensive rhythm pans are suspended from metal stands (usually home made) on lengths of nylon string looped over 'Z' shaped hooks made from bits of metal coat hangers! (Curious onlookers wonder why I always carry a supply of spare hooks, string, rubber strips and scissors in my bag).

Our first band 'costumes' consisted of loose-fitting cotton tops designed with orange tie-and-dye patterns which were made for us by a member of staff.

For the first few years the band was all male and all West

The Meadway Fiesta Steel Band

Indian and those pupils laid down the foundations of our local reputation on which future bands would build. In fact, two pupils, Ricky Greaves and Michael Romeo, went on to form bands in London. Then the Lower School was moved up to the Meadway site, the catchment area changed and we had the transition to a mixed membership with more girls. It has stayed that way to this day.

When Mr Seegobin left Meadway, another teacher, Trevor Smith, kindly offered to take over his role and has been the band's manager for the last 21 years. His cheerful, unflagging enthusiasm and tireless work has helped to build it into a successful outfit which is much in demand.

Transporting the band and its players to bookings was originally quite a problem. Saloon cars which were totally inadequate would be sent to take us to functions and sometimes they didn't even arrive. One summer day our 'transport' was very late arriving and we had been standing by the band equipment out in the playground for over an hour. The lads in the band got very bored and said, "Can we set up the pans and play while we're waiting? At least it will give us something to do!" So we set up the band and one of the tenor pan (melody) players started to make up a tune. The rhythm and bass players found which key he was playing in and began to add simple harmony and bass parts. By the time our 'transport' eventually arrived, a new melody (named *Meadway Calypso*) was ready to play and we included it in that afternoon's programme! It is still played, with a few additions, by the younger band to this day.

We started hiring our own van for bookings which was an improvement but often an organisational nightmare. The biggest change to our fortunes came when the school purchased its own minibus and we were almost self-contained. However, the pans had no cases and were strapped to the roof rack and covered in polythene sheeting. Going to a booking on one particularly windy day, the covering worked loose and we were alarmed to notice that while going down a steep hill we were 'overtaken' by one of our pans rolling past us!

Over the next few years we bought good quality chrome pans and cases to protect them, the minibus was updated and we bought a proper trailer for the four big bass pans. A valued friend of the band, Rick Legate made a covered extension for it and also a big tent. Now we could travel in style and be protected from the elements when we played. Only once was the weather so wet and windy that, try as they might, Mr Smith and the children could not hold the tent down long enough to peg it before the wind lifted them and the tent into the air.

During this time the band had increased in number and new 'costume' tops had been needed twice. The first replacement set was designed and made for us by another member of staff, Miss Guthrie, and when those had been outgrown, yet another patient member of staff, Mrs McDonnell, kindly made us another set from fabric chosen by a group of pupils from the band. Currently, with larger numbers in the band, it has proved more practical to have one-colour T-shirts with the band logo as an integral part.

Over the past 23 years, I have had the pleasure of arranging most of the music for the band and teaching a succession of wonderfully loyal, talented and keen children who have given up their time to rehearse, sometimes two or three times a week and willingly come out on bookings on most weekends during the summer months and quite a few during the rest of the year. When they have left school to go to university, college, or the world of work, they have been replaced from a 'learner' band of pupils from lower down the school.

As the band's fame has spread we have played at a very wide range of venues including London (Park Lane Hilton Hotel and Holiday Inn), Ascot (Silver Ring), Newbury (Racecourse), Elm Park football ground (England Under 21s International), TV appearances, Radio 210, and countless local civic receptions, fêtes, dinners, and weddings.

In the days prior to the pedestrianisation of Broad Street we regularly busked at Christmastime outside Marks & Spencer's by the covered bus stops. Our 'captive audience' would dance to the music while waiting for their buses, sometimes becoming so involved that the buses came and went without them even noticing!

We have built up an extensive network of liaison with local primary schools, senior citizens' organisations, and various charity groups and have taken part in the Tilehurst Eisteddfod many times, winning our 'class' on most occasions, sometimes with honours. We have recorded five different cassette tapes and our two most recent ones are available at the school office.

One of the earlier line-ups for the steel band

'Playing pan' gets into your bones and it is hard just to stop playing. We have many ex-pupils who have come back to play in the band – Greg Goodwin, Camilla Hancock and Katharine MacKinnon to name but a few – and our irreplaceable drummer Stephen Whale, who is now a professional drummer and has his own entertainment business has always stayed with us and still drums at our bookings. Many thanks Steve!

A group of ex-pupils have now been formed into an old pupils' band and take on the late night, more sophisticated bookings. A new logo and identity has been designed for the band by Neil Jones (who designed our original logo and business cards). Trevor Smith does the same magnificent job of managing all the schedules and bookings and of course drives the minibus to all the venues, loading and unloading the equipment with the help of the band members – and his unfailing sense of humour! New Millennium – here we come!

The steel band is a twentieth century Third World invention, having its roots in Trinidad and Tobago in the Caribbean. The legend of steel pans is that oil drums were left abandoned on the beaches of Trinidad by the American forces after the war. Like jazz was the music of the poor in the USA, so the oil drums became an instrument of struggle, not considered respectable, the panyards often being the centre of violent clashes. In time, however, the steel band came to be recognised for its worth.

The Trinidad government, after independence, encouraged major companies to sponsor bands, and pans began to be socially acceptable. Steel pans were first introduced to the UK in 1951 as part of the Festival of Britain. The band was called TASPO – Trinidad All Steel Percussion Orchestra – and was invited to play as part of the Commonwealth. August 1965 saw the first carnival held in London, where one steel band and 500 revellers represented little more than a makeshift operation. By 1973 carnival took on a mass creative form, more steel bands surfaced, supplemented by reggae music.

Mary Genis

'I Can Do That' MOBO

ANTHONY 'BIRD' THOMPSON has become well-known as a singer and now has become involved in helping other young musicians to get their music heard

It's very weird. There is no music in the family, although my mum has always had a voice, yet I have such a passion for my music that I would drop anything for it and my mum knows it. I don't know where it comes from. At school my music teacher came up to me one day, pulled me out in front of the whole class and said: "You have the most amazing voice." Then when we were studying *Joseph and his Amazing Technicolor Dreamcoat*, Joseph was being played by a young boy who couldn't sing. They wanted me to sing the part but said Joseph had got to be a white guy so they asked me to sing behind the curtain and he would mime it. I was only about 13 and I got a bit stroppy about it but it really did hurt and I almost stopped singing.

The music started when I was about six. I used to take my mum's knitting needles and start hitting them on the tables. My mum bought me my first little drum set one Christmas which she teased me with. She gave everybody else their presents and I got nothing. It wasn't until the afternoon and I was sitting there feeling miserable that she gave me the key to the house next door and I went in and there was this drum set. She says she will never forget going in there and seeing me banging those drums. As soon as I sat at the kit that was it. I taught myself to play and it just went from there.

The first time I got to play was with the West Indian Women's Circle Steel Band that was touring the area. The musicians were all young boys of about 15. The drummer didn't turn up and I looked at the drum kit and said, "I can do it". I was much younger than the others but I started to turn up to more rehearsals and it progressed from there. It was a full-size drum kit but I raised the seat and my head just appeared over the top.

I was playing at school in carnivals and things like that and Jeff Hinds was doing all the teaching. He was running his own band, Star Rhapsody, at the same time and I started doing gigs with them. They didn't have a singer and I said, "I can do that."

From there we started to do gigs at the Hexagon, going up north to Manchester, Liverpool, all over the place and we toured for three or four years. People started calling me 'Bird' and would ring me up and say: "Can I speak to Bird, please," and my mother would say: "Bird? What Bird? I haven't got any chickens in my house!"

Once my voice broke I got these really deep notes. I still have this big range from falsetto to very deep. My vocals have changed so much over the years and my voice is like an instrument which varies depending on what style of music I do. I have three types of vocals:, a very soft tone, a very powerful operatic voice, or I take both sounds and mix them together. I've never had any tuition, I've done

Anthony 'Bird' Thompson

everything on my own but now I would really like to learn the piano and practise the guitar because the two would aid me so much in what I want to do.

When I was about 14, I went in for a talent show at the old Central Club. People were going on stage and doing a little something and I was standing there when I felt this almighty shove in my back and I went flying forward. It was the organiser and he said, "Yes, you." I said, "No", but I went on and that was one of my biggest nights because the moment I started singing the whole place went mad and it just grew from there.

One of the groups I sang with did a lot of covers so I would write down the lyrics and listen to the artist so that I could portray how that artist did a song. I listened to a variety of artists and the good thing was it allowed me to vary my styles of music. People began to realise I could sing a lot of different songs and as I got older and did more talent shows, I began to cross over from calypso and reggae to soul and a bit of jazz.

I started to do shows at the Hackney Empire which was a real confidence booster. They had huge crowds and if the people didn't like you they would just boo you off. I'll never forget walking on that stage and seeing all those people there. The guy who went on before me was wearing a big white suit and he got his introduction and just walked on the stage and everyone went "Boo". He didn't even start singing. And the lady who was introducing the acts said, "You've got to calm down and give him a chance", but they just said, "Get off ,we don't like your suit, boo." He came off the stage and she just called my name and my heart started thudding. I thought I just can't go on, the crowd's still booing. She called me out again and I said, "I'm not going out like that. Bring the mic over." She brought it over to where I was, still hidden behind the curtain, and I just started singing and I knew I had them in my hands.

I came out on stage singing a new calypso I had just written and off it went and the whole crowd started dancing. I'll never forget it. It was one of the ways I managed to handle the crowd. I came off the front of the stage and went into the crowd and started dancing with them and shaking hands. All of a sudden I looked up saw this huge woman haring down the hall and she grabbed hold of me and started dancing round and round in circles and I'm singing and thinking, "Oh my God!" Then I thought I'd better get back on the stage but as I went to pull away the mic had wrapped itself round both of us so I couldn't get away from her. She noticed this and started dancing round the other way to loosen it. But she was carrying one of those dinky handbags and part of the lead was still wrapped around it so as she went back to her seat and I went back to the stage still singing, the mike just whisked out of my hands and I had to run back up to her. It looked as though I had gone back to take her to her chair and sit her back down and all the crowd started clapping.

I got back on top of the stage and it went really well. I didn't win – the girl that won had been on three weeks in a row and she had won it before she got to the mic – but it boosted my confidence even more.

Then I toured for two years here and in Europe with a group who were very big in Surrey, Spliff Riff. Now I'm busy setting up deals, writing my own material, helping people with their vocals, and doing a hell of a lot of recording. I still play drums.I've also been very involved in getting people to contribute tracks to this CD that has just been produced in Reading. *Talic* is a compilation CD of music of black origin by Reading artists, mainly from Oxford Road, and it was commissioned by Reading Borough Council African Caribbean Arts Development. We did not realise how big it would be; there were about 40 bands who submitted tracks and we managed to get them down to 16. Having that number of people coming forward was absolutely amazing. It showed us the amount of talent there is in Reading. If only someone could tap into that source.The feedback has been really something, there's such a variety of music in it and it has given a lot of people the chance to get their music heard. The only thing is I think it's a shame they didn't try to sell the CDs. People value them more and it would have raised funds to make another CD.

My dream is to play in front of at least 100,000 people. It was something told to me by a woman who read my palm. I'm not really into that but it was very strange – everything she said has happened. I've always drawn crowds. It gives me butterflies but the moment I start singing I'm in my element. It happens every show I do. I've built up enough confidence over the years to think, What have I got to lose?

And I really want my mum to see me sing. She has put up with a lot but she has never come to one of my shows.

'The Prophet of Reggae'
The influence of Bob Marley

The reggae star Bob Marley, who died in Miami on 11th May, 1981, aged 36, put reggae music and Jamaica firmly on the world map, influenced many, making him a symbol of rebellion, "the prophet of reggae", and a constant source of inspiration, not least among local people in the music industry.

Anthony 'Bird' Thompson said: "Bob Marley said so much and he did so much, and it wasn't till he passed away that people sat down and listened to what his music had to say. Bob's words will always say something. Obviously I listen to lots of others but with Bob it's the message that comes across that really helps and inspires me at the same time. I don't think I've ever come across another artist who has been able to do what Bob has done and still have the same significance years down the road. It's universal. That's the key to it."

Reading's reggae artist Aqua Livi remembers the first time he heard Rebel Music from the 'Natty Dread' album: "it inspired me to put the rebel into my music. Bob inspired me to locks up and understand the meaning of carrying locks." Aqua felt strongly that Marley was instrumental in making reggae more accessible. "Because of who he was and the time he was born as Joseph, with the coat of many colours, he fed the world with spiritual wheat that showed the uplifting of humanity."

Marley performed at Madison Square Gardens, New York, in 1980 with the Commodores, Curtis Blow, Dionne Warwick, Stevie Wonder. Reading saxophonist Izzy, privileged to be present, recalls the experience, one he will never forget. "Bob's performance was professional and natural, an inspiration. He brought strong lyrical content. His words are true, deep and meaningful, not about girl meets boy but more about things that matter in the world then and now. He put across lyrics 25 years ago that still stand strong today."

Izzy feels that reggae music has been exploited throughout the years, artists not getting enough recognition for the works and the media using reggae for advertising. He pointed out that reggae has become more experimental, fusing with other music forms where reggae artists are now chatting over drum'n'bass, garage and hip hop tunes. "Everything in life has it's time, our time is now!"

Reggae studio producer and musician Rej Forte said: "The first Marley album I bought was a Trojan release from the Lee Perry sessions, Soul Rebels. I liked it but didn't understand it at the time which intrigued me. Marley wasn't singing love songs. Once Marley signed to Island and released Catch a Fire, attitudes started to change. Listen to the guitar solo on Concrete Jungle played by Wayne Perkins, a US West Coast rock musician who just happened to be in the studio when Chris Blackwell was overdubbing the track. It works!

Mary Genis

'Big People' Dances MOBO

CLAUDETTE HENRY remembers how the coming of reggae was a musical turning point for young black people in Reading

In the late '60s and early '70s there was very little choice of clubs for the young black person in Reading. Pop music was the Beatles, the Stones, the Who, Englebert Humperdinck, Tom Jones or worse – country & western (in our house anyway!) – none of which really appealed. Like many of his generation, my Dad loved country & western and you would be hard pressed to find a black household during that period without at least one Jim Reeves album (he HAD to go!). However, from America came Soul, Motown, The Jackson Five, Stevie Wonder and other black groups with whom we could relate.

The musical turning point for West Indians in the UK came in about 1972 soon after the Black Power movement in the US which had us all in the biggest flares and matching Afro to assert our identity. That turning point came with Bob Marley and the influence of reggae music and the Rastafarian movement. At the time, no English person knew of Marley and other artists like Gregory Isaacs, Dennis Brown, U-Roy, and Aswad. It was a Black thing – as they say. However, locally there were not a lot of places to go and hear this new music. The only entertainment was what was referred to as 'Big People' dances which were held in hired halls by the adults usually with a live band (either steel band or calypso band). As teenagers we attended these with our parents (no choice) and at the time it was the only way we could go out to meet other teenagers. In general, provided you could wander off on your own, it seemed to work well with both generations going out together.

Other alternatives were to go to Top Rank /Night Owl in Station Road, a disco where you could get soul music – if you were old enough to get in. (It had closed down by the time I reached the right age and is now a bingo hall!) If you were a boy, of course, you could take in the music scene as far away as Skindles in Maidenhead or even London if you had that precious commodity – a car.

But when reggae came on the scene, there was no reggae club in Reading (and even today we still have to travel to London for these). However, many of the local boys came together to set up sound systems. This was much more than a disco, it was a cultural activity. The members usually made these huge sound boxes out of wood (at least six) with the biggest amplifiers they could find. They took up most of the space in smaller venues. Most times it took six or more boys to carry each box.

There was someone to mix the music, a 'toaster' who would rap lyrics over the records and get the crowd moving, there would be endless hangers-on (or box boys) whose job was to carry the boxes in and help with stringing up (this also meant they got in free). The boxes would be painted with the Rasta colours – red, gold and green – and other Rastafarian symbols like the 'lion of Judah' and the name of the sound. They often had their own slogans and jingles to announce their sound. It was very creative. Today most of the 'Sounds' use more powerful equipment but are not as big.

Claudette Henry

Being in a 'Sound' attracted lots of girls and as many of the sound guys were into Rasta and starting to wear dreadlocks, the girlfriends began to crotchet Rasta hats for their men. Ironically, these woollen hats, for which the Rastas were at first ridiculed, took off as fashion a few years later.

The sound systems brought new life to these big people dances, much to the disgust of many of our parents who found the music too loud, didn't like the positive messages, and 'back to Africa' themes. In our house reggae was banned and (like many others) we used to sneak around to hear Reggae time on Radio London on a Sunday afternoon (with the volume turned really low) and record it before our parents found out. Reggae was a Jamaican thing, of course, but I can recall now how almost all the guys I met said they came from Kingston, Jamaica, a few years later revealing themselves to be from Barbados and other islands.

We still went to big people dances but now there were always sound systems, and with them the opportunity for girls to get together with boys out of sight of parents. Eventually the sound systems began hiring their own halls and holding dances for young people with often two or more 'Sounds' playing, competing for the audience's attention. Every year there would be a cup match where different 'Sounds' from all over Berkshire would come to compete. The criteria, as I recall, was who could play the best tunes and also the very latest tunes to entertain the crowd. Many 'Sound' men spent a fortune getting stuff direct from Jamaica on export to be the first in town with the tune. The crowd would judge the winner.

I can't remember all the names of the sound systems but people tended to support different 'Sounds' because they were a group of friends or family and follow them whenever they played. For some girls this also depended on whether the guys were good looking or not. London 'Sounds' were always popular with the girls – which made the Reading guys jealous of the attention that guys from London seemed to get from local girls.

'Rockers' were in my opinion the most popular sound in town for many years and I remember when they won many cup clashes. It was really exciting as other sound systems such as 'Sir Marcus' and 'Masai' just didn't compare. Today 'Sweet Sensation' are probably the last of the 'old school' sound systems and are very popular. Many of their most popular 'revive' tunes today are the tunes us thirty-somethings grew up with first time round.

As for the reggae scene – well, everyone knows it now, but for me the early days of reggae through dub, lovers and more recently ragga has been a journey of developing a black British way of life linked to our Caribbean/African roots. For many of us growing up in England, we had to find our identity within British society, as we had either been brought here from the Caribbean to join families or were born here and did not know about our African /Caribbean heritage.

Many of the songs also dealt with and raised awareness of social issues when we had no other voice to express it, for example *13 dead and nothing said* – about the Deptford fire in which 13 youngsters at a house party were killed by an arsonist but no action was taken to find the person and the grieving families were ignored by both the press and the royal family. (When a similar incident happened two weeks later in Ireland, the Queen was the first to send a message of sympathy.) And *Police and Thieves* was a comment on the spate of inner city riots in the UK. This popular track led to several spin-off tunes with the same theme.

Being outside London it was often difficult to attract big names to Reading and whilst Sir Coxone Sound and also David Rodigan (a white DJ in London who promoted reggae music) would draw in crowds when they came to Reading, it was rare to see a live reggae artist. But I remember the time in the '80s when Gregory Isaacs came to Reading Town Hall to do a concert (the main hall was open then). Everyone just had to be there; here was the famous reggae artist in Reading. It was really exciting. His 'Lovers Rock' style was really at a peak then and for me he still is one of the best. I'm sure that many girls will remember whom they were dancing with when certain songs are played.

Since those early days, many reggae stars like Freddie McGregor, Alton Ellis and Frankie Paul, to name a few, have also played Reading in various venues like The Majestic (now RG1) and Central Club in London Street .

I still refer to dances with a caplyso band as 'big people' dances even though technically I probably count as one of the big people now. Those were the days!

Music in Lydda
Margaret Skinner

Margaret Skinner was born in Jerusalem and lived for 13 years in Palestine where her father was in the Colonial Service. She explains how her education in music started when she was living in Lydda.

"My mother could play the piano and organ; several cousins played instruments from the organ to strings; my musical tastes seemed restricted to Frank Crumit's The Song of the Prune and Down in de Cane Break, both charming tunes, and Ernest Lough singing O for the Wings of a Dove. Added to that, playing poker and chess with my godfather and devouring his collection of Peter Cheyney did not seem to my mother very desirable.

"In desperation she sent for my godmother, a Miss Willan, who owned a grand piano and was very musical. She arrived one afternoon carrying a parcel. The HMV wind-up gramophone was ready and on went the first side of Beethoven's Symphony No 7. We listened in silence until she had to change the record. My mother asked me if I was enjoying it but was severely reprimanded by Miss Willan for speaking between movements.

"Out went Frank Crumit and in came Dinu Lipatti playing Chopin and a catholic collection of opera and chamber music. Encouraged by the change, my mother sought out the only piano teacher in the district and we set off to see her.

"Unsure of what was happening, I was surprised when we arrived at the Convent School for Arab children. We were greeted by an Hungarian nun who was fluent in French and Arabic but could not speak English. This was no problem for my mother, fluent in French, but difficult for me, having no French and only a smattering of Arabic.

"The answer was simple. The nun, Sister Térèse, would teach me French as well. We started lessons straight away – Beyer, Books 1 and 2, all in French – scales, arpeggios and duets disguised as tunes. Hard work but we had a jolly time.

"Practice was another problem since we only had an old harmonium. However, undeterred my mother soon had it arranged. After what seemed to me a long walk down a sandy, prickly pear-lined lane, we arrived at the house of an Arab friend. While my mother drank Turkish coffee, I practised. Not the best of worlds but it worked until I went to school."

A Real Orchestra   Newbury Symphony Orchestra

The second oldest amateur orchestra in the country* started its life in 1879 as the Newbury Amateur Orchestral Union (NAOU), although since 1964 it has been known as the Newbury Symphony Orchestra (NSO). It began when six enthusiastic instrumentalists started their rehearsals in the loft above Pickfords' removal office in the yard of Queen's Hotel, Newbury, on 27th November 1879. They could hardly have foreseen that their efforts were to last into the next millennium. The founders were G H Bates, the first conductor, W Dines Eatwell, T B Mathews, F C Seymour, E L Staples and W T Toms, but by the following week they were joined by seven more players. One of these was Philip Davies, whose son Arthur, grandson Peter, who is still the president, and great-grandson Nicholas have made the Davies family unique in having an unbroken connection with the orchestra for the past 120 years.

Arthur Davies (1879-1978), son of the founding member Philip Davies, was born on 25th August of the same year it was founded and grew up with the orchestra. "This makes the first link between us," he recalled in the personal memoirs he wrote for his grandchildren. There has been a strong family interest in the orchestra. Two of Arthur's uncles were early members: – Will played the trumpet and Bert the trombone – and his aunt Bessie played the 'cello. Arthur's eldest sister Nell played timpani and was later a member of the English Ladies Orchestra, and his youngest sister Mary also played the 'cello.

Arthur Davies, who was timpanist, was treasurer for some 30 years until he retired at the age of 80 and his wife Millicent was librarian for many years until she took over the job of secretary during the war and kept it going during a difficult period with her hard work and enthusiasm. Two of her sisters, Lena Elliott and Dolly Neate, played double bass and viola respectively.

Millicent was also a musician as Arthur recalled: "For many years Millicent played the cymbals. She was a good player, very reliable, good on time and the crashes were right on the dot. At a rehearsal in the Corn Exchange, she was preparing for a terrific bang when one of the leather handles broke. The cymbal flew past the horns and the woodwind and settled down amongst the second violins. The noise would have fitted the *1812 Overture* towards the end of the finale, with good results."

By 1880 the NAOU was well established, with a membership of 15, and gave its inaugural concert on 13th April 1880 in the Old Town Hall. By 1881 the membership had grown to 25 and was to increase as the years passed. The earliest concerts were given to aid such local causes as the Steam Fire Engine and the Berkshire Volunteers.

The second conductor Dines Eatwell, a partner in Whiting & Eatwell, a men's outfitters in the Broadway, was succeeded in 1885 by a professional conductor, JS Liddle.

Arthur Davies wrote: "He was a very remarkable man. I think JSL did more for the cause of music in Newbury and district than anybody I know. Many were persuaded to take up the playing of instruments and he was able to make his pupils as enthusiastic as he was. He had four daughters Magdalen (violin), May (clarinet), Molly ('cello) and Monica (horn). They were all good musicians, especially Magdalen. I wonder why all their names began with 'M'?

"He came to Newbury in the late 1870s to take the post of organist at St Nicholas Church. He was conductor of the choral society and as it was founded in about 1880, I think he must have been one of its founders. The orchestra for the choral concerts was the NAOU practically en bloc. While he was conductor of both societies they were closely allied in a happy relationship. JSL also led the Temperance Band and formed a Temperance choir.

"JSL was most businesslike, very efficient and a great believer in punctuality. The platform at the Assembly Rooms was hardly ever ready for the rehearsal to start at the proper time. One morning it was in a state of absolute chaos. JSL looked at his watch, tapped his stand with his baton and said to Horton, the professional oboe player: "An A please, Mr Horton." H: "I have no chair, sir." JSL: "Can't you play it standing up?"

Mr Liddle managed to arrange concerts in towns including Wantage, Basingstoke, Reading and as far away as Bath. Sometimes members of the orchestra went by car though it was the early days of the automobile and once, when giving a concert in Reading Town Hall, the whole orchestra travelled by the Great Western Railway in specially reserved coaches. Arthur Davies remembered that the instruments were loaded on to a truck at Reading, to be taken to a waiting van. On the top of the truck reposed a valuable ''cello belonging to one of the players, Miss Dorothy Kingsmill (later to become Lady Sperling). To his horror, the porter rounded a corner too sharply and the 'cello fell off. Fortunately it was in a strong wooden case, so no damage was done.

During the winter, once a month on a Saturday night, the NAOU held concerts in the old Town Hall, a friendly and more or less draught-free venue. The charge was sixpence for the hall and twopence for the gallery and such was their popularity that the NAOU played to full houses. There are several fond memories of these concerts and one is recalled in the orchestra's centenary booklet .

"As the platform was flat, it was necessary to erect temporary staging and the exit to the platform was down a few steps at the back. On this occasion, in the programme was the *Farewell Symphony*. To give it the necessary atmosphere the lights were lowered and on each musician's stand there burned a solitary candle. The players one by one blew out the candles and left the stage by the back exit steps, but, alas, as Herbert Comyns blew out his candle and proceeded to leave he dropped his horn with a deafening crash and fell down the steps at the back. As one can readily appreciate, this was met with howls of delight from the gallery and shouts of 'encore'."

Another anecdote is told by Arthur Davies: "At this time I played the bass drum, and at one of these Saturday night concerts they were to play a piece called *Gamerra*, in which there was a bass drum solo. When the orchestra was assembled with Mr Liddle conducting, he beckoned me to come down to the front of the platform. Horrified at such a notion, I shook my head emphatically, but Mr Liddle beckoned again, with a very purposeful look in his eyes. Thereupon I succumbed and, picking up my bass drum, carried it like a bandsman, clasped in front of me. Of course I was unable to see too well, and so ended up by knocking his music stand off the platform down into the hall. This too was greatly appreciated by the gallery audience, who shouted raucously for an encore and that was before *Gamerra* had even started!"

In 1906 Newbury Town Hall was demolished and the only building large enough to accommodate concerts was the Corn Exchange. It was still a working market and on concert nights the exchange floor was hurriedly swept and hired chairs placed in rows. It was a cold and uncomfortable venue for performers and audience. Peter Davies, who was born in 1918, says: "There is a very blurred photo of the orchestra being rehearsed in the Corn Exchange, when I can't have been more than five. It was in an entirely unreformed state, even before they had a stage, just a rectangle with the corn merchants' desks shoved at the side."

After the First World War, there were, of course, sad gaps in the orchestra but by 1919 it had been built up again to 110 subscribers and 53 players.One of those players was an accomplished musician Marian Arkwright, a double bass player who joined the orchestra in 1885, and was one of the first women in England to be made Doctor of Music much to the pride of the orchestra. Dr Arkwright, who lived at Highclere, composed several works including *A Japanese Symphony*, inspired by a visit to Japan. She brought back with her a large gong which had a part in

Peter Davies at his 80th birthday celebration in 1998 flanked by the orchestra leader Peter Denny, conductor Adrian Brown and composer Samuel Becker
Picture by Newbury Weekly News

the score and now belongs to the orchestra. She was a great friend of Mr Liddle and succeeded him as a conductor when he died in 1921 but sadly only held the position for a year before her own death.

"Douglas Fox followed Dr Arkwright as our conductor," recalled Arthur Davies. "He was head of music at Bradfield College and was originally a pupil of Sir Hugh Allen who predicted that Fox would eventually be an outstanding pianist with a brilliant future. Unfortunately the 1914 war drew Fox into its hungry maw and he lost his right arm. It was a tragedy. Gifted individuals who had so much to give us should never have been called to serve in the Army.

"When he was discharged he felt very despondent about his musical career but Sir Hugh played with his left hand only and his right hand behind his back for three solid weeks and then said: 'Carry on, Douglas, it will be all right.' Fox did so with excellent results. He had a lovely touch. He played pieces specially composed for the left hand, which covered the keyboard almost as fully as those for two hands. Anyone outside the hall would never have known that the player was using his left hand only.

"Sometimes during a practice he would leave his stand, go to the piano and play a phrase to show us what he wanted without reference to the score. When conducting a scherzo or a piece scored for one in a bar, presto! he could turn over the score without missing a beat. He once gave me a lift from Bradfield to Newbury in his car. At the hill just out of Bradfield, he left the wheel, changed gear and was back at the wheel with incredible speed."

It was during Douglas Fox's time that Peter Davies has his first memories of the orchestra. "I used to be taken to practices in the old Congregational lecture hall in Newbury. I must have been quite young, before I was 10. It got me used to the orchestral sound. One of my earliest memories is of bassoon and clarinet played together as being a characteristic Beethoven sound. My mother started me singing octaves in bed before I could speak. The funny thing was when she asked me later which instrument I wanted to play I chose the 'cello not knowing my grandfather had played the 'cello. In fact there have been about 10 'cellists in my family including my oldest son and I played the 'cello from 1927 to 1990.

"I started playing for the orchestra before the war. On one occasion in the '30s when I was home from school, they were playing the *Portsmouth Point Overture* by Walton and needed a triangle player. So I played – and a devil of a thing it was to count, too."

This performance was conducted by George Weldon who succeeded Douglas Fox in 1931 when he was only in his early twenties.

> Arthur Davies recalled: "There was one outstanding event during George's regime as our conductor. It was a concert made up entirely of works by local composers. I very much doubt any other town the size of Newbury could put on a similar concert. It was well attended and caused a considerable amount of local interest. The programme contained pieces by Dr Arkwright, Peter Burges, Gerald Finzi, Robin Milford, Anthony Scott, Geoffrey Hartley, Guy Graham and Nelly Fulcher. The last item was the amusing Mice based on Three Blind Mice by George Weldon and was encored.

> "On another occasion we were playing Night on the Bare Mountain by Mussorgsky when an inquisitive little Welshman from the back of the second violins asked: 'Can you tell us what happened on the mountain, sir?' George Weldon replied: 'I would rather not'."

George moved on in 1942 and eventually became deputy conductor of the Hallé Orchestra under Sir John Barbirolli and later conductor of the City of Birmingham Orchestra. During his time the orchestra had enjoyed many peaceful years between the wars. Peter Davies remembers the pleasure of growing up in a musical environment. "It was so nice to be in a community as Newbury was in those days. Most of the people you knew were singers or instrumentalists. I remember going along the street with my father and he would remark somebody was a tenor or a violin. It was so pleasant. I never regretted not doing music professionally. I think it is very important to have a lot of amateur musicians. It's an awful rat race being a professional."

This pleasant existence continued until the outbreak of the Second World War after which the music was curtailed but not stopped. It was at this time that the committee decided to hold a Sunday afternoon concert

What music means to me
Arthur Davies

"Brahms Requiem is a choral and orchestral work which I like and enjoy more than any work I have ever known. Before I played the timps I sang it in the bass chorus. Since I started on the timps I have played it four times – in Bath Abbey, St Nicholas Church and the Corn Exchange.

"The part which Brahms wrote for the chorus, Behold all flesh is as the grass, is to my mind one of the finest parts ever written for the timpani by any composer. The triplets which he uses freely on each of the three drums form a rhythm which fits the words of the chorus in a very moving way. It was a wonderful experience.

"I think that devotional music, especially when performed in ideal buildings such as St George's Windsor, King's College, Cambridge, or Bath Abbey, transcends all other kinds of music. It always makes a tremendous impression on my emotions and transports me into another world. When I was a boy I was told I was a dreamer and I think I have been one ever since.

"The solo, As one whom his own mother comforteth, was not in the original score. It was written after the death of his mother whom he loved so well. The words, beautiful music and pathos of this solo make a valuable addition to an outstanding Requiem.

"I loved my drums; although they belonged to the orchestra I always looked on them as mine. When we were playing anything of which I was particularly fond, such as Brahms Requiem or the Enigma Variations (especially Nimrod) and they were in perfect harmony with the orchestra, they literally 'sang' their part to me. It was lovely. I used to hum quietly the part to myself too, so we all four of us enjoyed a quiet duet. They knew exactly what I wanted and always gave me of their very best. It was a sad day for us when we had to part company for all time.

"Every day I am thankful that I belong to a musical family. I cannot imagine what life would be without good music. Very, very dull to say the least of it."

as an experiment. It succeeded beyond their wildest dreams and the Corn Exchange was crowded to overflowing, with people standing at the back and many turned from the doors. The number in the audience and the money taken are still an unbeaten record.

Although the orchestra managed to survive a second war it was hard work building it back to its flourishing pre-war state. After keeping the orchestra going as secretary through those difficult years, Millicent Davies had had enough and gratefully handed over the post to her son Peter, who had returned from the Middle East in 1947 and joined the family business, J J Davies and Sons.

He recalls: "Up to 1939 we had a large membership under George Weldon who had done a lot for us; for instance we had 10 'cellists and everything else in proportion. Then after the war it was a low period. Music education had not had a great deal of attention. People who had been part of the community and played regularly were getting old and dying. When Mr Liddell was our conductor he had lived in Newbury, taught music in Newbury, and used to make children take up instruments which were going to be needed in the orchestra. That had been a flourishing time.

"After the war it had been really hard work getting one or two essentials like a bassoon or an oboe. It was very difficult getting enough wind players and enough good string players but we got by and kept our standard up pretty well. It is only comparatively lately we have got a full side of wind and we have a waiting list. We have three, sometimes four of each woodwind in the wings. We have practically everything including a harpist – we even have a contrabassoon."

There were also problems finding a home for the orchestra. During the war, they had to move wherever there was a hall, storing the instruments in unsuitable

"My wife Ann Davies ran a playgroup and nursery at our home in Enbourne where children were encouraged to play small instruments. Music was taken for granted. We had violins and 'cellos of different sizes and they were encouraged to pick them up and play them. One was Felicity Salter who later became leader of the Newbury Symphony Orchestra. Ann used to encourage children who had been discouraged from learning properly by rather unsympathetic regimes and they blossomed. One boy joined the Halle Orchestra and another girl went into the BBC Welsh Symphony Orchestra. I taught Ann the 'cello before we were married but as soon as we were married I said: "We can't have two 'cellists in the family." A viola was needed in the orchestra, so there you are. One of our sons plays the cello very well and my eldest daughter plays the flute and the harp and sings. One grandchild who is nearly two is particularly interested in the cello."
Peter Davies

places which were often cold and damp. After the war the orchestra moved back to the congregational hall until the difficulty of storing the growing library and their timpani and percussion instruments forced them to move on first to the college of further education and then to St Bartholomew's School where they have happily put down roots.

Conductors, too, have come and gone – there have been 11 since George Weldon. One of the most notable was John Fry, a very good professional violinist and teacher of the violin. With his work as a professor of violin at Trinity College of Music, conductor of three orchestras, and teacher at Douai Abbey School, he had to juggle a very demanding schedule – and all done by train and bus. During his time the orchestra celebrated its 75th anniversary in 1954. Ralph Allwood, who was director of music at Pangbourne College and is now precentor at Eton, took the baton from 1975-87. His successor, the talented Adrian Brown, who trained under Sir Adrian Boult, is still with the orchestra. Peter Davies says: "He is a very good professional conductor, and demands a lot – quite rightly."

It was in 1964 that the members of the orchestra decided that a change of name was necessary to present a truer image and it was as the Newbury Symphony Orchestra that it celebrated its centenary in 1979. During the anniversary concert, the orchestra paid musical tribute to its past by playing one of the pieces performed in its first concert, *Poet and Peasant*. Another notable anniversary was marked in November 1989 when the orchestra honoured its president Peter Davies on his 80th birthday with a piece of music specially composed by Samuel Becker. Peter was secretary for 47 years and took over as president in 1992, following in the footsteps of famous names like Sir Hugh Allen, the composer Lennox Berkeley, Lord Sieff of Brimpton, the broadcaster Johnny Morris who performed with the orchestra on several occasions, and the writer Richard Adams.

Newbury Symphony Orchestra is now enjoying its 121st season. It has about 60 enthusiastic amateur musicians and continues to encourage up-and-coming soloists by inviting them to perform concertos, one of its major objectives. Its reputation continues to be of the highest. At one rehearsal their conductor Adrian Brown told the players: "That sounds like an ordinary amateur orchestra. Now play it like a *real* orchestra." Few would argue that Newbury Symphony Orchestra is a real orchestra.

Ken Wickens and Alison Haymonds
with the help of Peter Davies
Newbury Symphony Ochestra: a centenary history
1879-1979 **Judith Warden Eykyn**

* The oldest is the Royal Amateur Orchestra in London

The Human Face of Policing
The Thames Valley Police Band

Police officer SERGEANT MERVYN CLARKE recalls his years with the Thames Valley Police band and mourns its passing In 1995

Playing in a brass band creates a unique fellowship among its members. This is difficult to describe but lasts for years, long after people have left or the group has disbanded. Such a band was the Thames Valley Police Band which was formed in 1973 and played its final concert in St Mary's Church, Thame, in March 1995 – 22 years later.

When the band started, permission had to be sought from the Police Authority. It was given a grant, which it had to repay, to buy instruments, many of which lasted the entire lifetime of the band. I was not a founder member but joined in 1984. Later I was for several years band secretary and deputy bandmaster, for a time fulfilling both roles at the same time. During my 11 years with the band, our musical director was Gordon Saunders, an accomplished musician in his own right, who joined the police as a civilian employee on his retirement as musical director at the Royal Military Academy, Sandhurst. The band often performed Gordon's compositions and he used to enthral audiences with his performances on the trumpet and post horn.

Initially, the band attracted sufficient interest from within the service to maintain its membership from police officers. Band members came and went and at first we always seemed to replace our losses, although not usually on the same instrument. In later years we failed to replace those who left and we had to widen the scope to offer membership to all police personnel, families and friends. The membership declined during its final years, which was both frustrating and disappointing, as there were many fine musicians in the service. Quite why we were unable to attract more members is still a mystery but I believe the band always performed to a good standard and was a fine representation of Thames Valley Police.

I can't remember a time when I wasn't involved in music having first learned to play the cornet when I was eight in the local Salvation Army band. Since that time I have played the tenor horn, baritone and now Eb Bass. Music has given me opportunities that I would never otherwise have had. I have performed in concerts throughout England, as well as Wales, Scotland, Belgium, France, Austria, Germany and Switzerland. I have played on several records, radio broadcasts and television and performed in most of our major concert halls.

Most band engagements took place within the Force area but we did on occasions venture outside the Thames Valley. We were invited on several occasions to take part in passing-out parades at Ashford in Kent, Shotley Gate in Suffolk, and Cwm Bran in South Wales. We provided the music at several charity launches for the Duke of Edinburgh Award Scheme in London, playing before celebrities like Bruce Forsyth, Val Doonican, Frankie Vaughan and Frank Bruno.

We had many memorable times, good and bad. When we visited Belgium, some of us with our wives, we were given accommodation in an Army barracks which we were led to believe was suitable for us with our spouses. When we got into the building we discovered that the couples were all together in a shared dormitory with windows from ceiling to floor without any curtains. The beds were all single, made of iron and bolted to the floor and our washing facilities were communal steel sinks with cold water only. Not our happiest memory.

On another occasion, following a passing-out parade at Cwm Bran, we marched from the parade square back across the front of the training school to where we had left our gear. The mace bearer, who proceeds the march, is always immaculately turned out, boots like glass and creases in his uniform razor sharp. As we approached our accommodation, the entire band dropped out save for the drummer who continued the beat for marching. At the end of the march the mace bearer, who had no idea of what had happened behind him, called at the top of voice for the march to halt. He turned round to be faced by a single drummer and numerous smiling faces peering around the corner of one of the buildings.

Undoubtedly the saddest occasions were when the band was asked to play at two funerals for serving officers. One of those was from the driving school, a motorcycle instructor who was tragically killed in an accident while giving tuition. The other, a former band member, friend and assistant secretary, died of cancer at only 41.

The band gave me the opportunity to expand my musical interests. I wrote several compositions, two of which were *Childhood Memories*, a selection of nursery rhymes which we played when visiting primary schools, and a piece dedicated to our final concert entitled *A Fond Farewell* which included the Scottish songs *Will Ye No Come Back Again?* and *Auld Lang Syne*. The music created a special atmosphere on a very sad occasion and has never been performed since.

Over the years the band took part in numerous fundraising events, played in schools, fêtes, old people's homes, police station open days and many official police functions, ceremonies and presentations. Above all else I believe the band presented a human face of policing which I believe is still sadly missed.

For a Dancer Nearly Blue It

Nearly Blue It was formed in late 1993 from the ashes of a very loud local band called Feverpitch, which deafened many a small club audience. The original idea was to play strictly blues music and the nucleus for the band was made up of bass player Chris Curtis, a superb drummer called Barry Clapson, a folk rhythm guitarist called Ian Tant and probably one of the best lead guitarists around in Berkshire called Rod Martin. The whole idea of Nearly Blue It was playing for fun; it was never intended to make any money out of it.

From the start, there were huge numbers of people coming along for auditions most of whom were never to be seen again. Some, of course, stayed including Andy Iddiols, the maestro of the keyboards, and Wayne Parker who until recently was the longest-surviving drummer. The band has had more drummers than hot dinners since Barry's carpal tunnel problem gradually got the better of his drumming and he had to take up the slightly less strenuous activity of singing. It is curently audtioning drummers yet again! Fronting the band with Barry on vocals is Lorraine Kuhl whose voice is like a cross between Maggie Bell and Connie Lush, and Mike Bishop is now lead guitarist replacing Rod Martin who left in 1997.

Past members include Martin Carter on harmonica, Jeffro Robertson on drums, Dave Sadd on drums, Damon Sawyer on drums, another drummer called Dean, Clare from Indecision and Kim McMahon from Slipstream on backing vocals and a few others whose names have long been forgotten.

Because of other commitments, the musicians are able to play only about a half dozen or so gigs a year with Blue It, but they are all memorable events in one way or another, usually because of the lack of space afforded by promoters who don't seem to appreciate the amount of room needed by a seven-piece band.

The band's involvement with the Leukaemia Research Fund began in July 1994. Chris Curtis tells the story.

"Charlotte Ruth, Nessa's and my daughter, was nearly 13 and showing signs of great talent as a dancer, following in her great grandfather's footsteps. On 9th July, she and her best friend Gemma Devereaux took part in one of Alison Knight's famous dancing school shows at Bearwood College Theatre. The following Wednesday, I came home from work to find that Chaz hadn't been to school because of a pain in the top of her leg. The family GP couldn't find anything the matter but suggested we take her to Royal Berkshire Hospital for an X-ray. The duty doctor there couldn't see anything on the plates but was a little concerned about her high white blood cell count so they kept her in overnight to do some more tests.

"The following morning, Nessa and I went to Kempton Ward to take her home. A bit odd, we thought, to find Chaz in a side ward on her own. Even odder when Chaz told us that someone was coming down to speak to us and that she'd got to go to Oxford. We were ushered into a private room with the consultant haematologist, Carol Barton who, very gently, very calmly, told us that Charlotte had leukaemia. You know how you feel when you are so deeply shaken by something? We didn't know whether to laugh or cry.

"She explained to us that leukaemia is a group of blood cancers, quite a large and diverse group, and comes in many different forms, and so we had to take her to John Radcliffe Hospital in Oxford to find out which leukaemia it was, to get it treated and, we hoped, cured. We also had to tell Chaz what was wrong with her.

"On Thursday we arrived at the Radcliffe, and were met by Dr Chris Mitchell and his wonderful team who, over the next five days, was to hit us with one sledge hammer blow after another. The first was to tell us that Chaz had acute myeloid leukaemia. Had it been acute lymphoblastic or one of the 'chronic' forms of leukaemia, it is apparently more survivable. Next he told us that she had only a 50/50 chance of surviving five years, and that she would have to undergo intensive chemotherapy every three weeks for the next six months.

"She started chemo on the Friday evening and by 11 o'clock on Sunday morning she was on 100 per cent oxygen because the oximeter was showing that her blood saturation was dropping – rapidly.

Later, in the lift going down to the ICU, Chaz asked me, "Am I going to die, Daddy?" I told her the biggest lie I've ever told anybody. These were to prove to be more or less her very last words to us.

"By 1.15 she was on total life support – ventilation, 100 per cent oxygen, you name it, the works. It was just like a bad dream, only it wasn't a dream. We had her baptised during the night and she hung on all night. Everyone was giving us the hope that if she

Chris Curtis

survived this crisis, all would be well in the long run. Then at breakfast time on Monday morning we were bleeped. Her kidneys had gone into failure and all her systems were shutting down. Now we had to make a decision: to keep on with her treatment in a totally hopeless manner, or to face the situation that she was not going to make it and switch off the machinery.

"Nessa and I were in a totally complete and utter daze. I prayed to the only one who has the power to give or to take away. I said if He had to take her, please take her now and end her suffering, and ours. There was really only one decision that we could make. So we switched off her life support machinery. Nessa and I both held her hand, gave her a last kiss and said good-bye. From being so full of life on the Saturday to 10 o'clock on Monday morning, our little angel had gone. When they had pulled out all the tubes, brushed her hair and given her a wash, she finally looked at peace.

"All this had taken just five days. It was now 18th July and it was to be her 13th birthday next week. As it turned out, that was the day after her funeral.

"What a terrible thing leukaemia is. It can strike anyone at any time and lots of further research is needed to find out the real reason why some people get it and others don't. There are still 18,000 or so people in UK who will be told this year that they have leukaemia, or Hodgkin's Disease, or Lymphoma or one of many other related diseases. The current survival rate is about 60 per cent, a little better than in 1994, so all the money we raise for research is actually doing some good. The Government pays for none of it, it is all financed by volunteers like us."

That is the reason that Nearly Blue It stages an annual fund-raising concert for the Leukaemia Research Fund. Once all the dust had settled after Chaz's death, and Chris had got himself back from his long period of deep depression, the band decided to hold a charity show every March. They turned for help and advice in getting the ball rolling to two well-known people from the music world: Dave Pegg, the bass player and mainstay of Fairport Convention, and John Dalton, who was at one time bass player for the Kinks. John also lost his son Matthew about 25 years ago through leukaemia, and he and his wife Val now stage a fund-raising concert in Broxbourne, Hertfordshire, every year.

With their encouragement,. Nearly Blue It staged its first show at in the Wilde Theatre at South Hill Park, Bracknell, on Easter Saturday 1995, accompanied by the backing vocal talents of the Vixens and the folk singer Kathryn Lincoln. The bill was topped by Dino Baptiste and the Mystic Mile and an audience of more than 100 helped to

Nearly Blue It playing at Wilde Theatre 1995

raise a total of £903. Not a bad start.

The following year the band shifted the venue to Bearwood College Theatre and topped the bill themselves, supported by the Gelfs, raising about £1,200. It had started to grow. The year after the show had to be cancelled at the last minute because Chris had an accident which damaged his left shoulder but two operations later, in 1998, they went back to the Wilde Theatre again. It was a sell-out performance, with a guest performance by the wonderful 74-year-old sax and fiddle player, Otto, supported by Small World, which raised £1,750 for the LRF. This was topped in 1999 by another sell-out show which made about £3,000 profit. Much of the cash comes from generous sponsorship from both local and national companies. This money goes towards things like theatre hire so that all the ticket money and cash from the raffle and merchandise stalls is profit. Sound and lighting systems are usually provided free thanks to the band's manager and sound engineer Slmon Procter and his friend Bob Kiddle of Gaslights. The band has also recorded an album on CD for the benefit of the fund.

The band usually plays straight rhythm 'n' blues, and soul but for the LRF shows a few special songs are slipped in, particularly one by Jackson Browne called For a Dancer, dedicated to Charlotte's memory. Often the band finds that songs learned specially for the show will end up in their repertoire, such as Pink Floyd's Comfortably Numb which has proved something of a show stopper.

Nearly Blue It is planning a special show for the Millennium year at South Hill Park, Bracknell, on Saturday, 18th March, 2000 and is hoping to raise more money than ever for the charity which is closest to all their hearts.

Stirring up the Suburbs New Wave, 1978 and after

What happened to the excitement of the 70s music scene in Reading? NEAL MARSDEN reflects on the passing of Reading's New Wave and wonders if he's just getting older

Moving to Reading in 1978, I suddenly realised what I'd left behind. Having seen the Sex Pistols at 'the Lanch'; The Ramones, The Clash and Talking Heads at Barbarellas (though not on the same bill!); The Coventry Automatics (soon to be re-named The Specials) at Tiffany's; and the 'Live Stiffs' tour at Leicester University (Nick Lowe asking "What's so funny about peace, love and understanding?", Elvis not "knowing what to do with himself"), there appeared little to match this in Reading – a town rarely mentioned in band tour dates, a suburb swamped by its closeness to London, a small place proudly portraying itself as 'average'.

But surely it couldn't be all that bad? Other, less likely, places had produced great surprises – even Hull. There had to be some energy, some excitement, some sounds in these suburbs; somewhere, surely? And there was – the 'Target'. Though not quite the Il Rondo or Barbarellas, it put on music most nights; and, in the best traditions of dark, dingy, stuffy, underground music dives, the music was (at times), new, exciting and different. And to confirm its place as a real venue, the landlord was grumpy; and it sold crap beer at inflated prices.

The Target; what was the attraction of the place? It had to be free to get in, some of the bands were so bad. It was that era when anyone thought they could form a band; they could, but some couldn't make us listen. But some were excellent; you went to see them, rather than just to meet your mates. The regular bands – Friction Groove, the Dave Knowles Band, American Train and Staa Marx, the one-offs of XTC and Spot the Fish (honest!) – they drew you there, keeping you away from Auntie Audrey's bacon and mushroom sandwiches and exquisite London Pride (and Ivor on his piano). They must have been good.

What a variety of music too. From great nights with Friction Groove, Staa Marx and The Dave Knowles Band, to forgettable and unbearable bands that not even six pints of Directors made seem OK (so why have I seen Sunfly twice?), and from the 'choogling' but conventional rock of American Train, to the 'Radios in Motion' of XTC. Great fun too, from the Great Mistakes and Die Laughing, and meeting like-minded people who became good friends. Friends in the Target crowd passed on news of where you could see and listen to new ('wave') bands;

of 'Bones' (a converted morgue I was told but, then, I'm very gullible) who put on Penetration and the Buzzcocks and of the 'Star', with its jukebox up-to-date with great new single releases. The music was starting to bring this suburb to life.

And other suburbs too! I would never have expected one of the best gigs I've ever been to would be at Bracknell Sports Centre. But when Elvis played his new songs from *Armed Forces* (including *Chelsea* twice), you knew it was 'special, so f*****g special'. Did Wreckless Eric really mean it when he sang "and she probably lives in West Wycombe" when playing the Nags Head? Did Reading Borough Council understand what they'd agreed to when they let Crass and the Poison Girls play Reading Town Hall (for that matter, did the promoters?).

But slowly, the local music scene changed. Between Pictures became Friction Groove (but Alison still had the

The Bundhu Boys provided a great moment

voice that sent shivers through you) and released an album; Dave Knowles became Turbo (but slowed down); Staa Marx's singer broke his leg falling off stage (but still kept singing); and Sunfly reformed to play a benefit for CND (but struggled to get all their gear on the Target stage).

The music scene changed; the music, the bands and the audience. Numbers watching bands fell; the centre of Reading sometimes felt like a ghost town; and the new, electronic music didn't seem to aspire to live performance. Bones, The Star and the Target closed in quick succession. A few clubs (Fives and Cherries) tried to maintain the momentum, but the 'punk/new wave' live music explosion was fizzling out. Though there were still great moments to come on the Reading music scene (Taxi Pata Pata and the Bhundu Boys at the Paradise Club opening up whole new areas of music; King Kurt throwing chickens at the After Dark; Chumbawamba politicising at the Trade Union Club; The Levellers shaking Rivermead; Carter USM stomping at the university), they came from outside, from beyond our suburbs; and from known acts. The local music scene appeared to be slowing down, unable to maintain the momentum and excitement of those days of the late 70s.

Or did it? Was it me? As I got older, did I search as much as before? Or did 'dance' really take over and side-track live music? I do think it's still there, just taking a new form in what now calls itself 'Festival City'. In 1991 a modern legend appeared; Nirvana (followed by another in 1996, Neil Young); and WOMAD came to Reading, with its acrobats from China, drummers from Burundi, dancers from Raratonga, sunshine music from Africa and sensual music from Latin America.

Yes, Reading changed; but now the sound in our suburb was the same as in Sydney, Seattle, Cape Town and San Francisco, where other WOMADs happened and Nirvana played! Reading's music was still around; it had just changed (as we all had). Let's hope it stays and changes, keeping us interested, excited and happy, bringing us new influences from the diverse world beyond our suburbs.

Famous Folk

Nettlebed Folk Song Club

Born at The Bull, Nettlebed Folk Song Club, which celebrates its 25th birthday in the Millennium year, is now one of the top folk venues in the UK. It was started in July 1975 by a group of folk song lovers from Maidenhead when the tenant of a local public house moved to the Bull Inn at Nettlebed, seven miles north of Reading. From a small start in a tiny bar (40 people), the club progressed to a converted coaching barn holding more than 100 and quickly established itself as one of the folk scene's major circuit venues.

Once again the club had to move in 1991 because The Bull Inn was closed by its owners Brakspears Brewery in Henley. However, the opportunity was taken to 'change gear' as the new venue, the Village Club in Nettlebed, holds 200 people.

The Folk Song Club is a volunteer-run, non-profit organisation and takes more than 15 people to keep it running smoothly and to organise the Monday evening concerts. The acts that are staged encompass the different types of traditional and contemporary music and song from the British Isles and North America with the occasional act from 'down under'.

Most of the major folk acts have appeared ranging from headliners like Fairport Convention, Steeleye Span, Ralph McTell, Lindisfarne, Richard Thompson and Show of Hands to club acts like Vin Garbutt, Martin Carthy, John Kirkpatrick, Eric Bogle and Huw and Tony Williams.

The club is also famous for its 'special performances' such as Feast of Fiddles and Folk on the Rocks where we mix leading national performers with local artists to provide unique themed evenings.

Mike Sanderson

It was Magic Newbury memories

GERALD BRADFORD played the double bass in symphony orchestras, dance bands and jazz groups for many years. He recalls his early life in Newbury when he was growing up and learning about music

I think I must have been about six or seven when I was first introduced to music. Our own home music was very primitive then. There were crystal sets with earphones – very few people had them then – and a big horn gramophone which you wound up. There was a smaller version, a little tiny thing like a box, with a horn about four inches in diameter and the voices always sound very falsetto.

We were fortunate because there were many bands in Newbury. The Newbury Town Band was a brass band and what fascinated us young children was their military-style uniforms, beautiful green tunics with epaulettes on the shoulders and soldier's hats that we used to call cheese cutters. Then there was the South Berks Silver Band wearing dark blue with red facings and piping, and playing silver instruments and, of course, the Salvation Army Band. They would always start in Newbury Market Place on Sunday evenings at about 6 o'clock. In those days Queen Victoria's statue was there with the four lions and the Queen up on the pedestal. The band would march up with the flag in the front playing *Onward Christian Soldiers*, cornets in the front, tenor horns, drums behind, and we boys used to march behind it triumphantly down Northcroft Lane into the Salvation Army Hall and sit there and listen to this music. They were all good musicians. There were two Piper brothers; one called Pip played a very good cornet and worked for the grocer's as a roundsman, and his brother played the tenor horn.

When I was a little boy, Sunday was a special day. We had Sunday school music in the afternoons, but in the evenings they held lovely outdoor concerts. Summers seemed to be so different then, there were sultry evenings and the men would wear their nice blue suits, polished shoes, no baseball caps, no trainers. Boys up to the age of about 13 would wear little grey flannel trousers, turned-over socks with the coloured rings round the top, and shoes or little leather sandals. Some would wear tennis shirts or cricket shirts, either white or cream, and little boys would wear blazers. Fathers usually had a walking stick and boys, when they got to the age of about 13 had a little walking stick with a silver coloured band round it, and would walk in front of their father with their walking sticks. Mothers would be in dresses, not trainers or those denims. There used to be something about music on a Sunday evening in Greenham House Park. The bands played lightish music, no jazz, and there would be pieces from operas, and the music seemed to fit into the period. There always seemed to be more flies about then, they used to bite, and sometimes you would get a thunderstorm. I remember the mothers used to say, "The lilac is out" and when the evenings were humid, the scent of the lilac was heady. There was no noise, very few cars, no ring roads, it was magic really.

People made their own entertainment in Newbury. We had Newbury Operatic Society, Newbury Amateur Orchestra, now Newbury Symphony Orchestra, singers, choirs, and Newbury Parish Church had a very fine organist called Gilbert Sully, a great humorist and a friend of mine. There was also a well-known lady called France Belk, who had a dancing academy in Newbury station, and ran a pantomime every year in aid of Newbury Hospital. She was a great benefactor and there's a little plaque in the Corn Exchange in her honour for what she contributed to Newbury.

It must have been around 1934 when I bought a ukulele. It was like a little guitar with gut strings and was very popular at the time. There was a lot of Hawaiian music then with steel guitars and ukuleles and girls in their grass skirts. I tried to learn to play that on my own, but not very successfully because you have to tune every string up differently. You need a piano or a tuner to tune the strings so you could play what they call the box of chords, like a chess board of dots.

When I got to about 14 I had a chance to buy a Spanish guitar with metal strings. I bought this in a shop in Newbury which was the Mecca of musicians, classical musicians, light musicians, dance band musicians, solo performers. I got half a crown a week pocket money and was paying one shilling and sixpence a week hire purchase for the guitar which cost two pounds, four shillings and threepence. I paid a shilling a lesson to a banjo player who taught me a bit but didn't know much about the guitar. Anyhow, I bought more tutors and practised very hard.

When I was about 17 I was introduced to a classical pianist in Newbury called Sylvia Nightingale. She started a little dance band called The Sylvians, and my friend, Harold Robson, who played the bassoon in the school orchestra, and I played in that until she gave it up and we started a band of our own called the Rhythmics. It consisted of Harold Robson on saxophone and clarinet, Harry Martin, piano, Basil Giles, drums, me on guitar, and Les Emberlin who played trumpet – he had the most silvery tone which could cut butter – and accordion. The accordion became very popular in the '20s and '30s, it was almost like these hip-thrusting electronic guitarists of today. Basil Giles, whose family had a baker's shop in Newbury called Giles Brothers, was the drummer and also a good crooner. He used to sing through a big megaphone, then later we got some amplifying equipment, two speakers. We finished up with a trumpet player called Ken Thomas who was quite a character. He used to bend his knees, put his trumpet in the air and shut his eyes – he thought he was Satchmo.

By 1937 we were playing in little village halls. We wore white shirts and with plain blue ties, grey flannel trousers, black shoes, hair sleeked with Brylcream. We were all young, quite good looking chaps really, and the girls used to flock. We got a bus cheap from Newbury District Buses when we were playing at Hampstead Norrys or Lambourne or Stockcross because we could fill the bus with all our followers, mostly girls.

There were some very good dance bands in Newbury at that time. There was the Embassy Dance Band with a chap named Walter Steptoe. He was a trombone player , a very good musician and could read piano music. He didn't know what the chords were, he'd just read them up as a bunch of notes. Terrible tone but he could read every note. We always used to say about him and Harry Pearce, a fine trumpet player, if a fly landed on the stave Walter and Harry would play it.

In summer 1938 we decided to run some Saturday night dances. The Corn Exchange, in those days, was used for hunt balls and other big occasions, so we started playing at St Joseph's Hall in London Road through Basil Giles's family who were Roman Catholics. The priest there, Father Green, had a nice Bechstein piano in the hall because in the '20s they ran little social evenings with perhaps a piano, drums and violins. Anyhow, we booked this hall on a Saturday night and he charged us £1 for the hall and 15 shillings for the piano.

"Be careful of the Bechstein," he said, "Don't put any cigarettes on it, don't put any beer on it." Of course we never drank in those days, we just had a little buffet – Basil made the cakes in his baker's shop and his sister used to serve. Our uniform was evening dress trousers, a very stiff shirt front, a black tie, and cut-away red jackets with black facings like bell boys used to wear. We wanted to look like the professionals, Harry Roy, Ambrose, all those big bands in London we used to read about but we never got anywhere near their standard.

We did very well. We'd sometimes get 50 people there and we'd come away with perhaps 12 shillings and sixpence, and when you were earning about 30 bob as a junior draughtsman or a shop assistant, it was quite a bit of pocket money. Sometimes we earned nearly as much in two evenings as we probably earned a week. Sadly that little heaven didn't last long. In early 1939 most of us

The Gerry Bradford Quartet, from left, Gerald Bradford, Bill Renshaw, Len Hidden, and Les Newman in the 1950s

chaps joined the Territorial Army, we could see something coming, and some joined Territorial units in the band and the last dance we had was the week before the declaration of war, and we were really doing quite well then. But most of us got called up.

Music has always seemed to be a part of me. I just love to hear the sound of the various instruments. But it's strange. In the wartime, when times were hard, the music was always happy. Today when it should be happy, people aren't happy and the popular music is dreadful.

In 1947 some of us chaps in different dance bands got together and created a jazz and a dance band called The Gold Star Players because we liked to improvise. Ken Thomas, who started it, was on trumpet, Les Newman, who was a church organist, on piano, Tony Robins on drums, Ken Thomas on trumpet, Denis Kemp on guitar, and I played double bass. We used to play on Sunday nights. Very often we'd play for other big dances. I played with Don Turk and his band quite a lot, at the Olympia three nights a week, depping for his bass player. He had the most wonderful big band. The Reading and Newbury musicians worked quite well together.

In 1950, Les Newman and I, with other musicians, started our own band called Gerry Bradford and his Music Makers. We played all the tunes of the day – in fact I believe we were the first people to play the music from *South Pacific* over here before UK copyright was granted.In the '60s we had a big band in Newbury with the full complement of four saxophones, two trumpets, four rhythm, piano, double bass, guitar and drums.

I've played the double bass in symphony orchestras, dance bands and jazz groups, and nowadays when I hear the electronic bass guitar, I feel there's something which is gone out of music. I seldom play now but when I play some of my old records of the dance band years and hear those wonderful dance orchestras of the '30s and '40s, the professionalism is wonderful.

'Great Emotions, Noble Concepts' Dame Gillian Weir

DAME GILLIAN WEIR is a world famous organist. Born in New Zealand she has lived in Tilehurst, Reading, for many years mainly because it is well placed for her to continue her constant travels. She is also first patron of The Berkshire Organists' Association

Background music has now become so much a part of our lives that we seem to expect it to always be there, almost like an act of God. People often don't like background music in shops and supermarkets but feel they must have it. In one restaurant when I asked, "Could you please turn the musak off", they looked at me incredulously saying, "We can't possibly turn it off." Recently in a shop I asked the assistant about the musak and was told, "But the people like it." So I turned to the person next to me to ask if she liked musak and she said, "No, I don't like it, but you have to have it, don't you? Anyway I can switch it off'. That's what most people say; "Oh I don't really hear it. I can switch it off mentally."

This has tremendously important results, particularly for musicians, as many people now take it for granted that music is only for background. If you spend most of your day trying consciously or unconsciously to switch off the sound so that it doesn't drive you crazy and you can get on with thinking about what you're going to buy at the supermarket or how to do your job, how can you possibly expect to switch it back on again when you come to a concert?

People are becoming more and more desensitised to the intricacies and subtleties and the nuances which are part of what we call 'high art' or 'fine art'. It has been said that the average attention span is now three minutes, it's certainly very short. People are increasingly leading a digital life rather than an organic one; always passive, waiting for the next instruction, rather than engaging in the kind of organic thought,which is the one that produces an imaginative life of the mind.

A musician, or indeed any person in the arts, must be able to use the faculty of imagination so that they can enrich the piece they are playing or the picture they are painting. Great music is about great emotions, noble concepts. These you can't see; you can't put them on a table and look at them, or type them out on a computer. These are abstract qualities, endangered by the inability of people to think on abstract terms . It has tremendous bearing on the arts. Music, of course, has a huge part in entertaining but the core of it is that the great works have a thrillingly intellectual level – and people are

terrified of saying that. Somebody has proved that playing Mozart to seriously disturbed children quietens them instantly. The children came thundering down the corridors as they normally did, burst in the door, heard the music and stopped, stock still. After a week of playing Mozart she played rock music instead and they went back to exactly as they had been before. The Greeks knew the power of music. This is something we don't entirely understand but which they understood, and we should try to explore it. One of the most enormous arrogances of the modern world is the rejection of something until you understand it, even though you can see that it works.

Dame Gillian Weir

I first really responded to music by dancing. I can still remember where I was in the house when I first heard Brahms' *2nd Piano Concerto* on the radio. And I danced to it, which I think was a huge, huge advantage because it gives you an idea of the size of the phrase, and that's an important issue.

Nowadays, doing master-classes, I find there are many people who are unable to decide what tempo to engage for a piece. They will often have a technique which enables them to play it at a speed, but at the same time they don't quite have the feel or the stimulus that is needed when you want to create a hypnotic effect; and so they just choose it by extraneous things, like the time signature or when it was written. But this is not an intrinsic part of the piece. They are not able to make musical decisions through musical criteria.

It's amazing how many people learn instruments but they are only thinking externally. It's rather like learning a language without ever speaking in the native accent, or ever thinking in the new language because you are always translating it. There's always something missing. Responding with your body, which always makes fluid gestures, you have a much greater understanding of how a phrase is shaped – the lines of music are for the most part curved. Also you have a concept of the size of your gesture in the space around you, and since the music has been written by someone who is engaged in the same relationship with the space around themselves, you then have an innate understanding of that piece.

When I was growing up there was music all around me. We had a national orchestra which came around to my little town once a year; we also had the radio and a wonderful music service. My mother was a very good singer and her sister was a pianist of professional standard I started playing the piano and was very quickly an addict. Now often students say to me, "I'm thinking of taking up music professionally, do you think I should?", and I always say no, and the reason is that they have asked me. I never ever asked anybody. I was so terrified somebody would say no, so I never gave them the chance.

I started playing the organ by mistake. When I was about 16, my local church was without an organist for a couple of weeks, and they said to my mother, "Your daughter plays the piano, will she come and play a few hymns?" So I went over there, trod around on the pedals and tried to understand how this terrifying piece worked, then got rather hooked on it and eventually fell in love with it.

I had some wonderful teachers. I myself love teaching and the interaction with my students, and I'm very interested in the psychology of teaching. I think of it as releasing someone from limitations, rather than instilling facts; more that you are drawing something out. My first teacher was not only a very good technical teacher but she was a natural philosopher, and I still find myself now thinking about things she said.

Then I came to England and I had the great Cyril Smith, the concert pianist, as my teacher, and that was marvellous; terrifying, but wonderful. He taught me a huge amount. He taught me how to hear – not just listen, but how to hear. You have to teach children what real listening is. It's an active not a passive occupation. I used to sight read very easily, right from a child, and that was great fun as I would just plough through music, take whole volumes of anybody, Haydn, Mozart, chamber music. But I didn't always actually hear it; my brain didn't engage. Cyril Smith dealt with this in a magical way so that when the moment happened, when it changed, it was just as if I'd been blind and I'd had an operation to see. I could hear in quite another way.

My organ teacher was excellent too, an individualist, and a thinker, not someone who just says, "Do it this way." I get students who come to classes who have been pressurised to the point of a nervous breakdown sometimes. They have been told to do things this way, you lift your fingers here, you do that there, never any concessions to their own individuality, which means that they don't actually see what there is to be seen in the piece of music. A piece of music is an endless treasury of images, feelings, sounds, colours, shapes, everything. You can get five great performers and they will play the same piece in five different ways and they are equally valid. There are, of course, styles for each period which should be adhered to but that should never be a strait-jacket. Unfortunately it becomes a strait-jacket in many ways, partly because of the excessively scientific way of thinking we have at the end of the 20th century.

I travel all the time and it is fascinating playing different instruments in different environments. It means that you can play every kind of music from every period. You can be playing Renaissance dances and early music on a tiny antique organ in Italy, with a touch rather akin to that used on the virginals. Then you go to a 19th century organ with a much larger scale and you play the great organ symphonies. Then you move to a very modern organ which has other characteristics and you play a different repertoire again because the environment has a different acoustic. Japan is amazing, for instance. They have so many new concert halls, and every one has a magnificent organ.

Everyone should travel, especially organists because the instruments are so different in each country and unless you see the originals you have no idea how to play them musically. The sounds are so different. Of course it's hard for everyone to go to these countries but there is one place that everyone can go to, and that is the wonderful land that you discover in a book. To play French classical music, for example, which was written at the time of Louis XIV, the Sun King, you must read the wonderful books about that extraordinary period. Then you get all these images in your mind, and they inform the music as you play. It is not possible to play the music without having those images.

Millennium Choice
Gillian Weir

My favourite music always has to be Mozart. There's so much music really, but the Mozart Requiem, for example, is a magical piece. So is the G Minor Piano Quartet - that's beautiful, and in fact any of the concertos, let's say 488. It grips people without them not neccessarily knowing why. There's a lot of work in music that isn't immediately beautiful but nevertheless does things for you later on.

All these pieces have marvellous melody, and warm and effective harmony. They also have that indefinable extra quality, which makes you feel that someone is speaking to you. What it is they are saying you can't be sure, and indeed if you could put it into words then you wouldn't need the music. That's the whole point about music, that it transcends words, but you do know that it is saying something.

'Closer Communion' The Berkshire Organists' Association

Organists have been employed to play in churches and in places of entertainment for many centuries but it was not until the mid-nineteenth century that many more musicians were needed to play on the newly-built organs in rural churches and on the large organs appearing in town halls up and down the country. During the Civil War in the 17th century a number of church organs had been destroyed and, as a result, in the 18th century many churches had a "West Gallery Band" to provide their music. Following the Oxford Movement in the Anglican Church, there was a proliferation of organ building. With greatly improved communications at the beginning of the 20th century, which could be described as the heyday of the church organist in England, it was felt necessary and beneficial for this large number of serving musicians in Berkshire to get together to share their experiences and widen their horizons.

The Association was formed in 1921, the first AGM being held at Hickie's music shop in Reading. Objects and bye-laws were drawn up. The objects were: 1) to bring the organists of Berkshire into closer communion, and to deepen the feeling of brotherhood among them; 2) to hear lectures and papers, to give recitals, and to discuss matters affecting organists and their work; 3) to further means of co-operation with organists of kindred associations and to safeguard the interests of organists generally; 4) to further whatever tends to the improvement and development of music used in divine worship.

The Berkshire Association was affiliated to the National Union of Organists which became the Incorporated Association of Organists in 1929. The first president and leading light for many years was Percy Ravenscroft Scrivener who was the organist at St Giles-in-Reading for 63 years from 1895 to 1957. During this time he exercised immense influence on the musical life of Reading generally. Subsequent presidents have all been well-qualified professional musicians or good amateur organists who have brought experience and know-how from other walks of life to enrich the Association.

For better or worse, separate organists' associations were later set up in Newbury, Abingdon and Windsor and the title 'Berkshire Organist' now applies to those living in or around Reading.

Looking back over the activities of the Association in the 20th century, a pattern emerges of talks, recitals on local organs and visits further afield to look at, learn about and sample different organs. The very first talk entitled Church Music from the Free Seats given by H C Colles in 1921 conjures up visions of a past era when some churchgoers could not afford to 'buy' the better seats in the church. In 1925 the tercentenary of the composer Orlando Gibbons was celebrated with a visit to Newbury.

The National Union of Organists' Associations Congress was held in Reading in 1927. As well as many musical events, details of which are preserved in a glossy programme among the association's archives, there were visits to Huntley & Palmer's biscuit factory and Sutton and Sons' seed trial grounds, a river trip to Goring and a char-à-banc trip to Windsor and Eton for the entertainment of the delegates. As an example of the music performed at this time, the following is a programme from the 1927 Congress:

Short organ recital at the Minster Church of St Mary the Virgin, in the Butts, Reading, by the Organist, E O Daughtry, Esq, MA, Mus Doc, FRCO

Voluntary Maurice Green

Adagio and Allegro from Sonata in C major Corelli

Prelude and Fugue in C minor JS Bach

Sonata in F Sharp minor Rheinberger

Slow movement (5/4 time) from *Sonata in C minor* Chopin

a) Chorale: b) Priere Jongen

Sonatina, lst movement Karg-Elert

Programmes given by a variety of good local organists today in lunchtime recitals at the same church are similar to this with the addition of the not inconsiderable organ repertoire of the 20th century.

Church organists are guardians of their instruments and in the historic churches of central Reading there are some fine and interesting organs. The Minster Church of St Mary possesses a 'Father' Willis built for the London Exhibition of 1862. It stands on the north side of the chancel and has a case designed by Harold Rogers of Oxford. It has four manuals and pedal organ with 51 stops, 2,886 pipes, 33 couplers and three tremulants.

In the parish church of St Laurence there is an organ built by John Byfield in 1741. It has been restored several times including once after bomb damage in 1943. It retains its original case but the early keyboard is preserved in a glass case.

At St Giles, an organ was built and erected in a gallery at the west end of the church in 1829 by JC Bishop. Subsequently it was rebuilt on the north side of the chancel and recently has been moved to its original position after renovation by Harrisons of Durham.

But by far the most treasured organ in Reading has been the 1882 "Father" Willis in the Town Hall. The Association has played a large part in saving this magnificent instrument for the people of Reading. During the 1960s and '70s a sub-committee made all the arrangements for celebrity recitals and brought such well-known names from around the world as Fernando Germani, Pierre Cochereau, Jean Langlais and Marie-Claire Alain to Reading to perform on the Town Hall organ.

The Association encourages young musicians to become interested in and take up the organ and has sponsored an organ section in the Woodley Festival. Young players from Reading Blue Coat School and Reading School have won the cup given in memory of Albert Barkus, one of Reading's distinguished former organists.

An international performer with an illustrious career and many awards for outstanding achievement in the arts, Dame Gillian Weir, whose home is in Reading, was recently invited to become the first Patron of the Association and all were delighted when she accepted.

The Association looks forward to a bright future for organs and organists in the town of Reading and its surrounding areas.

Christine Wells
President 1998/2000

Millennium Choice Christine Wells

Purcell's Songs – very English and exquisitely beautiful

The Dancing Years
Palais de Danse

The Hammersmith Palais de Danse opened in 1919 and its immediate success led to the creation outside London, of other dance-halls run on broadly similar lines. One of these was the Reading Palais de Danse, occupying spacious premises in West Street (on part of the site which was later occupied for many years by Reading Co-op).

Miss Vere Leslie was the hostess and exhibition dancer, and her style and personality would probably have ensured the success of the venture, but the financing of the Palais turned out to be unsound and the business came to a sudden end in 1922. The company was found to be insolvent and Major George Herbert, who owned most of the shares and was managing director, was found dead in the kitchen of the Palais. He had comitted suicide.

A number of local hotels and restaurants held regular dances. For example, in 1925 the French Horn Hotel at Sonning Eye ran fashionable Saturday night balls and the HTE Edwards Sonata Jazz Band had a contract to play at these events. It also provided music for club dances at The Pearson Hall, Sonning.

By 1927, Attfields Tea Dances, held at the Binfield Hall in Friar Street, Reading, had become a feature of social life. The tickets were relatively expensive (at two shillings and sixpence) and the dances were held in the afternoon and on Saturday evenings. At the end of the '20s there was a trend towards dances held in the restaurants of large stores like McIlroy's Jacobean Restaurant.

Tony Barham

Peace celebrations in Wokingham – the bands play for Children's Day, Wednesday, 22nd July 1919

The Bulmershe Connection Primary school festivals

GWYN ARCH remembers the pleasure of working with young singers during his years as Director of Music at Bulmershe College of Higher Education

If you want to sing, and if you are at school, and particularly if you are at primary school, then Reading is the place to be. The opportunities for singing en masse are possibly equalled elsewhere, but are unlikely to be exceeded. When I first arrived in Reading in September 1964 to join the staff of a brand-new teacher-training college in Woodley (Bulmershe), I soon became involved in schools' festivals in the old Town Hall. Noel Hale was the borough music adviser and there was an annual secondary schools event and another for the juniors. It was the first time I had seen serried ranks of white blouses and grey skirts and trousers, and the beginning for me of working with ensembles measured in hundreds rather than dozens.

The second half of the sixties was a period of frenetic activity in the education business. The training period for teachers had recently been expanded from two to three years, but there was also the problem of providing enough teachers to cope with the post-war 'bulge' in the birth rate, so during this decade the number of teacher education students in England and Wales doubled.

Bulmershe came into being principally to train primary school teachers, and the students were to be trained in the methodology of all the subjects that formed the primary school curriculum. They also elected to take one subject as their specialism, so I, as the newly-appointed head of music, had to devise short 'curriculum' courses for all and sundry as well as an academic but practically-based programme for the 15 or so music specialists. This turned out to be something of a challenge initially. There was I, the only 'musician' on the staff, with no one to turn to for advice, and with no teaching experience of any kind whatsoever with young children. Worse, I had never taught music as a classroom subject. I had been the head of the English department of a large grammar school in Hertfordshire, dabbling with music on the fringes; starting a girls' choir in school, directing the music of the local operatic society, giving piano lessons to eke out the pitiful salary, and doing a bit of composing and arranging.

How I got the job at Bulmershe, indeed, how I had the cheek to apply for it, is too complex a matter to deal with here, sufficient be it to say that the education world is mightily impressed with the printed page. If you've

published something, you are taken seriously, and – fortunately – I had. As head of English, I had been landed with the job of running the school dramatic society, and it attracted hoards of budding actors. The average play with a cast of 12 disappointed the 73 who didn't manage to get a part. Solution? Write a musical and bung the leftovers in the chorus. So I did, and amazingly, Boosey and Hawkes liked it, and so did the appointing committee in Berkshire – not that it helped me in any way to devise an appropriate syllabus for all those unsuspecting students.

Right from the start we had to build a professional relationship with every primary school within reach of the college. By 1967 there were well over 700 students, and every one of them needed a teaching practice place in each year of the course. Fortunately, most of the schools were only too willing to help, and college staff spent many weeks of the academic year working in the schools supervising the students, and sometimes doing a bit of teaching themselves. In my case, this was a much-needed opportunity to acquire a bit of primary school experience, to experiment with various schemes of music pedagogy. I found myself adapting Carl Orff's ideas for use in English classrooms, along with Kodaly's methods based on the voice. The voice! Here I *could* claim a little experience. My Hertfordshire girls' choir had given me the opportunity to work with voices, and I'd loved it, too. Maybe I could transfer some of that experience to these younger, and even keener voices?

What made these children keen, of course, was the enthusiasm of their teachers, and here I was very lucky indeed to find myself frequently visiting a group of schools where singing flourished. As I write this article more than 30 years later, I can readily recall with pleasure the standards achieved by the music teachers in many of the schools nearest to the college – Beechwood, Earley St Peter, Alfred Sutton, and so on.

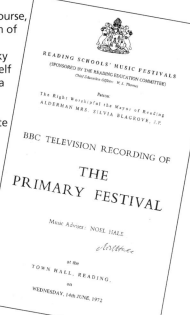

READING SCHOOLS' MUSIC FESTIVALS
(SPONSORED BY THE READING EDUCATION COMMITTEE)
Chief Education Officer: W. L. Thomas

Patron:
The Right Worshipful the Mayor of Reading
ALDERMAN MRS. SILVIA BLAGROVE, J.P.

BBC TELEVISION RECORDING OF

THE PRIMARY FESTIVAL

Music Adviser: NOEL HALE

at the
TOWN HALL, READING,
on
WEDNESDAY, 14th JUNE, 1972

The first year at Bulmershe College was a strange one. The buildings were still in the process of construction, so all the teaching happened in Bulmershe School, where the buildings were complete but at that stage occupied only by its first intake of 12-year old children. I was their music teacher, too. Although the students had no classrooms of their own they did have living accommodation - the first phase of building had concentrated on making six hostels ready in time for the initial intake of 225 students. However, although you could boil a kettle, if you wanted to eat, you had to walk a good half mile across an increasingly muddy field to the school, whose kitchens provided breakfast, lunch and dinner.

We all ate lunch together, *theoretically*, the children all huddled in one corner of the dining room, overwhelmed and outnumbered by seemingly hundreds of teachers, and it was *their* school. In line with 'progressive' thought, the staff ate with their students, again theoretically. What actually happened was that some tables came to be regarded as staff ones, and the students diplomatically joined their peers elsewhere.

On an autumn day in 1965, at one of those tables I found myself sitting next to a member of the college's staff I hardly knew. He was Pat Rooke, an educationist and historian, and by the end of the meal we had decided to write together. We were going to make our own distinctive mark on primary school music! We were ambitious and energetic, and I'll bet we thought the existing repertoire old-fashioned, out of touch and boring. Such is the arrogance of the truly inexperienced. We thought we could persuade some of those keen music teachers to use our material with their children. We would then rewrite or modify in the light of its reception, and then be able to submit it to publishers as tried and tested!

In 1966 we completed our first effort. It was called *A Day with a Difference*. We persuaded the Keith Prowse Music Publishing Company to take it (at that time they did more than just flog theatre tickets). In the introduction we set out our stall, modestly stating, "It offers a new kind of educational experience for the child in the junior school. At one level it is a play with words and music; at another it is the focal point of a project which brings together a variety of creative subjects – drama, art, music,

Primary Schools' festivals

Roy Nash, former chair, festival committee

The 55th primary schools' festival in Reading falls in the year 2000, but their predecessors date back before the war. For years, popular children's concerts were held at Reading Town Hall, organised by local teachers, and there were also musical appreciation concerts featuring eminent conductors such as Sir Malcolm Sarjent.

After the Second World War, Reading Education Committee appointed Dr William Veitch as music adviser, and the first secondary festival took place in the Town Hall in November 1946. Programmes were varied and not only gave children the experience and joy of singing together, but included string and woodwind groups, generally showing the extent of musical work promoted in schools day by day. The festivals, both secondary and primary, became an integral feature of the musical life of our town. John Russell succeeded Dr Veitch as music adviser in 1950 and in turn he was followed by Noel Hale in 1955 who held the post for the next 17 years, retiring in 1972.

The festivals often marked special occasions. In 1950, as part of the Reading Christian Arts Festival, the secondary schools gave a bicentenary concert as a tribute to the memory of J S Bach whose death had occurred 200 years before. The Reading Youth Orchestra and Choir also supported the concert which included the F minor Piano Concerto, the piano soloist being a pupil of Leighton Park School who, according to the press, gave an 'excellent performance'. Unfortunately, the secondary festivals were discontinued in the mid-1960s due no doubt to the gradual changes taking place in secondary education.

The primary schools' festivals also date from 1947 and still continue, transferring to The Hexagon in 1979. In many ways this proved more convenient but unfortunately lacked the fine "Father" Willis Organ which had been used to such good effect in both the secondary and primary festivals. The programmes follow a customary formula of groups of songs for massed singing interspersed with various pieces which have included strings, recorders, wind bands, percussion, steel bands, drama, dance, narration, choral speaking, plus a short musical work.

Noel Hale very much extended the instrumental teaching in schools which has gone from strength to strength. During his final year before retirement, the festival was televised by the BBC entitled, Come Lassies and Lads. In 1974 they also televised Songs of Praise with local junior choirs from St Giles Church, Reading, conducted by Bryn Williams, music adviser to Berkshire Education Committee.

The festival committee had eventually to find its own conductor and was fortunate in securing the services of Norman Morris of Phoenix Choir fame. Norman conducted the festival for some 17 years, his place now taken by Clive Waterman, well-known in school music circles.

The festivals have always aimed at inculcating in children an enjoyment of music and experience of the concert platform. These festivals could not have taken place had it not been for the festival committees of dedicated teachers responsible for quite a daunting task of organisation including, of course, the music teachers in our schools. For those children taking part, the concerts have made a memorable impression which most regard as one of the highlights of their primary school days.

imaginative writing, etc. The play is meant for production in the classroom rather than on the school stage for public performance. What matters is the enjoyment and the involvement of the participants." It is hard to know how many children actually became involved in it, but judging from the sales figures, very few. This day made no difference at all.

Undaunted, we pressed on. Our next notion was to produce a sort of cantata for children, a kind of mini oratorio. Pat came up with the idea of rewriting the first two chapters of the Book of Genesis, up to the point where God creates woman and the real trouble begins (naughty!). Genuflecting in the general direction of Haydn, we thought we would call it *Creation Jazz*, little realising that anything with the word 'jazz' in the title would be seized on with interest, as it meant exciting and 'with it' and likely to appeal to youngsters.

As with everything else, we were interested in what children thought of it before going any further, so I asked Eileen Day at Beechwood School if she would like to do the first performance, and I would play the piano for it. Eileen was an enthusiast for choral music and an excellent music teacher, and that first performance took

place in late 1969. It went well, and most important of all, the children loved it. And with children there's no dissembling. When you hear them singing your music in the playground, that's a real thrill, and encouraging, too. Unbeknown to us, a bigger thrill was to follow. The school secretary had sent a tape recording (on a big spool in those days) to the religious broadcasting department of BBC television, and they liked it too. So one Sunday morning in February 1970 those children went on a bus to All Hallows Church in the city of London and sang it for the cameras. In that era it wasn't a recording, either, but a live performance, and the bus broke down, and we only got there with ten minutes to spare…

After that there was no stopping us, and mini-cantatas were produced at six-month intervals, most of them ending up on BBC One on a Sunday morning or in ITV's 'God-slot' at 6pm, usually coming from Southern Television's studios in Southampton. Naturally, they were tried out in local primary schools and many a busload headed due south, filled with children convinced they were going to be famous.

I don't know whether the Woodley and District Primary Schools Music Association existed before the opening of

The Primary Schools massed choir at The Hexagon in November 1994

Bulmershe, but my (incomplete) collection of concert programmes reminds me that the Association staged its big concert of the year in the main hall of the college from 1971, and this venue was used for about ten years. My programme for the 1972 event indicates the schools taking part in the festival. They were Beechwood, Crazies Hill, St. Dominic's, Woodley CE, William Gray, Southlake, Sonning CE, St John Bosco, Twyford Polehampton and Wargrave Piggott Junior. After singing folksongs from Hungary, Scotland, Brazil and France, the choir gave the first performance of our latest piece *A Golden Legend*, the story of Crios and his search to find the most powerful ruler in the world. (He ended up carrying an infant on his shoulders across a raging river and was renamed Christopher – 'bearer of Christ'). An average junior choir would have 30 or so members, so this particular one would have had 300 voices or so. This concert, I notice, was repeated on the following night. There is never any problem in getting audiences for concerts involving young children, and they are invariably enthusiastic, irrespective of the merits or otherwise of the performance. "If our Melanie is in it, it must be good!".

Over the years I have established a reliable statistic. A primary child 'sells' an average of 2.5 tickets. Mum and dad usually come, but Grannie is often keen as well. Today, the Woodley Association has its annual concert in the Hexagon. Its director is Clive Waterman, head of Southlake. Sometimes they perform one of our cantatas, with actors in costume and dancers in leotards, and it's lovely to see. They did one in 1999, *Mighty Mississippi*, originally written for a similar festival in 1980. The Hexagon holds an audience of about 1200, so Clive gets a choir of 400, guaranteeing that the place will be filled. It needs no advertising, and the box office of the theatre plays no part. The 2.5 ratio remains reliable.

It's not only Woodley's children that get to sing at The Hexagon. So do the Reading Primary schools, year after year, for as long as I can remember. Every year, too, Reading Male Voice Choir invites another 400 to share a special concert, creating, at some point, the spectacle of them all singing together – eight-year-olds to going on 80. That doesn't happen everywhere.

The Central Berkshire Music Centre, based in Reading (part of the Berkshire Young Musicians' Trust) has got in on the act, too. They have the advantage of being able to use some of their talented teenage instrumentalists to accompany the (obligatory?) 400, so I have had the honour of being asked to conduct some very ambitious projects, such as the 'environmental' musicals *Ocean World* and *Yanomamo*. Here, the singers shared the stage with dozens of dancers, costumed actors, narrators, huge child-executed visual aids, and – soloists.

The competition to get a solo spot in the show is always strongly contested, and in going round the schools to audition the many aspirants I never cease to be amazed to find so much natural ability in so many places. And they are all going to sing in a professional theatre, into a professional amplification system, and with their very own personal spotlight shining on them. It's *got* to be good, even better than singing in the choir, but of course we do that, too, and aren't we lucky to be living in Reading?

Poet's Pleasure

Playing for John Betjeman

In 1947 we had a terrible winter which turned into the most magnificent summer. At the time I was playing in a band called The Lyricals, which started in Thatcham in about 1938. Most of the musicians had played in the local brass band and Charlie Packer who ran The Lyricals, had played in an Army band in the First World War so of course he played like a military musician. He was a damned good timekeeper, you couldn't fault him. He was like a human metronome.

One day he told us we had an engagement to play Farnborough Rectory, the home of John Betjeman. The house was on a hill outside Farnborough, right on the downs, south of Wantage, and as the band drove up the hill in a big taxi we noticed there were oil lamps all the way.

When we arrived, we were told: "You're playing on the sunken lawn." On the lawn were two farm wagons pulled up together where the band was to play and there were searchlights and amplifications ready. It was buzzing with flies attracted by the lights.

We were getting our kit together when out of the doorway came John Betjeman. He looked like an artist, like Augustus John, with a sweeping artist's hat and a cloak with a red lining. He came over and said: "I'll show you where the refreshments are. Follow me." We followed him thorough a side door and down some steps. It smelled like a cellar and it was a cellar and in the middle was a trestle with a barrel on it – a 20-gallon barrel of cider. He said: "There are your refreshments – it's very good cider."

So we drank up and the band played well. The only trouble was the flies. They kept settling on the music so we had to brush them away and lose a note or two.

That's how I met John Betjeman.

Gerald Bradford

Wearing the Tartan with Pride Reading Scottish Pipe Band

Bagpipes can be very temperamental as members of the Reading Scottish Pipe Band know to their cost. The pipes can freeze if too cold as happened on the band's trip to Yugoslavia, or the reeds go out of tune if the weather is too warm or humid as on their trip to Japan, where the instruments had to be dried out before each performance. The traditional leather bags also have a tendency to dry out if not used for a while but this can be overcome by using pipe seasoning to make them airtight. Failing this, Pipe Major Ron Patterson recommends using whisky!

In the early days, band members learned a salutary lesson about the necessity of caring for their temperamental pipes. The band was parading at a Remembrance Day ceremony in Bracknell and before going into church the pipes were stored in what was thought to be a cupboard. Unknown to the members this housed a radiator and when they started to play again after the service the sound was distinctly unmusical.

The difficulties don't stop there. The band can also experience problems with their kit which can weigh up to one-and-a-half stone. With their elaborate feather bonnets, the pipers can become very hot and uncomfortable when parading in the summer months. On the other hand, on a bitterly cold day, kilts can be a bit draughty. Dress for the various shapes and sizes of band members can cost up to £1,500 a person – £90 alone to refurbish a feather bonnet if it gets caught in the rain.

But it's all worth it and in the 40-plus years of the band's existence there have been any number of memorable moments – moving, exciting and exhausting. One of the more dramatic was when Pipe Major Ron Patterson and ex-Pipe Sergeant, Sandy Walker became film stars for a day and played the pipes for the third wedding in Four Weddings and a Funeral. The scene is supposed to be Glencoe in Scotland but was, in fact, filmed much closer to home in Hampshire.

Home for the Reading Scottish Pipe Band since it was formed in 1957 has been St Andrew's Church, in Reading, and this is reflected in its original name, the Reading St Andrew's Pipe Band. The fortunes of many musical organisations in Berkshire have so often depended on their venues (or lack of them) and the unbroken use of the church and its facilities for almost half a century must be a major factor in the continuing success of the band.

Sandy Blythe, an ex-Sergeant Piper who had served in the Cameron Highlanders, was instrumental in organising the band. He wrote to the commanding officer of his old regiment for permission to wear the Cameron of Erracht tartan and to use the regimental St Andrew's Cross cap badge. Permission was granted and the tartan and badge

Reading Scottish Pipe Band at the Bicester Scouts Church Parade, 1997. This was the largest band (13 pipers and six drummers) Reading has turned out in 10 years. Front row: SandyWalker, Ron Patterson, Michael Barnes, Dennis Davis and Keith Youldon

Pipers Sandy Walker, David Henson and Charlie Sim

have been worn with pride by the band ever since.

Throughout the years, members who joined usually came in two categories, either those who had been taught from an early age, usually in the Boys' Brigade, and therefore had a wide experience of performing, or those who longed to play but had not had the opportunity to learn. What the beginners may have lacked in dexterity they more than made up for in enthusiasm and loyalty.

The main problem for the band officers in the early days was to get enough members to make up a reasonable band, in order to earn money to buy kit to attract new members – and so it went on. This meant that the learners had to turn out if they were capable of keeping the pipes up when 'corked out' or holding the drum sticks in the correct manner. "Make it look as though you're playing," was the order of the day. The pressure on those who could play was enormous and a great debt is owed to those stalwarts who soldiered on, carrying the band and encouraging those 'coming along'. A good band in those days would consist of six pipers, one or two side drummers and, if lucky, a bass. Of the pipers, probably only one or two would be good; the others would be in various stages of learning.

As the years passed, piping and drumming greatly improved and successive Pipe Majors and Pipe Sergeants left their mark. The instruction became more organised and the repertoire of tunes gradually increased. A young soldier stationed at Arborfield Camp joined and spent most of his time practising anywhere he happened to be; eventually he transferred to the Scots Guards as a piper, became a sergeant and passed all the exams to qualify as a Pipe Major. Another young lad joined, was a quick learner and entered the King's Own Scottish Borders travelling all over the world with their band. The

Reading Pipers should take credit for their initial training and enthusiasm.

The uniform of those early days was a real hodge podge of what anyone owned that resembled highland kit, so that many tartans were worn. Gradually more Cameron tartan kilts and plaids began to appear, mainly because members bought their own. Ex-army battle dress blouses were acquired and dyed green by a non-playing member (female of course) in a large pot on her kitchen stove. The same lady also took white shop overalls and cut and fashioned them to look like military dress jackets. Another member, George Lovering, was generous with financial help to get the band under way.

As the band increased in size and playing ability it was able to take on more engagements and as its reputation for performance, dress, discipline and reliability grew, so did these engagements. The first ones were very local and for very small fees. One was a Scout parade for which the band was paid £5; the fee for the same parade in 1997 was £320. Members in those days did not ask for expenses so that all the fees could go towards kit.

In 1970 the band joined the Royal Scottish Pipe Band Association (RSPBA) and through them took part in massed band performances. In 1972 (the year the band entered its first competition at The Highland Gathering in Richmond, Surrey) there was a move for the band to become The Royal British Legion Berkshire County Band but after several meetings it became clear that no sponsorship would be available. It was decided to remain independent and in 1973 the band formally changed its name from Reading St Andrew's to The Reading Scottish Pipe Band.

All the hard practising was paying off and the turning point for the band came when it was invited to Belgrade, Yugoslavia, to play for the New Year celebrations in 1974/5. They were to be one of the first bands to go behind the 'Iron Curtain'. There was feverish activity to put together a stage performance and ensure marching tunes were up to standard. The whole visit was a huge success with the band playing in the streets, at a children's hospital, and in a theatre performance that was televised to other Iron Curtain countries. Many stories are told of this time, one of which was the introduction of the band to slivovic, heated plum

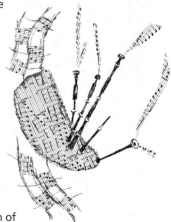

brandy. It was gratifyingly warming for the bandsmen playing outside in the bitter cold, but it did make the spats curl back!

The following summer of 1976 is remembered as being the hottest one for many years and there had been no rain in June, July and most of August. All through that time, the main period for engagements, the band sweated through in its thick uniform, hoping it would dry out before the next parade. Then towards the end of August, on a Saturday night when parading in Newbury Carnival, the weather broke halfway through the march. The heavens opened up and it poured, or as the Scots would say, 'It fair stotted doun'. Normally any spectators would disappear when this happened but because the rain was so welcome and it was a warm rain, nobody moved and the band received a tremendous ovation for continuing to march and play. It took days to dry out.

The band participated in massed pipes beating the retreat in Henley-on-Thames to celebrate the RSPBA 's golden jubilee in 1980, and in the same year, the band was honoured to parade for the Dunkirk Veterans Association. It was a memorable occasion. As the parade ended someone started to clap the band and this was taken up by the whole parade. Even the hard-bitten Drum Major did not have a dry eye.

In 1981 the band went to Meaux in France which led to several bi-yearly visits to a small village nearby, Changis-sur-Marne, to play at their carnival. This proved a very popular venue thanks to the hospitality of their hosts. Band members stayed in the homes of the villagers and were plied with champagne and wine. The band returned the hospitality by entertaining their hosts in Reading.

The 50th anniversary of the end of the Second World War was celebrated in 1995 with the band performing on 8th May to a large audience at Bracknell for VE Day, and also on 13th August for VJ Day when the Royal British Legion Veterans paraded their colours at a church in Henley in newly-acquired shirt-sleeve order.

During the years, members of the band have played at venues all over England and have visited Germany, Norway, Sweden, Switzerland, Finland and Japan, but probably none of these will compare with their forthcoming Millennium engagement. Hundreds of pipers and drummers from all over the world are meeting up in Edinburgh for what is believed to be the largest ever pipe band gathering to perform in aid of Marie Curie Cancer Care – and, of course, the Reading Scottish Pipe Band will be there.

Members of The Reading Scottish Pipe Band are of all ages – from 10 to 74 – and varying levels of expertise. Pipe Major Ron Patterson, who has been playing the pipes for over 30 years, is now in charge of 18 pipers and seven drummers,

Drummers Geoff Booth (tenor), Steve Kinghorn (bass), Terry Marriott-Lodge (tenor) and Bob Clifford (side)

with 12 pipers and two drummers who are learning to play. It takes on average between two and four years to become proficient in the band. The hardest part is memorising the tunes – currently the band has a repertoire of about 140 – and as it is impossible to carry music while playing the pipes and marching so all must be learned by heart. The band also has to practise drill movements under the command of the Drum Major. He marches at the front of the band and gives his commands by various movements or signals of the mace, indicating when to start, stop, and change direction or pace. Regular band practice sessions are held at St Andrew's on Monday evenings.

Anne-Marie Dodson
with the help of Ron Patterson, Pipe Major

Information from
The Reading Scottish Pipe Band – A History 1957-1997,
with kind permission of the author David Henson,
one of the original members of the band

'The Show-Off Stuff' Mayfair String Quartet

The Mayfair String Quartet can be busking one day and playing in Windsor Castle another. It's a tough life but an interesting one as HEATHER BURNLEY has found since she started the group in 1995. A New Zealander who grew up in Australia, and trained at the Hochschule in Berlin, Heather came to England seven years ago and has become a familiar and welcome sight playing with her quartet in Windsor Royal Station

When I was three, my mother says I saw her teaching herself the violin and lay down on the floor and screamed until she said she would go and buy me a little one. My first violin teacher only accepted me because I started playing on an eighth size violin. She'd never seen one before. It all just went from there. Now, it's as if the violin is my right arm.

I've worked with all sorts of orchestras all over the place, and it's only during the last three years we've been focusing on the string quartet. Sonia and I started it. We met in 1993 working for an agent in London playing gigs in various orchestras and other string quartets, before we broke away on our own to do an all-girl thing – a bit sexist but it seems to work.

We started the group in 1995 and we met both Claire-Louise, our second violinist who has only been with us a year, and Ann, who plays the viola, working for the same string quartet agent in London. It's very hard to find a perfect match, people who are looking in the same direction, who are prepared to put in the effort for work we don't get paid for, who will market the group.

All of us have been on the professional circuit for the last seven years in orchestras, string quartets, solos and recording sessions. Our second violinist works as an orchestral freelance musician, and our 'cellist and viola player work in 'Garden Opera' in the summer. I also teach part-time in schools in Bracknell and Wokingham for the Berkshire Young Musicians' Trust.

It can be hard, particularly when everyone does other things. We all have to cancel our own dates occasionally and get 'deps' (deputies) in for the job to go ahead, but within reason. If you've got recitals and recording sessions and you start cancelling them, it's mucking around a lot more people than the four of us. You're screaming down the phone, changing this, making arrangements, just trying to find a date we can all get into a recording studio that works out with the guy that runs the studio. It can be a nightmare.

Out of all the work we get, more than 75 per cent is directly through busking or street performing – there isn't a term for it that I like. We've got a deal with Windsor Royal Station where we perform and sell our tapes and CDs, and a couple of times a year, they'll hire us for recitals. We also busk in other towns in the area.

It's not like street busking or on the tubes, it is under a roof in a nice shopping centre. Because of the set-up in such a nice place, people realise that it must be kosher and that we're professional. We have a violin case to collect the money, or a 'cello case when we're feeling really desperate. You can do very well there and we get numerous enquiries.

Sometimes we work with a flute player, Charlotte Palmer. She's also a stand-up comic, so she really works the audience a treat. It's fantastic when she does that. She plays at Windsor Royal Station on her own as well doing what we're doing – advertising herself for private functions.

There are scary moments at Windsor station; for example when a whole lot of 14 or 15 year-olds ride by on their bikes and lob fire crackers or tomatoes or things like that. That has happened and is very worrying.

A friend we used to work with in London was busking in Watford and someone threw a tomato at the violin. Unfortunately it landed on the bridge and the whole violin exploded. It was worth about £18,000 – it was insured but damage like that can't be undone.

We've had people who walk by saying we are no better than beggars which upsets me quite a bit as they don't actually hear that we're making music at all. Sometimes a member of the crowd will get in on the act

and start conducting. We had an opera singer once who happened to be walking by when we were playing *Nessun Dorma* and he just started singing. Suddenly there were people running around because he sounded the spitting image of Pavarotti!

We play all the heavy classics but we really prefer playing the lighter material, the stuff that brings all the cheers. I love playing new music, anything written after 1950 or in a different style, but you don't earn much money playing that.

We're all madly in love with Rumanian gypsy music and want to focus on that, with a slight input of rock 'n roll perhaps; something that's a little bit different, a little bit quirky. That's what we'd really like to try.

We've got all of the classical Slavonic dance music but also the more traditional, where it begins really slushily, and gets faster and faster and faster. The whole thing shows every bit of emotion you can possibly put into your instrument and every bit of virtuosity at your fingertips. It's really show-off, crowd-stomping stuff but also shows that we can put as much emotion into that as you would be playing Tchaikovsky or Debussy, or any of the greats.

We do work in London, but mostly in Berkshire and the Home Counties. We've played at Windsor Castle in the old library, at Cliveden, and on the riverboats for Maidenhead Steam in the summer. We've also played at Legoland Windsor – that was bizarre.

You have those really horrible jobs where you are sitting outside in the garden and someone has billed you as being the main attraction for their garden party but it's rainy and it's windy. People never understand you can't play in the rain and you can't play in the sun because the varnish gets severely damaged. My violin is 290 years old and people often don't understand that we have to protect our instruments.

At functions, some people show great appreciation whereas others barely notice us. Nevertheless we give our best and try really hard to make a difference for someone's occasion. That's the whole point. They're hiring us so we've got to do our best.

We often put on a big show at these official functions where they want us to show off. We meander between the tables in big sweeping movements, though people have to be seated because we can't risk the instruments. It's very effective and brings the house down. Sonia balances her 'cello on a pad on her shoulder, walking as she plays.

We can play for an hour-and-a-half from memory. The idea is based on the string quartet from the Titanic, though that wasn't strictly a quartet. When they played, the leader would just say number 19 or number 25. They'd all know that number 19 was *God save the Queen*

The Mayfair String Quartet

and number 25 was Pachelbel's *Canon*. That was the way they did it. They played 100 or 200 things from memory and now nobody does that. It's a lost art. The things those musicians who played on the boats could do, they were amazing. We're trying to do that.

It's very hard to live off a string quartet. The weddings, gigs, the garden parties, the bar mitzvahs – they help us to raise the money to put on a recital. A recital doesn't make money. It is also how we raise the funds to make CDs. It's the only way short of taking out gigantic bank loans.

Our dream is to record the things we want to do. The tape we have made has just got straight classical music on it but the CD we are making has pop music on it as well as the theme music from *Titanic* and *Unchained Melody*, and classics like *Bolero*, *Eine kleine Nachtmusik* and Pachelbel's *Canon*. No string quartet has ever recorded anything quite like that.

At the moment, we don't do our own arranging. One of our deputies is an extremely good arranger; otherwise we try and pay for exclusive arrangements. We've got the Mozart *29th Symphony*, *The Barber of Seville* overture and the *Magic Flute* overture that have been adapted for four musicians and they work beautifully.

Every client is sent out a repertoire list and quite often

they'll choose the Beatles or Abba, particular music they want. You'd be surprised how many people come up to us and ask for the most outrageous stuff. We can put together something that's quite simple on the spot – someone asked us to play *Match of the Day* and we did that – but not a complex, established piece, particularly if we don't know it!

We had *Unchained Melody* arranged because somebody asked to walk down the aisle to it – a lot of our music develops that way and then it proves to be very popular. We're now going to record it and put it on the CD because people want it, and it works so well for strings. It can be just as moving without the vocal.

What we really want is to have a quartet of electric instruments. We would like to be able to play outdoor gigs as a fully electric string quartet.

I played on an electric violin about four years age when we had to beef up the sound for a particular venue. On my violin you can make it cry; on an electric violin you can't get that sort of emotion out of it. But electric is really easy to play because the sound is fairly constant.

The difference between a violin and an electronic one is not like the difference between a family car and a Formula One car where everyone is going to presume the Formula One car is better. It's not.

The classical instruments are the better instruments but the electric ones look funky and they all match in sound, so you are not having to work to create a sound that matches each other like someone who plays in a string quartet has to do.

At the moment we don't need it. Nobody needs an electric string quartet at their wedding – it would be too loud if you're playing for someone's meal. But it's certainly another avenue we would like to explore.

 # Newbury String Players

Two memories of the composer Gerald Finzi

I knew Gerald Finzi well until his death in 1956. While I was in Cairo during the war I had letters from him saying, "When you come home be sure to come and play with the Newbury String Players." Before the war Gerald and Joy Finzi came to live at Aldbourne and Joy joined Newbury Symphony Orchestra as a violinist. Then Gerald started the Newbury String Players because he thought something like that was needed and he used to take them round village churches for concerts. He wanted me to join but I couldn't because Saturday afternoon was rehearsal time and that was my busiest time in the family china and glass shop, and I didn't like to leave it. I did occasionally play with them. I had started Enbourne and Hampstead Marshall Choir and I have a programme which shows Gerald and myself as conductors at a concert given by the Newbury String Players and the choir.

Gerald Finzi was a nice little man, rather precise. My mother used to say he was a bit like a dancing master, pointed toes and a neat appearance. He had all sorts of interesting friends. I remember going up to Ashmansworth and meeting the poet Edmund Blunden, who was a professor of English at Hong Kong University. Vaughan Williams was also a great friend of theirs, always known as Uncle Ralph.

Peter Davies, Newbury Symphony Orchestra

Concerts at Bradfield College had attracted wider attention than is usual for school events since the end of the 19th century. Choral works by Mendelssohn and Handel were performed with enthusiasm and seem to have reached a reasonable level of competence. More ambitious productions followed. The December 1903 concert was devoted to the works of British composers. This gave an opportunity to hear such rarities as Thomas Frederick Dunhill's Tubal Cain, a movement from the Piano Concerto in F Minor by Sterndale Bennett and a song from Arthur Sullivan's The Martyr of Antioch.

This event paled in comparison with the concert given at Bradfield College in May 1942 by the Newbury String Players when no less than three distinguished composers were in attendance. Gerald Finzi was conducting (he had founded the Newbury String Players in 1940) and there to hear the music was Benjamin Britten, newly returned from the United States, after a nerve-wracking voyage in a small Swedish cargo boat, and George Dyson, representing an earlier generation of composers.

It seems that Britten was quite critical about the performance (Finzi's conducting abilities, as he would freely admit, hardly came up to Britten's remorseless standards). Dyson, it is said, was more encouraging. Since Dyson had been a music master himself at a succession of English schools from 1908 to 1937 he was probably less critical.

It would be interesting to know how Britten and Dyson got on together. Sir George Dyson (now remembered mainly for his Canterbury Tales music) was of a different temperament to the young Benjamin Britten. Before the 1914 war he crossed the Alps on a motor-cycle and during the war, a sixpenny handbook on hand-grenade throwing called Grenade Warfare, written by Dyson, was widely used in the training of soldiers.

Tony Barham

Quaint Music 'Hurdy-gurdy man'

GRAHAM WHYTE describes how he became a hurdy-gurdy man and discovered some unexpected help via the Internet when he was building his own copy of a 15th century instrument

Say 'hurdy-gurdy' and most folk think of a Victorian street piano. But the true hurdy-gurdy is a very different beast, the only thing in common being a handle, which is turned in a circular motion. The hurdy-gurdy is an ancient instrument, appearing in ecclesiastical carvings a thousand years ago, yet it is still a popular folk instrument in Europe, especially in France.

I first fell in love with it when I heard one at the Early Music Exhibition and determined to build a copy of one dating from 1480 from a kit. It is really just a violin in a box, with the aforesaid handle turning a wheel, acting as an endless bow. There are six strings; two of which play the melody, plus four drone strings. You can choose to have just one of these sounding (giving the home note of the key) or you can add others to give notes an octave and a fifth higher, so that it sounds like a constant chord.

This is why many people think it sounds like a bagpipe - the only other instrument I can think of that also has a constant drone. Like the bagpipe, it is an outdoor instrument, ideally suited to accompany peasant dances. As well as providing the tune and the bass, it also provides rhythm. If the handle is rotated in a jerky manner, it causes a tiny movable bridge, the 'dog', to vibrate and make a short buzz.

When I received the kit, my spirits fell. There were umpteen bits of roughly finished wood, all of which needed accurately finishing and sanding. The back needed steaming and curving, and I needed a replacement after I broke the first one. The melody strings are played with a keyboard, but these are not plucked like a harpsichord, neither hammered like a piano. Instead, the depressed key presses a tiny tangent of wood on to the string, in the same way as the fingers of a violinist shorten the string to make a higher note. This really was a job for an experienced woodworker! Eventually, after endless inlaying, sanding and waxing, it was finished.

Imagine how demoralised I was when the only sound which came out of the thing was a raucous squawk which frightened the cat and led to my family's demand that it should be consigned to the loft, where it remained for some years. Then I was introduced to the world of historical re-enactment and rashly signed up to be a strolling player in the year 1588, so I had to get the thing

to work. Advanced geometry was needed to enable the strings to touch the wheel at the correct angle and pressure. But, surprisingly for such an ancient instrument, the greatest help came from the USA via the Internet. A warmhearted Californian lady who runs a business making hurdy-gurdies provided me with the correct weight of strings and some tiny packets of fibre for cottoning the strings. This involves twisting Just the right amount on to each string where it rubs against the wheel, in order to produce the sound, but I had been totally unsuccessful in laying my hands on the appropriate cotton in the UK.

At last! I could get a sound from the infernal machine. The melody strings were tuned by altering the angle of the tangents – all I had to do now was to learn some authentic tunes and I could be 'the hurdy-gurdy man', but it was not all plain sailing.

Because of the way the hurdy-gurdy is strapped on to one, you cannot see the keys, and have to play them by feel. Just so, I hear all you pianists say. But remember that the keys vary in size as you go up the scale (remember the violinist's fingers?), so an interval of any given number of notes covers a different length, depending on where it is on the keyboard. Added to that, one has to remember to turn the wheel constantly or the bowing stops.

So if you can rub your tummy and pat your head at the same time, this could be just the instrument for you!

It was all worth it, though. Although she plays up during extremes of temperature and humidity, my hurdy-gurdy gives pleasure both to the Tudor re-enactors who dance to it, to the many thousands of visitors who are entranced by such an unusual instrument, and to me.

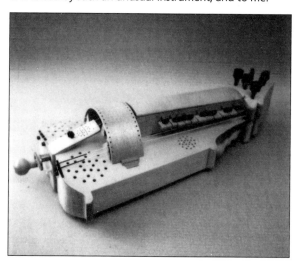

The completed hurdy-gurdy

A Feeling of Community   The Royal Free Singers

The Royal Free Singers started modestly with a group of parents meeting one night in 1973 in the geography room of the old Royal Free Boys secondary modern school in Windsor. Among the songs they sang on that occasion were *All through the Night* and *Drink to Me Only*, which may or may not have been significant. What was significant was the night – it was a Wednesday which has never changed – and also the man who had brought that first choir together, Benedict Gunner who is still their musical director after 26 years.

The Royal Free Singers has now grown to a highly-regarded and well-established choir with about 150 members. It retains its link with the Princess Margaret Royal Free School in Windsor, where it still meets for rehearsals in school term, but is primarily for the people of Windsor and district. It gives three major concerts a year, undertakes overseas tours and hosts choirs from abroad.

The moving force behind the Singers, Ben Gunner, was formerly a geography teacher at Royal Free, then director of music at Princess Margaret Royal Free. He is now a freelance conductor, principal conductor of the Orchestra of London, and director of Musica Europa, an agency specialising in the organisation of international concert tours, workshops and exchanges. He tells the story of the Singers, with interpolations from several of the long-term members.

"It's an awful shame I didn't make more of a record of that first meeting but of course I had absolutely no idea that it was going to develop into what it has," says Ben. "It wasn't an important choir at all, it was a very small, simple organisation. I would say we muddled and bumbled along from week to week. Success was not important, enjoyment was, and we went along like this for several years."

Ben says he was appointed geography master at the Royal Free, by the head Geoff Finney, largely on the strength of agreeing to organise the Christmas carol concert. After that, anything remotely musical landed in Ben's pigeon hole. Although he played the organ and had been involved in choral singing at school and college he had never thought of himself as a musician.

"After a year or two – I don't know whether it was my initiative or the headmaster's – I started a boys' choir – fairly unusual in a secondary modern school. I do know we entered the Tilehurst Eisteddfod and the boys sang

Jack the Carter Lad. The great feature in it was that one of the boys had to crack a whip."

Ben thinks one or two parents may have approached him about forming a choir but whatever the reason he sent a letter out in 1973 inviting parents to come along to a meeting to discuss forming a Wednesday night choir.

"It is quite clear now that the very first meeting of the Royal Free Singers – and the name was easy because they were parents of Royal Free boys and they were singing – set the tone all the way through. We still have singers from that time. There is a sort of core in the choir which has grown and it's picked up the style and the character from these earlier people and from me because that's how the choir was."

It was at the beginning of the autumn term in 1973 when my son brought home a note from Ben inviting parents to join him in making music in a small choir. The invitation seemed to be an excellent opportunity to rekindle my interest in singing, which really had been confined to my days as a choirboy and the usual home-spun entertainment at Christmas and other festive occasions.

"I went along to the school on the appointed evening and found myself to be one of about a dozen in all. There were about three men and a couple of us took the tenor line. (It was the only occasion I can recall when the tenors outnumbered the basses!) I am not quite sure how the ladies sort themselves out but they eventually managed to divide more or less equally between sopranos and altos. We were ready to tackle our first piece.

Nigel Jeffries, founder member

Singing is in Ben's blood. His father was a fine bass who sang with the BBC Choral Society and ran The Woburn Choral Society in which his mother also sang. Ben had already joined the Oxford Bach Choir and the English Bach Festival Chorus in London when he started the Singers.

"I was young, enthusiastic, enjoying my job. Starting something new appealed and I loved singing. There was a lot of fun and not much refinement in those early days. Neither the Singers nor I had too much idea of how to achieve a high level of performance. However we went along happily singing, giving concerts and entering competitions.

We sang at the George VI Hall in Windsor to a group of old ladies and gentlemen. We were very proud of one merry little song called The Whistling Gypsy. One of the singers whistled the melody, we had guitar accompaniment and we all joined in the verses. Les announced the number and called it The Gistling Whipsy. We couldn't stop laughing and the old people loved it because we all looked so happy.

Joan Harris, founder member

Ben says: "Some of the earliest memories I have are going in for the Slough Festival doing part songs, whatever I could lay my hands on. We did *All in the April Evening* which seemed to hang around for ages. It's quite chromatic and not easy to do nicely, very easy to sing flat with quite sophisticated choirs. We did pieces like *My Love is Like a Red, Red Rose,* which was tuneful and seemed to suit us, *The Lark in the Clear Air*, and some madrigals which are quite sophisticated and not everybody's cup of tea. We sang these in Slough and Maidenhead Festivals and the adjudicators were probably primed by the organisers to say nice things about us so that the festival wouldn't collapse the following year. A landmark was when we sang a motet in Latin, *Exultate Justi* by Viadana."

> We were introduced to Latin early on in our choral learning. One of the first pieces was called Exultate. We were given photocopies and when I look at them now I wonder how we read them at all. This piece was a firm favourite with May Shaw and it became a standing joke that wherever we sang, May liked to sing Exultate. "I do like a bit of Latin," she used to say.
> Joan Harris, founder member

By the late '70s Ben had become deeply immersed in singing and belonged to several London choirs. "I used to watch other conductors and wrote down what they said in rehearsal. I looked to see how they started movements and how they ended them. I had an innocent formula – if the conductor I was singing with was well-known, then he must be doing it correctly and therefore I could do it too."

Years of practice with the Royal Free Singers as well as a year at Trinity College of Music in 1976 played a significant part in Ben's development as a musician. "My present conducting opportunities result from all those years of practice with the RFS. We've grown together. Our performances have improved as my own experience and confidence have grown.

"An important step for me was the discovery some years ago that I was no longer reproducing somebody else's performance by listening again and again to their recording."

The choir's repertoire has changed over the years to match its size and non-auditioned status. It performs best singing large choral works accompanied by a first class symphony orchestra.

> I've enjoyed all the concerts – some more than others of course. I enjoyed St Matthew Passion, Carmina Burana, opera choruses, Verdi Requiem – a terrific sing, Elijah – I'm very keen on Elijah. And I could sing Messiah every year, I love it. In fact I think it should be part of everyone's education to learn the Messiah.
> Ann Ayres, Secretary

Although the Royal Free Singers don't have auditions they have always attracted enough people who know what they are doing; the others learn.

Ben says: "There is often a lot of humbug talked about how you should sing as though there were techniques that everybody should possess before they can sing. It's one thing if you're going to be a professional singer or take part in high quality chamber choirs, where you need to be really good of course, but it's quite another if you're singing in an average choir like the Singers.

"It isn't helpful if you get somebody coming into choir who doesn't sing in tune, or without the slightest idea of

The Royal Free Singers

what they are doing and doesn't improve. On the other hand, providing the majority are musical to a degree and most people are (that's the one thing we all have, a voice) we can all have a go. For me the beauty of the sound is the most important thing.

"There are some people who find it difficult to sing notes in tune – and I don't just mean singing flat. I mean singing almost any note. This is why I am always saying, 'If you can't do it, don't do it.' In a large orchestra, much of it gets hidden. It's more important to me that all these people come along. After all, they're not professional; they're in it for an interest, why make it heavy?"

> Singing in the Verdi Requiem in St George's Chapel was the highlight of our singing but a close second was singing The Messiah with the school in 1985. Another grand occasion was when Princess Margaret came to hear us sing in Eton School Hall.
> June Smith, founder member

Ben Gunner says that the Singers have something very special which he has not found in other choirs, a sense of community.

"I think the Royal Free Singers, as a club or society, is probably as successful as any you can get. I don't think you go to RFS principally for the fine music, You go because it's got a very all-in complete feeling about it of 'I like it here'. I like the atmosphere. There's always something happening, always something to look forward to."

> I went along to my first rehearsal, my stomach full of butterflies, but determined to make this first step in order to "find myself". I felt welcome as soon as I walked in the door and a great sense of anticipation as the rehearsal began, as I

had joined just three weeeks before the Messiah was to be performed in Eton School Hall. I really wondered if perhaps I was out of my depth, but even I surprised myself when I realised that all the years of painstaking piano lessons were really now being put to good use, and I could manage to sing along by sight-reading. This gave me a feeling of self-worth as I felt capable of something other than home management. I left that evening feeling very uplifted and looking forward to the next Wednesday.
> Ann MacLennan

An important part of the RFS programme are the outings and tours abroad, including a visit to Hungary in 1994 and to the Czech Republic as the Silver Anniversary tour in 1998. One member recalls: "Royal Free Singers tours over the years have become great landmarks in our lives – how else would we learn map-reading by torchlight, or learn how to negotiate steep paths up to a church for rehearsal, or climb hundreds of steps up to the highest part of castle ruins for a team photo, or even learn various pieces of music on the coach?

"Together we have seen great areas of Europe and, thanks to Ben, have been taken to places that ordinarily we would never see. Who would take us to a restaurant, perched on a high cliff overlooking the Danube, just so that Eifion could buy another double bass to add to his collection?"

Ben said: "When you're young, you've got your whole life ahead of you. But as you get older you realise that the most important thing is having friendships, a good sense of belonging, a feeling of community, and that's what RFS possesses. It has real friendships, a real feeling of community, a real feeling of caring."

> As long as we've got Ben we'll carry on. Everything revolves around him. Without Ben, it would alter considerably. The committee's job is to make sure it's a viable organisation – and to control Ben!
> Ann Ayres, Secretary

Millennium Choice

Ben Gunner's top eight

Bach's St John Passion

Bach's B minor Mass

Brahms' Symphony No 4

Richard Strauss' Four Last Songs

Schubert's String Quintet

Shostakovich's Piano Concerto No 2

Mozart's Haffner Symphony

Dvorak's String Quartet The American

Look To The Light Reading School

Since its foundation in 1125, Reading School has continued to exercise an influence on the lives of the local populace, and those further afield, not only through its educative processes in the classroom, but also from positions of musical authority and leadership in the town and beyond. This last century has seen no change to its role despite continued attempts over the last two decades to question the purpose and existence of the school, dedicated as it is to the pursuit of excellence.

It is the school's fervent hope that it will be singing the school song way past the millennium, with perhaps a chance to change to the opening lines,

Eight hundred years or more have passed
since Reading School was founded.

At the end of the 19th century and the beginning of the 20th something of a musical renaissance manifested itself in England. Concerts and recitals became much more numerous, and the level of performance at them was greatly raised. The love of music and the desire to learn something of its mysteries spread far and wide throughout the country. Music was admitted as a legitimate study in the universities, and in the schools, from its humble beginnings as a despised extra, it became a recognised part of the curriculum.

For many years, provision for formal class music lessons in the public school system, had been grudgingly given. If it did exist, then it was a diet of chapel practices for the whole school in preparation for the daily acts of worship, with the occasional lesson listening to a record of a particular composer's symphony, which one constantly read about.

The Director of Music at Reading, in common with those at other schools, was usually the chapel organist who gathered around him a group of promising players. In this context we think of Dr E O Daughtry who joined the school in 1913 as music master. He trained the school choir, produced a long series of successful school concerts, and operas, a custom which persisted up to the 1980s. The Minster Church of St Mary the Virgin in Reading proved to be the focal point for the training of such promising organists. Dr Daughtry was organist there inspiring his pupils to great heights, and starting a tradition of Reading School organists, who were destined to occupy some of the most prestigious organ lofts in the country.

Geoffrey Tristram followed this path to success. He played daily in the school chapel with his contemporaries, and rose to be one of England's finest recitalists, spending the rest of his time as Organist and Master of the Choristers at Christchurch Priory, Dorset. It is fondly rumoured by one of Geoffrey's living contemporaries that the school organ was the worst he had ever played on!

In 1997 the present Director of Music represented the school at a memorial service to Douglas Guest 1916-1996. Douglas had been Organist and Master of the Choristers at Westminster Abbey from 1963 to 1981, bringing great distinction to the Abbey's music. He owed much of his success to the musical influences exerted on him at Reading School, and was held in high esteem by those who subsequently came into contact with him in the world of professional music out of the organ loft.

Today the school boasts one cathedral organist, Michael Harris, who is organist at St Giles Cathedral, Edinburgh, and also lectures at Napier University. His brother is Chorus Master for the English National Opera.

Dr Daughtry was able to combine his work at St Mary's with a tutorship in music at The University of Reading. He was one of many whose contribution to the world of academia has been quite distinguished. We are proud of Sir Hugh P Allen (1869-1946) who was appointed to the Heather Professorship of Music at Oxford University in 1918 in succession to Sir Walter Parratt, who had recently resigned the post.

No records exist of any phenomenal scholastic success at Reading School (then the Kendrick School), but the first hint of music as a future profession came when Dr F J Read came to Reading as the organist of Christ Church in 1877. He too was a fine organist, and deeply impressed the young Hugh Allen. In 1908 he was appointed Director of Music at Reading University, a post which he held until his appointment as Director of the Royal College of Music at the beginning of 1919.

Coming closer to home we often read articles by Basil Lam. An eminent musicologist and expert on early music, he combined his love of scholarship with a position in the BBC. A fine example of his integrity and far-reaching scholarship can be read in his notes accompanying a boxed issue of Bach's Christmas Oratorio in 1977 by EMI.

And what of the last 20 years I can hear you ask? Is Reading School keeping abreast of the constant changes in curriculum emphasis and still managing to support a sympathetic environment in which music can continue to flourish? Recent Head Masters have realised the value of maintaining music as a high profile subject, and have given it their wholehearted support. It is one area where an academic discipline can be coupled with the development of practical skills totally suited to the type of boy with any musical ability who enters Reading School.

Reading School

The need to ensure the continued success of the music department in promoting this aim was recognised by Lady Beecham, widow of Sir Thomas Beecham, the legendary conductor and impresario. When re-establishing the Sir Thomas Beecham Archive in Norfolk, Lady Beecham came across some cuttings relating to Herman Lindars. It was then 1986, the year of the quincentennial celebrations for the refounding of Reading School in 1486. Lady Beecham noticed that Herman Lindars had been at Reading School in the early 1920s, and had gone to the Royal Academy of Music graduating from it with distinction. He had risen to be not only a steel magnate in Sheffield, but also a composer and conductor of considerable talent. It was in this connection that the Lindars family formed a lasting friendship with Sir Thomas and his family when Herman Lindars was given the opportunity to conduct Sir Thomas's Royal Philharmonic Orchestra.

To perpetuate his links with the school and to maintain the high standards of music in it, the Sir Thomas Beecham Trust has endowed three valuable prizes. These recognize not only high academic achievement, coupled with well-developed practical skills, but also a willingness to participate in the musical activities of the school. A well-rounded musician results from the Trust's encouragement and generosity.

The school also benefits from the Trust's concern that boys should not be prevented from receiving practical tuition because of financial hardship, and provides funds for this purpose. It is also aware of the costs incurred when studying music at university, and provides a leaving scholarship for a Reading School boy to defray costs of purchasing music and books during the three-year course. Far from being mere onlookers, members of the trust attend several of the important school functions where music features prominently, and are able to take a personal interest in the recipients of its awards.

Other awards have followed from former pupils. An annual prize, the Geoffrey Tristram Organ Prize, to encourage the highest standards in organ playing, has been established by a contemporary of Geoffrey. This prize was established at the time when the school embarked on an ambitious scheme to replace the ageing organ in the chapel. For a number of years now the chapel has resounded to the fine sounds of a fully restored Hill organ, standing to the front of the extended gallery at the west end of the building. Several boys now occupy organ lofts of some description in local churches as a result of their experiences and training at school. To commemorate a relative, a local music outlet has endowed a James Elphick Prize to be awarded to the most promising pianist in the upper school.

Reading School orchestra with Director of Music Graham Ireland

We now have sufficient stimulus to draw the best out of our boys. These set an example to their contemporaries, and an infectious move begins to raise the standards of all pupils to even higher levels, from the ablest boy to the beginner.

What is the present state of music in the school? Very healthy I would say. Recent trends in education and cuts in budget allocation have necessitated severe restrictions on the provision of music in the average school's timetable. It is not always offered as an examination subject. Enlightened management at Reading sees the value of music in the school, and seeks to support the subject come what may. Its task has been made easier with the advent of the computer, and the various courses combining music and technology, music with recording techniques, for example, which now abound, and offer the ideal course for the Reading boy. More pupils each year subscribe to these types of course as the number of boys wishing to read pure music diminishes.

Those who do not follow a university career can be seen in the music retail business, in the recording industry, in teaching, in private music teaching, in opera production, and the training of opera choruses. Many boys still in the sixth form run their own bands and play regularly at venues recommended by their peer groups. The groups are as knowledgeable of the pop scene as are the musicologists and academics of the present state of the so-called classical scene.

At the time of writing, a rumour is being widely spread that a former Reading pupil is about to release a single on to the eagerly waiting public. It is the school's intention to continue to foster its links with the town and to lend its expertise to many of the musical institutions which flourish in the county. Music-making is one of the school's specialities, one which helps to form the well-rounded and well-educated citizen, fit to take his place in society and protect that which is good. Its aims are firmly rooted in the chorus of the school song:
Look to the light,
Strive for the right,
Floreat Redingensis.

Graham Ireland
Director of Music, Reading School

Music and movement
Teaching dance

As a dance teacher, music plays a vital role in my work. It can be used as a way of communicating in itself or be the inspiration needed for someone to express themselves through movement. Music is important in the setting of the mood or atmosphere in which to work or create or explore ideas. The atmosphere that is created will influence the movement.

Those fortunate enough to be able to work alongside musicians may enjoy the luxury of having the music tailor-made to the mood or movement of the moment. In this way the music may accompany the movement rather then the other way around.

Over a period of two years I worked with a young woman who was brain damaged and had lost most of her sight as a result of recent serious illness. Before her illness, she had enjoyed going to discos and this was the music to which she loved listening and moving. She was most comfortable with pop music which had an obvious and regular beat. It drew familiar movement 'vocabulary' when I used it in our sessions together; the dancing tended to remain on the spot using mainly the lower half of the body.

As this young woman's confidence grew and we developed a good relationship through our dance sessions, I began to challenge her with different styles of music and explore new ways of moving. I discovered that to move very slowly was the greatest challenge. I began by using a specific part of the body, for example the hands, and deliberately focused the movement on the top half of the body. I used ambient music, a gentle exploration of sounds without an obvious beat. We danced together and took our hands on a journey but we had to move as slowly as we possibly could.

Gradually it became more comfortable and as this young woman became stronger she was able to link more pieces of movement together. When we improvised and explored movement together, the resulting dance was richer and more interesting because we were able to use a contrast of speeds. In this way the music had been a great influence on the development of this new way of moving.

Interestingly, when we came to choreograph a piece of dance that we wanted to perform together, I gave her the choice of what type of music we should dance to. She chose a piece of slow gentle music.

Helen Joseph

Bringing out the Talent Readipop

It's every local band's dream to be signed up by a major record label, but the reality often involves a lot of hard work to get your music noticed by the people who count. Musicians in Reading, however, are being given some added support through an organisation set up to promote local bands. Readipop is a promotions company that was founded in 1998 by Russell Alsop, Pete Brookes and Gavin Lombos – all of whom are stalwarts of the local music scene themselves. Funded by the Arts Council of England and through corporate sponsorship, this non-profit making organisation has already succeeded in stirring up interest in Reading music. Three CDs have been issued featuring local bands and various gigs have been held in Reading and London to promote the music even further. Plans for the future include a fringe festival, which would be held just before the Reading rock festival as a warm-up event before the main festivities.

The ethos behind the venture is to generate interest in local bands, particularly during the time of the Reading Festival when interest in the town is at its strongest.

Russell, who sings with local band burt, feels that Reading has much more to offer than just the rock festival and sees Readipop as a means towards making this known. He also feels that the townsfolk of Reading are somewhat left out of the picture during the time of the festival and hopes that Readipop can act as a mediator between the two. It is hoped that the planned fringe festival will not only showcase local bands but also generate interest in the town and encourage Reading festival-goers to stay around a bit longer than the Bank Holiday weekend.

Soulster Mazz Marilyn

The first Readipop CD was produced in 1998, with the financial support of John Madejski, chairman of Reading Football Club. Many of the featured artists had already made a name for themselves in the town through

Young Reading group M4 (Explosion)

Left: Reggae artist Aqua Livi Above: The team behind the Talic CD celebrates

playing at local venues and this helped the Readipop organisers to decide which bands to include. A total of 9,000 CDs were distributed at the Reading festival that year and copies were sent to radio and TV stations both locally and nationwide. Four bands – burt, Chocolate Starship, Powis Square and Saloon – went on to release singles as a result of the CD and the four bands have subsequently acquired the name 'The Reading Four' along the way. A series of gigs followed, including an all-day event at London's Dublin Castle and a season of Readipop nights at the Fez and Firkin pub.

Another CD was completed soon afterwards, entitled *Talic*, this time featuring music of black origin. This particular project was supported by Reading Borough Council, who were impressed with the first Readipop CD but wanted to redress the musical balance.

"The first CD was based around the Reading festival," says Pete, who has now left Readipop to pursue his own musical projects, "so what we had was a glut of indie and metal bands but no emphasis on other styles of music such as reggae or funk."

Of the 16 artists featured on the CD, four bands from the Oxford Road area of Reading were given added support through workshops to help with the production of their songs. As Russell explains, "They had come to a point where they needed a recording of a professional nature in order to promote their music. We helped them on to the first rung of the ladder and we hope this will give them the ammunition to go on to approach record companies."

Pete is quick to add that the other tracks on the CD were of such a high standard that you would be hard put to tell which groups received additional help.

A second Readipop CD was released this summer and there is a noticeable difference between this one and its predecessor. The music featured is far more diverse with a more underground feel, a fact that Pete attributes to the lack of live venues for bands to play in Reading. Whereas the artists on the first CD were chosen because their music was well-known on the live circuit, this time around the music was chosen on the basis of demo tapes.

The advantage is that all kind of bands have sprung up from the woodwork and even Pete, who prides himself on his knowledge of local music, admits to not having heard of some of them before. Strict criteria were also used in the selection process this time. Bands were chosen not only for their songwriting skills but for their commitment to their music, their involvement in the Reading scene and a willingness to make it into the music industry.

As Pete says, "It's no good putting a band on the CD if a record company rings them up and they say they're only doing it for a laugh."

It is obvious that all involved in these projects have an enormous amount of enthusiasm and belief in what they do. As a result of their commitment to promote local music a lot of exciting new bands are coming out of Reading and it is hoped that more bands will follow their example. There is a lot of musical talent currently simmering under the surface in Reading and organisations like Readipop are just what is needed to bring it out into the open.

Liz Alvis

High Notes, Low Notes Reading Symphony Orchestra

One of the casualties of the Second World War was Berkshire Symphony Orchestra which gave its last concert on 15th March 1939. With so many male members, the orchestra faced the exodus of most of its musicians into the forces and the players disbanded .It was to be five years before the music started again.

In February 1944, committee members of the orchestra decided to circulate an advertisement to gauge the level of interest in forming a new orchestra.

The response was enthusiastic and the newly-named Reading Symphony Orchestra was formed. Rehearsals were held in the restaurant of WE McIlroy every Thursday and after only five months the first concert took place, presented by the committee of Holidays at Home, an organisation set up to raise money for wartime holidays for children.

At first, concerts were usually held on Thursday evenings, with the occasional Sunday afternoon, but the starting time of the evening concerts – 7pm – proved too early for many of its audeince and affected the attendance. By 1947 the starting time had changed and Wednesday or Thursday evenings became recognised as RSO nights at Reading Town Hall.

The early years saw as many as seven concerts a year but it eventually settled into a routine of three annual concerts. The orchestra travelled to Swindon, Basingstoke, High Wycombe and as far as Portsmouth to perform, and there were also special concerts by the string section only and later the wind section.

In the early 1950s the RSO performed at a wide variety of events ranging from celebrations for the Festival of Britain and the Coronation of Queen Elizabeth II to concerts for the patients of Broadmoor Hospital and the inmates of Reading Gaol. However by 1952 the orchestra was struggling financially and was suffering from a shortage of players. Money was a continual problem because of the high cost of engaging professional soloists and the need to pay for extra players to augment the woodwind and brass sections for the bigger concerts. Unable to gain grants, the RSO was forced to introduce voluntary donations from members.

The problems began to mount up, culminating in a real annus horribilis in 1956 with the sudden death of the first conductor, the loss of rehearsal venue as McIlroy's closed and an overdraft which forced the committee to suspend all concerts as each one lost more money.

A fee from Reading Education Committee to perform two concerts for local schoolchildren was a lifeline for the orchestra and allowed it to present its own concert that year. Following the success of these performances the education committee continued to offer support for two children's concerts and two adults' concerts a year.

Throughout its financial worries the orchestra still managed to book many world famous artistes, and by 1962 had regained its former status and was reckoned to be one of the three best amateur orchestras in the country.

In 1978 the orchestra began a new and successful venture, the Reading Symphony Orchestra Young Musician Competition for players of school age from the Reading area. The winner receives a cash prize and the chance to perform a concerto with the orchestra.and many of the young musicians have since become well established in the music profession.

1994 saw the 50th birthday of Reading Symphony Orchestra and as part of this celebration a new chamber orchestra was formed. The Reading Sinfonietta was designed to put on one concert a year after the main orchestra season had finished and to concentrate on a repertoire no longer performed by the full orchestra. This marked a return to the sort of music played by the RSO in the early days. It also signified the confidence of the orchestra in its future after surviving a difficult first half century with its high reputation intact.

Ken Wickens

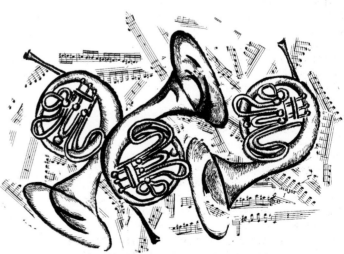

This is my Island...   Sisserou Folk Group

As the rain began to fall on a typical summer's afternoon, the crowd in Reading town centre stopped to watch as the group began to sing. "*This Is My Island In The Sun,*" they sang, umbrellas high, dancing and smiling until eventually the sun did come out.

Such is the impact of Sisserou, a Caribbean Folk Group who live in Reading but originate from the Commonwealth of Dominica (not to be confused with the Dominican Republic). Dominica is an independent British Commonwealth country situated between the French Islands of Guadeloupe and Martinique, known as 'Nature Island' of the Caribbean due to its unspoilt green and mountainous terrain.

But even if you have never heard of this beautiful island, after one performance by Sisserou, you long to sample the warmth of its shores and its people.

> **The Dominican culture is unique in the Caribbean because of the influences of the various inhabitants on the island - the Caribs, the original settlers who gave the region its name and who still live on the island today, the French, African and British. However, the French influence is prevalent and forms the basis of their native Creole language.**

In the UK, very little is known about Caribbean folk music. Most people assume all Caribbean islands have steel bands and calypso. But with their arrangement of traditional Dominican folk songs (more lively and vibrant than folk music is perceived to be) Sisserou has introduced a new aspect of Caribbean culture to the people of Berkshire, which is yet to be explored.

The group began singing as Dominican Folk Singers (UK) in 1983 – initially to raise funds following the island's devastation by Hurricane David in 1979. Most of the members are related, as there are fewer than 10 Dominican families living in Reading. There is also one member from St Lucia.

As the only group of this type in the UK, they later renamed themselves Sisserou after Dominica's national bird, a rare parrot unique to Dominica. Also unique is that the group members consist of the older generation of Dominicans who came to England in the 1950s and '60s, and one of their own songs, Streets of Gold, tells of their experiences.

Sisserou wear hand-made traditional national costumes with brightly coloured madras cloth and whether dressed in their Robe Dwiyet or Jipre (skirt), Fulla (scarf) and Tete-Casse (head-dress), you are transported back in time to the early days of the Caribbean.

Sisserou sing in their native Creole and also in English but often include drama to interpret visually their Creole songs. (Umbrellas are also particularly handy!)

Their first CD was produced in 1997, entitled Streets of Gold which is one of four songs written by Claudette Andrews, her father Watson Andrews (both members of the group), and her brother Derick Andrews who also composed and arranged the music on the CD. As a local voluntary association they were unaware that they could have sought funding and raised the money for the CD from their many performances. They recorded it at Mike Sparkes Recording Studio at South Hill Park, Bracknell, and the CD is now used to help raise funds for projects in Dominica.

This adaptation of Dominican folk songs (including their version of Island in the Sun) has also added a dynamic quality to this traditional music whilst keeping the cultural feel, for the enjoyment of future generations in the UK – wherever you're from.

One of the highlights of the group's career was in December 1987, when the Dominican Prime Minister, Eugenia Charles, invited all Dominicans abroad to return home any time from 1st January till 31st December 1988, to help celebrate Dominica's tenth anniversary of Independence in 1988. A massive celebration was being planned for carnival in February and Independence Day itself, 3rd November.

Claudette Henry takes up the story:

On behalf of Sisserou (then called Dominican Folk Singers UK) I eagerly took this opportunity to contact the Dominican Government to offer our services. This was warmly accepted and we were given an official invitation to perform as part of the Independence celebrations. For two members of the group, this was an opportunity of a lifetime as they had not been back to Dominica since leaving 30 years ago.

The group organised an excursion for 48 people including friends and family and got a group booking with British Airways which included our own specially chartered plane from Antigua to Dominica. Then the hard work began – rehearsal after rehearsal preparing for this most important performance.

It is one thing to sing your folk songs in a foreign country, but the challenge was how to make it interesting to people who had seen it before and understood the language. In the UK we had adapted the songs to have a strong visual impact so that people could understand their meanings even if they didn't understand the words, including some small acting scenes to introduce some of the songs.

However, we felt that for this special performance we needed to bring something of our own to the celebration, and decided to compose two songs as our 'gift' to our island.

The first song, *Coute Nous* (meaning – 'Listen to (hear) us'), was written in English and Creole, as a plea to Dominicans not to 'disinherit' us just because we now live abroad. In the Caribbean, people who left their island and never returned to live there are often thought to have rejected their island and no longer care about it or its people. Our message was to tell them that nothing could be further from the truth, to express how much we loved our birthplace and that Dominica will always be home in our hearts – wherever we are.

The second song, *Streets of Gold* (in English), tells of the hopes and ambitions of those who left for England in search of the promised 'riches' and the harsh realities they experienced in the late '50s and '60s. We felt it important to share what it was like to be in a foreign land, far away from your families and people you love.

We wanted both songs to express real feelings, which the group members had experienced and wanted to convey. We were very pleased with the result; *Coute Nous* was our favourite with its catchy up-tempo celebratory feel, whilst *Streets of Gold* was more sombre and emotional.

Suddenly the time approached and we arrived in Antigua, the first taste of the Caribbean for some, for others the first emotional return. The excitement and anticipation was electric as we moved to board our chartered plane – soon we'd be in Dominica! After a 20-minute flight we saw Dominica with her wondrous green mountains, and valleys, and touched down to a loud cheer. On landing at Melville Hall airport, at customs we were all given a special souvenir welcome letter from the Prime Minister before going our separate ways. Most of

Who, where, what...
Sisserou

The members of Sisserou are: Claudette Andrews, Watson Andrews, Andrea Andrews, Monica Alexander, Theresa Charles, Matilda Noel Justina Prosper, Eric Prosper, Bernie David, Ken Pascal.

Sisserou have performed at various events from fêtes and schools to festivals and weddings in and around the Reading area, plus fundraising for local charities like Sue Ryder, Macmillan Nurses, Save the Children and Huntingdon's Disease Association and Afro-Caribbean Leukaemia Trust among others.

Amongst their achievements are:

- A special welcome performance for Eugenia Charles, then the Dominica Prime Minister (1987)
- Being filmed for a BBC Documentary
- Successfully organising and staging own sell-out concert at the Albany Theatre, Bristol
- Performing at the Inauguration of Reading's first black Mayor, Rajinder Sophal in May 1993
- Performing for Reading Cosmo Festival (1993-6) and the Dusseldorf Twinning celebrations in Broad Street, Reading (1997)

Especially memorable was –

- Being invited to perform in Dominica for the 10th Independence Anniversary celebrations in 1988
- Performing at Reading's first WOMAD International Festival in 1990.
- Having recorded and produced their own CD of Dominican Folk songs called Streets of Gold in 1997.

Sisserou

us stayed with family; the others stayed at the Anchorage hotel in the capital city, Roseau.

The journey from the airport was long, but so beautiful, with coconut palms, winding mountain roads and the sight of the sea crashing against the rugged rocky coastline. It was too much to take in, and for the children visiting their parents' birthplace for the first time, it was breathtaking. We spent the next day acclimatising at a beach party organised by some friends. But soon enough, after a few days of sightseeing and relaxing, we had to organise ourselves for the performance at the Arawak Cultural Centre.

We all found the heat difficult to work in and just three days before the performance most of us had either lost our voices or caught colds. I couldn't believe it. So we searched the town for all the cough/cold medicine we could find (which was difficult, as they didn't have stuff we knew) but to be honest, a lot of it was probably nerves as well. This was a big performance for us after all, and we wanted it to be perfect.

We had organised the lighting and sound, the local cultural contact had arranged the ticket sales, and soon everything was ready. The evening of the performance arrived and we were very nervous. The lights went up and on we went. The audience was taken by surprise as they'd expected us to sing as a choir and not dance and act our way through the songs. The loud applause at the end made it so worthwhile, and we were very proud to be there. Everyone told us how impressed they were with the way we had interpreted the songs and made them alive and new.

Come rain or shine, Sisserou performs

Not only that, we were then invited to do a repeat performance at another village by a member of the audience who was so excited by what she saw. Praise indeed since she was one of the original Dominican Folk Singers from whose albums we had learned the songs. We were also invited to sing at one of the hotels as part of its celebrations for guests. After that came the big street festival to celebrate independence- the singing might have been over but the partying continued!

Back in England, we were revitalised by our success. As the group consists of mainly older people it was a real achievement to see them perform – they had worked so hard. On a personal level, I was thrilled by what we had achieved. My dream of performing in Dominica and to receive recognition for our work made the trip worthwhile and an everlasting memory.

Now we perform all over the UK but mainly in Berkshire providing a glimpse into our beautiful island in the sun, and its culture – come rain or shine.

Claudette Henry

The Entertainer John LIghtfoot

JOHN LIGHTFOOT, who is one of the best-known entertainers in Slough, was a founder member of Slough Musical Theatre Company (formerly Slough Operatic Society) and is a life member of Maidenhead Musical Comedy Society. He looks back over his career which still continues even though he is now disabled

Music is my way of life – I entertain – and have done ever since I first came to Slough as a teenager.

Do you remember singing lessons in the Boys' Club? Agar's Plough? Youth Steps Out? There were so many things that went on in Slough. It was lively. The war was on, people were dying, times were hard but there was life. In 1940, I was 17 and hadn't been called up. I had joined the Boys' Club, which at that time was at Baylis Court School, when I moved to Slough in 1938 to stay with a cousin. The sports organiser was Bill Yates and his wife, who had been a singer, started giving lessons in the Boys' Club. I joined it because I was singing mad and had been singing all the time since I was a child. I had the lessons, learned songs and so forth, started entering competitions, mostly as an individual. We'd do a little show in the club. I'll always remember *Where'er You Walk*. To us kids, you know, it sounded bloody marvellous.

When I got called up, I served in the Fleet Air Arm. I travelled quite a part of southern England at the latter end of the war singing with a group from the Navy and Army – it was a great let-out from normal work. You had your perks from that, doing something you really liked. We used to rehearse at the Hotel Metropole, Padstow. Those were great days.

Towards the end of the war and into the early '50s, we had Youth Steps Out dances and they were fantastic. They'd be packed with young people but I think we behaved ourselves a bit more than they do today. I mean, there were fights going on but Leslie Morby, the Boys' Club leader, had a wonderful way of controlling people. He had an authority but it wasn't a bullying authority. He guided you, he didn't lambast you.

During that period, I entered numerous talent competitions. Just after the war, Slough had Agar's Plough for Holidays at Home. Eton College gave them permission for part of the playing fields to be used and people came from all over the place – big tents, talent competitions, flower shows – every night of the week there was something going on.

The cinemas in those days ran talent competitions between films , the prize being a double ticket to watch films there for a year. I had a couple of pairs of them from the Adelphi in my time. The Adelphi and the Granada had big Wurlitzer organs and the top players used to play them. Cinemas were not like they are today – then they were a complete night out. Of course, the first type of karaoke was the old Wurlitzer. The words came on the screen and you got your bouncing ball over the words and the audience would sing. Community karaoke was a regular feature.

John Lightfoot (right) with comedian Tommy Handley

I broadcast in 1950 on a programme called *Spot the Winners*. I won the night I was on and was in the All England finals. Kenneth Horne fronted the show. I was on stage at the Centre with Jack Train, set up with Tommy Handley. I could have gone professional after the broadcast but I was married by then and Mary didn't want me to travel.

I was involved with theatre when I saw an advertisement in a paper asking for those who were interested in forming an operatic society to meet at Manor Park. Then we had a formal meeting in the Ambassadors' Cinema on the Farnham Road. The prime movers were there, including Mary Morgan, a Welsh lady who was later Mayor of Slough. That first meeting was in 1952 and from it we decided to form the Slough Operatic Society. We had our first show *No, No, Nanette* in 1953 in the Orchard School, which is now known as Arbour Vale.

I was a founder member and did not know that there had previously been another Slough Operatic Society which had become defunct in the 1930s. As far as I was concerned, we were a newly-formed body. We had a wonderful musical director, Bob Plowright from the Guildhall. He was a marvellous fellow for getting choruses going. He'd come down and sing everybody's part. We had big choruses in those days, eight-part harmonies, stuff like that. Singing was the forte.

Our second show was *The Vagabond King*. I played one of the leads in this show. It made me laugh to be a villain. They said I was too nice a person for such a role. My son was also in that show – his one and only theatre appearance. The last show we did at The Orchard School was the *White Horse Inn* in 1958, the only show we did two weeks running, with a week at the Orchard School and a week at Langley Secondary Modern School.

Carousel was our first show at St Joseph's and our last was *Brigadoon* in 1964. During that time we had Lord Astor, Admiral of the Fleet Lord Chatfield, Lady Howard Vyse and others as patrons but we've lost them all now. We're losing our grip, you see.

It was then that we hit the big time. With sponsorship from a couple of members and a grant from Slough Borough Council, we took the bull by the horns and went into the Adelphi, a 2,000-seater theatre, with *Oklahoma* in which I played Curley. We often played to 7,000 to 8,000 people a week when we were at the Adelphi. Our rehearsals for our main shows were at the Centre so we performed two pantomimes there – *Dick Whittington* and *Robinson Crusoe* – in 1966 and 1968. Our last show at the Adelphi was in 1970 when we had 2,000 kids in on a Saturday afternoon for our pantomime in which I played Baron Stoneybroke.

We continued to rehearse at the Centre for *Orpheus in the Underworld* which we performed at Slough College in 1971. *Guys and Dolls* required a larger stage so we moved to the Farnham Road Centre in 1972 and continued performing there with *Fiddler on the Roof, West Side Story, Kiss me Kate* and a funny show, *Lock Up Your Daughters*, which is not done often enough.

Then, to our delight, the Fulcrum (now Virgin Cinemas) was available to us. Our first show was *My Fair Lady* in 1977 and continued with one pantomime and one major show a year – *Hello Dolly, The Music Man, The King and I, Half a Sixpence* and *Oh What a Lovely War* – with small productions in between until 1982 when it closed. It was heartbreaking. That had been our heyday and we came down to earth with a bump when the council sold it.

After the Fulcrum, we lost our way again. I put that down to the fact that we had no home. The one thing about Slough that makes me angry is that there is no central place for the arts. It's been like that for years. Before the war there were more venues in which one could entertain than there are today. I'm not suggesting that the arts in Slough are dead – they're there but they are all in little niches and need knitting together.

We went back to the Centre for a number of years, then a change of treasurer brought about a change of name to Slough Op, or sometimes the SODS, to try to get more people interested. What people don't seem to realise is that opera has music and songs and drama. It's not Grand Opera – the nearest we got to that was *The Vagabond King* with its eight-part harmonies. Therefore a change of name wasn't necessary and, in fact, most of those who wanted the name changed are no longer members.

I had been wanting us to do an Old Time Music Hall as we had done after we left the Adelphi. It is great entertainment for an audience and it makes money. There are two methods: a pub scene where somebody

John Lightfoot in performance

plays the piano and everybody joins in the singing; or a wartime scene with soldiers and officers. The first we did had wartime numbers in which we involved the audience. We had an army dressed in first World War uniforms and they sang *Oh What a Lovely War!*

We tried out various techniques such as a silhouette of a steamboat with cut-outs while singing *Way Down the Levee* – the audience loved them. I've found that the Old Time Music Hall audiences are there for a good time and many of them dress for the occasion. The only instrument I play is a mouth-organ so, at one stage, I played *Keep the Home Fires Burning* back-stage while the audience wached the silhouettes of the soldiers – very haunting.

We used to build a ramp – a proper platform as they do for the fashion shows – down to the double doors half-way down the hall. The band was on the left-hand side, down in the hollow. During the finale of the first act, we came on singing *Let the Great Big World Keep Turning*. We were holding hands and the audience spontaneously joined us, making a huge circle.

We also invited a speciality act to perform , such as magicians. Tommy Cooper's brother, David, who not only looked like Tommy but also had a similar act, appeared once and that night there was a queue a mile long outside the Centre hall. We had catered for about 400 people paying £4 for a ploughman's supper and we had double that number.

I still do an Old Time Music Hall show for the elderly in sheltered housing but it's not given that name any more. Now they call it a 'presentation with a chairman'.

Millennium Choice John Lightfoot

I love musical theatre particularly Rodgers and Hammerstein's Carousel, Fiddler on the Roof and Lehár's The Merry Widow

Stick, Hat and Dance Slough Musical Theatre Company

More memories of Slough Musical Theatre Company (formerly Slough Opeatic Society) from JEAN KEENE, an honorary life member. During her 34 years with the company she has experienced a variety of musical shows and a variety of venues. She recalls theatrical disasters and triumphs, prompted by secretary Bob Simpson

It was a good-looking young actor in the front row of the pantomime chorus who was responsible for getting me involved in Slough Musical Theatre Company. I was 18 and I went along to the Community Centre with my mother and her friend, whose little girl was dancing in the pantomime. I thought, 'That's a good-looking fellow in the front row, how am I going to meet him?' So at the end of the show, when we went to pick up the little girl who was dancing, I said to her mother, "I bet it's fun doing that." I was introduced to the cast – and 34 years later I'm still there. But when I saw the young actor with his make-up off, I didn't fancy him any more!

We started in the Adelphi and I helped backstage for the first time in 1965 in *Oklahoma*. My first stage appearance was in *South Pacific* – I walked across from one side of the stage to the other singing *Bally-Hai* in French – then I was in the chorus of *Carousel* and that was it, I was hooked.

After a few pantomimes, we performed *The Pajama Game*. We had a huge society then, about 70 strong. A new director came along and he thought, 'I'm not going to do The *Pajama Game* with this amount of people.' He auditioned the society and chose about half of them. Of course half didn't get in and I believe they formed the Unity Players.

I remember one year when we were at the Adelphi, a general election was called at very short notice during the week of our show. They wanted the Adelphi for the count on the Thursday night. They asked us if we would give them the night and lose all the ticket sales. Yes, we would. For doing that, Sir Anthony Meyer, who was MP for Slough, invited us to the House of Commons for dinner. He arranged the carriage and we dined at the palace of Westminster, the whole works.

After we presented *Call Me Madam*, we lost the Adelphi because it became a bingo hall. We spent some time at Slough Community Centre but in 1976 we had the chance to put on *My Fair Lady* at Slough's new theatre, The Fulcrum. It had just opened and we were the first society to put on a big show there. We had no money to perform this show, none at all, and this was big time. However,

the chairman of the committee actually put his house up as guarantee against a loan. Because we knew this, we sold out every single seat four weeks before that show. You couldn't get tickets; there was a waiting list of 300. Those heady days have gone.

We performed quite a few shows at the Fulcrum: *Hello Dolly*, *The Music Man*, *Brigadoon*, *My Fair Lady* again in 1985, when they closed it down and made it into a cinema. So back we were in the Community Centre for about three years until the Planet Theatre at the Fulcrum opened again and there we stayed until we lost it after *Me and My Girl*.

We put on one main big production in the Spring and a Christmas show, usually a pantomime. In days gone by we used to have quite an active society, doing little cabarets and travelling shows. We really want to get back to that field again in a way, that's where the money was. We were very motivated in those days. I don't think people have quite the same interest in it now, they tend to have more home-based activities. But we work at it.

We were active socially as well. Before Nigel Lawson was

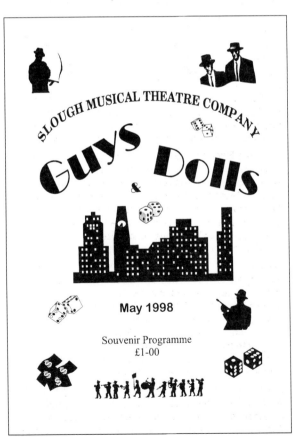

SLOUGH MUSICAL THEATRE COMPANY

Guys & Dolls

May 1998

Souvenir Programme
£1-00

Chancellor, he was Tory candidate for Slough and used to come to many of our dinner-dances which were held annually at Monkey Island, Thames Hotel at Maidenhead, places like that. They're not fashionable now but they were at that time. We used to go away to the seaside for the day, most bank holidays there was a group who went camping – fun and romping, but relationships survived. We held sponsored walks and one of our musical directors, Geoff Biggs, spent the whole of his 21st birthday on a sponsored sing at the Fulcrum.

There are no auditions to join the society. We hold open auditions for every show. Even people who've been around for as long as I have, still have to audition but we make it lighthearted. We don't have any back-biting. Everyone joins in, claps whoever goes up and does an audition, whether they do a good one or not so good. We're very close friends; we root for each other even if we're both going for the same part. Once or twice we've lost people and open auditions are one way of getting new members.

We have quite a range of ages and talents. Una Stubbs was in the chorus of an early show, we've had people go into Summer Season, end-of-pier shows, pantomime. Some of the members have been with us for years.

Marion Bray will soon be retiring from work but she is such a character, she always makes us laugh. Then we have Jean Johnson, who is not one of life's natural dancers but is another of the society's personalities. There's a piece in *Stepping Out*, where the girl who can't really tap-dance is told she must have a hat, a cane and she's got to tap-dance, and she says: "What, stick, hat and dance?" We call Jean Johnson 'Stick, Hat – and I've got to dance as well'!

We've had some funny times. Once we were asked to go on Breakfast Television when Russell Grant gave the horoscopes in the morning. We would be riding on an open-deck bus, one of the sightseeing ones used round Windsor, and we would be a background to Russell Grant. But we were not going to just sit back humming a pleasant tune, we decided we were going to be big. So, to the tune of *Old Rafferty's Motor Car*, we paired off into twos and each did our bit. And we dressed up as clowns.

I would love to have a photograph of Russell Grant's face. I think he expected twin-sets and something nice from one of the gentle shows, *The Mikado* perhaps. Well, of course he wouldn't have it so we never sang that number. How he put it to us was that he had a bit of a sore throat and he would have difficulty shouting over our singing.

We always used to play last night practical jokes. We had a young chap join our society, very keen. We were doing *Cinderella* first time round at the Fulcrum. There's a part

in the show where the Ugly Sisters are waiting for their dresses for the ball. We had eight little tots who all came on carrying boxes. The scene was set round a green dress that was in the green box, so Cinderella would open it up and hold up the green dress. One night it wasn't in the green box. It was in the last parcel he opened up. He was searching for this green dress with Cinderella standing there saying: "Oh, come on Buttons!" He never ever came back to us.

I remember one time when we were doing *Orpheus*, there is a part where you sing, "Behold my new balloon", and a balloon comes sailing down. It was the launch of one of the Apollo rockets and the backstage team had dispensed with the balloon and on stage a small Apollo spaceship was flown with a parrot on the back, and we had to carry on singing.

Unfortunately those fun things were stopped as the society got bigger and more money became involved.They decided it wasn't professional. Once you started spending £13,000 –£14,000 on a show these jokes had to go.

We've had our disasters too. When we performed *The Wizard of Oz*, we had a nasty accident, the only big accident we've ever had. At the very beginning there is a tornado. We had a house on stage, the biggest house I've ever seen on a stage. It was on a runner so when the storm raged, and the stage went black with thunder and lightning effects, somebody in black pulled it round. But they pulled it too far forward and it caught the blacks across the top and the lights. There were about four of us standing there waiting to come on and be The Munchkins and all we could hear was this crashing and ripping noise as the overhead blacks were torn. They had to bring the fire screen down.

It did £2,000 worth of damage. But fortunately the show managed to go on; we cleared the stage and off we went.

One of my worst experiences was when my husband planned a special present for me – to go to Paris in the spring – but that weekend was the dress rehearsal of *Hello Dolly*. We worked out I'd get back in time if I left my costume at my mother's. But there was a storm and the flight was delayed. While I was in Paris, my purse with the long-term car park ticket inside had been stolen so they wouldn't release my car without a hassle and it was pouring with rain.

The show had been running for about an hour and my number was coming up. I came flying in, all bedraggled. They had my costume down in the quick-change wing. They said: "Jean, where have you been?", ripped my clothes off, stuck my hat on all skew-whiff and I went straight on and did that number. What a nightmare that was!

Giving God the Best Tunes Salvation Army music

Music has always been important in the Salvation Army, writes BERNARD SPARKS who has been involved in Corps music in Berkshire for about 70 years. He recalls some memorable moments during that time

Ever since the formation of the Salvation Army, music has played a major part in worship. In fact, the Founder General William Booth is reported to have said, "Why should the devil have all the best tunes?"

There are a number of musical sections within the normal activities of Corps (Church) life. The brass band is for personnel over the age of 15 years, and many Corps have a Young People's Band for the under-15s. Then there is the choir, known in the Salvation Army as the Songster Brigade, for those over the age of 15 years, and for the under-15s, there is the Singing Company. A number of Corps also have musical groups comprising stringed instruments, such as guitars, double bass, keyboards and drum kits, sometimes referred to as Worship Groups. All the Musical Sections take part in the normal services on Sunday on a regular basis.

The Salvation Army has its own music department, which approves all music used by bands and Songster Brigades, which has been composed or arranged by Salvationists. The Salvation Army is very fortunate to have many brilliant composers and new music for bands is issued frequently; new music for Songsters is published in book form three times a year, consisting of anything up to 10 pieces per book.

Salvation Army Bands have been in existence in Berkshire over the last 100 years at Corps in Reading Central, Reading East, Reading West, Newbury, Wokingham, Maidenhead and Slough. We would have a very large band if all current playing members were to assemble at one time – there would be approximately 150 players. Similarly with the singers, we would have a Songster Brigade of about 170 voices.

The individual bands have many demands for their services but the main priority is to accompany the congregational singing at the Sunday, weekday and open-air services.

The Lower Earley Band (formerly Reading East) with which I have been associated for more than 60 years, pays regular visits to Reading prison to assist with the services held in the chapel and have been doing so for many years. Visits to hospitals, old folks homes, and concerts with other Corps or denominations are regular occurences. Requests are received frequently from local organisations to provide music for marches, parades and even garden parties.

One engagement the Lower Earley (Reading East) Band has been attending for more than 20 years is the annual Cenotaph Service held on Armistice Day on the bank of the River Thames at Caversham, organised by the Caversham Section of the British Legion.

I think the most memorable occasion in the past 50 years for this band was in 1950 when it was asked to lead the march of the St John Ambulance Brigade to Windsor Castle on the occasion of the presentation to Berkshire County Brigade of a new Standard in St George's Chapel. It is believed that the Reading East Band were the first non-military band to play within the castle walls, performing outside the chapel before and after the ceremony.

Over many years, humorous occasions often occur. Once the band and Songsters were 'specialling' (Army terminology for conducting services) for the Sunday at Fleet. We had conducted an open-air meeting and were marching back to the Salvation Army Hall when we came to a crossroads. Unfortunately the Flag Carrier misunderstood the instructions he had been given and

The Salvation Army outside Reading Gaol

turned right, only to discover that the band had turned left!

Another occasion was when the band was heading a procession in Caversham of the local British Legion. The sky was very black when the parade started and we had been marching some ten minutes when the heavens opened! Then, starting from the back of the march, people began "falling out" to find cover from the rain. This was not a mass exodus but a gradual line-by-line dispersal. Members of the band, left marching on their own, started doing the same thing, until the only people left were the Flag Carrier and the officer in charge! If only a video recording had been made of the event, I am sure it would have made excellent viewing as the whole incident happened over a distance of some 300 yards.

The Salvation Army at one time had its own Assurance Society with its head office in London and, just before the Second World War, it was evacuated to a very large house in Caversham Heights called Rosehill. From the staff that worked at the office a band was formed, taking for its name The Rosehill Band of the Salvation Army, which became known all over the world. I was privileged to be a member of this band, starting on the first cornet bench, then taking over the percussionist position when the previous percussionist, an officer, was transferred to another area.

This particular band had a very varied range of engagements, including local concerts for various organisations, concerts at the bandstand in the Forbury Gardens in Reading, and 'specialling' for the weekend at a number of Salvation Army Corps, where we were able

to incorporate concerts for the Troops. I can remember two occasions when we went to the BBC Studios in Maida Vale to take part in the series Listen to the Band, which is still broadcast today.

I had my 'most embarrassing moment' when playing with the Rosehill Band. I had played with the band for two years when I volunteered for the RAF, only to be discharged after 10 months on medical grounds. A short time after coming home, the bandmaster contacted me to see if I could help them out as they were going to Bristol for the weekend and had no percussionist. This I readily agreed to. Come the Saturday evening, the hall was packed with 1,500 people; the stage was tiered and I was perched on the fifth tier behind the band for all to see. The 'star' piece for the evening I had never played before, so I was having to sight-read. The bandmaster, Colonel Jakeway (very renowned in Army circles) explained to me that towards the end of the piece when the music builds up to a great crescendo, he would 'cut off' the band and I had to come in with a mighty crash on the large cymbal. The concert starts, we have come to the 'star' piece, the music builds up to a great crescendo; the band 'cuts off', the conductor points to me and, would you believe it, with hands poised ready for the off, I completely missed the cymbal. In the ensuing silence, a whisper went around the hall, "He missed it – he missed it!" Was my face red.

On another occasion when we were giving a concert at the Larkhill Army Camp on Salisbury Plain, the music called for a 'treble forte' drum roll. I was attacking this with great gusto when one of the drumsticks shot out of my hand, straight across the band, narrowly missing the conductor. This incident was well received by the soldiers, as you can well imagine!

The famous Rosehill Band of the Salvation Army

Millennium Choice

Bernard Sparks

As my likes in music are very varied I find it difficult to select a favourite piece but one I like very much is Judex from Mors et Vita by Charles Gounod. Brass bands have always been associated with playing hymn tunes and my favourite is Fewster composed by Ernest Fewster (1905-1973).

Weekends Only The Saturday Morning Orchestra

RAYMOND JONES, Conductor of the Saturday Morning Orchestra, explains how, despite numerous snags, this unusual orchestra has survived and flourished

The origin of this unusual musical phenomenon dates from late 1970 when as a newly-appointed head of music at Highdown School I encountered Arthur Legge, a newly-appointed head of adult education in Caversham. Arthur had previously worked at Woodley, where a very successful adult orchestral workshop had flourished for several years as an evening class and he was keen to explore the possibility of forming a similar group in Caversham. Highdown was his chosen location and I was the 'instrument' so to speak, targeted to establish the new initiative.

But there was a snag. Commitments to a demanding new job and a young family meant that I could offer time only on Saturday mornings. This was agreed and with many misgivings we set out in September 1971 to tempt adult players to Highdown to perform at arguably the least musically time in the week. (It should be understood that the proliferation of children's musical activities on Saturday mornings which now enrich the cultural life of the county was some years distant at that time.)

As feared, the first meeting was none too promising, yielding only a violinist (later persuaded to take up the viola), two clarinettists (one of whom didn't come again), and myself. But Arthur was determined. He said, "I don't care if we only have a class of three for three years, I'll have got this bee out of my bonnet!"

The end of his initially proposed time span however signalled three significant events:

1) The 'class' had grown to a respectable 14 diverse instrumentalists.

2) A successful residential weekend course at Ufton Court, recently opened to the public, had been undertaken and greatly enjoyed.

3) We had welcomed into our midst Jimmy Mutch, a former professional violinist who would become our 'Messiah', leading the 'orchestra' for the next 25 years, inspiring us all with biennial performances of the great violin concertos.

The 'class' continued to expand and by 1980 had reached forty players. But there was another snag. That year the Local Education Authority decided to double its enrolment fees! The move was resolutely resisted by the class which elected democratically to become self-supporting as Reading Orchestra Workshop (although some queried the initials!) under my 'benevolent despotism'.

Still based at Highdown, the orchestra continued to explore the classical repertory, on occasions enjoying magical collaborations with local soloists Pamela Chilvers and Sally Ann Goodworth (Schumann Piano Concerto) and Paul Cox ('cello concertos by Elgar and Saint-Saëns).

But in 1990 came another snag: an unfortunate confrontation with 'local authority' on site at Highdown resulted in a swift change of base to Meadway School in Tilehurst. Here we were able to utilise a larger rehearsal area and improved social facilities. During this period the orchestra was invited to give concerts at Hurley and Reading Blue Coat School for Mike and Janet Robson's charity (the International Spinal Research Trust) and twice at Chiltern Edge School for Save The Children Fund, both with Bernard Strauss as piano soloist.

The move to Meadway coincided with a major change in the administration of the orchestra, with 'benevolent

The Saturday Morning Orchestra at a Save The Children concert at Chiltern Edge School, Sonning Common, c 1992 photo by S V Spoliar

despotism' giving way to equally successful committee management. A new name for the orchestra seemed in keeping with the change and 'The Saturday Morning Orchestra' was suggested, approved and adopted with professionally designed logo and corporate identity.

In 1993 there was another snag. Meadway School had recently changed administration to Local Management of Schools and we were told that our hitherto subsidised booking charge could no longer be sustained. Where to now? At last fortune smiled on us. The Beansheaf Community Centre at Calcot, a new purpose-built building with excellent facilities including a sizeable hall, had just been completed and was about to open. Hearing that the orchestra needed a permanent base on Saturday mornings, members of Theale Parish Council welcomed us warmly and as a result we have been very much at home there ever since.

At time of writing the Orchestra numbers 45 players. It meets on 26 Saturday mornings a year and is prepared to tackle most composers in the repertory from Scarlatti to Shostakovitch. Recent collaborations (just as magical as those mentioned above) have been experienced with local singers: Ruth Thatcher (soprano) with Mahler's *Des Knaben Wunderhorn* and Berlioz's *Nuits D'Été*, and Martin Harding (baritone) with Vaughan Williams's *Five Mystical Songs*.

Although having prepared concerts in the past for charities, most members seem happier to rehearse self-indulgently, entertaining only friends and loved ones at the end of each term. There is no age limit and there are no auditions, but the instrumental constitution of the Orchestra is monitored where necessary to preserve a reasonable working balance. Competent string and brass players are always welcome.

Apart from the outstanding service to the Orchestra's cultural development rendered by our leader Jimmy Mutch, now retired – a further outstanding service has been carried out by Dinny Barker, who over the years has assumed selfless responsibility for organising the refreshments so essential to our well-being at every rehearsal and who now also presides as the very business-like chairperson of our committee. Dinny has kindly hosted committee meetings at home and all committee members will attest to the unrivalled quality of her chocolate sponges.

As the millennium approaches all the positive factors which have contributed to our modest success seem set to continue and the quite recent appointment of Steven Wellman as a young and enthusiastic assistant conductor, together with the loyalty and long-standing membership of the Orchestra, auger well for the future of what must still be a unique musical enterprise in Berkshire.

Out of Tune
Solomon and 'Hutch'

During my years as a musician in and around Newbury I came across two pianists, both famous but quite different in style and character. One was Solomon, the great international pianist, who played at the Corn Exchange, Newbury, in 1944. He was on the same bill as Edmundo Ros, the South American dance band leader, who gave a remarkable performance – Latin-American music was very popular at the time.

Solomon, who had a cottage somewhere near Inkpen during the war, was known to be very temperamental. For the occasion a piano was loaned by Alphonse Cary, the music shop in Newbury. Under the supervision of Mr Brooker, this huge concert piano, kept for special artists, was pushed very carefully through the town.

Les Newman, who was playing in our dance band as a pianist at that time, was a piano tuner, organ repairer and tuner, and he could take a piano to pieces and put it back together again. He tuned up this piano on the stage and got it ready for the great Solomon.

Mr Booker attended the rehearsal to see all was well. He was quite a debonaire man, and used to wear old-fashioned collars that turned up at the ends, a black jacket and striped trousers. At the rehearsal, Solomon played a few chords and he said: "This piano is out of tune." Mr Booker almost had a nervous breakdown on the spot. He said: "I had my best tuner doing this." But Solomon said: "This piano is out of tune."

Actually I think it was in tune but I understand that Solomon had a reputation for saying that nothing was ever right.

In the 1960s I played in a big band called The Hi-Fi led by Bill Ward. One spring evening we had an engagement to play at Donnington Castle House about the time of the Newbury Spring Handicap. Someone hinted that the Queen Mother might be there. If so, none of us saw her.

We were engaged to play from 8pm to 7am, with breaks of course, and were asked to assist in the cabaret from 10pm to 11pm. We arrived early and were astonished to see Leslie Hutchinson, 'Hutch', a well-known name from the 1930s to the 1960s. He was one of the best popular entertainers of the time, a wonderful pianist and singer.

The dancing started with Derek Hart, then well-known on TV presenting the news programme 24 Hours, as the compere. After an hour or so Hutch came over and asked if some members of the band would accompany him. We weren't really prepared but I said: "Well, I'll watch your left hand", and he said, "That's fine." Then Hutch played and sang Smoke Gets In Your Eyes and other great songs of the '30s. It was one of the most enjoyable half hours that I've spent in my life. It brought the house down.

Gerald Bradford

Blue-eyed Plaice and Shiny Windows Songwriter Terry Clarke

TERRY CLARKE, singer, songwriter and musician, combines fame in America with hard graft in Reading

I would say about half the songs on my latest album were written at Friar's Tea Bar in the morning while I'm taking a break from window cleaning. I get in there at 8am with a notebook, a couple of coffees, a bacon roll, and sit there quietly and work away. There's no one to bother me. Some people have writer's block, but I never get a chance to record everything I write. I write very quickly. Once when I was recording in the States I needed a bridge and a couple more verses so I went and sat at the back, rolled a couple of cigarettes and came back half an hour later and said, "I've got it, let's do it." So far they just keep coming.

Window cleaning is hard work, but it's outside, keeps me fairly fit, and I'm meeting people all the time. In fact one of the songs I've written is called the *Union Street Smelly Alley* march, and the first verse is about the Smelly Alley fish shop where I clean the windows. I remember about eight years ago I was down there one morning at about half eight, and it was pouring with rain, all down the gutters. Kevin who runs the place, was standing in the rain with his grey bushy beard, trying to sell fish. He was saying, "Who wants to buy these blue-eyed plaice, blue-eyed plaice, lady, come on," and there I was with my mop and bucket and I could hardly wait to get back in the car and write it all down: "There's a man in the alley with the rain on his face, saying who wants to buy two blue-eyed plaice." That was the beginning of the song. It's one of the songs I'm planning to record on my next album, which I call My Reading Songs, songs about Reading, inspired by Reading, growing up in Reading.

I wasn't from a particularly musical family, though my parents liked listening to music a lot. My father, being Irish, loved the old ceilidh bands and the radio was always on when I was a child. My earliest memories of music are of that radio. Music was somehow always important to me. In the '50s, it was the BBC Light Programme – everything stopped for that – and then there was Radio Luxembourg and all the country stuff. That was the first music I really loved, the Everley Brothers, Johnny Cash, Jim Reeves.

By the time I had left school the Beatles had happened, so everybody in the town was in a band. I played the guitar straight from the start. My parents bought me my first one, and when I left school I started trading them and collecting them and I've had dozens ever since. My

Terry Clarke

oldest one, an Everley Bros model which I've had since about 1969, is still as good as ever. I had a few lessons at the very beginning but I was pretty much self-taught.

The first band I ever worked with after school in 1963/64 was a band called The Statesmen. They were all local guys and we played lots of pubs in the town. Then in the late '60s I played in soul bands, playing the guitar more than singing. At first I just wanted to be a hot-shot guitar player, but it normally worked out that whatever band I was in I was the best vocalist so I ended up by default being the singer. Then when people started writing stuff, I was normally the most accomplished songwriter so I kind of fell into that by default also. Within a few years, before I was 20, I realised I was going to be a singer and a writer rather than a guitar player. Other people had come along who had more facility on guitar; they could play better and faster.

I hung out for a while with a guy in Reading called Mike Cooper. He was probably the first local person who impressed me. I learned a lot from him. I played with him on and off for a few years in the late '60s, early '70s, and then I did my first single, which I wrote myself, called *Lady* with Polydor in London in the early '70s. We got good reviews but didn't sell a lot. So I just stayed around playing locally and with Mike Cooper on some of his albums. In the late '70s, early '80s, I had a band, Domino Effect, and we had lots of gigs. After that broke up, I stayed pretty much solo, playing round the Irish scene in Reading, andlearning the mandolin and the bouzouki.

I ended up going to the USA in 1986, to Nashville first, then Austin, Texas, where I met somebody who produced my first album. It had a lot of musicians on it who I'd met over the years and had offered to play on it and that got picked up by an English label which actually financed the next two albums. Some of the musicians I've met over there have played with me here in Reading. I'll book a gig locally as it's nice to have people from West Texas playing in town here. There's a guitar player who I met in 1992, and I've worked with a lot, Henry McCullough, who was in Joe Cocker's band in the late '60s . He played Woodstock with Joe and then he ended up in Wings with Paul McCartney for a while. Henry lives back in Ireland now and we toured together quite a bit in the early '90s.

When I was young and growing up I was, like most people of my generation after the punk days, totally enamoured of America and American music – Elvis, country music, soul music. All through the '60s, everyone was into it. Interestingly, what I found when I started going over to America and meeting all those musicians was that, at the same time, they were totally infatuated with England and English music. There's a friend of mine, Jesse from West Texas, who comes from the same town as Buddy Holly. At the same time that I was growing up in love with Buddy Holly's music and looking at photographs of bright pink Cadillacs on desert roads, Jesse was combing his hair forward and wanting to be in The Yardbirds. The grass is always greener. I think it's the same with the younger ones now; the kids over there are totally into Oasis and Blur; it still goes on.

I go to America about once a year. The album I've just cut there is actually for an Italian record label. It won't be out for a while but it's the third one I've recorded for them. I've got another one coming out soon which is totally acoustic – just me on guitar. I recorded it at The Rising Sun, and that's been taken up by a record label in Vermont. It will be my first release on an American label. I recorded it here, did the art work here, all in that little studio at The Rising Sun and it's actually coming out on an American label. When I was in America last time I did three radio interviews, a television show, and played live; it's easier there to get that kind of exposure and I'm beginning to be better known there than here.

There's a lot of people who say songs and poetry are the same. You like to think the songs are poetic, but I believe that's a totally different discipline. Some people in reviews have said, "As well as being a songwriter he's a storyteller" and it's nice, it's flattering. There's certainly a storytelling element but I would never call myself a poet. You can have words which on a blank page might look trite but when you put the music in, once they are sung,

they can become the classic '50s, '60s pop song. I think my writing is a mixture of folk themes, jazz, Irish, and rock 'n' roll. The funny thing is I can write the song and be recording it and to my ears it might sound jazzy or country, and then people in America turn around and say "Wow! That's so much like the Beatles." You have these influences but you're not aware of it.

I'm a big fan of Johnny Mercer and his lyrics, *That Old Black Magic, Come Rain Come Shine, Moon River, Days of Wine and Roses*. He is regarded by a lot of people as one of the greatest lyricists; he didn't write a great deal of music himself, and most of his songs were collaborations of great lyrics to other people's music. His comeback to people who he thought praised his lyrics too much was, "You can't hum a lyric!". Nine times out of ten the lyrics come first for me. A lot of song writers would maybe start with the melody, but I don't usually do that. Sometimes I have the lyrics alone and then put music to it but even if I do that there is a kind of rhythm, a bit of a groove, starting in my head. So even if I haven't the music at that stage I know it is going to be a ballad, up tempo, major key or in a minor key. I have got most of that intuitively as I am doing it.

Obviously I'd like just to do music all the time. I know people who only do music for a living, but they don't make any more records or write any more songs. I think a lot of people have this idea, with pop music, that there are fortunes to be made. There are for a few people, but it's like all the arts – photographers, writers, painters, even a lot of the ones who are very well known, I don't know if they'd be able to survive on the royalties from their books. They all have had other posts, lecturing, teaching classes I worked in retail in Reading in the '60s, and 20 years ago took up window cleaning. Most of the time I've needed to do it, but I don't mind it being tough.

I've always lived here in Reading. When I was eight years old I used to walk through the market place in the morning to St James's School. I remember these things now when I'm in town in the mornings. You see the past and also see how things are now. I can remember in the '60s a cafe in Friar Street where all the bus drivers and conductors used to go with their billy cans and get them filled up with tea, just like it was yesterday. It's the present and the past all mixed in together. It reminds me of Dylan Thomas's *Under Milk Wood*. He wrote that about Swansea, but if he had lived in Reading he could equally have written it here with all the characters in the town. An inspiration really can be from anywhere.

 Millennium Choice Terry Clarke

Miles Davis playing Sketches of Spain

'Tis Music in the Sinners' Ears' The Spring Gardens Band

It was really thanks to the flying fingers and fundraising abilities of the Ladies' Sewing Meeting at the Spring Gardens Mission that the renowned Spring Gardens Band came into existence. If it hadn't been for them, the faithful might still be listening to the sound of concertinas.

Music was always seen to be a useful tool for drawing attention to the church and encouraging others to come to its services and meetings, as well as catering for the spiritual and musical needs of church members. This was where the concertinas came in, as the souvenir of the 21st anniversary of Whitley Hall (1927), explains: "For many years the only instrumental music for the out-door work was that supplied by the concertinas of Messrs C H Coppuck, J Meredith and F Coppuck.

"Then, largely through the efforts of the Ladies' Sewing Meeting, brass instruments were bought and a Band formed. Mr James Morris was the first Bandmaster and he was succeeded by Mr W Sopp."

Although the importance of the band was recognised in relation to the evangelical approach of the church, we know little about it during its early days at the Spring Gardens Mission, except for gleanings from the Methodist Times. For instance, in the January 1934 edition, bandmaster James Morris is described as "an accomplished musician, being the first musical instructor of the Old Spring Gardens Mission Band. He can play almost any instrument and has been the mission choirmaster for about 35 years, the latter quarter of a century at the present Whitley Hall Methodist Mission of which he is a trustee."

Since James was described as being the first musical instructor of the band and the same article tells us that he moved to Reading "about 50 years ago", having been born at Timsbury, Somerset in 1869, we can date the start of the band to between 1884 and 1893 when it is mentioned in the minutes of the Leaders' Meeting of Spring Gardens Mission.

The Spring Gardens Wesleyan Mission Band prospered, gaining a high reputation and a growing pile of prizes. In a caption under a photograph of members taken in 1908, it was recorded that the band were winners of "the Southern Counties Band Association challenge shield (Second Section) 1907; holders of five Association Certificates; two Berks, Bucks and Oxon Musical Festival Certificates; winners of 12 prizes (five firsts) and a set of 26 silver medals."

The band continued playing in the Tin Hut Mission Hall in Lynn Street until the much more spacious Whitley Hall was completed. Catherine Montague recalled that her father, Benjamin Cox, played in the band for the first service at the new purpose-built Whitley Hall Methodist

The Spring Gardens Wesleyan Mission Band 1902

Church on 14th March, 1906. It was not until 1909 that the band was again mentioned in the minutes of the Leaders' Meeting when, on 20th July, a meeting was specially convened to consider the report that the band had arranged to give 'Sacred Concerts' in one of the public parks on Sunday afternoons. From the bandmaster and band secretary, it was learnt that three such concerts had been arranged "of which one had been given, one abandoned owing to unfavourable weather and one was to be given on August 15th. No Church Official had been informed." After a long and earnest discussion, it was agreed that the following letter should be sent to the band secretary:

"Having been informed by the Bandmaster and secretary of the Spring Gardens Wesleyan Band that a sacred concert is to be given by the above Band on the afternoon of Sunday, August 15th, in one of the Public Parks, the Leaders' Meeting of July 20th, 1909, strongly deprecates such action and earnestly requests that the Band reconsider the matter, taking into serious consideration the earnest and unitedly expressed wish of the Leaders' Meeting that this concert be not given."

At the next meeting we read that "developments had made it unnecessary" for the matter to be pursued, so presumably the band did not play. Instead they were asked to take part in the aggressive Christian work planned for the winter, by marching round the neighbourhood on Sunday evenings once a month "calling attention to the Hall Services, instead of conducting the usual Open Air Service at 5.30 pm, and that the Church should accompany them."

Many ex-scholars of Whitley Hall's Sunday School, including Len Rapley, A. Rosa Wilson (Ags Dixon) and Bob Cooper remember the Spring Gardens Band leading them to Leighton Park for the annual Sunday School treat, and Bob recalled it used to lead a parade, which included Pastor Spargo and the entire Sunday School, round the streets in the Spring Gardens area on the day of the Sunday School anniversary.

Not all occurrences connected with the band bring back pleasurable memories. Len Rapley remembered that the band, which often played at a short service on a Sunday before marching to Whitley Hall for the evening service, played *Nearer My God To Thee* on the corner of Spring Gardens and Milman Road on the Sunday following the sinking of the Titanic, when 1,500 people perished after the ship struck an iceberg during its inaugural voyage from Southampton to New York on 14th April, 1912 .

In the same year the band became involved in more controversy, and this one got into the papers. The Reading Observer of 4th May, 1912 , reported in an article entitled (in the three-deck headline common to the period): Trades Unionist Demonstration – Coming of

Age Celebration – Prominent Labour Leaders at Reading:

"Speaking at No I platform where the crowd were awaiting the arrival of Mr Will Thorne, Mr J G Butler, the prospective Socialist candidate for Reading, referred to the absence of one of three bands (the Spring Gardens Wesleyan prize band) advertised to take part. A section of the religious community in the town had, he said, brought influence to bear on the bandsmen and it was as much as they dared do to come so they did not turn out. (Shame) But that was a religious movement as they saw it and they saw in that action another example of the great difficulty they had in trying to help the workers of the town. It was a great pity that such a blunder should have been committed as the withdrawal of the band. He wished to say that the bandsmen were willing to come (cheers) but were stopped by those in power."

The band, which was conducted at the time by Mr J Hodges, broke up during the years of the First World War, and when it reformed in 1919 Charlie Coppuck (of concertina fame) took over as conductor.

He was still in charge when GE 'Ted' Watkins, a member of the well-known Watkins family, joined in 1930 at the age of nine. He had been taught to play the cornet by his father, a member of the band since 1920, and its secretary at that time. He took over as conductor in about 1937 and remained so until he retired in 1975.

Ted who continuing the family tradition as the band's conductor from his father, recalls: "When I joined the band we rehearsed in Whitley Hall Tuesday evenings and played concerts in the chapel. The pastor then was J W Spargo and the Whitley Hall representatives to the band were Messrs G Morris, W Tucker and Upton."

He remembers the band was later embroiled in another controversy which led to a complete break with the chapel: "The band broke its connections with Whitley Hall in 1933/4 and then rehearsed for a number of years at Christchurch School. I think the break up was brought about by the selling of scent cards and football tickets to obtain new uniforms and instruments, which the leaders of the chapel did not agree with.

"The band still has 30 members (a similar amount to the 1902 and 1908 ones) and do quite a number of charity concerts, but years ago we would march around the town in hospital parades and to fetes. We are still self-supporting – that is one reason we don't do contesting now, because of the expense and the lack of rehearsal room. We now rehearse once a week at St George's Hall, St George's Road – we can't afford any more because of the price of instruments and music.

"We have quite a number of young people – boys and girls – in the band, so there is still plenty of interest in it."

Daphne Barnes-Phillips

The Benevolent Fiefdom Sainsbury Singers

In 1920, 29-year-old Frank Sainsbury returned to his native Reading from London. A well-known amateur singer with a good baritone voice, he had had several offers to join professional opera companies, including Carl Rosa and D'Oyly Carte Touring Opera, but had had doubts about the prospects for supporting a wife and family in such an peripatetic fashion.

Getting a settled day job, he treated music as his hobby. At first, this was confined to singing in concerts around Reading, mainly in recitals to aid local good causes. However, using his evenings, he also set up as a music teacher and was soon taking some of his pupils to these concerts with him, both to show off their talents and to give them experience of performing in public. The group soon becoming known as Frank Sainsbury's Singers.

There followed a series of small concerts which he organised specifically for his pupils. Consisting mainly of operetta or oratorio selections or individual items from popular music of the day, these were given in church and village halls. Then, in Reading's Small Town Hall on Wednesday, 17th February 1926, he organised the first of what was to be an annual Programme of Recital by pupils of Frank Sainsbury.

By 1930, with a growing reputation as a gifted teacher, he had some 40 or so pupils. With the help of a talented and supportive wife, Kathleen, as accompanist, he began the more formal concerts which were to become a sustained part of Reading's pre-war musical life. However, by 1936, he felt that a more stable grouping was possible with the main aim of presenting large scale works in their entirety. The first of these productions was still in concert format but, by 1938, he had a group of singers and players he deemed capable of presenting fully-staged performances of light operetta.

'Founded 1938 for the study and performance of Operatic and Choral Work' – the Sainsbury Singers had arrived.

By 1998 – during its first 60 years – some 68 different major works were performed in 113 productions. Venues ranged from small halls such as at Park Church to the Hexagon Theatre. Its repertoire has featured Gilbert and Sullivan, Viennese operetta, American musicals, Broadway musicals and Grand Opera. There was one commissioned first performance:– Michael Sharman's *Pirating Pinafore*, based on music from Gilbert and Sullivan operettas and parodying the story of the copyright and royalty problems associated with unauthorised performances of Gilbert and Sullivan works in the United States of the late 19th century.

The Sainsbury Singers' first production, *HMS Pinafore*, was given at the old Palmer Hall in January 1939, rehearsals having begun in Grovelands Hall late in 1938. It was conducted by Frank Sainsbury himself and he was to conduct another 35 productions up to 1962, shortly before his death in 1963.

It had been a marvellous start but, almost immediately, came the Second World War. The male chorus was almost decimated by the call-up. Materials for costumes and scenery rapidly became increasingly scarce. Nevertheless, productions were still planned with the additional aim of contributing to the sustaining of wartime morale and, with the exception of 1940, at least one production was given each year of the war's duration.

It was in pursuit of getting professional-level performances from what was now an enforced imbalance in his company that, in 1943, Frank Sainsbury persuaded Clare Henderson, a well-known London producer who had recently retired to Henley, to become its producer. She was to remain in that capacity for most of the next 30 years. Following several short tenures in the meantime, Evie Bence took over in 1986 before being succeeded by another professional producer, Stephen Salter, in 1998.

Frank Sainsbury

The end of the war had seen not only a rebuilding of the company but also a new venue. Most of the war-time productions had been in the Park Institute, but 1947 saw a move to Reading's Town Hall. Providing the opportunity to put on large-scale productions – the first was *Merrie England* – the Town Hall was to be the company's main home for the next 30 years. But, the Town Hall was not really a working theatre. For each production, it was necessary to build not just the set, but also a performance stage – everything from footlights to the full proscenium arch. The stage area – though much larger in area and considerably higher than any previously available to work on – was nevertheless somewhat cramped. The dressing rooms (as they were called in polite conversation) were mostly down in the bowels beneath the stage and varied from cleaners' cupboards to day-time offices. Then there was one of Reading's (and England's) chief glories – the magnificent 'Father Willis' Organ. Alas, this was also one of the company's chief nightmares. It prohibited 'round the back' communication between the two wings at stage level. This resulted in a penalty of several exhausting minutes (two flights of narrow stairs – a climb down, a dark corridor and another climb back up) for any off-stage movement between opposite sides of the set. This was bad enough when the production demanded it – worse still, if the result of a faulty memory!

Then, at the end of an exhausting show-week, the whole lot had to be dismantled – often by early Sunday morning after Saturday's last night.

In 1977, Reading's new Hexagon theatre complex was completed. On 7th November that year, the Sainsbury Singers were invited to celebrate the opening with a concert performance of Gilbert and Sullivan's *The Gondoliers*. With comfortable seating for a large audience, a large West End-sized stage, a sunken orchestra pit, real dressing rooms, an available curtained proscenium, scene dock, and (most welcome of all to the on-stage performers) one-level freedom of movement between the two wings backstage, The Hexagon was a most attractive venue. It was to become the new home for the company and its productions have been given there twice a year since then.

The new facilities also enabled the company to expand its horizons in terms of the type of works which it could perform. A taste for the Broadway show had been engendered by the production of *My Fair Lady* in 1976, but it was the availability of The Hexagon's spacious stage area which enabled a major change of direction in its repertoire. Shows which demanded many changes of scene – such as *Hello Dolly*, *Half a Sixpence*, *Oklahoma* and *Showboat* – could be produced with the slick changes to the set which are an essential part of such performances. Extensive dance routines could be set for shows such as *Guys and Dolls* or *Me and My Girl*. These also naturally demanded a wider range of personal expertise in individual performers with acting and dancing abilities comparable to that of singing. The development of stage crew members was just as important.

From its beginnings, Frank Sainsbury ran his society much as a benevolent personal fiefdom until his death in 1963 although, as the enterprise grew, a management committee had been formed in 1950 to help organise its affairs. Over the years, the company steadily developed its own wardrobe, stage management, lighting, sound and business management teams – all vital to the putting on of large productions.

Frank was its musical director until 1962 when he was succeeded by Robert Ladkin, himself succeeded in 1974 by Michael Evans who in turn handed over to the present musical director, Michael Sharman, in 1996. Choreography, always important in stage productions, became a key requirement with the onset of performances of grand opera and, later, modern musicals. Pixie Denzey, Beryl Cooper and latterly Isobel Stebbings and Kim Hughes (jointly) have expanded both the repertoire and individual expertise of the company's members. For many years now, the business affairs have been handled by business manager John Jones and treasurer Stephen Fisher and stage management by Chris Stebbings. Stage performers receive their appearance preparation from teams led by make-up director Bob Fennell and wardrobe mistress Pat Spinks. And the Sainsbury family connection (not part of the Supermarket dynasty) is still going strong with Keith Sainsbury as its current president.

To celebrate its Golden Jubilee in 1988, in conjunction with The Phoenix Choir and Reading Male Voice Choir, a gala concert was given in the Hexagon. Nearly £9,000 was raised from this and other events during that year, to equip a reception room in The Radiotherapy Department at The Royal Berkshire Hospital which, coincidentally, was celebrating its 150th anniversary that same year. In 1998, the Sainsbury Singers' Diamond Jubilee was celebrated in a gala concert given at the Bearwood Theatre.

The company has a distinguished cohort of patrons. Indeed, 1974 saw three of the present patrons – Sir Colin Davis (then director of the Royal Opera House, Covent Garden), Valerie Masterson (principal soprano with English National Opera) and Graham Clark (the operatic tenor who was then actually singing in the production) – in the Town Hall together for the Sainsbury Singers' production of Faust.

Further confirmation of the company's standing came in 1996 when, as part of the National Trust's Centenary Celebrations, the Sainsbury Singers were invited to give the Saturday Evening Concert at Basildon Park.

John Southall

Getting the Mix Right   South Hill Park

PAUL JAMES was a professional musician until he came to South Hill Park arts centre in Bracknell, as music programmer and later deputy director. He left in 1996 after five years to become first ever director of Farnham Maltings arts centre. He remembers his times at the Park: "It really wasn't like going to work at all."

South Hill Park

Arts centres always have a battle getting across the message that they are inclusive not exclusive. British people have a bit of a problem with the word 'art'; there are all those prejudices about so-called elitism. South Hill Park is a rather imposing mansion and doesn't lend itself to giving out an informal, friendly message to passers-by. Nevertheless I think it is a fantastic place and one of the best arts centres in the country. I've played in most of them so I know.

From 1980 to 1991 I was a professional musician (saxophone, bagpipes, woodwinds) touring round the world and making records, mostly with a folk band called Blowzabella. I also composed and performed for theatre companies and worked as a session musician in studios for all kind of artists from reggae, Asian pop, folk, world, rock and jazz. Touring was great but by 1991 I had had enough. I was always the one who did the organising in the band so it was a fairly natural progression to work as a music programmer in an arts centre.

What attracted me to South Hill Park was that I had played there as a musician. South Hill Park had always had a reputation for good music. There was Bracknell Jazz Festival in the late '70s and most of the '80s. Bracknell Folk Festival had a long history, and there was jazz and classical music throughout the year. So when I saw the job of music programmer advertised I thought I'd apply and was genuinely amazed when they offered me the job as I'd had no previous experience apart from playing in arts centres. I had been to arts school and love all kinds of music, theatre and dance, so it was a great place to work and be involved in the arts as an organiser.

The famous Jazz Festival had finished a few years before I got there and the Folk Festival was in decline. I think the weakness was that the Park used outside organisations or promoters to think up the festivals and the arts centre provided the facilities. I thought it would be a good idea for South Hill Park to provide the facilities and the ideas as well.

I felt it should have its own music festival as a key part of its arts programme so I organised the first Bracknell Festival in 1992 and built it up until I left in 1996. The idea was to bring together all kinds of music – indie, hip hop, techno, ambient music, world music, jazz, everything – because my theory is that festivals that just do one kind of music only appeal to one narrow part of the potential audience.

Also I felt strongly that apart from a bit of tokenism, local musicians had been largely left out of previous festivals and I sought out local promoters and bands and gave about a third of the programme to them. It worked well because we began to get a majority of local people in our audiences instead of a small minority. A community arts centre like SHP is there primarily for its local community and the programme should reflect that. The problem was that when they started doing festivals back in the '70s there were hardly any houses near the Park. By the '90s it was surrounded by new housing estates so it became more of a battle to balance the neighbours wanting peace and quiet with the rights of the festival-goers.

Getting Bracknell Festival started in 1992 was hard work. We had to overcome a lot of "it's not the Jazz Festival… it's not the Folk Festival" but by the second year people started to get the message that it was a broader kind of event where you could experience all kinds of strange music. I loved the way the staff used to get behind it and work as a team. One of the things I really enjoyed was getting together a gang of what local councillors would probably describe as "disreputable youths", who used to drink in the bar on Fridays, and convincing them they should form themselves into the backstage crew. They were absolutely brilliant at it and still are; the main stage always ran to time.

Musically, a lot of it blurs together, but I remember Jah Wobble doing a wonderful set on the main stage and Ian Dury backstage writing a little poem for my son. I also got a lot of satisfaction from bringing in a more visual approach, multimedia, live computer art and street theatre.

When I worked there I thought our funding wasn't as good as it could be. Now I realise that South Hill Park was very well funded by comparison to most other arts

Bracknell Jazz Festival, South Hill Park, 1987

I enjoyed putting on a year-round programme of jazz and contemporary music and building up a bit of a music scene for local bands. The programme works best when it is a mixture of professional artists of national and international reputation and local amateur and professional artists. When you get the mix right you break down the barriers and people get more personally involved.

As a programmer, it's really easy to fall into the trap of just booking the things you like yourself. You have to be inclusive and listen to what others want and try and react to that creatively. It's all about balance; if you don't have any original ideas and you only book whatever other people want, the programme lacks focus, but if you are too dogmatic about your own ideas the focus becomes too narrow. It's impossible to get it right, you just have to try your best. The great thing is the programme is a living, breathing thing that should be changing and developing all the time in response to the changes in the wider world.

The problem for people nowadays is the massive and baffling range of choice they have. Pick up any newspaper in Berkshire and on any one night you can go and see gigs, theatre, cinema, dance at several venues within a 30 minute drive. Developing audiences gets tougher and tougher as competition increases. It isn't just the product though; if you have a great venue with atmosphere it contributes to people's decisions about where to go. South Hill Park has the disadvantage of being on the edge of a town with little public transport but it's got bags of atmosphere and good facilities so it will always get audiences as long as it gets its marketing right.

I don't think things have changed in any fundamental way. People are the same mixture of ultra-conservative to the very eclectic in taste. The biggest change in music was the explosion of independent and specialist music labels and magazines which started with the punk thing in the late '70s. Since then, music audiences have had more choice and more information and its easier now to get into a particular type of music in detail. The Internet works well for music in particular and like a lot of people I use it all the time to find out about bands, gigs, festivals and CDs.

It's as hard as ever to make a living as a musician in Britain. The main reasons are that it's still considered not to be a proper job and there is a lot of competition because this country produces so many talented people. One of the driving forces which makes talent emerge is that the latter happens despite the former. People with original ideas love to rebel.

At its best, music (like all contemporary art forms) is about ideas. I hope that never changes.

centres. Bracknell Forest Borough Council and Southern Arts really supported the place. Bracknell Forest were always pretty generous with grant funding. I think this was because it's a new town so the council were interested in investing in reasons for people to live and work in Bracknell and the arts were a part of that.

I was also lucky to have had a great boss. The director, Christine Bradwell and I started there around the same time – she went on to be chief executive of The Anvil and I went to be director of Farnham Maltings – and she was brilliant at encouraging the staff to express themselves and take risks to create an imaginative arts programme. Nothing is ever without its problems but for most of the five years I was there we had a great time. It really wasn't like going to work at all.

A Fairly Rare Breed Slough Philharmonic Society

Slough Phil, as it is affectionately known, has been providing high quality orchestral and choral music in the town since it was founded as part of Slough Estates cultural life. DAVID WILSON, a winner of the Mayor of Slough's Award for Individual Contribution to the Arts, has been their musical director since 1959 and describes the pleasures and perils of running a large amateur society

Slough Philharmonic Society is actually an orchestra and a choir – I don't know in which order one should put them, choir and orchestra – but it is both. Amateur societies like this with a dual role are a fairly rare breed; in fact of the 700 amateur orchestras in the country, fewer than 50 have a choir attached. So it is Slough Philharmonic Orchestra and Slough Philharmonic Choir and the orchestra exists to provide accompaniment for the choral concerts.

Having an orchestra that has time to rehearse for a choral concert is unusual and an important asset. The fact that we can give six or more rehearsals before a concert means that the orchestra has been thoroughly rehearsed to accompany the choir and it makes an important difference to the standard of the whole performance.

The very first performance by the society was of *The Messiah* in 1942, the year after it was founded by Slough Estates Ltd. When they formed the enormous trading estate in the '30s, Slough Estates set up a social fund to provide housing, medical facilities, and sporting and cultural pursuits to serve the people working in the factories.

The original Slough Community Centre, which had been opened by King George VI and Queen Elizabeth in 1937, was the concert hall we used for many, many years. Slough Estates asked a retired Army musician, a regimental conductor, to form an orchestra and a choir at the Community Centre and rehearsals started in 1941 for their first concert. That performance of *The Messiah* in 1942 was followed by nine other concerts in the first year.

After that the Society held eight concerts a year throughout the war under great difficulties and would perform at 3 o'clock on a Sunday afternoon in order to ensure that air-raids did not affect the concert.

Because the RAF Central Band was based at Uxbridge and there was a Guards Band at Windsor, the orchestra was able to call on them for extra players. Some of the outstanding orchestral players of the next generation served their time as bandsmen during the war, and

musicians such as Dennis Brain, the horn player, Leonard Brain, his brother who was an oboist, and the flautist Gareth Morris, played for Slough Phil. As a result the standard was very high and the Community Centre was packed out with audiences of 800 or more.

However, things changed after the war, with diminishing audiences, and we have steadily been rebuilding since then. At present the orchestra has 68 to 70 members and it is pleasing that the average age of the musicians has come down dramatically recently. We have many new young players in their late 20s and early 30s, generally those who've been to university, or are starting a job and are sufficiently settled to have time to join.

David Wilson

Our longest-standing member is Margaret Harkness who is treasurer of the Society. She was a professor at London University and joined the orchestra as a violinist in 1942. She is still playing, and a much-respected member of the Society. We have professional players in all sections of the orchestra who it to keep up their playing standards.

The choir tends to have longer-term members – one has been there since 1948. For various reasons its size has fluctuated over the years and membership has been as high as 120. At the moment there are 75 members and the are singing very well under chorus master Kenneth Weller. We are very proud that one of the choir members has now become a professional and has sung at Glyndebourne and at Covent Garden.

Slough Phil is a sociable society and the coffee break in the middle of rehearsals is an important part of the evening, when like-minded people can chat together. We also have social gatherings such as barn dances.

I am the seventh conductor of the Society. Soon after I came to Slough in 1956 as Head of Music at Slough Grammar School, I joined the orchestra as a bassoonist, and when the position of musical director and conductor at Slough became vacant, the Society asked me if I would be interested. I started in September '59 and conducted

Slough Philharmonic Society

my first concert in November and still consider myself fortunate to be in this position.

We give five concerts a year; two are choral in December and May, and three are orchestral in November, February and March. It normally rehearses as a complete choir but we have now appointed an assistant conductor so there will be sectional rehearsals for the choir as well as for the orchestra in future.

One concert I clearly remember was a performance of The Messiah, in the days when we had terrible fogs. The fog had been fairly thick in the afternoon, so after we had held the pre-concert rehearsal one of the soloists who lived on the other side of Slough went home. However, she was unable to return to the Community Hall for the concert because all transport was cancelled. We started the performance on time but without all the soprano arias. Then the fog started creeping into the Community Centre hall and it eventually reached a point when you could not see the back of the hall.

At this point we terminated an unfinished Messiah in agreement with the audience so that everybody would actually get home. After that, experience we took out an insurance against bad weather.

The biggest bone of contention over the years has been finding a satisfactory concert venue. If we go back over the years, the history of Slough Phil has been a history of worrying where to perform and where to rehearse.

We didn't move out of the old Community Centre until 1977 when The Fulcrum complex in the centre of Slough was built. We gave just 17 concerts there before Slough Council decided to close it. The Thames Hall was good for orchestral concerts and we had the largest audiences in our recent history of up to 800.

We now give three concerts at Eton College and two at the new Centre in Slough, which opened this year. We gave our first concert there in February 1999. The acoustics are good but the main drawback is that there is very minimal staging and it's on the flat, so beyond the first few rows the audience cannot see the orchestra at all. We hope that is going to be addressed before the next season

Our repertoire is very varied. Most of our concerts are concerned with classical music but we are flexible and this year we gave an American programme which included Gershwin and Jerome Kern. But it is the main symphonic repertory that the players are interested in. The most successful modern work we have presented recently was Bartok's *Concerto for Orchestra*, which was a fine performance for an amateur orchestra. I hope I am not blowing our trumpet too much, but we do like to think that our standard is very high and we can tackle difficult works.

We have just performed Haydn's *Creation*, which I consider to be a wonderful piece. I have conducted it before but this was very special. Clearly, the audience enjoyed it. It was one of those celebratory evenings when everything goes perfectly, when the choir and orchestra all gel.

We cannot afford to pay the highest fees for soloists such as Nigel Kennedy, but we have engaged some soloists at the start of their careers and who have now become famous.

I suppose the most outstanding must be Peter Donohoe, who came just after he won the Moscow Piano Competition, and being impressed with the orchestra, came a second time. In our artists' autograph book he wrote: "The Slough Philharmonic Orchestra is terrific. It is a privilege to play with the orchestra for a second time."

Millennium Choice

David Wilson

Asked for my favourite piece of music, I would say Elgar's Enigma Variations. But I have varied tastes and I could equally say Abba's Thank You for the Music, and this aptly sums up my professional life as a musician

Busking in Berkshire
Street musicians

Music has found another outlet in our everyday lives in almost every town in Berkshire. Where there is a shopping precinct or pedestrianised area it provides a permanent stage for a many-talented society. Buskers abound. Students of music unable to find work during holiday periods play their chosen instruments for our pleasure. Guitarists strum through every range of style from Segovia to Dylan.

In Maidenhead a violinist charmed everyone with sweet tunes played on his electric violin. When a large enough audience gathered and he ended his recital he sold them tapes of his recording. Good business sense.

In Broad Street, Reading, shoppers are treated to the hurdy-gurdy sound of children's roundabouts. There are bands, classical and rock, and troupes of dancers of every kind. On one occasion a young couple in full evening dress delighted everyone with their ballroom dance routine.

A welcome addition to our culture are the many ethnic groups who entertain us with their colourful costumes, graceful dances and unusual instruments such as the South American pan-pipes. The foot-tapping beat of the steel bands invite everyone to join in the dance. They are all a joy to watch and listen to.

Many of the buskers have their own pitches. One regular always performs with his faithful dog keeping him company.

Some performances are organised, for charity or for advertising. There are the carol singers at Christmas time.

Always somewhere there is someone ready to play, dance or sing for the passers-by in the hope of payment of a few pennies and while they continue to please who would deny them some small recognition of their talents.

No longer do the streets echo to the screech of traffic but to the sound of music.

Carol Whelan

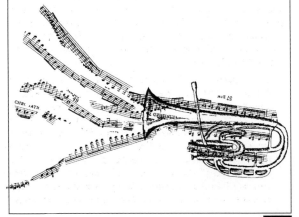

The Sound of Silver Sandhurst Silver Band

Not surprisingly, it was to the army that Sandhurst Silver Band owed much of its early success, for after its formation by the local Coombs family in 1908, musicians were regularly 'recruited' from the nearby Military College.

Fred Coombs, who lived in Albion Road, Sandhurst, had long thought that the village needed its own band to play at local functions, and with that in mind, set about contacting others with a similar interest.

However, it was in 1912 that the band became firmly established when, under the baton of Fred Bennellick, who worked as a saddler at the Broadmoor institution, it bought its first set of uniforms and became instantly recognisable, not only for its music, but also for its smart appearance.

Not only did Mr Bennellick become Sandhurst Silver Band's first conductor, but his four children and one of his grandchildren also became a playing member.

As with so many of the brass bands of the '20s and '30s, Sandhurst was at that time very much a local family affair, with the Birds and the Clarkes, as well as the Coombs, contributing heavily towards its make-up.

Sadly, though, by 1954, as with many similar organisations, numbers had tumbled to such an extent that the band's conductor, Gerry Hughes, occasionally played the cornet solos from his rostrum as well as conducting.

But despite the shortage of musicians, the band continued to add cups to its trophy case, including a first at the Southern Counties Contest at Cirencester.

One thing which partly accounted for the reduction of the band to an all-time low of 20 members, was a split which took place in 1960, when the conductor left to form Camberley Band, taking several other musicians with him.

However, there were high spots as well as low, and at the time when cornet player and current president Brian Attewell becoming band secretary, the musicians temporarily deserted their instruments to take up hammers, trowels and paintpots and build their own headquarters in Green Lane (now Brookside) – a building that is still in use today.

Sandhurst Silver Band in 1959. *Photo by Gale and Polden Ltd*

In the late '60s, the band staged a remarkable recovery in size with the influx of several high-calibre players and the introduction of a new musical director. Under the leadership of former Royal Marines conductor Roger Palmer, from Wokingham, Sandhurst Silver Band achieved success at numerous competitions, winning five trophies at the Southern Counties contest at Portsmouth Guildhall.

Then in the early '70s, Albert Lack, of the world-famous Grimethorpe Colliery Band, became MD, taking the 35-strong Sandhurst ensemble to third place at the National Area Contest before handing over the baton to Jim Brewer, a musician from Woodcote with many years orchestral and choral experience.

A succession of musical directors followed Mr Brewer, including Jack Clark, a second ex-Royal Marines musician who joined the Sandhurst Band from Morris Motors, and Steve White, who travelled down from Yorkshire to become conductor, eventually marrying a fellow musician and member of the Bird family.

Under Roger Burke, its current musical director, who was formerly with the Royal Corps of Transport Band, the ensemble continues to add to its list of impressive contest successes but, more importantly, it is an engagement band, playing at fêtes, concerts and other musical events.

Although a wider sweep for competent musicians has broadened the membership from its original local family days, there is still a strong social bonding that keeps the secretary busy organising bowling evenings, barbecues and dinners with even a trip to Alton Towers thrown in for good luck.

As Roger Burke himself put it: "I know we will never challenge the country's top brass bands in terms of musical achievement, but I do know that this band can really perform when it puts its minds to it. Couple this with the its undoubted enthusiasm and there you have a recipe for success."

Ron Pearce

St Sebastian Wokingham Band

While it is to the factories, quarries and pits of Northern England and South Wales that so many brass bands owe their existence, it was often the churches and chapels that were the motivators in the south.

That was certainly the case in Wokingham in 1931, where like-minded members of the congregation from St Sebastian church, in Nine Mile Ride, together launched an ensemble to play the hymns and lead local fêtes and festivities. Those pioneers could have had little idea how their brainchild would prosper.

Although membership is now drawn from a much wider area, links with the Wokingham church are still strong and following that pre-war launch when the vicar actually played in the band, a succession of church leaders have held the presidency to this day.

However, one man more than any other can claim the title 'Mr Brass of Wokingham' for 84-year-old Alan Clacey joined the band when it started and is still a key member of the trombone section after a period of 68 years during which he was conductor for 25 years and also secretary and treasurer.

During the past 18 months, the band has been collecting trophies and certificates for its wall,

The St Sebastian Wokingham Band, with its conductor Bruce Gentry and two of the cups it has won in recent years   *Photo by Studio Carr Ltd*

the most recent being at the National Championships of Great Britain where the band came a creditable fourth.

During 1998, the band won its section in both the Spring and Autumn contests organised by Southern Counties Amateur Bands' Association. It has also won the local Battle of the Bands for the past three consecutive years and, taking on the competition in Lancashire, the traditional hotbed of brass banders, on their own territory, came first in one of the Whit Friday Festival contests .

Wider fame came when the band was filmed while playing in a Whit Friday procession in Yorkshire, leading to a fleeting appearance in the award-winning film Brassed Off.

Ron Pearce

Voices in Unison Jackie Tate

JACKIE TATE remembers the fun and the hard work of singing in a girls' choir

I was in the Central Berkshire Girls' Choir for a couple of years before I left to go travelling in a year out before university. To join, I had to sing a few notes for Gwyn Arch, the conductor, as a sort of informal audition. I remember being terribly nervous as I really wanted to be in the choir. One of my friends, Katy, who was already in the choir, was always raving about how great it was, and I was desperate to get in. I was also in Basingstoke Choir at the same time, so I had done a similar type of audition before, but the two choirs were, of course, very different. In Basingstoke Choir we would concentrate on a long classical work, whereas in the Girls' Choir we'd sing much shorter pieces, both classical and more modern works. Both choirs offered very different experiences, and I wanted to sing everything from Grieg to Gershwin to *Godspell*.

I remember Girls' Choir rehearsals were great fun - exhausting, but I always looked forward to them. We practised first at the Reading Activities Centre on Crescent Road, and then later moved to Earley St Peters, Church Road. I would come out from rehearsals absolutely buzzing and sing all the way home in the car. I think my parents knew all the songs off by heart long before they heard them performed on stage.

Gwyn certainly made us work very hard, repeating phrases over and over until they were perfect. It was incredibly satisfying when we'd get it just right and Gwyn would bring the tips of his fingers together at the finale and we'd all fall silent totally in unison. You could cut the air with a knife at those times.

There were several performances with the Girls' Choir, but the most memorable for me was when we reached the televised quarter-finals of the Sainsbury's Choir of the Year Competition in 1995. ! still have the video now that mum recorded from the TV, (and that I remember desperately scanning afterwards to see what shots there were of me and my friends), and even watching it now brings back the nerves I felt at the time.

Out of an original 300 choirs that had entered, 12,000people in all, the Girls' Choir performed with seven choirs on our day, of which only two were to go through to the semi-finals. It was a day trip up to Manchester by coach from which we returned in the very early hours the following morning. We performed two pieces: to open, *We Beseech Thee* from the musical *Godspell* by Stephen

Schwartz and arranged by Gwyn (Gwyn once said that we were ideal guinea pigs for his arrangement experiments!); to finish, *Hymn to Vena*, from the *Rig Veda*, by Gustav Holst. One of the most terrifying moments was when we could hear backstage, just before we were due to go on, the choir that was performing in front of us drawing to a close and the applause from the audience.

In *We Beseech Thee* we made tick-tocky movements in time with the song; left, right, left, right. Gwyn was equally energetic and all that the audience must have seen is him jiggling from side to side. He was certainly the most lively and energetic of conductors there. I was standing right in front of him, centre front, as I was the shortest, with the TV cameras weaving in and out of us all. It was very hot, and we were all wearing matching scarlet scarves round our necks. The judges later said that they thought these restricted our singing, though we didn't have them tied tightly at all; it was far too warm.

Of course, most tension was felt when waiting for the results, announced after what seemed an enormously long wait. After singing all day, the choir now sat in silence, fingers, everything, crossed. We really thought we deserved to win, but there were some very good choirs and we didn't go through. Nevertheless, though we were disappointed we had all enjoyed ourselves. The only problem was not showing our enjoyment too much, as the TV presenter said that the girl who smiled the most had the prize of kissing him – not a pleasant prospect!

You would have thought after working so hard on two pieces in such detail that we wouldn't want ever to see them again. But we had grown to love them and in rehearsals afterwards back in Reading we would always go back to sing them over and over again.

Dedicated to music Temperance bandmaster

Many long-time fans of Reading Football Club will remember the upright figure of Frederick Percy Hill singing and conducting Reading Temperance Band at all the home matches at Elm Park. Mr Hill, who died in 1960 at the age of 75, was not only bandmaster of Reading Temperance Band, later Reading Military Band, but leader of the Broad Street Brotherhood Congregational Church Orchestra. He was also conductor of several prize-winning choirs including the Great Western Railway Choir, the Labour Choir, the Co-operative Ladies and the Co-operative Mixed Choirs.

"He dedicated his life to music," says his daughter Norah Ham, now 83, and the only surviving member of Frederick's three daughters and one son. "He had a wonderful tenor voice and I grew up with music all through my life. We had a family quartet. I sang soprano, my mother Edith sang alto, my dad sang tenor and my brother George sang bass. We won many cups and medals at different music festivals."

The Hill family lived in Elm Park Road, Reading, and Frederick worked as an electrician at the Signal Works for Great Western Railway. Outside work, all his time and energy were devoted to music.

"I don't know where his musical ambition came from or whether he was trained," says Norah. "Both his brothers were organists, Uncle Bert at St Mary's, Beenham, and Uncle Arthur at St George's, Reading, but my father couldn't play the piano. He was a clarinettist and played in the band before he became conductor. Conducting was his life."

As a staunch supporter of the Labour Party, Mr Hill's first choir was the Labour Choir at Minster Street, in Reading. He was also a member of the Temperance Society, so it was not surprising that he joined the Temperance Band, eventually succeeding Mr Wicks as bandmaster.

Norah, who has always loved brass bands, remembers keeping in step with the Temperance Band, in which her father was playing, all the way along Oxford Road towards the Pond House. "When I got back home I got a hiding for following the band."

Her uncle Bert taught her the piano and she would accompany the family when they practised – "anything within reason I could manage but nothing too hard."

She always remembers the hours her father spent copying out the different parts of orchestral music. "He would buy sheets of manuscript so that he could copy out the music for higher or lower parts. It was wonderful to see him sitting at the table copying out those notes for hours.

"He would practise at home in our little room and no doubt frighten the people up the street!"

He won many challenge cups and trophies with his band and choirs and also put on many charity concerts. The Broad Street Brotherhood Orchestra played in the church every month for Sunday afternoon concerts (recalled by one of the youngest players, young George 'Ted' Watkins), and the Sunday night concerts in the Town Hall were very popular.

Frederick Hill

"He was never in," said Norah. "He was out all over the place with his band and his singing. He had a marvellous voice and won the Great Western Railway Festival veterans class for several years running and many other awards. I regret he was never recognised for all he had done for music and for local charities."

Norah loved singing, was a member of the GWR mixed voice choir and sang with Broad Street Brotherhood choir. "We sang a lot of Sankey's hymns and I particularly loved *The Old Rugged Cross.*"

She sang at Sunday School in Elm Park Hall and with her classmates at Wilson School she would take part in the Children's Concerts at the Oxford Road Schools for Harvest Festival.

"Schools came from all over Reading to take part and Mr Marsh was the leader. I remember singing the *Harvesters' Night Song* and *What a Friend We have in Jesus.* Those concerts were packed out."

Norah's brother George was also a fine amateur singer and was a member of the BBC Choir. Now his grandson, Darrel Forkin, who is Frederick HIll's great grandson, is continuing the family tradition as a professional singer.

Although Norah had to give up her music because of the demands of work, marriage and children, she has a young granddaughter, Sharnie, who is also showing signs of the family's musical talent.

Rising from the Pit Theatre organs

In the sixties, as film audiences began a long slow decline, cinemas all over the country were closed down or converted into bingo halls. This meant that the unique theatre organs, built specifically for cinemas, became redundant and if it were not for a few enthusiasts would probably have disappeared. One such group of theatre organ lovers is based in Old Windsor, and founder member and chairman IAN STEWART describes how The Windsor and District Theatre Organ Trust was started and how it rescued and restored a beautiful Compton organ. Thirty years on the organ is still in regular use, is played by professional organists in four public concerts each year and is available to be played by theatre organ enthusiasts

The first theatre organs were built in the early 1920s to provide background music for the silent movies – they were originally used to fill in the intervals when the cinema orchestra was having its tea breaks. Cinema owners soon realised that a single organist was much cheaper than an orchestra so the orchestras were sacked leaving the organist to do all the work. These organs were provided with "toy counters" which could provide all the sound effects needed for silent films (indeed all subsequent theatre organs had toy counters up until the last organ was made in 1939).

The theatre-style of organ originated in America where the Wurlitzer Organ Company was predominant although, ironically, it was an Englishman, Robert Hope Jones, who designed the Wurlitzer organ. The first British theatre organ was built in 1924 by the John Compton Organ Company for the Shepherds Bush Pavilion, one of the first purpose-built cinemas. Previous cinemas had been adapted music halls, some of which had contained pipe organs of the church type. The first Wurlitzer organ was imported into this country in 1927 and installed in the New Gallery Cinema in Lower Regent Street where it remains, the cinema having long been converted into a mission church.

Several church organ builders, both in America and this country, began building theatre organs when they recognised the boom in cinemas would offer them another sales outlet. In this country, Compton was by far the largest builder with more than 500 made in the 16 years of manufacture – others include Hill, Norman and Beard who made organs under the Christie name (John Christie of Glyndebourne fame), Conacher of

Huddersfield, and Spurden Rutt (East London).

Our story – the story of the Windsor and District Theatre Organ Trust – starts in 1965 when Ted Lawrence, who lived in Old Windsor, decided to fulfill a lifelong ambition to own a theatre organ. After meeting some fellow enthusiasts at an electronic organ concert in Slough, he formed the Windsor and District Theatre Organ Trust. Three of those original members, Ian Stewart, Reg Cudworth and Jim Stewart, are still involved, with Edwin Brown and Ron Tibble, who have been members since 1967.

Towards the end of the trust's first year, Ted was told by ABC Cinemas that the 1937 Compton organ in the Regal Cinema, on The Old Kent Road, was redundant and for sale. He liked what he saw and purchased it for £250 on the understanding that the removal was supervised by a professional organ builder. The result was that over three snowy weekends in January 1966, six novice but keen members of the trust, under the supervision of organ builder George Barlow, removed the organ from the cinema. To aid re-installation, photographs were taken and the building frames were marked with felt tip pen (still clearly visible).

The organ was removed to storage in a wholesale sweets and tobacco warehouse in Windsor where it stayed while lengthy negotiations took place over its new home in Old Windsor Memorial Hall. At last, after protracted discussions with multiple authorities (the Old Windsor Memorial Hall is on Crown land so even the Queen had to be consulted), approval was given to install the organ in the hall.

Chambers for all the pipework were built on the back of the stage with the organ trust members acting as labourers under the supervision of a friendly local builder. The big day came when the large holes were knocked through the rear wall of the stage for the installation of the shutters which control the volume of sound entering the hall from the two pipe chambers. We were very fortunate to have friends in the right places – even ICI was persuaded to paint the chamber walls with a very hard paint normally used in toilets because it was graffiti proof. Unfortunately,

Ted Lawrence

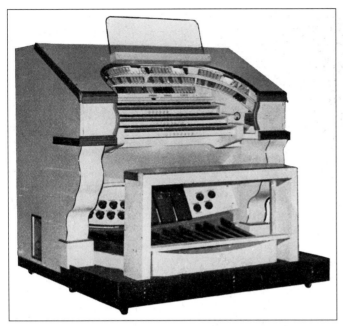

The restored Compton console with the illuminated surround removed, new contours, new music desk and 'organza'-and-gold finish, looks less typically Compton. The functional stool was replaced by a Wurlitzer-type bench

photo by Reg Cudworth

the resulting smell as the paint "cured" was not appreciated by the audiences of the village pantomime being staged in the hall that week.

Our organ was eventually reinstalled during 1967/8. We were learning fast by this stage but still made many mistakes. This was the era of the mass destruction of theatre organs in cinemas and so we were able to pick up extra ranks of pipes very cheaply (£20 per rank including chest). The organ was finally playable in early 1968 and used for various village functions while it settled down in its new home. It was formally opened in January 1969 by the Mayor of the Royal Borough with Vic Hammett and Jackie Brown (who were made vice-presidents of the trust) at the console.

The organ, as installed, is a three manual instrument with electro-pneumatic action and its weight is estimated at 10 tons. It has a detached console (which used to come up on a lift) and 11 ranks of pipes, the smallest being the size of a pencil and the largest about 18 feet long. The total number of pipes is about 1000. There is also a piano, xylophone, glockenspiel and vibraphone, all on electro-pneumatic action controlled from the console. The organ is fully equipped with the sound effects of the silent film era such as bird whistle, siren, cymbal, castanets, and drums. John Compton was a very advanced organ builder for his time and many facilities were provided to help

control all these devices. Second touch (press the key harder for a second function) is provided on two of the three manuals. There are also pistons (buttons) between the manuals for instant changes of stop combinations and these are adjustable while the organist is sitting at the console.

Thirty years on, the organ remains in regular use. We have suffered 'shortage of wind' problems on several occasions (hardly surprising since the organ is now twice its original size) and, following consultation with the British Organ Blowing Company in the early '80s, we added a three horse power blower to supply wind to the four Accompaniment ranks. We have just replaced the failing 60-year-old five horse power motor on the original blower with a modern 7.5 horse power unit.

The majority of the pipes are made of metal, mostly an alloy called "spotted metal" which is about 70 per cent tin, 20 per cent lead with traces of copper and antimony. These pipes will last forever if treated carefully – most damage can occur in the tuning process, which is needed before every concert. The rest of the organ, like the pipe chests, wind regulators, building frames, are made of wood with all the pneumatics made of high quality leather which looks like a very thin version of the chamois leather used to clean cars. Over the years the leather dries out and cracks and the chests then have to be releathered.

Spare parts for the electrical action are unobtainable (the last bits were made before the Second World War) but there is a supply of pieces from cannibalised organs to be found through the "organ grapevine" if you make your case known.

The original wiring is cotton-covered copper which gets brittle and is now replaced with modern colour-coded cable of the Post Office type. The "relays" which interface between the organ console and the pipework are rather like a telephone exchange, beautifully made with many thousands of silver wire contacts and magnets all working on 12-15 volts. When these give trouble, it is time to light the josticks and get out the prayer mats!

Of the 500-plus organs built, there are probably about 50 left, mostly in private ownership. There are only two remaining in cinemas in London. Fortunately there are several preservation groups like ours which have managed to install organs in public venues, the nearest being in Abingdon Abbey Hall (another Compton) and Birmingham (a Compton in a school) with Wurlitzers in Woking, Worthing, Manchester, Glasgow, mid-Wales and Shrewsbury.

Sadly our founder chairman, Ted Lawrence, died in 1982

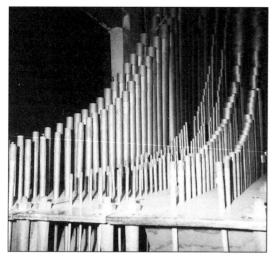

The accompaniment chamber pipework

but the rest of us are still going strong even if a lot older and wiser. Many of us recently assisted with the transplant of the ex Granada Welling Wurlitzer into the Woking Leisure Centre. In the process I broke my big toe in two places – who says that you never learn!

Why do we do it? The theatre pipe organ has a sound which is unique and not yet copied by the electronic organ or keyboard. Many of the modern generation have never seen a theatre organ in a cinema, in fact very few of the cinemas built in the 30s remain that have not been "tripled", turned over to bingo or replaced by the 10 screen multiplex. As a result, our concert audiences are getting older.

Most of the original cinemas were built in the "atmospheric" style, with ornate decorative plasterwork, plush seating and subdued lighting, which was supposed to transport the audience into a delightfully carefree world even before the film started. The organ interlude was intended to help create that relaxed atmosphere. We hope to recreate the atmosphere in our concerts for as long as we get the audiences and the organ keeps playing.

Millennium Choice Ian Stewart

A piece of light music for a small orchestra, Songs of Paradise by Reginald King

'Round up the Usual Suspects'

'Round up the usual suspects' – that's how you pretend to investigate a crime in Casablanca or how you can assemble an all-purpose band in Reading. It's not a formal band with a fixed line-up, but a loose affiliation of musicians who may find dinner jazz, folk dance music, rock 'n' roll, chart hits and pub songs all in an evening's work.

Forming the stalwart support to the bold musical enterprises of Hugh Crabtree, they can be seen joining forces with Pete Lincoln and saxophonist Alan Whetton at the Eldon Arms or the ICC in Birmingham, . They appear with drummer Dave Mattacks for the 'Folk on the Rocks' events and the annual 'Feast of Fiddles' at the splendid and very broadminded Nettlebed Folk Club run by Mike Sanderson.

Martin Vincent is a regularly featured guitarist among these Usual Suspects. A graduate of The University of Reading and former deputy headteacher, he has a keen interest in music education. He teaches guitar and has provided live performance opportunities for many young musicians by running school orchestras, bands and choirs and writing music for school and community concerts, festivals and theatre projects.

At university, he played in student jazz bands and afterwards with Clem Adelman in the days of the Cap & Gown.

After this he fell among folk rockers Whittaker's Patent Remedy for a series of performances at the Hexagon and also joined the Aldbrickham Band and the Albion Dance Band with Ashley Hutchings at Berkshire Midsummer, Towersey and Bracknell Festivals.

There followed a spell with the blues band Jive Alive In the mid-eighties this was occasionally augmented with a powerful brass section borrowed from Graham Parker and the Rumour.

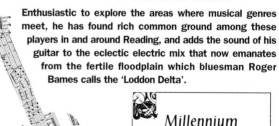

Enthusiastic to explore the areas where musical genres meet, he has found rich common ground among these players in and around Reading, and adds the sound of his guitar to the eclectic electric mix that now emanates from the fertile floodplain which bluesman Roger Bames calls the 'Loddon Delta'.

Millennium Choice

Martin Vincent

El Noy de la Mare, a traditional Catalan lullaby transcribed for guitar by Andres Segovia

Expressing what cannot be said Therapeutic music

The power of music as therapy was known long before the birth of Christ, when David lifted the spirits of a king with his harp. For music therapist **PAMELA CHILVERS**, the language of communication and healing is music and her new career is another stage in a life full of music. She trained with Fanny Waterman and studied piano with Ivey Dickson at the Royal Academy of Music gaining her GRSM, LRAM and the Professional Certificate in Performance. After taking her PGCE at the University of Reading, she worked for three years as assistant director of music at Highdown School in Emmer Green. In 1977 she took a year out to compose a music drama for local churches based on Acts of the Apostles called Acts, a community project, involving about 80 people. She taught piano at Reading Blue Coat School, St Joseph's Convent School and Leighton Park, and continues to compose, mainly piano pieces and songs

Yehudi Menuhin said music is therapy and it has always been so. In the days of the Old Testament when King Saul could find no comforting words from any of his advisers when he was depressed, David, a shepherd boy, came to play the harp to him and Saul's depression lifted. Shakespeare famously said "Music has charms to soothe the savage breast" and "A man that has no music in him is dark as Erebus – such a man is not to be trusted", and Victor Hugo wrote: "Music expresses that which cannot be said and on which it is impossible to be silent." All these express the essence of music therapy.

The language of communication and healing between client and therapist is music. For an autistic child, that might be the only way her or she can articulate their world, which has very different social and personal expressions from those with normal development. An elderly person, particularly someone with Altzheimer's disease, may not remember how to put a coherent sentence together but can remember a song from the 1920s and be able to sing it all through perfectly. It can help someone come to terms with loss, after an accident or a stroke, when physical and/or mental faculties are badly damaged, because the ability to respond to music is not damaged. Music is addressed to the healthy, functioning mental and spiritual aspects of a person to bring encouragement and hope.

My own involvement in music began when I was four years old, and saw the pianist, Russ Conway, playing and winking at me from the television set. That was my cue –

Pamela Chilvers

thinking that Russ had singled me out, I made a bee-line for the piano. Then from the age of eight, I distinctly remember setting my sights on the Royal Academy of Music in London, an ambition which I achieved in 1970. After years of training, teaching music, composing and bringing up my family, I began a music therapy course at the University of Bristol in 1993.

Part of my work as a music therapist is in homes for the elderly in Berkshire and Oxfordshire. In Berkshire, I work at Goldendale Retirement Home in Caversham, which is a small residential home, privately run by Maureen Schwartz, with the emphasis on individual care and attention. There are between seven and ten residents, mostly over 85 years old, and music therapy takes place once a month. We begin by singing songs from the 1920s while playing instruments such as bells, drum, wind chimes, ocean drum and rainmaker. Then I go round to each person individually, playing my recorder or harp, and we improvise duets. These improvisations will inform me, clinically, of the emotional and physical condition of the resident and I can then work therapeutically with that, helping to build confidence and self-esteem through the music, and helping to bring a measure of God's healing through the restorative power of music.

The other nursing home is Holyport Lodge near Maidenhead. There the group is larger and so I adapt my sessions to fit in with the needs of the day. Up to 15 residents come to a session, some with feelings of loss – perhaps depressed because they have had to forfeit some measure of independence – and some with physical difficulties such as Parkinson's disease, stroke, or dementia. Some are able and just come to enjoy the music. I also work at Thamesfield Nursing Home in Henley which is similar to Holyport Lodge.

In January 1999 I began a scheme for Windsor and Maidenhead LEA at Holyport Manor School, a special needs school for children aged two to 16. The pilot scheme was funded by the East Berkshire Autistic Society and the PTA of Holyport School. The scheme ran for two terms and involved a half-day of music therapy with autistic children, and a group of children with moderate to severe learning difficulties. Windsor and Maidenhead's music adviser, Graham Sanders, also helped initiate the pilot with a view to providing music therapy to the school in a broader sense from September 1999.

My job is to assess children for suitability (most have an innate response to music), provide half-hour sessions and, in the case of autistic children, to provide a means of expression of stereotyped behaviour, a container for challenging behaviour, a means of helping to relieve anxiety, and help with forming social relationships through musical interaction with the therapist. I focus on communication through music and I have a psychodynamic approach to my work. The group involves three children of varying ages and difficulties, including epilepsy, dyspraxia and severe learning difficulty. I use songs known to the children, improvisations and one-to-one work.

The client-therapist relationship takes time to build and therapy is a process which can last for example six weeks or six years, depending on the needs of the person. I also see a boy with severe learning difficulties privately. For a child who cannot speak or move very much, music is of vital importance, and the therapist has to enter the child's world, which may be at a much slower pace than the normal frantic pace of life we normally tend to live.

I have recently released my first CD, entitled *Therapeutic Piano*, which includes three of my own compositions, *Kites*, *Clouds* and the *Communion Song* from Acts, Part 3. Music was researched for its therapeutic effect, notably to test whether or not the music played reduced high blood pressure and promoted a feeling of well-being and relaxation. Satie's *Gymnopedies*, and other slower pieces, Chopin, and Debussy's *Clair de Lune*, and, of course, Beethoven's *Moonlight Sonata*, 1st movement, all produced that effect, and the album was tried out on friends and family (my best critics) and colleagues before it was recorded on my Steinway Model M piano at home.

As a musician, every week is different. I have about 40 pupils to fit in a week and am also a mentor for the MTpp (Music Teacher in private practice) course run by The University of Reading as well as an examiner for the Associated Board of the Royal Schools of Music. I might be loading my instruments into the car to be used in music therapy with the elderly or I could be driving to play the piano for a conference at Heythrop Park, where I am resident pianist, or visiting Inglewood Health Hydro, Kintbury, to present an evening of music therapy. I am always looking for ways of enhancing a person's life through the joy of music. It is a wonderful gift and I feel very privileged that this gift has been entrusted to me.

Music therapy at Inglewood Health Hydro, Kintbury, with Ensemble Galant

Millennium Choice

Pam Chilvers

Rakhmaninov's 2nd piano concerto. I used to play the record all the time when I was about 16 but my hands were never big enough to play it myself. Now my son's are and he can play some of it for me.

Violin Virtuoso
Kreisler in Reading

In 1929, the great virtuoso violinist, Fritz Kreisler, gave 32 recitals throughout Great Britain, between 24th January and 28th February. On 31st January he visited and performed in Reading Town Hall.

This programme consisted of Bach's Partita in E major and the Concerto No. 22 in A by Giovanni Viotti – not a well-known name in the modern repertoire but since known as the father of modern violin technique.

Viott was a man with an unusual career, having been a member of the National Guard at the time of the French Revolution and later becoming a wine merchant in London, a founder member of the Philharmonic Society and a Director of the Paris Opera. He died in poverty in 1824.

Kreisler's Town Hall recital ended with a selection of six short pieces, including some of his own arrangements such as Songs my Mother Taught Me by Dvorak, and the traditional Londonderry Air.

The time of the recital, 3 pm on a Wednesday, indicated the custom of the time when shops and many offices closed for a midweek half day. My father attended this recital and recalled that the town hall was packed to capacity.

Scholes' Oxford Companion to Music is rather less than generous in commenting upon Kreisler, claiming that he tended to ignore contemporary composers of standing and 'entertained an infatuated public with trifles of his own arranging or composition... bits of melody picked up here and there and recast'. This appears to be a somewhat curmudgeonly appraisal of an outstanding performer.

My father, himself a violinist, regarded it as a privilege to have attended such a remarkable event.

Kreisler continued to give recitals until 1950. He died in New York in 1962 at the age of 87.

Bob Russell

Harmony between Town and Gown The University of Reading

Music has been taught at The University of Reading for more than a century largely due to the foresight of a group of music lovers from the town. Their determination meant that Reading has benefited over the years from the musical talent and expertise attracted to the university, and the town has had continual access to musical events there. It has been an harmonious collaboration between town and gown as DERMOT O'ROURKE explains

The University Extension College, Reading, was founded in 1892 (its name was changed three times, but I'll just call it the college until the period when it became the university in 1926). In 1897 a number of people from the Reading Philharmonic Society, the Reading Orpheus Society and the Berks Amateur Music Society, aware that the college's premises in Valpy Street were due to be extended, asked that provision might be made for practical and theoretical music teaching. The extension plans could not be altered but the college managed to acquire a three-year lease of YMCA premises, conveniently also in Valpy Street.

In so many of the archival papers remaining, the questions of expenditure looms large. In Valpy Street, the argument for furnishing a fourth room and equipping it with a grand piano was not to promote piano teaching but to enable the college to host TCM examinations and thereby make some money. A later example comes in a pair of letters from the Director of the Brahms Centenary Festival, 1933, the first proposing a Guarantee Fund to 'lighten the load of the organisers'. The second letter tells supporters: 'You will be glad to know that the Brahms Festival has paid its way, in some miraculous fashion which I do not attempt to explain – for in these days it seems almost ridiculous to expect Music to pay'. No mention is made of the musical success of the concert which, inevitably, included the *Academic Festival Overture*.

The whole college moved out from Valpy Street in 1905 and by Easter was installed in London Road. The main teaching and administration departments occupied the row of houses east of Crown Place. Music had the next, detached house (Green Bank) and the Library and Staff Common Room had Acacias, Alfred Palmer's former home. The whole block was right next to a building which was said to look much more like a college, namely the Royal Berkshire Hospital. The School of Music was to remain there until its final move to 35 Upper Redlands Road in 1965.

In terms of staffing, Music had by far the most teachers of any Department in the college – many had only one lecturer. As a local paper puts it in 1897: "A staff of professors has been appointed, under the immediate supervision of Sir Walter Parratt, Mus Doc. It comprises most of the professors of music in Reading, supplemented by some well-known professors connected with the Royal Academy of Music and other institutions."

Well, of course, the word 'professor' was often used very widely, for teachers of dancing, even of boxing, as well as music. (An American immigration officer once said to me on seeing I was a librarian: "Say, what kind of a professor is that?"). Reading's college had to wait for University College status before it had a Professor with a capital P; two were appointed in 1907, with the country's first woman Professor the following year. The title was given sparingly, and there was no Professor of Music here until

The University Orchestra, conducted by Thornton Lofthouse, playing in the air-raid shelters beneath the cloisters, London Road, 1941. *From the painting by Frank Ormrod*

Ronald Woodham's appointment in 1951. Sir Walter Parratt, the College's Honorary Director of Music, was in 1897 yet to become the Professor of Music at Oxford and Master of the Queen's Music.

From the start in 1897, individual tuition was available, daytime or evening, in singing, pianoforte and organ, violin, viola and violoncello. There were also classes on Monday afternoons in rudiments of music, harmony and counterpoint up to the standard of the RAM/RCM Associated Board's local examinations. In the following session they added an ensemble violin class and a sight singing class to the daytime programme. As the Department developed the overall programme fell into two parts: courses leading to the LRAM, ATCM and ARCO qualifications either in teaching or in performing; and later teaching for the College Diploma and possibly for the Associateship of the College, automatically awarded to any Reading student who obtained a degree, usually a London degree, as a result of their studies here. Once University status had been achieved, it became possible to get a Reading degree in Music, and the Diploma qualification gradually fell into disuse. Diploma and degree students were not necessarily local residents, any more than they were in any other subject. Teaching for the lower level examinations continued to be offered to local students, and is still available today. A registration fee is paid to the University, and the Department undertakes to provide the tuition, the fee for which is paid direct to the tutor.

In *The University of Reading: the first fifty years* (1977), Professor J C Holt tells us that the School of Art and the three year Diploma in Fine Art were abolished in 1965, and 'by then only the School of Music preserved the old general educational service for the locality. In this case the [academic] Department of Music benefited from the broader School, for it enabled it to provide a wider range of instrumental tuition for its students than would otherwise have been possible; it also reinforced the University choirs and orchestra' .

Shortly after the First World War, the school attracted some of the musical great names of the century. Adrian Boult succeeded Professor Allen as conductor of the Choral Society and Orchestra in 1918, and stayed in this post for two sessions. In 1919 Edmund Rubbra gained a composition scholarship to study at Reading and after a year he won an open scholarship to the Royal College of Music where he remained until 1925, after which he is said to have taken 'whatever work came his way'. This included being back at Reading as a part-time tutor for two years.

Gustav Holst was Rubbra's composition teacher at RCM and from 1920 he also was on the staff at Reading. He succeeded Boult as conductor and was also tutor in

Composition and Theory of Music. At a concert in Reading in February 1923 Holst slipped off the rostrum, falling on the back of his head. Although the after-effects of the concussion were not all that serious it spurred Holst to take a year off from his very demanding workload and simply rest and recuperate; this, in retrospect, was a major turning point in his career.

Both the college community and Reading's music-loving public were to benefit from a number of early innovations. In 1903 the Music Club was founded, organised as a Student Society; its members enjoyed making their own music as well as listening to lectures and recitals by visiting musicians. Hard on its heels came the University Orchestra (1904) and Choral Society (1906). Together these ensured that the town had continual access to local musical events throughout the century. For concerts they used both the Great Hall and outside venues such as the Town Hall and where appropriate the churches. The long run of annual series of subscription concerts only came to an end when the Hexagon came into use.

The college musicians played their part in providing charity concerts, perhaps especially around the time of the two World Wars, for example a performance of Bach's *St Matthew Passion* in 1915 at St Mary's Church, in aid of the Red Cross and St John. They provided the music also at another town event – the unveiling in 1913 of the plaque in the Abbey grounds to *Sumer is icumen in*. In 1925 the college provided a venue for the British Women's Symphony Orchestra.

It should be mentioned that from the early days in London Road, the college possessed a valuable asset in the shape of the Great Hall, a multi-purpose building as we would now say, used for meetings, lectures, examinations and theatrical performances, but by no department more extensively than by Music. Even the most unmusical of students heard some music there, when the organ played at the graduation ceremony. A generation ago, when university academic dress was confined in colour almost entirely to black except for the maroon or scarlet gowns of the Doctors and the Vice-Chancellor's blue and gold robe, one outstanding exception was the cream and pink watered silk gown of the organist's Oxford Doctorate of Music.

Other societies came (and some went) within the college and university. There was a Madrigal Society. There was the Operatic Society, offering a performance one evening in 1964 comprising a première of Purcell's complete *Dido and Aeneas* linked with Gilbert and Sullivan's *Trial by Jury!* In general however, the lighter side of music was left to the town to provide, though nowadays it has a presence in the university at Bulmershe Court.

Sounding Brass Watership Brass Band

A brass band started modestly as a works social club by a Newbury chartered surveyor has built a lasting reputation. The story of Watership Brass is told by PAUL TWYNING

The beginnings of The Watership Brass Band were not auspicious. At its first meeting five people turned up, none of whom could play. But this did not deter John Norris whose extraordinary idea it was to form a band at his work as a form of social club. Work was the Royal Institute of Chartered Surveyors and the RICS band began its life in 1980.

After that first meeting John began to teach the new members the rudiments of brass and augmented the band with his own family, his wife Carol, and two daughters, Nicola and Becky. Further recruitment through advertising began and practices were held at the RICS office building, Norden House, in Basingstoke.

The band made its debut at at a Catholic school fête in Basingstoke in that first year, and was appalling! However, from such humble beginnings was born a band with a sense of comradeship. The RICS were a friendly group and there was always a tea break at practices to allow people the time to get to know each other.

In early 1982 John realised that he needed to hand over conducting to someone more experienced in order for the band to progress. They advertised (again) and an ex-Army bass and trombone player called Colin Bell took up the baton and began sorting out players and music into some sort of order. For instance, one bass (tuba) player was really a cornet player at school and he was promoted to front row cornet after volunteering to swap back for one fête. He is now the principal solo cornet.

In late 1983 , Colin Bell had to leave because of pressure of work and he brought in his fellow Sandhurst player Ted Howard to conduct in his stead. Ted oversaw the move to the Methodist Church Hall ,in Kingsclere, from the RICS offices where practices were still being held. The move had become a necessity because of lack of space and a feeling from the non-banding surveyors that the RICS band was not the suveyors' social club it had started out to be.

Kingsclere Methodist Church was very welcoming and became the band's home for some years, with the standard of music improving enormously.

During this time, 1987, Ted Howard had to leave, and yet another advertisement brought them the band's present musical director, Zander Grieg, a descendent of Edvard

Grieg. Zander has a background of Salvation Army banding and choral work which held him in good stead as he pushed the band further towards its present standard.

At this time it was suggested that, as the band was no longer connected with the RICS, the name should be changed. Various suggestions were put forward but the winner was proposed by Alan Dyer. Alan said that the band's proximity to Watership Down and the fact that players travelled from as far apart as Hungerford and Basingstoke meant calling it Kingsclere Brass would not be appropriate. He suggested Watership Brass and it has remained so ever since.

Late 1987 saw the roof blown off the practice room, not by the band but by the October hurricanes. This forced a move to Newbury Baptist Church Hall and Newbury has become the band's permanent home.

Watership Brass now has its own training band formed in 1993 under the leadership of Helen Grimsey (née Sampson). Thanks to Helen's hard work tithas proved a training ground for players of any standard (or age) and a future supply of players is assured.

In 1997 the band moved again, though still in Newbury, to the Sea Cadets' Hall, the TS Victory on the A4 towards Thatcham, where it practises on Tuesday nights.

As the quality of the music has grown so the band has appealed to wider audiences at home and abroad. Watership Brass has been on tours to The Netherlands in 1991, Germany in 1996, and America and Canada in 1998, pleasing audiences wherever it went with its mixture of good music and good spirits.

A high point for the band came at the start of 1998 when it won a National Lottery grant which paid for a full set of new instruments. These were presented to the band in front of television cameras at a special concert by the host, Sir Peter Michael.

Watership Brass has always been a friendly and approachable band and, thanks to the guidance of people like the late Andy Westall (Watership's chairman for a number of critical years who tragically died young), the band has steered away from competition banding. Instead it has concentrated on giving good quality entertainment to its audiences, a policy which has given the band a high reputation over the years and has helped it to live up to the motto on its programmes: "Serving the community – musically."

Millennium Choice Watership Brass

Our favourite is probably the march Aces High because it is in memory of our chairman Andy Westall who died young

Notes on a Musical Line The Watkins family

Berkshire music without a Watkins would be unthinkable for it was in 1885 that the family began its takeover of the county's sharps and flats – and is still supervising their continuity with more than a little gusto.

However, the story begins a little earlier in 1855, when one suspects that William Watkins was given a cornet instead of a rattle as he began life in Symonds Yat, Herefordshire

Like so so many of the country's leading brass instrumentalists, William began his musical career when he joined the Salvation Army, becoming a major before moving to Reading with his family to live in Southampton Street in 1885.

He transferred to a corps in the town and was soon helping to brighten up Sunday mornings with the local band – one engagement leading to an incident that could so easily have led to the end of music making for the Watkins family.

During bygone days, Silver Street was not a place for the timid, and at one Sunday service a brick thrown by a passer-by struck William in the mouth, damaging his cornet and doing little to improve his embrochure.

The remaining five musicians decided that enough was enough and disappeared leaving William to the ministrations of two Italian ladies who bathed his mouth and cleaned the blood from his face before persuading him to carry on with the service – which he did, leading the prayers and playing the hymns on his cornet.

For his bravery, William Watkins was taken to the hearts of the tough Silver Street residents and for a long time he was the only Salvation Army musician allowed to take religion to the area where he 1ed services until he died in 1935 at the age of 80.

One of William's great delights was to know that his love of brass band music was shared by his sons and he taught George Edward to play the baritone horn and his brother Fred, the cornet, the latter going on to perform with some distinction with the Reading Temperance Military Band.

However, it was principally George who carried the family banner forward until he died in 1979 aged 85. George joined the Spring Gardens in 1926, when the band was attached to Whitley Hall and was conducted by one Charlie Coppuck.

When Charle decided to call it a day in 1935, George took over the baton continuing until 1970. Altogether he devoted 53 years of his life to the Spring Gardens Band as both musician and leader.

George passed on his immense enthusiasm to his son – also christened George Edward, but soon becoming "Ted" to his many friends and colleagues in the music world – and to his nephews, Les, who played the cornet, and yet another George, who soon became proficient on the tenor horn.

With Les and George III living next door in Southampton Street, music was seldom far away and every evening the four Watkins musicians performed brass quartets in one or other of the houses.

George had first introduced young Ted to the trombone when he was seven years old, but soon realising that his arms were not long enough to reach the last two slide positions, he decided that the cornet would be a better option.

However, it was not only the family that benefited from George's ability to pass on musicianship to others. He became a peripatetic music teacher, first at Ashmead School, where he formed a band of more than 100 musicians, and later at Prospect, Highdown and Blue Coat schools. He also took over conducting responsibilities with bands at Thatcham, Cholsey and East Woodhay, winning many trophies with his various charges.

Always one for a challenge, George was persuaded to provide music for roller skating at Reading's Palmer Hall, before moving with promoter Ron Bamford to the Corn Exchange in Caversham Road. Here he also formed a dance band for what quickly became the town's number one ballroom – the Majestic – in the late '40s.

Realising that life was becoming just a little too hectic, George handed over the running of the dance band to son Ted, under whose leadership it went from strength to strength. It was reformed in 1960 to coincide with the take-over of the ballroom by the Rank Organisation.

Going back a few years, Ted had joined the Spring Gardens Band in 1929 when he was nine years old, becoming principal solo cornet when he was 13 and also playing with the Broad Street Brotherhood Orchestra under its conductor Fred Hill.

In those tender first year of his teens, Ted was entered for a senior championship event at Oxford under the adjudication of the legendary Harry Mortimer, and to his surprise won awards for the best cornet player in the junior, under-18, senior and championship soloist classes. These were to be followed by more than 50 trophies in the years that followed.

His first broadcast came when he was still only 14 after he received an urgent call from a band in Leicester whose principal cornettist had succumbed to a sudden attack of mumps.

Three generations of the Watkins family, from left: George Edward Watkins (Ted), Derek Watkins, George Edward Watkins senior

Ted's musical career is still flourishing after 65 years with the Spring Gardens Band – 28 of them as conductor following the retirement of his father.

He has, however, forsaken the dance band world and retired from teaching posts at Coley, Ashmead, Prospect and Highdown schools and at The University of Reading.

Despite this, Ted still finds it difficult to turn down any youngster who comes to him for help or advice providing that he or she shows genuine keenness to learn an instrument.

The fourth generation of this remarkable family, Ted's son, Derek, was taught the cornet from the age of six and quickly joined his elders in the brass band. He was recruited into the 14-strong dance band at the Top Rank Ballroom when he was just 13, taking over the lead trumpet chair when his brilliance became apparent.

Ted said: "Derek was very fortunate to join a group of excellent musicians at the ballroom, absorbing all the experience they were able to offer."

At the age of 17, the then youngest member of the Walkins family turned professional, joining the Jack Dorsey band at London's Astoria Ballroom as a first step towards becoming one of the most sought-after musicians in the country – if not the world.

However, it was not only the brilliance of his playing, but also the diversity of his skills that made his name a byword in a chosen profession. In his favourite field he has played with the bands of Dizzy Gillespie, Benny Goodman, Count Basie, John Dankworth and Buddy Rich, to name but five of many.

He has backed scores of international stars including Frank Sinatra, Tony Bennett, Sammy Davis and Barbra Streisand – appearing on stage with her during the London run of *Funny Girl*.

Groups from The Beatles and Bros to those led by Eric Clapton, Paul McCartney and Georgie Fame have sought his expertise for recordings and live dates and he has been featured on the soundtracks of dozens of films including the James Bond series, *Indiana Jones, Star Wars* and *Shirley Valentine*.

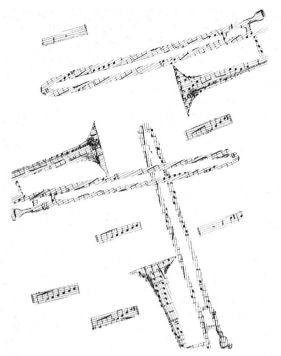

Television viewers who know Derek will have recognised him on hundreds of television shows and he has been featured with Bob Hope, Benny Hill, Tom Jones, Oscar Peterson, Johnny Mathis and Sarah Vaughan. However, his many gigs do not end with jazz and pop music, for as well as 20 years of world tours with the James Last Orchestra, Derek is sometimes called on by the London Symphony Orchestra and the Royal Philharmonic.

And when you finally believe you have exhausted this man's extraordinary talent, you learn that he also runs brass masterclasses at music colleges in Britain and Austria and as design consultant for Smith-Watkins Trumpets, has originated an instrument used by many of the world's top players.

Maurice Murphy, principal trumpet with the London Symphony Orchestra, said: "I sit beside Derek in the studio and still do not believe what I hear", whilst composer John Barry said: "It's always a good feeling when one walks into the studio to know Derek is leading the brass section. He never fails to deliver the goods."

Sadly, Derek's children have not become musicians and so four generations of superb achievement will almost certainly come to an end when he closes his trumpet case for the last time. But Berkshire would indeed have been a poorer place without this remarkable family and its century of of music making.

Ron Pearce

When I was Very Young...

Linda Maestranzi

In the early '60s my mother worked in a café/restaurant in Milk Street, in the City of London. It had a strange mix of clientele, from bowler-hatted bankers to Irish bricklayers and ink-stained printers, and served everything from full English breakfasts to steak dinners.

When I was four, my mother would sometimes take me with her. It was a great adventure – a world away from the east end of London. I used to be fascinated by men in pin–stripe suits swinging their umbrellas to some strange rhythm that only they could hear. I would embarrass my mother by walking behind them, matching them step for step. Even the journey on the underground was fascinating. Where were all these people from? Where could they be going? Would I ever be tall enough to hold on to the handles that hung down from the carriage's ceiling? (Only just.)

The café must have been fitted out in the '50s because every table had what looked like a mini juke box on it. Clients could drop money into it and choose records which then played on a much larger juke box against one of the walls. This too was heaven! We did not have a radio or record player at home so I rarely listened to music but I still loved to dance.

The café was always busy and music would be playing all day. Regular customers would put on my favourite songs and I would twist and twirl away the morning, dancing between the tables. Then when the record was finished they would applaud me and sometimes give me sixpences for my efforts. There were days when I took more in tips than my poor mother did!

This only stopped when I became old enough – and tall enough – to serve customers. Even then I would dance my way to their tables, balancing plates and cups of tea in both hands.

Thirty-six years later I still find it difficult to keep my feet still when I hear particular songs and I remain a source of embarrassment to my family when I drag them on to the dance floor at family weddings. Classical, pop, Latin American, if it's got rhythm I'll dance to it. Anyone fancy a spin?

Little Linda

A Feast for the Senses WOMAD

When I first heard the name WOMAD, I thought it sounded very odd and had no idea what it would be about, still less how much I would enjoy it, writes TORSTEN LOULAND. So, like many others, I stumbled on something unknown. It was some while later that WOMAD was elucidated as World Of Music, Arts and Dance, which gave a clue to its contents but not to its scale and impressiveness. Now, having tasted the delights of six Reading WOMAD festivals since 1992, I can describe some of the flavours of WOMAD

WOMAD is a feast of sound, colour, smell, taste, warmth, and atmosphere, a refuge from the mundane, where you can come across unexpected delights of music and culture. It is an oasis in the middle of Reading, yet far away from Reading. When spending the weekend at WOMAD, it's easy to forget where in the world you are, and arriving home afterwards seems as deflating as returning from that fantastic summer holiday abroad. But you may well return with new tastes and enthusiasms to keep you excited and occupied. At WOMAD you can hear new music, ancient music and music never brought to these shores before.

For the fact and figure hungry, WOMAD is a three-day festival at Rivermead, with five or six stages where 60 or more musical acts perform. The musicians come from far and wide, from Algeria to Argentina, from Gambia to Greece, and from Tokelau to Turkmenistan…from 90 countries around the world so far. Brightly coloured flags will greet you as you arrive and walk into WOMAD. They dominate the site the whole weekend, with different colours every day, populating the open spaces, vivid in the sunshine against blue skies.

Between watching musicians, you can peruse and purchase the goods and wares of around 120 stallholders and sample cuisines from around the world at some 30 food stalls. For those who want to get more involved, there are workshops and master-classes given every day by many of the performers, at which you can hear some of their secrets, learn some of their culture and be taught some of their techniques. For children, there are play areas, activities, a pool, story telling and the Sunday carnival procession to prepare for.

If a moment's peace is what you need, when wearied by so much richness, if not by the heat, you can take a break on the banks of the River Thames while distant music drifts over. If a different kind of break is what you need, there is always the big wheel, helter skelter or the

'Blues special' WOMAD, South Hill Park,1989 *photo by Ron Pearce*

carousel at the fair. One hot year there was bunjee jumping for the brave. It was definitely a good way to cool off,because of the nice breeze on the way down, and it gave an unbeatable view of the festival, the river and Reading, if you didn't mind it being upside down.

At night, many of the shops prefer candles and lanterns to bright light bulbs, making the atmosphere all the more enticing. One even had an Arab-style lit charcoal brazier outside, hoping to grab the attention of those waiting to warm chilled hands and limbs. The food stalls have their brightly painted signs lit up by strings of lights and people wander back to the stage carrying plates laden with goodies. Brandy coffee gives a kick in the evening when one might flag, and delicious hot mulled cider, neglected during the heat of the day, seems to be absolutely the best way to fend off the encroaching chill of the night. Then there is a wonderful choice of breakfasts the following morning which is great for starting another day of sensory feasting.

The campers can claim to be the core WOMAD-goers,

One of the 'blues' greats, singer, guitarist, and fiddler Clarence 'Gatemouth' Brown at WOMAD 1989   *photo by Ron Pearce*

Romanian Wedding Band. Layered samba rhythms provided by local drummers, Reading's Beatroots Bateria, with the underlying thumping bassy drums, hyper whistles and rackets are perfect for getting itchy feet to join the procession.

WOMAD started as an idea of Peter Gabriel's in 1980. It was nurtured with the help of friends at The Bristol Recorder and bore fruit in the first WOMAD festival at Shepton Mallet, Somerset, in July 1982. Creatively, it was a huge success, pioneering the same mix of ingredients that we love so much today – friendly atmosphere, many bands, diverse talent, colour, food, shops – though at that time they were ground-breaking. Another festival was tentatively organised the next year, just breaking even, and gradually the WOMAD organisation began to take shape with a festival in some form every year, often nerverackingly close to making a loss.

WOMAD's first visit to Berkshire was in 1989 with a Blues special at South Hill Park in Bracknell, a year in which it also went to Denmark, Canada and Spain. It visited Reading, Rivermead, in 1990 and has been here every year since. In recent years, each day has usually been attended by a full capacity crowd of around 17,500 people. The atmosphere is friendly, relaxed, has no prerequisite to follow fad or fashion and welcomes a healthy mix of all ages from those still in nappies to the walking stick-aided, diehard, veteran culture explorers.

WOMAD hastened the break out of world music from eclectic radio shows and specialist shops into the open, to be heard and seen by not just the followers of up-and-coming music but also those who happened upon it by chance or adventure. Early visitors to WOMAD may have been fans of world music, or just festivals in general, but over the years the festival has drawn in more people who are just trying it out because it is local, and then discover something wonderful. Festivals are now big business, but WOMAD does have something unique about it – a combination of diversity of performers, championing of unsung acts, colour and carnival spirit. This is the festival where stage security staff are more likely to be seen helping children to sit on the front of the stage than throwing people off it. While other festivals may tempt with impressive lists of well-known performers every day, WOMAD's jewels are usually secrets waiting to be discovered: the names are often unknown but, as has proved the case so many times already, many will go on to befestival headliners years hence. One thing that will never wear thin, however, is the surprise of being amazed and inspired by the music of someone unknown.

Reading the programme is like reading the menu of a new restaurant, with each dish made to sound irresistible. Choosing is not easy and a long considered ponder is essential. WOMAD is about the unknown waiting to be discovered, as well as reprise of the well-

generally civilised, with some decking their pitch out like an open-air front room or reception area. The experience frays at the edges a little with the expanding mud pools round the water pipes, the meandering queues for the dribbling showers and those new neighbours who have complete faith in their ability to pitch a tent in one of the remaining spaces at 2am on the first night. I am amazed at the number of spiders that take up residence in my tent just two hours after I have pitched it.

Sunday's procession marks the start of the last evening of the festival with a celebration of colour and two days of children's creativity: flags and banners, huge paper animals and monsters, and tall headdresses all fight for the sky line as they flop and jolt along to the rhythms of the marching bands. Every year there are some of the performers that can bring their music to the procession – this year (1999) the Bollywood Band, last year a known. Everyone comes away with different tales of inspiration. My memories are snapshots of unique moments, and here are some of them:

Irish Band – Boys of the Lough

Boys of the Lough are an Irish fivesome. The flute player turns his hand to a small tin whistle for a couple of tunes; his rapid playing dances over three octaves with an uplifting liveliness that is impossible to resist, while in slower tunes his seamless sliding between notes evokes the sad voice of a plaintive soul. His mastery of such a modest instrument is matched by the other players and when their performance ends and the atmosphere they created begins to subside, I feel really sad and wish they could play all their songs again. 'I'm sorry we can't play any more, but there'll be another great band along in a short while' – that's what they all say, and it's true. I resolve to buy a tin whistle and learn some Irish music and watch out for them again.

African bands and Femi Kuti

WOMAD always has great singers and fantastic bands from Africa: Salief Keta, Papa Wemba, Remy Ongala, Lucky Dube and many more, most recently, Femi Kuti. The music is vibrant, rousing, with upbeat tunes, and moving ballads, a whole family of musical richness. The music is never restrained, always exuberant, unafraid to celebrate, projecting warmth with a flurry of notes layered with harmonies, encouraging one to throw off the shackles of English/Western stiffness, and get up and dance. In quieter moments, soulful ballads are sung with beautiful African voices, stirring the emotions even further.

Femi Kuti's band, all in bright costume, enter with a cheeky dance. His three backing singers, tease and egg the crowd on with their athletic, seductive shaking and dancing. Femi Kuti leaps on, and fires up the audience from every side of the stage before breaking into the first song with powerful solo and emotive words. He sings with passion about issues that affect Nigeria and its people. The band are his partners and he regularly swaps places with members of its horn section while they solo, centre stage. Such is his presence that the whole crowd – and there must be as many as 5,000 of us – are moving to the left, then to the right, 'cleaning it down' as Femi says, and trying to see how low we can dance!

Latin America and José Luis Cortés

Just before the 'all things Latin American' craze swept the UK, WOMAD brought us José Luis Cortés. This Cuban king of cool is backed by his band NG La Banda, and it is huge – five vocalists, a five-piece horn section, keyboards, guitar and bass, and of course plenty of hands at the rhythm. They produce such a big sound. José Cortés leads the band with his vocals, but occasionally plays a flute, which he makes really fly. The trombones, saxes and trumpets frequently play dizzyingly fast runs in perfect unison to punctuate the verses,

Femi Kuti – singing and playing with passsion

followed by fat, fanfare chords. Their repertoire ranges from the seductive, smooth and mellow tunes that you might hear in the most high class hotel, through to carnivalesque, rhythmic tunes to lead a night-long procession of dancing and celebration.

Just when we think we've seen it all they depart the stage and show us how its done carnival style. The drum kits are dismantled and anyone who is not playing a horn, is holding the rhythm up with a drum, or a bongo, or anything they can hit Tracked by spotlights, they weave a procession through the packed crowd. Everyone claps to the rhythm, and we applaud as they pass near us, a chance to show off our admiration.

Japanese Drummers

Another memory is of the Kodo Drummers. They stood like Japanese warriors, one on either side of a single large drum on supports, chest high, hitting the drum as if it were the sport of Hercules, demonstrating precision, power and stamina. This year this Japanese art was demonstrated again by the Taiko Drummers from Hiroshima. Their highly-polished wooden drums have a beautiful grain which makes them look like giant rounded nuts with the ends chopped off and replaced with skins.

Workman rig the lighting on stage for WOMAD 1990. *Picture by Reading Evening Post*

One drummer starts playing the largest drum peacefully and slowly; boom…boom…clack…(on the rim), as slow as the last raindrops dripping off a tree into a pool. But the pace soon picks up. Other drummers join in ones, in twos, in groups. The silent accent of the sticks held in the air is as important as the loudest strike of the drum at the other end of their trajectory. When they lie down with drums between their legs and then play one of their fastest most aggressive pieces in an unsupported half sit-up, they show us that this art is not complete without power, stamina and discipline.

The Bare Naked Ladies

Another day and Bare Naked Ladies amused us with audacious lyrics and provided comical counterpoint to the other styles we gorged on, but there was no chance of remembering their witty words as each new line made me laugh and forget the one before. Now they are much more widely known after their chart success, only five years after WOMAD thought them a talented band to bring to our attention.

Hukwe Zawose and Nephew

Last year (1998) we saw Hukwe Zawose and his nephew play. They came from Tanzania and brought with them their brightly coloured tribal costumes of fur, feathers and teeth, their dancing and singing accompanied by music on their illimbas. The illimba is also known as a thumb piano and has many variants in Africa. Their version has on top of the hollow resonant box two sets of pins with varying lengths; on the outside ones, intricate, elaborate tunes are played with the thumbs, while those inside add a resonating depth.

In addition a bead dangles on a string between the front corners, which they swing back and forth so that it 'clacks' rhythmically against the underside of the box. Hukwe was training his nephew on the techniques of his music and dance, which was no mean feat given that while producing wonderful music on their illimbas their dancing took them around the stage, jumping, shaking, lowering themselves onto the ground unaided by spare hand and then back up, again, all the time never losing balance and never slowing in their perfectly-timed flurry of notes.

To add to this, they also sung. Hukwe uses a rare technique only known in a few tribes whereby he can sing two notes at the same time: it seems that by poising his neck in a certain way he alters the shape of his mouth and throat so that he can produce a resonant note that underlies the melody he sings.

The whole is incredible and awe inspiring, and we stand with jaws dropped in amazement and admiration. Hukwe Zawose was one of the artists to give a workshop. We scurried along to hear about his singing and hopefully join in. A packed hall listened intently. He talked a little about the music of his home through an

Otis Grand leads the Dance Kings at the 1989 WOMAD   *photo by Ron Pearce*

interpreter, and then started to demonstrate it with the help of his nephew, this time using a stringed instrument called an isezi. Then he started to teach us some harmonies, first everybody, then splitting the audience in two for an overlapping part.

Getting 200 people to sing their parts with one voice was difficult at first, but he did not stop until we had achieved it, and the result was profound and moving. Finally, he embarked upon an ambitious attempt to get us to learn a single melody line which six groups could sing in a cannon. We got half way there before our session was curtailed to make way for the next, but I, and many others I'm sure, were moved and left in no doubt about this man's magic.

The Pandeæmonium Marching Band

Every year WOMAD allows one local band a place on the bill. One year, the Pandaæmonium Marching Band, playing anarchic tunes and rhythms, took delight in using their performance opportunity to cause pandemonium: whenever an audience gathered to see them, they marched off quickly, upturning the idea that bands must stay put while the audience has the prerogative to come and go.

A Lucky Break
Sisserou at Womad

The first time I went to a WOMAD tent was at the Glastonbury Rock festival in the mid- 80s and the rich mix of culture and music to be found there fascinated me. So when I heard that they were planning to hold a festival in Reading, I was very keen to go. Then it occurred to me that as it was for world music, there might be an opportunity for Sisserou (then Dominican Folk Singers UK) to take part – after all we were a local world music group.

I found the telephone number for WOMAD from directory enquiries and spoke with one of the organisers and the director Thomas Brooman, introducing the group and myself. After a half-hour conversation, we were offered a place on one of the smaller stages in the Rivermead main hall. It was a real lucky break. We could hardly believe our luck. Not only a place but we had been offered a fee too. Unfortunately we were too late to be on the main brochures for artists but we were on the sheet handed out to people coming on the day.

I received confirmation and our stage passes and I remember feeling very nervous about it. We felt like pop stars as we were swept through the artists' entrance to our dressing rooms. The rest of the group was in awe of the set up but had a really enjoyable time. This was a really big deal for us, with all the stages, banners and famous world acts – there was our little local group. It was a wonderful experience but I think we were overcome with the importance of the show and although we performed well, I didn't enjoy it as I was so stressed out worrying if we had enough mikes, how well we were using the stage (it was huge), etc.

The audience seemed to like us and afterwards many people enquired where they could buy our music and if it was available at the Womad stall. Another opportunity missed!. However I'm really proud to say that we performed at the first WOMAD in Reading – and we'll also be there for the tenth WOMAD in Reading 1999. This time we'll be ready for the music sales!

Claudette Henry

It's the Timbre that makes it Woodley String Orchestra

STUART FORBES writes about the pleasures and problems of running a local string orchestra

Woodley String Orchestra dates back to 1968 when Elizabeth Weitz, a local music teacher, gathered together local players for musical enjoyment. It was informally known as Woodley Workshop Orchestra which also trained people in string and ensemble playing and orchestral techniques.

My involvement with the orchestra came about in 1981 just after Elizabeth Copperwheat, a well-known violin teacher, became conductor, and it was formally made into Woodley String Orchestra. Elizabeth always had her fiddle by her side and was constantly demonstrating better techniques. It was almost like a very inexpensive violin lesson. I owe her an awful lot because she did help my string technique. I was a very rough sort of player when I first went there and the discipline of the orchestra helped my playing a lot and indeed that of many others.

The orchestra still has some of the members who were there in 1981. Elizabeth was conductor for about six or seven years and she has now come back to the orchestra as a member. She has actually taught the fiddle to my son Alex, who is now principal double bass player in the orchestra, and who wasn't even born in 1981 which makes one feel a wee bit on the senior side.

After about 1986 Elizabeth was very heavily committed with her teaching and work with the Central Berkshire Music Centre and she felt she had to relinquish this position. The orchestra then moved to a new building in the Church of England school where we still rehearse and our next conductor was David Carter who was a music teacher at Bulmershe School. He brought a very able principal cellist with him, Edward Longstaff. David moved on to greener pastures after a few years and Edward took over as conductor. He was an exceptional person. His ability to get people focused on the task in hand was quite exceptional.

The first violin leader at the time, a young girl from Bristol attending The University of Reading, ended up with a first class degree in music. After four or five years, Edward left to take up a job with the Purcell School of Music in North London, then Elizabeth came back for a couple of terms, after which we found our present conductor, Ken Moore, who was a bass player with Reading Symphony Orchestra. Ken has been with us now for about five years. Unfortunately the numbers have declined a little over the past six or seven years, with

many people retiring.

We are trying to perform more concerts at the moment. It makes sense, after rehearsing for 10 weeks, to be able to go out and do the same concert at two or three different venues. We are trying to do more concerts now, although we are struggling with numbers at the moment. However, the people we do have are very loyal. It's not so bad having so small a number, as we always all turn up because we rely on one another. With larger numbers you're never all there on the same night.

We have been very fortunate in the last few years to have had some of the best soloists in the area to give concerts with us. We had two young ladies, Jennifer LeCocq, and Chloë Barnett who sang well together. I always remember as we rehearsed one evening, Concorde went over but those girls could certainly hold their own against Concorde and the orchestra. I was quite impressed.

There is no doubt that many string players like playing in a string, as opposed to mixed, orchestras. When you get one of those nice chords played from the bass, the cello, the viola, and the second and first violin, and it's all exactly in tune, it just gives this little ring you don't get with other instruments; it's the timbre; that's what makes it. Also, the string orchestra repertoire is quite interesting, the Elgar *Serenade for Strings*, is very popular, as is Barber's *Adagio for Strings*, and Mozart's *Eine Kleine Nachtmusik*. The earliest work we do is the Bach *Double Violin Concerto*, right through to Barber's *Adagio for Strings*, and a wonderful piece called *Air of Excitement*, written by Geoffry Russell-Smith. Edward Longstaff composed a *Serenade in D*, an interesting piece. It always sounds a lot easier than it actually is.

To be able to write a piece which the players and the audience are going to enjoy is quite a challenge. Music can be adapted for strings. At one notorious concert we actually performed Eine Kleine Beatles music, which consisted of Beatles compositions written in that style. You could just about pick out the tune. That tends to be the exception, however, and we usually stick to pieces which were written exclusively for string orchestras. It all depends on the conductor's preference, and some are more particular than others.

Gerald Finzi, the conductor who founded the Newbury String Players, bequeathed his library of music to the University of Reading and we have been able to borrow from it occasionally. In the last few years we have tried to build up our own library because the cost of hiring music has become very expensive. Once you have bought it and performed it a couple of times you have got your money back. We have been able to borrow one or two orchestral scores from Central Berkshire Music Centre and in return we were able to lend some of ours at short notice. We all try to help each other.

We used to hold some smaller events, what we call 'tea-shoppe' music. We run one event annually at the Coronation Hall in Woodley at the time of the carnival. That was fun except for one year when, for some reason, we were down to about six musicians. We were playing away quite happily when it started pouring with rain and the hired military band was herded into the Coronation Hall. There were six of us with our little fiddles in one corner and in another a full 30-piece band absolutely blasting the place out. It was no contest.

We would like to get our numbers back up to strength so we can participate more in the community. We've got ourselves into the situation where, because we are low in numbers, we are unable to get a higher profile in the community. If we had a higher profile, we would be better able to recruit more members. It's a bit of a vicious circle. At the moment, if two or three key people are unable to turn out we struggle rather badly. With more members, we could play more.

It's hard to get the youngsters now because they are under a lot of pressure. There are a lot of orchestral groups available for people of their age. They go to college and university and get jobs and can't come back. It is a shame. I am convinced that there are musicians out there and we will attract more members.

These things have always been cyclical and in time the fashion will swing back to orchestral playing. Think of all the sporting fashions, and how they have come and gone. Maybe we should offer free exercise while you play! I have tried playing the fiddle on an exercise bike. It's all right when you are playing steady music, but when you're playing something like The Arrival of the Queen of Sheba you have to pedal very quickly to keep up with it. And it didn't look very good when someone came to the door!

Ringing the Changes
1st Taplow and Hitcham Packs

Music has always played its part in the Scouting and Guiding Movements – think of the Gang Shows and singing round the campfire. Anyone who has had a Cub or Brownie in the house knows all about the doubtful joys of working for badges, which encompass activites as wide-ranging as knots and music.

Guides and Brownies from the 1st Taplow and Hitcham Packs are working towards a more ambitious badge – and are enjoying ringing times and harmonies on belle plates in the process.

Belle plates are flat plates of metal with handles and clappers and are tuned diatonically, enabling them to be rung as ordinary bells.

The Guides and Brownies meet once a week and have learned to ring tunes, simple harmonies and arrangements of well-known pieces, both classical and modern. Practising is rather cramped as they have to meet in a small room with limited ringing space but nevertheless they enjoy it.

The children are working through the staged Guide and Brownie Bellringer Badge and also through the Crescendo Scheme organised by Handbell Ringers of Great Britain. Most of them have achieved at least Stage 1 of these awards.

This all sounds rather serious, but the aim of it all is to teach them how to make music together – and above all to have fun.

Debbie Mitchell

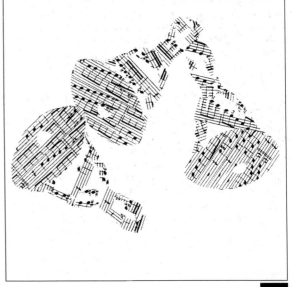

The Service of Music Lay clerk at St George's Chapel, Windsor

TREVOR CRADDOCK became a Lay Clerk at St George's Chapel, Windsor, in 1978. Since then he has also become well-known as a singer and teacher. He describes his life and work at St George's and as a solo singer

Auditioning for a lay-clerkship is actually a rather gruelling process. Going back 21 years, I remember I was called fairly early, I think shortly after 9am, which meant getting up very early, 'warming up' the voice and then driving over from Reading to Windsor Castle to be there on time. The initial auditions take place in what is called the Song School or Merbecke which is part of the Assistant Organist's house in Denton's Common within the castle. Candidates are required to sing a prepared piece of their own choice and then two sight reading samples, perhaps an early period piece such as Byrd or Tallis, followed by a more taxing 20th century piece, typically a piece by Francis Poulenc, or Lennox Berkeley. I think I had a piece from Lennox Berkeley's five-part mass for my audition, and then a certain amount of aural tests to test the quality of the ear; from that a short-list is made of two, three or four singers who then go and sing in the Quire of the chapel and face what could be future colleagues. There they are required to perform their chosen piece with the organ, together with an unaccompanied ensemble piece to test the balance with the other choir members. In my case I sang the baritone solo in Stanford's *Nunc Dimittis in G.* Nowadays the boys are not normally present at this audition process which involves men's voices only, so that if a tenor is auditioning, an alto and a bass will come across and perhaps sing an extract from the Byrd three-part mass.

The final stagr is an interview with the Chapter (the Dean and Canons) who confer with each other and the Director of Music, and then come to a joint decision in offering the post. There have been occasions when nobody was actually thought suitable which meant that the advertising process had to be gone through again, and lists drawn up. The rigorous nature of the audition process is a reflection of the demands and disciplines that the job of Lay Clerk actually entails.

The Music Director who took my audition and with whom in fact I sang for 13 years, was Christopher Robinson who left St George's in 1991 to become director of music in succession to George Guest at St John's College Cambridge. We were joined in 1991 by Jonathan Rees Williams, who had been organist at

Trevor Craddock sings Banquo's aria from Verdi's Macbeth for Berkshire Shakespeare's Players in the '80s

Lichfield Cathedral for 13 years.

Lay-clerk duties used to be more onerous with Matins and Evensong commitments for most days of the week, with very little opportunity to accept outside engagements. Conversely, Lay Clerks did have security of life tenure, which meant that they were guaranteed accommodation throughout their life and in many cases kept singing until the very end. Over the years Matins was dropped and was partially replaced by morning rehearsals. Now our commitment is a rehearsal from 4.40 to 5pm from Monday to Friday (Wednesdays excepted unless it happens to be a major-Feast day), followed by Evensong at 5.15 to about 6pm. There is a rehearsal from 4.30 till 5pm on Saturdays, followed by Evensong; also a rehearsal at 10 till 10.30 on Sunday mornings followed by matins at 10.45 and Eucharist at 11.45, and an afternoon rehearsal at 4.30

till 5pm with Evensong at 5.15. We normally have a Friday evening rehearsal from 6.00 to 6.45pm which gives the Director of Music a chance to rehearse part of the weekend music or indeed music for any forthcoming concert that has to be covered.

Nearly all the services are open to members of the public; it is only services such as Easter Day Matins, Christmas morning Matins, Garter Day, extra Royal services, funerals and memorials where admission is only by ticket.

It is not normally known in advance what the size of the congregation will be for a service; it could be two members of the community, perhaps during January and the dark winter months, to possibly up to 200 people who spill over into the nave; it depends on the time of year and whether we have visiting groups.

Of late we have undertaken a lot of extra concerts, both in and away from the chapel. For instance in chapel we have a contract to sing for British Gas, the Wine Society, and SmithKline Beecham, and away from the chapel we sing on a regular basis for JP Morgan in London for their managers' Christmas dinner and for the Macmillan Cancer Foundation gala which is a biannual event held in the chapel at Eton. In addition, we normally have two Christmas concerts on consecutive nights just before Christmas, and normally an Easter concert during Holy week or the week preceding that. We have featured works by Francis Shaw, whose father was a former Mayor of Windsor, and who has a long-standing collaboration with one of our canons, Canon John White, who is also our Precentor. We made a CD of their work last year, including a commissioned work called *Bright Phoenix*, composed to complement the consecration of the High Altar 'Phoenix' frontal by Thetis Blacker.

The choir has also undertaken first performances by Stanley Glasser, a South African composer who lectures at Goldsmith's College in London; we broadcast live on Radio Three his *Magnificat* which features substantial use of African rhythms.

We operate a verse-week system whereby solos go in weekly rotation; there are three voice parts, and four voices to each part, so we have four altos, four tenors and four basses, which means that solos pass from Decani (those who sit on the south side) A to Cantoris (on the north side) A, revert back to Decani B and then across to Cantoris B.

To enable colleagues to undertake outside engagements either as a soloist or session singers, we have a system of hiring deputies whereby not more than two voices of the same part can be away at the same time. We are allowed up to 20 leaves in any one term with a maximum of 48 in any academic year. The first eight leaves of each term are gratis and then any leaves taken between eight and 20 incur a fee towards deputy costs. Most of my colleagues

Starting to Sing

Trevor Craddock

When I was eight I became a chorister at St Albans Cathedral where my eldest brother had been head boy. As St Albans Cathedral has no choir school, when my father was required to move, I had to follow. I was 12 when we moved to Reading and attended Henley Grammar School, now Henley College, from 1963-1970. I embarked on a law degree at Cardiff and sang for an academic year at Llandaff Cathedral. I was advised to take my singing more seriously and as a consequence moved to London and commenced vocal studies with the celebrated baritone John Carol Case. I was also coached by Paul Hamburger, and became a member of the Temple Church Choir, London, under the direction of the late Sir George Thalben-Ball. In September 1978, I became a lay clerk at St George's Chapel and I also resumed my piano studieds with Robert Jones and Iris Loveridge and obtained an LRAM teaching diploma. I consider that I have been fortunate in gaining many insights through my teaching of singing and piano.

fit other work around their singing commitments. The salary is not quite enough to live on, but we do have the important concession of rent-free accommodation. We are normally paid extra fees when we undertake concerts, that is anything outside our normal chapel commitments. Obviously when TV is involved, our fees are further enhanced. We also have the security of living in the castle and are actually part of the College of St George, which does involve a certain amount of community living and responsibility.

I have sung at several memorable occasions, services and concerts in chapel over the years, including Prince William's christening, the Duchess of Windsor's funeral, and the installation of King Juan Carlos, as a Stranger Knight of the Garter, which was also the only Garter ceremony that has been televised since I have been here. The choir also sang at the William Harris centenary concert, a former organist and choir master of St George's and composer of the very beautiful and well-known anthem F*aire is the Heaven*, at the Queen's 70th birthday concert on 27th April, 1996, and on various Songs of Praise and Christmas morning BBC and ITV transmissions. Most recently we performed at the Royal wedding of Prince Edward and Sophie Rhys-Jones in June of this year.

During the year our main services are Ash Wednesday Evensong – the *Allegri Miserere* with the top C (trebles permitting!), Easter Day, Garter Day (normally the second Monday in June) and also the Garter Requiem for departed Knights of the Garter, which takes place the

Trevor Craddock (right) and Lesley Garrett (left) perform in Judas Maccabeus with the Ware Choral Society conducted by Julian Williamson

day after Garter Day – an anti-climax after the glories of Garter Day itself. Various settings of Requiem Mass performed have been by Fauré, Mozart, Victoria, and Duruflé.

Other big days are Advent Sunday which features a major carol service, sometimes attended by Princess Margaret and once or twice by the Queen herself, and Christmas Eve Nine Lessons and Carols which is always a packed affair. It has included for some years the John Tavener *Christmas Proclamations*, which is a wonderfully dramatic work; it has a tenor cantor, with interpolations by the chorus, and then a sudden full organ chord in C sharp minor providing an electrifying moment after such a long period of unaccompanied singing.

The service finishes with the very gentle accompaniment of the Eucharistic hymn, *Let All Mortal Flesh Keep Silence*, the first verse of which is sung as a baritone solo. All the chapel lights are dimmed and it is sung by candlelight. This hymn is designed to lead into the Eucharist of Midnight Mass.

My solo singing career outside St George's has taken me from Queen Elizabeth Hall on London's South Bank and York Minster, to the recording studios of Wardour Street for the occasional backing for adverts. For instance I conducted a group of 12 boys drawn from St Albans Cathedral and the Berkshire Youth Choir for an advert

for an American insurance company which I hope may lead to future work.

In a more classical vein, my solo work for opera and concerts involves much preparation and care. Depending on the size of a role and its technical demands, I try to allow between one month and six months gradually working it into the voice. I often devise a technical exercise based around a particular problem to try to alleviate it. I also try to keep in good physical condition; I go running down the Long Walk whenever I can and go walking and generally try to keep myself fit, both for breathing efficiency and general stamina.

When singing, the convention is to use a copy, but I do try when singing oratorio to learn as much as possible from memory. One is sometimes asked to memorise something completely but this is the exception rather than the rule. Singing from memory avoids being hidebound by the copy as this tends to form a barrier between the performer and the audience. The flow from performer to audience must be as seamless as possible.

If I am singing in a foreign language, time is needed for the text to permeate and become natural-sounding thus avoiding any stiffness in sound production.

When I am using the voice on a normal basis, I try to spread my practice sessions over the day, avoiding a 'blitz' session. I try never to sing for more than about 45 minutes in one go, because this does tend to 'take the edge' off the voice. The muscles around the larynx become tired and consequently do not support the voice sufficiently. I tend to work on the lower register early in the day and then adjust the pitch upwards as the day progresses.

On the day of a concert, I keep as quiet and as self-contained as possible; that is very important. I like to go 'into my shell' and harbour my resources and my concentration. This can sometimes be very difficult, especially when being offered hospitality between the rehearsal and performance and meeting new people, but I do try to keep as quiet as I can and concentrate on the job in hand. Similarly, I try to leave plenty of time for travel on the day, and to try to write-in a period for relaxation at some point on the performance day. I gradually warm up the voice to cover at least the full compass of the work or works being performed, so that for instance if I have a work with a bottom 'E' in it, I will try and go down to at least an E-flat at the bottom, and perhaps if it goes up to an 'E' at the top I will try to prepare an 'F' at the top, to allow some margin for error in performance.

When preparing a piece new to my repertoire, I don't always practise it from the beginning. I sometimes work from the end of the piece backwards, so that the work is prepared to a uniform standard, otherwise it is very easy to find that you know the beginning well and perhaps the middle; the end is always a bit hazy. So for a balanced knowledge of the piece I do try to work from both directions.

When having to memorise a piece, or when performing a recital programme, I start that learning process early, because when under pressure, the memory will fail unless it has 100 per cent recall. I always try to concentrate on short sections at a time, trying to absorb all the musical markings such as 'mezzoforte', 'crescendo', 'parlante', 'con la voce', all expressions which should be learnt in parallel with the sung text.

Millennium Choice Trevor Craddock

The Domine Deus from Bach's B Minor Mass – it is the synthesis of the three independent parts, the obligato flute part, against the soprano and tenor soloists, which together weave an ingenious musical tapestry.

My favourite piece from a personal performance point of view is the Verdi Requiem. It has wonderful scope to give every ounce of one's interpretative skills. I feel it was absolutely written for my bass-baritone voice and the sheer drama of the work never fails to move one. I would go anywhere to sing this work.

Memorable moments
Trevor Craddock

I have sung the Messiah in Romsey Abbey when it was desperately cold. It was in the depths of winter, and I was trying to sing 'Why Do the Nations?', which is a very challenging declamatory aria, and my diaphragm was so rigid I could not articulate the long runs as I would have wished because I was shaking from head to toe from the cold. A really distressing experience! I think it is probably better on balance to be too hot than too cold when performing because when feeling cold the powers of concentration also seize up. It just became a test of endurance to get through the concert.

Another time I agreed to perform C P E Bach's 'Magnificat' for the Camden Festival and luckily I was asked to do it six months before the actual concert. This gave me time to look at it and work it into the voice because it is one of the most difficult pieces I have ever sung. It involves vocal gymnastics all the way through, covering a very wide vocal compass, and that is where I used my full six months preparation time.

Probably my most taxing sustained oratorio role is Mendelssohn's 'Elijah', because the baritone as Elijah sings at various points all the way through the oratorio and finishes with a very high tessitura aria, 'For The Mountains Shall Depart'. It is a very difficult aria to sing, perhaps two to two-and-a-half hours into the performance when one's stamina is running low.

One of the most enjoyable and moving performances was the Quaker schools' performance of the Messiah in Durham Cathedral. Leighton Park is one of the Quaker public schools and every four years the schools come together to perform a major oratorio, normally in an important venue nearest to the host school. It was the first concert in which I sang for the Quaker schools and the scaffolding for the choir went right up to the nave screen. It was wonderful hearing these young voices projecting down the nave. They worked extremely hard to make a very stirring performance.

I have had a long and happy association with the Reading Bach Choir, principally under the baton of Julian Williamson. I had a chance under his conductorship to perform some quite unusual repertoire pieces, for instance, Arthur Bliss's 'Shield of Faith' (which was written for the quincentenary of St George's Chapel) at the old Reading Town Hall, and Vaughan William's' Epithalamion. I owe a lot to Julian.

It is not generally known that the John Lewis Partnership have their own well-equipped theatre above the store in Oxford Street and, for a number of years, they have undertaken productions of rare operas. The two such operas in which I have had roles are 'Geneviève de Brabant' by Offenbach (Charles Martel) and 'Si j'étais Roi' by Gustav Adam (Prince Kadoor).

A Folk Tale Woodley Yeomen

There are few folk musicians averse to a pint or two at the end of a long and stressful gig but for a band to adopt the name of its local public house is, perhaps, a little more unusual. It was in early 1968 that this decision took place, as university lecturer Ian Graham and maths teacher Malcolm Clarke met in the bar of the Woodley Yeoman pub to contemplate the formation of a folk band with a difference.

The Bull and Chequers had been an early runner in the title stakes but after a few more beers, lightning struck and the Woodley Yeomen it was. This was the name which would eventually become famous in the folk world.

Originally a trio consisting of Ian (accordion), Malcolm (guitar) and fiddle player Derek Walker, the group's first engagement was at Reading's Park Congregational Hall in October 1968, and at the end of the evening the three musicians split the princely sum of £4 12 shillings and eightpence.

An early decision had been made that the band would perform traditional folk music for dancing, but with a modern amplified jazz approach and it soon became clear that a rhythm section was needed to ensure the desired sound. By chance, Ian Graham had received a letter from bass player Harry Elliot, a male nurse recently employed at Broadmoor hospital, who was keen to join the local music scene after leaving his previous band, the south-coast-based Blue Door. The rest, as they say, is history and the trio quickly became a quartet and then a quintet as drummer Fergus Laidlaw left The Reivers to add badly-needed punch to the back line.

The first major change in the band's line-up came in 1970 when Derek Walker graduated from Reading University and moved to Shropshire to take up a position with British Steel. With this move, the educational link became even stronger as teacher John Roberts, previously with the Buckinghamshire-based Riversiders, took over the fiddle chair and a second change occurred when jazz drummer Graham Heffernan replaced Fergus Laidlaw.

The only other alteration in the permanent line-up happened when bassist Ron Pearce forsook the big band palais scene to try his hand in an entirely different field, taking over from Harry Elliot. By now, though, the band's diary was bursting and it was often necessary to call in one-night replacements so that regulars could have an evening off.

To provide a full list of personnel would be an impossibility, but the task to find able 'deps' often necessitated hours of telephone calls to all parts of the country, particularly after Ian Graham left to take up a teaching post in Swansea. Among the noteable musicians who sat in with the Yeomen were Brian Willcocks, Linda Martin and John Barber from The Ranchers, and Dave Green, Rick Smith, David Springall and Linda Bradshaw from the Blue Mountain Band – both internationally-known groups with impeccable credentials.

As with personnel, the list of important engagements undertaken by the band would fill a volume, but the booking which changed the Yeomen from local band to one of national status could well have been disastrous.

Cecil Sharp House is the mecca for everything folksy and a booking to play at the London headquarters on Saturday night is rare indeed. Caller Brian Jones, who often worked with the Yeomen, had recommended the band to his father, Cyril, who was responsible for all bookings at Cecil Sharp House.

Although Cyril had never heard the band, he accepted Brian's word that it would not let them down, and the heavily-amplified group was booked to appear in front of a packed house of very experienced dancers, perhaps more used to a traditional acoustic sound. Fronted by caller John Chapman, from the Midlands, the band's improvisatory style front line, backed by what was really a jazz rhythm section, threw caution to the wind and the result was instant success. The audience had heard nothing like it before and loved it.

But the final triumph came when members of the Sunday Club – the nickname for the English Folk Dance and Song Society's top demonstration team – heard the commotion and left a rehearsal on the lower-floor to see what all the noise was about.

It was one of those risks that paid off, for the 'experts' – puzzled by not having heard of the band before – quickly added it to the lists of significant bookers, resulting in invitations to top festivals throughout the United Kingdom and abroad.

there was a second feather for the Yeomen's caps when they were invited by BBC television producer Ron Smedley to play for the Royal Ballet School. Ron, also a member of the Sunday Club, had been engaged to teach folk dancing traditions to the aspiring ballet dancers, and the band was booked to play before the Queen Mother at a gala performance at Covent Garden.

As founder-member Ian Graham said: "On the night in 1968 that Malcolm and I sat in the bar at the Woodley Yeomen pub, we never dreamed that we would one day share a stage with Rudolf Nureyev and Margot Fonteyn."

The experience was, however, not without its hairy moments. Throughout all rehearsals the band and dancers had performed with full stage lighting but at the actual production, without warning, the lights were switched off except for spots which followed the dancers.

The musicians were forced to play the entire evening from memory, but the result must have been satisfactory because they were later booked for a repeat concert at the Richmond Theatre.

1978 was the year that the Woodley Yeomen made their first record when, at the invitation of the EFFDS, they laid down 13 tracks to accompany one of the society's Community Dance Manuals. The session took place at the RG Jones Studio in Morden and the musicians involved were Ian Graham (accordion), John Roberts (fiddle), Malcolm Clarke (guitar), Harry Elliot (bass) and Graham Heffernan (drums).

At the other extreme and in its earlier days the band was engaged to play for patients inside Broadmoor and bassist Harry Elliot spent most of the evening pointing out inmates who had only recently been household names in the pages of the National Press.

Among major festivals played by the Woodley Yeomen were the international week-long events at Sidmouth, Whitby and Broadstairs and also, memorably, in 1978 the band was invited, together with groups from the United States and South America, to play in Israel at a series of concerts to mark the 30th anniversary of the founding of the state.

The tour got off to a bad start when El-Al overbooked the plane, resulting in Ian Graham and Graham Heffernan missing the scheduled flight and having to wait until the following day for seats on another aircraft.

Nevertheless, once all had arrived, the band found itself on a constant roll of engagements, playing in most major towns and even in front of the President of Israel in an underground theatre in Tel-Aviv which doubled as a nuclear fall-out shelter.

Another 'event to remember' occurred when the band was booked to play at a gala night to commemorate the opening of the new suspension bridge in Hull. Transport in those days was an old Bedford van and during the journey to Yorkshire in a relatively serious snowstorm the engine developed an aversion to the extreme cold. Repairs in Nottingham saw the band on its way once more, but after an extremely successful performance at the Guildhall in Hull, the vehicle again refused to start, which was not surprising as the snow was now dangerously deep and the temperature many degrees below freezing. Hours of attempting to fire the engine meant that the townsfolk were all asleep and so covers were stripped from instruments and amplifers and used to protect the musicians against the cold as they tried to sleep in the back of the van.

The band finally arrived at Reading on the back of an RAC breakdown truck the following lunchtime.

The circumstances that led to the Woodley Yeomen's second recording date – this time at the Woodcray Manor Studios in Wokingham (now a golf course) – could alone fill a book. Ian Graham, his wife, Barbara, and Malcolm Clarke were active in an organisation called Forest School Camps, a body derived from a pre-war experimental school that believed in the value of the outdoor life in a child's education.

Post-war, the school having closed, the experience and capital were put to the foundation of yearly camps, where young and old would live together under canvas in as simple a way as possible. Country dancing was one of the many activities that formed a basis for the annual two-week holidays and after attending and enjoying one of these aptly-named Folk Camps, Eric Limet decided that he would organise similar events in his native Belgium, accordingly founding Mains Unies.

The story then moved to 1978 when David Kettlewell, then on the staff of the EFDSS, mentioned to Ian Graham that Eric was looking for musicians, prompting him to take his family (every one of whom played an instrument) to the Continent to camp with Mains Unies – which he did for many years. This led to the Woodley Yeomen being commissioned in 1982 to record 15 tracks, to which Eric Limet added the caller's instructions in his own language, with the added difficulty of making the translation fit the timing of the music. The musicians featured were Ian Graham, John Roberts, Malcolm Clarke, Ron Pearce and Graham Heffernan.

Sadly, it was not long afterwards that the band played its final engagement. It had become increasingly difficult to find musicians worthy of the Woodley Yeomen's reputation and an even greater headache to bring them together for bookings throughout Britain. The final straw came in 1983 when Malcolm Clarke took up an exchange teaching post in America and although it was hoped that the band would reform following his return to Britain, the revival of those heady days was never to come about.

Ron Pearce

It's Great to be Young Reading Youth Orchestra

KEN WICKENS, who was Reading Youth Orchestra percussionist from 1969 to 1977, remembers the pioneering RYO which brought him music – and romance

The people of Reading should be very proud of Reading Youth Orchestra. Over the years it has been responsible for many marriages (including my own).and has also, of course, played an important part in the life of numerous young people of the town.

At a time of great shortage in the 1940s, Reading Education Committee, a very forward looking authority, allocated funds for the purchase of musical instruments and set up a scheme to allow the loan of instruments and tuition for a small fee, and a handful of children took up this opportunity to learn to play. At this time Reading Youth Club Music Committee proposed an orchestra of a number of youth club members between the ages of 14 and 20. The new orchestra was to be arranged and conducted by Humphrey Hare, senior science master at Leighton Park School and accomplished amateur musician. It was from this small handful of children that Reading Youth Orchestra was formed. The first rehearsal

was held on 29th October 1944, with 11 young musicians.

The early days saw difficulties with the players at different standards and also the woodwind instruments not at the same pitch but in March 1945, only six months after the first rehearsal, the orchestra gave its first small concert. The first major concert of RYO, however, was an orchestral and choral concert held at South Reading Community Centre on 16th November 1945.

Rehearsals for the orchestra started at Reading School but soon moved to the Garden Room of Watlington House on a Friday night. The orchestra made steady progress and in 1947 it was felt that they could accept an invitation to undertake a tour of Holland. This was a considerable challenge as the war in Europe had only ended less than two years before. In following years the RYO was touring Germany and Denmark.

1950 was tinged with sadness for the orchestra with the death of Humphrey Hare, and for the next two years it was conducted by Mark Wigram followed by John Russell. Then in 1954 Edward Underhill, who had been connected with the orchestra from the very beginning, became the conductor. His wife Doris had been Honorary Secretary since 1952.

All members of the orchestra who played under Ted Underhill will have fond memories of his military style conducting and his strong opinions about music. They will surely also remember Doris who sat at her table on a

Founder Humphrey Hare puts the pioneering Reading Youth Orchestra through its paces at a Watlington House rehearsal in 1946

small platform at the far end of the Garden Room, her raised position giving her a good view of events. She would keep the register every week and record who had paid their subscriptions (and who had not!) Once the rehearsal had started she would pick up her knitting and give smiles of encouragement whenever a player looked in her direction. In latter years she was accompanied by a small dog (a pug, I think).

Ted cared deeply for young people and wanted very much to encourage them through a sense of friendship and fun to develop their talents and ability to perform. Ted and Doris were a unique pair and the orchestra were very fortunate to have them. Throughout the '50s the orchestra continued to grow with 96 players performing at the 15th anniversary concert in 1959.

It was in 1960 that the annual vacation course in Torquay began. The orchestra stayed at the Castle, a local YMCA, and had the routine of sectional rehearsals in the morning with the afternoons free, followed by a full orchestra rehearsal in the evenings. The week ended with a concert at Torquay Town Hall. In 1970 this course moved to Portsmouth YMCA but the format remained the same with the end-of-course concert held either in Portsmouth Cathedral or in the Guildhall. The courses were hard work but also a huge amount of fun and anyone from this era will recall the infamous Portsmouth beach parties!

In 1974 Ted Underhill felt that it was time for a younger person to take over the running of the orchestra and his last appearance was at the 30th anniversary concert.

Roy Goodman, head of music at Bulmershe School and an accomplished violinist, was subsequently appointed the next conductor. Roy introduced the orchestra to the modern idiom in music, and in his two years as conductor, he led the orchestra from Bach to Boyce, and Shostakovitch to an experimental work for percussion and electronics which was performed at Christ Church Festival of Music. During this time the rehearsals moved from Watlington House to Alfred Sutton Boys' School, from there to Bulmershe School and then to the Green Road site of Reading College. Roy retired as conductor in April 1976 to pursue his own performing career.

Robert Rosco, the next conductor, continued to introduce the orchestra to a wider repertoire of music and at the same time encourage the young people he worked with to grow socially and personally with the experience of European tours and vacation courses.

Since the early 1950s the major concert venue was Reading Town Hall with the principal concert of the year in July, usually the hottest day of the year! When the Town Hall closed, concerts moved to other locations around Reading with one at the Hexagon in the presence of the Queen and Prince Philip for the formal opening of the Civic Centre. Since 1986, a new concert venue out of Reading has been St John Smith's Square, London which has become a great regular event.

1994 was a special year for the RYO, being its 50th anniversary. Gala and reunion concerts were held at the Hexagon in Reading. The reunion concert brought together members across the life span of the orchestra many of whom have gone on to the professional world of music and those, like myself, who continue to play for fun. Robert Rosco retired in 1997 and the baton has now been taken up by Rupert D'Cruze with whom the orchestra has since continued to grow .

With help from FRYO (the Friends of Reading Youth Orchestra)

The Yattendon Hymnal

The Yattendon Hymnal was a collection of 100 hymns which appeared towards the end of the 19th century.

It included some hymns written by the poet Robert Bridges (who co-edited the Hymnal). There were also some ancient hymns which he rewrote in 19th century English. The hymn book was regarded as one of the best of its time and seven of the hymns from it were included in the 1950 edition of Hymns Ancient and Modern.

Bridges was in charge of Yattendon Church Choir for many years and he was also involved in music teaching at Yattendon C of E School.

He was made Poet Laureate in 1913.

Tony Barham

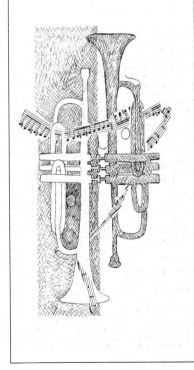

From Arthur Askey to The Hollies The Excel Bowl

In the 1960s, Reading had its first and only bowling alley, The Excel Bowl, in Caversham Road. Hundreds of local teams played at the 24-lane 10-pin bowling alley, open 24 hours a day, and for a time there was a flourishing members' club run by a committee. Musicians and entertainers, some famous, some completely forgotten, appeared there until the place became a victim of its own success and, unable to get planning permission to expand, the management pulled out. **NORRIE HART**, who used to be on the members' committee, remembers those days.

The Excel Bowl members' club was sited conveniently upstairs immediately you entered the Bowl so that anyone who wanted to be a member but not get involved in ten-pin could do so for the princely sum of, I believe, £2 a year. Of course there was nothing for your £2 initially, just a watering hole away from the thunder of bowling balls downstairs and the crash-bang-wallop of the machinery.

My involvement with Excel began a couple of months after the Bowl opened. Yes, I was invited. I seemed to be involved in quite a lot in those days – football, fishing, local politics even. An invitation to this American dream coincided with something else (I dimly remember Reading Football Club playing away somewhere). Anyway, who wants to spend an evening chucking a big rubber ball which weighed a ton (it was actually 16lbs) down a long wooden lane at 10 plastic covered wooden pins? There surely are better things to be doing?

I was then sent some free tickets for instruction and a bowling session after a couple of months. With nothing to do I wandered off down to the Excel one Tuesday (or it could have been a Wednesday). I was offered a coffee, which was also free, and my feet encased in new bowling-type shoes by a rather nice young lady.

The only real thing I remember of that introduction to ten pin was a) I actually managed to knock some of the pins over and b) I dropped one of those heavy balls on the foot of Fred Purdy, then the number one bowler at Excel who was playing in the next lane.

That free lesson became very expensive as I soon decided to have a go at league bowling one night a week which soon stretched into six nights a week and Tuesday afternoons.

That left Saturday with little to do as there was no league play. So I did the next best thing. I went down to the

The (very) Small Faces

Excel Club with a gang of friends, soon nicknamed the Clan, and either stayed in the club for a drink or went wild by dashing down to Hayling Island or the like for a bit of entertainment.

Being now fully integrated with all that went on at Excel, I suppose it was no surprise when the then centre manager Sid Vaughan asked me and some other regulars to form a members' committee. Our brief was to take up any complaints from bowlers and club members and discuss things with management. The main objective was, in fact, to make Saturday nights as interesting as possible with the proceeds of a one-arm bandit (and they really were in those days) and a small charge at the door on Saturdays only, so the committee began a series of club nights on Saturdays.

I compered the shows initially and booked most of the acts through Consort Entertainments, an agency run by Jim and Marion Cookson from a first-floor office in Cheapside. The other committee members that I remember were Olive, a lovely lady, a treasurer who was a treasure, Frank and Mrs Nicholson, Larry the bar manager and a Roy whose other name escapes me.

Our first venture was a tramps' ball, for which everyone (and I mean everyone) dressed up. Music played little part in the Saturday night revels unless the artistes provided their own.

We paid £25 for the first band, provided by Consort, name now unknown but they also dressed the part. Curtains were courtesy of sacking from anywhere and everywhere, half the seats were replaced with bales of straw dowsed in some flame-retardent liquid which smelled vaguely of mothballs. How we managed not to set the place alight I do not know.

The next Saturday Arthur Askey was top of the bill with supporting acts – a lady quick-draw artist (paper and charcoal – not guns) and a girl dancer who brought her own music tapes.

With the profits from the first two ventures we had a solid stage built and from a second-hand shop in Caversham Road we also bought an upright piano which tuned up beautifully.

The next dance night was a revelation. Jim Cookson played me a tape in his office one afternoon which sounded like the Beach Boys with a female choir backing.

"As a one-off," said Jim, "I'll let you have them for £75."

"How about the backing?" I asked.

"What you heard from the tapes, you get."

I shall always remember Jim smiling and tapping his nose. What a great little fellow.

And two weeks later our next big dance night was Hawaiian night with – The Cameos.

It was their first live performance in Reading and certainly not their last. Why no one promoted them I'll never know. They were superb, their vocals out of this world.

They were headed by Guy Fletcher, who later wrote and appeared in the European Song Contest with songwriting partner Doug Flitt. The Cameos also had a special cabaret piece, the 1812 Overture where the band all changed instruments as they played the classic faster and faster.

The Frank Jennings Syndicate fronted our country night – there were so many great nights. These dance nights were interspersed with variety acts of all kinds for which we needed backing. Jim found us the Richard King Set, who could actually read dots (sheet music) and fill an evening with good music and vocals or back artists on other weeks. They rapidly became resident band

We had comedienne/singer Joan Turner, hypnotist Peter Casson, and many local artists made their first live performance at Excel. Bob Monkhouse cost, I believe, £200 and gave us three hours instead of one after we had seen three other acts.

The group scene was now upon us. We never managed to book The Beatles or The Rolling Stones (although the Stones did appear at Reading Town Hall) but the very, very Small Faces before they made it cost us 50 notes (which was less than they actually played on their guitars). They were noisy, scruffy and the younger club members thought they were good.

I don't think we would ever have wanted them back but, as they never ceased to tell us in between numbers, they did make a record and appeared on Top of the Pops. So six months after having the group for £50 for the whole evening, £5,000 would get you only one song.

Slade played only because Noddy Holder was local and

also unknown. The Hollies were on the fringe and gave us a splendid night for a bit more than £50. Millie, even though she was virtually a one-hit wonder with My Boy Lollipop, was a big hit with the younger set.

And then the committee were taken over. Head office in London realised we were making money, albeit every penny went into the club, and the committee was disbanded. The Saturday night fever continued. Anyone with 15 shillings to spare could dance the night away to rock.

Probably as a sop I became an employee of Excel, working away from Reading at Tolworth, Cliftonville and other Bowls. When I returned to Reading I rarely went upstairs on Saturdays, and I moved on to employment elsewhere. Then Sid Vaughan had returned as bowl manager and telephoned me to tell me the bowl was closing. There was nothing that could be done.

I wonder where Sid and Roger Polly, the former managers, Larry and Martha, joint hosts in the upstairs bar, and many, many regulars at Excel are now? Some I still have as friends, some have passed on.

The fact that Excel had provided one of the first rock spots in Reading and some great memories for a lot of people makes me proud that I was part of the Excel era.

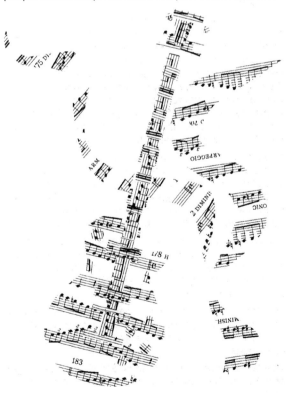

Sweet Singing in the Choir · Berkshire Youth Choir

The name of GILLIAN DIBDEN is synonymous with excellence in choral singing not only in Berkshire but to a far wider public. Her success with the Berkshire Youth Choir in winning the Sainsbury's Choir of the Year competition in 1996 was seen by millions on television. She is Head of Voice and Choral Music for the Berkshire Young Musicians Trust.

I think I am a teacher at heart but I discovered that it was standing in front of a choir that really switched me on. I was thrown in at the deep end. I had been singing in the choir at St Mary's Church, Langley, when they opened St. Francis Church in 1961 and desperately wanted someone to start a choir. The vicar asked me if I would lead the choir at St. Mary's as a singer and start a choir at St. Francis and between these things I found this was the world that really excited me. I hadn't had any training although there was something nominal, called 'choir training', at the Royal College of Music which was my favourite session of the week. We would gather in a room at the top of the building and sit round in a big circle singing mostly sacred church music. The chap running it used to say: "Who knows this piece?" and it was always the same boy who would go out in front and do it. It was more like a sing-along than formal training in conducting.

My parents were both musical, but they would have described their abilities and interests differently from each other. Father ran a dance band in Burnham. As a child he went to a local piano teacher who after one term said he knew as much as she did so, based on one term's tuition, he continued to play by ear because he didn't read music very well. My mother learnt both violin and piano as a child and also had a superb ear for music. Clearly as they were both so musical they were keen for my sister and I to start piano lessons. I went to a good piano teacher at St. Bernard's Prep School, in Slough. I wouldn't describe myself as a real star on the piano but I was always in the top few at festivals. As a teenager, in a fairly bolshy mood, I was keen to give it up. My mother threw all the arguments at me about the time and money she had spent and it was the best thing she could have done, because if she had let me give up then, my life would have been very different. I am very grateful for those battles.

At Senior School at St. Bernard's they introduced violin lessons but it was a woodwind instrument that I wanted to learn. However, because I was born with a cleft palate

I didn't find the clarinet possible. I had air coming down through my nose as well as my mouth, so I couldn't blow well enough to do it. I was hugely disappointed but went on to the 'cello. This too was a very good move.

Then a new music teacher called Susan Hall came to St. Bernard's and she absolutely livened up the music. From being a fairly insignificant pupil, I became one who was important in the school because my subject had become an important one in the life of the school. I think the people who influence you when you are young have a huge responsibility. I lost touch with Susan Hall because she went abroad but my parents were so grateful that there was someone like her who knew what to do with a musical youngster. She was tremendous. In my mother's declining years she often said: "I wonder what happened to Susie?" She so much wanted to tell her how much pleasure she and everybody else had derived from my music. So after mum died in 1993 I decided to trace Susan as I knew she was married to a head of music in a public school in Scotland. I wrote to tell her the joy I had gained from music and how it had influenced my life and we met again when she came down to London.

Having taken up the 'cello, I went along to the Royal College of Music on a three year graduate course and even though I had only been learning for a short time they seemed impressed with the amount I had covered. Piano was my first study and 'cello second. When I graduated I decided to take up teaching – I always wanted to be a teacher – and I went to a school in Oxford first then back to St Bernard's.

I had enjoyed success with the choirs at St Bernard's in the ' 70s and I was becoming known for my choral work – Hamish Preston, the music adviser of Berkshire, had often been to my concerts and was a great supporter. Roger Durston, head of Instrumental Service in Berkshire, also was encouraging. He invited me on several occasions while I was at St Bernard's to help him with a Berkshire Summer Youth Opera Course which he was conducting. In 1984 he asked me to consider setting up a Berkshire Youth Choir. They had never had one as an ongoing entity and would I do it? All my life I have responded well to people I feel inspired by so through Roger and Hamish I said I would start a Berkshire Youth Choir.

I then learnt that Roger was leaving to go to East Sussex. My heart sank because I had thought I would be working in partnership with Roger. I was disappointed and wondered: "Do I really want to do this?" But I thought I would be a fool not to give it a go, so I did, and the Berkshire Choir really began. Although my life at the RCM had meant that I had sung under the baton of some exceptionally good people, my inspiration has come from local people, like John Wellingham, an Eton master who ran the Slough Philharmonic Choir and, of course, Ken

Weller, the present chorus master of Slough Philharmonic Choir. I learnt so many tricks from him which I still use. Coincidentally he is organist at Taplow where my husband Alan is now vicar.

Since those first days The Berkshire Youth Choir has become very large – about 90 members. I have not always wanted it to be so large, but it has a very healthy, fantastic sound. A large choir can sing with a very punchy sound and if they are technically good enough they can also sing with a very small sound, which is the test. So it's worth hanging on to a large number of singers.

There are three youth choirs now because we have The Berkshire Boys' Choir and The Berkshire Girls' Choir as well. The Berkshire Boys' Choir was formed in 1988. Up and down the country there is a shortage of boys' singing. In a youth choir it was always difficult to have enough tenors and basses. Richard Hickman, principal of

the Trust at that time, called me in one day and said: "I'd like you to start a boys' choir." I found the thought daunting as up to that time my choirs had been all girls. But I have to say that it was the best thing that ever happened. I wondered what was the smallest number that could be called a choir? I supposed if 10 or 12 boys applied I could hope to start it. But it was amazing. Despite a postal strike, we had 130 applicants and I had to audition the lot. The parents were so excited that the opportunity was there. They had remembered their own singing days at school when their choir was at the heart of school life.

We resisted the need to start a girls' choir for a time. The Berkshire Young Musicians Trust has a good structure of choirs in all its music centres and there were a lot of children singing, predominantly girls, so I saw no need to have a county level choir for the younger girls. They

Berkshire Youth Choir

Gillian Dibden

could always graduate on to the youth choir if they had the ability to do so. But parents, seeing how well the boys had done, were keen that something similar was started for the girls. So in 1996 we started that. That's going well too. The girls went to the National Festival of Youth final in 1998 although I was in hospital at the time. My daughter who was a founder member of the Berkshire Youth Choir, conducted them and they got the outstanding award.

I suppose the highlight of my professional career was winning the Sainsbury's Choir of the Year Award in 1996 when the youngsters not only won the mixed voice category but the overall award as well. We had been entering the competition for some years. I think we learned a fair bit over the time we'd entered and we always did well – we'd got to the quarter finals before we won it. We went from strength to strength and each set of choir members who entered this competition absolutely loved it. Kate Jones organises it and she has great skill with people.

There is great excitement at these competitions, an atmosphere that choirs can create in a way instrumental ensembles can't quite do. There is this network of support and mutual appreciation with choirs saying well done to other choirs. It has an atmosphere which is very special and which the Sainsbury's competition captures

and really enhances. The right programme is crucial. It has to have a certain combination of winning pieces. We have a large repertoire, an excellent librarian at the Berkshire Music Trust, Judy Bullock, and a big collection of choral music. If they are short programmes I believe in a short snappy lively opener, a statement of what you're about.

In the final of the competition which we won I took a very daring step and let them deliver the opening piece without me conducting. Not many conductors would go that far. Although I think the conductor is of paramount importance to every choir, every choir is different if you stand a different person in front of it. I feel that a strong conductor like myself has to play a balance between leading and guiding the singers and not imposing myself on them. I am working with a lot of very musical youngsters and the teaching element is very important but leaving them alone to make the music is an interesting step.

When we've been going home in the coach after a competition, they sing their hearts out over a long journey. Sometimes I've sat there, feeling tired out, listening to them and I've thought "Wow! they sound good. They really sound good." They've been trained up to the hilt and then they deliver the music spontaneously from inside them..

Television coverage makes it a different kind of competition because presentation rates higher than in other competitions. I have learned over the years how to make the visual presentation exciting. If you stand people in straight rows in black and white concert dresses on a television screen, it makes pretty boring viewing. Viewers are likely to turn over to another channel if they see something boring. I always believe in these short openers – one or two pieces. There is a huge danger in letting a choir sing on its own. The ensemble has got to be very tight, and getting 60-65 singers to sing as one without hurrying is the worst thing. They'll hurry and there's no conductor to hold them back. If I say "Don't hurry", they may go the other way and they will lose spontaneity or have a plodding rhythm.

In recent competitions, I got one of the percussion players, who has a smiling face and high communication skills, to stand at the front (not facing the choir) with a tambourine and that held the pulse. It meant that the camera could focus on the faces of the choir not the back of the conductor and it gave a new perspective. On another occasion I made a triangular formation, three people in the front row, seven in the next then eleven, something different to look at.

We changed our concert dress about four competitions ago. The members pay fees to be in the choir and because the parents pay to come to the concerts and for petrol to run around the county to be in this choir, I feel strongly that I can't ask for an expensive concert dress. I don't feel educationally that it is right for me to ask the parents to provide this. So a few years ago I asked for suggestions from the choir. Because we'd been told black and white was fairly boring on television I asked choir members to think of an economical way of colouring things up.

Firstly we just had a blue neck scarf for the girls and a blue bow tie for the boys. But when I saw it on the screen those items were so small they didn't have any impact. So then one of the girls came up with the brilliant idea of a royal blue waistcoat – royal blue being a Berkshire colour. It seemed like a good idea and these waistcoats were made by the parents, not desperately expensive, and they've made all the difference. I'd still love to be able to put them into some lovely dresses but we don't do enough concerts a year to merit the outlay. They grow so quickly too. The blue waistcoat for girls has been a real boon and it doesn't matter about the bow ties being small because we have enough colour now to succeed.

Another thing we did with presentation was that in some of the pieces we mixed up the boys and girls and that gave a different angle to look at in the grouping. In our final piece, which is usually a spiritual or a light music piece, I have them standing about all over the stage rather than in conventional rows. That too looks interesting from an audience point of view.

What we have done in concerts, though not on TV, is to stand the choir among the audience in a huge circle. Audiences feel quite excited by that. They have said that although the blend is still there you feel quite excited if you suddenly hear a beautiful voice near you. It is an intimate kind of music making.

The Berkshire Youth Choir didn't enter the Sainsbury's Choir competition in 1998 because of an unwritten rule that the winner does not return immediately. Every competition is a gamble. It depends on how you sing on that particular day, whether the adjudicators like you and your programme. I think the likelihood of coming up with the goods a second time round is highly unlikely. It's not right for the second lot of students to think, "Oh, we didn't get anywhere we're not as good." I'm sure the choir will be back for the next competition in 2000.

> **Some funny memories: I can remember losing my baton in the early days, so I conducted with a size eight knitting needle. Once I asked a little girl who was going to sing at an old people's concert which carol she was going to sing and she said: "Home and Away in a Manger". Too much television! Another child called me Mrs Dibley – and she doesn't even know I'm married to a vicar.**

My work has developed under David Marcou, principal of the Berkshire Musicians Trust. He has enabled me to

Berkshire Girls' Choir

Berkshire Boys' Choir

stretch my own work as well. I've been invited to speak at conferences and conduct courses abroad. David has been so encouraging. He recognises in his own staff people of talent, encouraging them in everything they do within the Trust. but also giving them the head to stretch their own talents, to keep their own development alive which is very important. Music in Berkshire is extremely healthy and young people in Berkshire have a huge amount going for them. There is such a call for the work that the Berkshire Musicians Trust does that I think it will go from strength to strength.

> **The Berkshire Young Musicians Trust was established in 1982 to safeguard and enhance music education for young people in the county and aims to provide for the aesthetic, intellectual and social development of young people and to develop performing and creative skills. Under its principal David Marcou, who joined the BYMT after a distinguished career with the London Philharmonic Orchestra, the Trust gives instrumentaL tuition to about 10,000 pupils in primary, middle and secondary schools. The philosophy is that music is fun and the priority is that no young person is prevented from learning music because of financial constraints.**

> **The Trust, which receives financial assistance from Berkshire's six unitary authorities, operates from four musical centres in Central Berkshire (serving Reading, Twyford, Pangbourne and Theale), East Berkshire (Windsor, Slough, Maidenhead and Ascot), South Berkshire (Wokingham, Bracknell, Sandhurst and Crowthorne), and West Berkshire (Newbury, Thatcham and Hungerford).**

Come, Listen to the Bands! Marching to a different drum

Above: The Reading Air Training Corps Band at the head of the town's squadrons as they march through West Street on their fourth anniversary parade during the Second World War

Right: Drums and bugles of Reading's Sea Cadet Corps leads "tomorrow's sailors" to their wartime headquarters at Huntley and Palmer's canteen in Gas Works Lane

Reading Borough Band entertained audiences in Berkshire at the turn of the century but, despite research, very little has been learned about either the band or its musicians. The only names known are those of the Piercy brothers – Richard Henry (front row, third from right) and George Harold (second row, seventh from right), both from West Reading. Readers may be able to fill in some missing names